Drawing Programs: The Theory and Practice of Schematic Functional Programming

Tom Addis · Jan Addis

Drawing Programs:
The Theory and Practice
of Schematic Functional
Programming

 Springer

Tom Addis
University of Portsmouth
School of Computing
Portsmouth P01 3HE
United Kingdom

Jan Addis
Clarity Support
Southsea PO4 9QU
United Kingdom

ISBN 978-1-84882-617-5   ISBN 978-1-84882-618-2 (eBook)
DOI 10.1007/978-1-84882-618-2
Springer London Dordrecht Heidelberg New York

British Library Cataloguing in Publication Data
A catalogue record for this book is available from the British Library

Library of Congress Control Number: 2009927007

Cover design: KuenkelLopka GmbH

Printed on acid-free paper

Springer is part of Springer Science+Business Media (www.springer.com)

To David Gooding
Who is a good friend and is a colleague who has enhanced this work with his scholarship. He has done more than most to make this book possible. In particular, he listens and engages in real debate.

Preface

Drawing programs is a personal response to some very practical problems. To explain this I need to go back in time to when my greatest toy was the Mechano set; a mechanical construction kit with instructions on how to build your own toys. I soon found that although the kit was boundless in one sense it was also very limited. I spent many hours trying to do things that were well beyond the intention of the kit designer. Much later I found electronics where circuits provided me with a much wider scope for model building but it still took a long time to make devices. It was not until programming was introduced during my time at University that this really flexible tool was made available. No more bleeding fingers from the iron work and no more burnt ties from soldering irons. Modelling was going to be easy and fun. However, there was snag. I had a natural inability to spell or even to construct coherent written sentences. It is true that I had evolved many strategies to successfully overcome this problem but the strategies only worked within a limited framework. The problem with programs is that they are written and involve the accurate use of characters. Most of my time was spent in pursuing typos and very little time on the programming. Sometimes it was necessary to ask someone to look for me and usually they could identify the problem within seconds; natural ability is a wonderful thing.

Functional programming in the form of LISP came along and the power of this language for expressing formal systems in an elegant way was very exciting. It was one move away from having to worry about the actual physical computer with all its storage management problems and one step closer to a language designed specifically for modelling. It was like stepping into an automatic car after years of struggling with manual gears. Even though practical computer languages had moved a long way from machine code it was still only a change from the crash gearbox to synchromesh. The computer structure was still in the background in that everything was forced into the framework of data and processes thus reflecting the fundamental dual distinction within the machine itself. The problem with functional programming was that it was constrained by its own formal framework and stopped short of being able to extend itself. LISP overcame this problem, to some extent, by slipping back into the computer framework by introducing special 'program' type functions. It also overcame another limitation by allowing the language to be extended beyond the original formal functional description. In some cases it was still very clumsy and from my point of view still required being written.

As an engineer, electronic circuits had been no problem to read, to find errors or to remember. If only programming could be made that easy. It was this drive to create a tool that would sidestep issues of spelling and yet still provide a professional tool for developing models and other kinds of programs. This led us to create Clarity, or rather, led Jan to develop the Clarity environment for me. Also, while we were at it, we could also eliminate some of the restrictions found in current text-based languages.

Clarity has been introduced quite slowly in this book simply because it seems to be slightly at odds with the normal windows approach. This is not too surprising since it was developed well before windows had become generally available and it was also driven by different requirements. The theory related to designing models has been included right from the beginning but for practical purposes it can be skipped.

The justification for Clarity given in Chapter 1 is in response to criticism of the diagrammatic approach to programming. These other diagrammatic approaches have usually been stimulated by a desire to make programming available to non-programmers. This is not the purpose behind Clarity. Clarity has been driven by a need to provide a sophisticated tool for programmers that would rather work with diagrams than with text. Projects are given at the end of each chapter. These follow the style of the Mechano instruction book in that every step is described. The purpose of doing it this way is to show how drawing programs should be done and to give an illustration of good techniques.

Clarity has been developed over the last 23 years for a wide range of different projects. It evolved out of an IKBS project (CARDS) in 1986–1990 with the General Electric Company, the University of Reading and the Imperial Cancer Research Fund to build a special hardware device that would allow those involved with DNA research to create models of DNA behaviour. For this a modelling language was needed. Originally the researchers had used Prolog. The next SERC/ESRC/MRC project in 1991–1996 was with the Universities of Bath, with Professor David Gooding, and the University of Reading with us, to construct a model of scientific discovery from the history of science. This work is still going on. Another project started in 1996 and funded by Ship Analytics (now MPRI, part of the L3 consortium) was an expert system used as a teacher replacement for Mariners training on a ship simulation for gas and oil management. Work on the automatic assessment of these students is also almost complete. Other work involving modelling of the negotiation process (Billinge and Addis 2008) at the University of Portsmouth has come up with some surprising results requiring us to reconsider the motivation behind reasons for conversation.

We have also taken on some really good post graduate students from the Technical University of Delft, The Netherlands. These have been provided by Dr, Drs Leon Rothkrantz almost every year between 1996 and 2006 to work on various projects. Many of these projects have helped to start new research directions such as those described in Chapter 10. In particular, Dr Bart-Floris Visscher was one of the visiting students who led a team that used Clarity to construct a planning system for a multi-legged robot (Portech Ltd). He was an outstanding student. He came back to Portsmouth to do research with me and his Thesis (2005) *'Exploring Complexity in Software Systems: From an irrational model of software evolution to a theory of psychological complexity and cognitive limitations based on empirical evidence'* went well beyond my own work started in 1977. It was thrilling stuff. He also designed the embellished Clarity icon on the front cover.

There have been many others that have helped us develop the Clarity Environment. Simon Gray (Sharp Edge Systems Ltd) was invaluable at the system level while we working with Apple Macintosh computers and he was always a source of new ideas. Dr. Carol Small introduced us to the functional database language (Poulovassilis 1988) during the CARDS project and wrote the core interpreter for the Sun UNIX system based on Field and Harrisons work (1988). John Chewter, an undergraduate student at the University of Portsmouth, showed considerable programming aptitude by constructing the Faith to Clarity interpreter for his final year project in 1995. It has been surprisingly useful. Ray Gillett (Director, MPRI, UK) has provided us with a set of excellent practical industrial projects since 1998. These projects have not only tested the system to its limits but many of the techniques developed for the belief system (model of science) have found a natural home. We thank him for his patience in allowing us to develop the system in our own way.

The Clarity schema has allowed us to work closely with many technically competent people. This close working with a fast implementation leads directly to the models needed. Any system that is useful requires to be continually modified to keep pace with technology and changing perspectives. For this reason we are giving away Clarity in all its forms with example databases and source code. At the time of publishing these will be found at the publisher's web site http://www.springer.com/978-1-84882-617-5, the University of Portsmouth web site http://userweb.port.ac.uk/_addist/978-1-84882-617-5.zip and a special Clarity community web site http://www.clarity-support.com

Southsea, March 2009   Tom Addis

References

1. Billinge D. and Addis T., (2008) 'Seeking Allies: Modelling how Listners Choose their Musical Friends', Special issue of Foundations of Science, Vol 13, No1, March, pp 53–66, ISSN 1233–1821.
2. Field A. J. and Harrison P. G., (1998) 'Functional Programming' pub Addis-Wesley Ltd, ISBN 0-201-19249-7.
3. Poulovassilis A., (1988), 'FDL. An Integration of the functional database Model and the Functional Computer Model', BNCOD 6, CUP, Cambridge, pp 215–236.

Contents

Chapter 1
Why Schematic Functional Programming?

> *Though I speak with the tongues of men and of angels, and have not charity,*[1] *I am become as sounding brass, or a tinkling cymbal.*
>
> Corinthians 13, 1.

Introduction

Schematic functional programming uses diagrams, or more precisely schema, to specify a functional program. We will describe a particular example of such a programming environment called Clarity. At the time of writing, and as far as we know, this is the only example of a professional programming language that is based on a combination of schema and functions.

Clarity was originally written by the authors simply because we were tired of struggling with computer coding when all we wanted to do was to create computer programs that solved our problems. The problems we had to solve were hard enough without being worried by the difficulties of getting the coding right. We could spend days hunting for some minor error such as a missing or misplaced bracket while the real issue we were trying to solve was held up. This seemed a tremendous waste of time.

Having had some experience of electronic engineering we had found the drawing and design of electronic circuits not only fun but also very productive. The translation of a drawing into an actual implementation was never a problem, so it did seem a good idea to try for something equivalent in programming. We needed the clarity of diagrammatic representation so that we could cope with the complexity of large programs. However, we were not the first to consider this and there are a few examples of successful electronic style diagrams that generate computer programs (e.g. Prograph and Matlab). Unfortunately they hit several problems with their visual

---

[1] For meaning of the word 'charity' we prefer 'generosity of heart'.

T. Addis, J. Addis, *Drawing Programs: The Theory and Practice of Schematic Functional Programming*, DOI 10.1007/978-1-84882-618-2_1,

approach as has been shown by those who study computer psychology (Addis and Addis 2001). We will discuss this in the next section.

It would seem that with the complexity of professional programming there was a danger of getting lost in the same way as a child might get lost in the puzzle "Who is linked with which shape?" (Fig. 1.1). This and the view that visual programming languages were only toy languages and not worthy of consideration are the two main reasons for such languages not being adopted by serious or professional programmers. On the other hand many of those developing such languages have done so with the explicit intention of opening up programming only to novices.

The exceptions are those languages that were specifically designed to create interfaces to programs, such as Visual C++ or Visual Basic. This class of visual languages still has the difficult job of programming the processes that lie behind the constructed interfaces. The buttons or sliders still need to do something and to describe this means delving into the details of C++, Fortran, Pascal or Basic programming. So if we were to do anything serious with a truly visual language and assuming that such a language would help us cope with the difficulties of constructing large complex programs then the question arises as to what needs to be done to take advantage of a schematic representation.

We will explore these and other questions while we introduce the schematic functional language Clarity. It is possible to skip these explorations and just jump to the sections concerned with the practicality of programming using diagrams (or schema, etc.). Whether you skip or not we recommend that the exercises be attempted. We will indicate those sections that can be skipped with an arrow followed by a page number for those who want to just learn the practice of programming with diagrams. An example of this is shown at the end of the next heading below. The start of the practical headings on the page will be prefixed by *. Exercises and projects that are designed to give the reader practical experience are provided in most chapters.

For the reader, what will eventually emerge from these explorations, tests and a practical experience of Clarity is an elegant view of programming, a view, we believe, that will benefit his or her designing ability with any style of programming language.

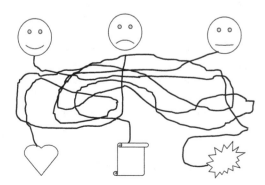

Fig. 1.1 The problem with pictures

The Collapse of Visual Languages [→ Page 12]

First it is worth considering the problems and criticisms of a visual language of the kind we had in mind. The arguments between the supporters of graphic and text programming came to a head in June 1996 at the MIT Laboratory for Computer Science which hosted a workshop on Strategic Directions in Computing Research. The 300 participants were divided into 22 working groups where each group explored different topics. Their reports were eventually published in the ACM Computer Surveys (Wegner and Doyle 1996). One of these reports was concerned with Visual Languages (Citrin 1996). The report noted that despite the great intuitive appeal of such languages they have not been adopted except as curiosities. Citrin suggested that there are three distinct areas that make visual languages unacceptable for programming. They are

- *Appropriateness of mapping*; deciding which aspects of problems map naturally into visual representations and which are best left as text.
- *Scalability*; the ability to construct and comprehend very large visual programs.
- *Transparency of the interface*; allowing changes and modifications of visual programs to be as easy as editing text.

The suggestion here is that if these were 'solved' then visual languages would become more acceptable.

Some 6 years earlier, Green (1990) had already asked the question

Is there evidence that diagrammatic notations genuinely offer something that symbolic notations cannot match?

and noted that

It is disturbing to observe that many workers have not even asked this question, and instead assert uncritically that 'Pictures are more powerful than words. Pictures aid understanding and remembering . . .. Pictures do not have language barriers. When properly designed, they are understood by people regardless of what language they speak.' If the more dewy-eyed propositions of program visualisation enthusiasts are accepted, then we can expect diagrams to be better for all purposes.

Soon after this observation Green with Petre (1996) published the results of a series of careful studies exploring different graphical and text notations for ease of programmer interpretation. They concluded that

- Overall, graphics was significantly slower than text to interpret.
- Moreover, graphics was slower than text in all conditions and the effect was uniform.
- The intrinsic difficulty of the graphics modes was the strongest effect observed.

These damning results were illustrated by selected observed behaviour and they concluded that

Far from guaranteeing clarity and superior performance, graphical representations may be more difficult to access.

Their most vivid description was concerned with 'Knotty Structures and Working Memory Load':

Program structures can contain 'knots' which force working memory load on the reader. . . . The sight of subjects crawling over the screen with mouse or fingers, talking aloud to keep their working memory updated, was remarkable . . . . One of the distinctions between expert and novice behaviour was that the experts made better use of their fingers, occasionally using all 10 to mark points along a circuit.

These are indeed remarkable observations that were supported by further work published in 1996 (Green and Petre 1996). These observations are particularly remarkable since engineering of many flavours, such as car design, architecture or electronics, would be impractical without diagrams.

On close inspection of their study it is evident that the experiments are only concerned with interpretation. Even so this does not limit the apparent uselessness of visual programming since it would seem reasonable that design should depend to a large exent upon interpretation. So the questions needed to be asked are as follows: 'What might be the difference between engineering a computer program and other engineering practices that seems to cause diagrams to become a positive disadvantage?' 'What is it about interpretation for programming that causes the problem?' 'Is it possible to overcome these difficulties and obtain the gains that diagrams clearly have in engineering, etc. for programming?' 'Is there something unique about programming that is different from other design processes?'

It is worth noting at this point, and as we will show later, that knotty structures are a result of imperative programming. Functional programming avoids this problem because of its properties of referential transparency and pattern match (of components). These properties will be fully explained (see pages 126 to 140).

Engineering Drawings [→ Page 12]

There is no problem in understanding the utility of an engineering drawing that represents such things as the design of a bridge, engine or aeroplane. A scaled schematic provides a means of trying out a design on paper and before the expense of manufacture (Fig. 1.2). It is a skilled task involving considerable precision that requires training from an expert in the field. The diagrams are drawn from views employing many established conventions. There is no pretence that the diagrams are easy to produce or necessarily simply understood. The drawings are scaled and are surrogates for the real thing (Davis et al. 1993) providing images that allow some direct measurements and that act as a guide for the creation of equations and the construction of the item.

Electronic circuit diagrams are also surrogates, as are ordinance survey maps. Icons that reflect something of the physics of how the component objects work represent switches, uniselectors, relays, electric motors, valves, transistors, resistors

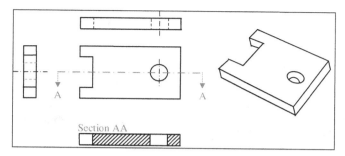

Fig. 1.2 Engineering drawings

and capacitors. There is sufficient in the abstract representation of these icons to remind the engineer about the nature of the devices to the extent that their unusual properties can be deployed. For example, screen grids of valves can be used to mix signals, the coils of relays can replace an inductance, and transistors can be used (with care) symmetrically (Figs. 1.3 and 1.4, first diagram). Logic circuits are also surrogates even though they are not so well endowed with icons that represent their workings. The logic gate in its entirety is too complex to represent its structure compactly.

In this direct case of engineering drawings it would appear that the formal and the informal semantics are folded into each other; what the notation represents in the working system and what the engineer intends it to represent in the world are one and the same thing. However, this simplicity diverges slightly when VLSI is introduced to replace the normal components of electronic circuits. Transistors and other components are now intersections of laminar areas of different materials (see Fig. 1.4, last diagram). To cope with this, a new kind of diagram was introduced to bridge the gap between the implemented device and the electronic circuit. This is the 'stick' diagram (see Fig. 1.4, middle diagram) (Mead and Conway 1980). Sometimes the engineers combine both kinds of notation into one diagram. The

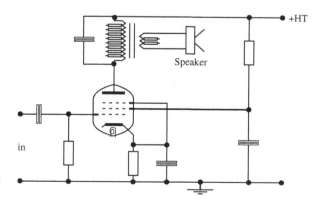

Fig. 1.3 Valve amplifier
(valve basics by Harry Lythall
SM0VPO)

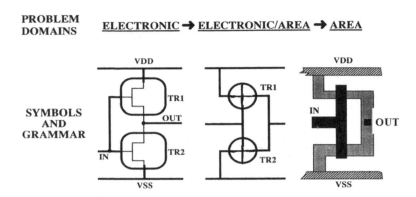

PROBLEM DOMAINS

ELECTRONIC → ELECTRONIC/AREA → AREA

SYMBOLS AND GRAMMAR

Fig. 1.4 Different VLSI drawings of the same circuit

equivalence of the formal and the informal semantics no longer holds directly because each kind of diagram now represents a different abstraction of the artefact for a different purpose (problem domain).

However, in all cases of engineering drawings they are also used to help create calculations and thus make predictions of behaviour or performance. This involves looking up information in tables and deploying laws of physics, such as Newton's three laws for mechanical devices or Ohm's and Kirchoff's laws for electrical circuits. There is no need to carry out experiments to demonstrate the value of these drawings for the design of artefacts. They may not be perfect but they would not be used if there were any significantly better method.

Engineering Drawings Used for Programming [→ Page 12]

The notion of a surrogate has its place in software engineering. A typical set of diagrams are those used for systems analysis. The example analysis shown in the first diagram of Fig. 1.5 is a variation of data dependency diagrams (Addis 1985). This shows the many-to-one relationships between the set of catalogues and the set of parts supplied by a set of suppliers. In this analysis suppliers must show at least one part in their catalogue. As for VLSI each of the three diagrams is a different abstraction concerned with different aspects of the design procedure. The first diagram is concerned with identifying classes of objects and their existence dependency. A part cannot exist unless there is at least one supplier of the part. The key to the effective design of this first diagram is familiarity with and the skilled use of the normalisation process as applied to data structures (Codd 1971, Maier 1983) just as Kirchoff's and Ohm's laws are needed for electronic circuits. The last diagram describes the actual physical pointer system in the memory that links information together. The middle diagram, similar to the stick diagram for VLSI, bridges the gap between the two abstractions.

Fig. 1.5 Three representations of the same data

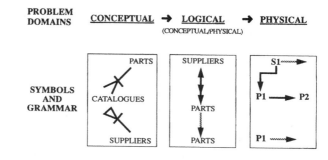

Something in the use of engineering diagrams has changed for systems analysis. The change is that the elements referenced by the icons (e.g. PARTS) are fluid. They are no longer easily identified objects, as is a logic gate or a switch. They are sets or concepts. The focus of design has shifted towards the relationship between the design process and the designed artefact. The involvement of the designer in deciding what the nature of the elements of the world is to be, although rarely acknowledged, is paramount to the ultimate design. What exactly is defined as a part or a supplier or a catalogue item is never expressed except in terms of attributes. Catalogues is a part and supplier relationship that has a reality as separate catalogue lists but these have disappeared. In the world in which we operate and in time this usually leads to confusions. What attributes are common to every part? Do all parts have a colour? Who may be defined as a supplier? Is your colleague with whom you work a supplier because he supplies you with information? This problem of indefinable sets is referred to as 'irrational' (see Addis et al. 2008 and c.f. page 76).

LabView, MatLab and Prograph are all graphical languages that draw upon the circuit diagram as their representational paradigm. The obvious appeal is to the skills that engineers already have in understanding and designing with such languages. The advantage of such languages over normal engineering drawings is that a circuit can be tried out before being built. This gives security of design; it ensures the artefact works as expected.

The oddity about these languages is that people would ever choose to use them as a general programming tool given that the elements have been fixed for reasons that have little to do with the potential of a von Neuman machine or the possibility of abstracting elements from a problem domain. It is thus not too surprising that they are confined only to certain well-defined areas of work.

The current design methods for software such as SSADM which were developed during the early days of computing (Stevens et al. 1974) are inadequate and do not provide the same security of design as found in electronics. We will now ask the question 'Given complete freedom of choice on a representation, unbounded by physical constraints, what would it be?' As we will justify later the answer is an approach to programming that can use simple diagrams to represent many levels of abstraction that allows different perspectives of the same program and is based on a handful of simple principles. This is the style of 'functional' programming, a style that is tremendously powerful and capable of programming very complex ideas compactly.

Functional programming is the process of programming using functions. Functions map types (such as integers, reals, characters, strings, lists) into (or onto) other types. An example is the function 'integer-multiply' which maps pairs of integers into a set of single integers. An example of this mapping is $2 * 3 \rightarrow 6$. More will be said of this later (see pages 15 and 48).

The simplicity of functional programming comes from the fact that there are really only four principles that need to be known. These are the *function, type, recursion* and *pattern matching of function components*. In imperative programming terms,

- Programs are *functions* and so are data, procedures and sub-routines.
- A class is a *type* such as Boolean or String but the strength of a functional language is that you can also create your own types.
- The basic processing controls of programming showing when to stop, where to loop and where to go next in a program are the self-referential mechanism for looping. This is the *recursion of functions*.
- Pattern-triggered function calls, such as a case statement or an array indexing (reference by index pattern), are governed by the *pattern matching of function-components*. However, pattern matching goes beyond these examples and will be described in detail later.

The snag with functional programming and another reason why it never really caught on is because it appears too mathematical. However, we found that if you convert such a language into its diagrammatic equivalent then the resulting pictures are easier for non-mathematicians to follow than formulae once a user has learnt how to interpret them. Figure 1.6 is a typical diagram used by those teaching functional programming (e.g. Reade 1989). The function illustrated is to copy string S n times. Here the string to be copied enters at the bottom left of the diagram (S) and the number of times it is to be written at the top left (n). If the number n is zero (0) then a blank string ("") is returned and that is the end of the processing. If n is not zero but is (say) one (1) then a one is subtracted from n and the string (S) is concatenated with whatever comes out of stringcopy [0 S]. In this case a blank string (""). For a number greater than one the process is repeated n times. So stringcopy [3 "Fred"] $\rightarrow$ "FredFredFred".

This suggests that diagrams like these should be used to program directly and we have called this kind of programming 'schematic functional programming'. So the schematic programming is the process of programming a computer directly through the construction of diagrams. Such diagrams are also referred to as schema, graphics, visuals or pictures.

Functional programming can be compared with the normal imperative programming that refers to named storage locations (memory) and processes (programs) on the contents of these locations. Imperative programming is more in line with the actual way that a computer works and is structured. Computers consist of distinct

Fig. 1.6 Stringcopy : int ×
string → string fun
stringcopy (n, s) = if n=0
then "" else stringcopy (n–1,
s)∧s

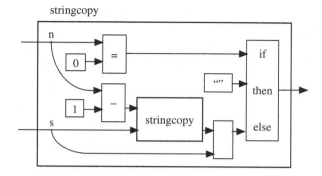

memory and a processor where the processor transforms information from memory and returns the result to memory. Functional programming is derived from the mathematics of lambda calculus and does not necessarily correspond to the computer structure. There is clearly a similarity in the respective practical outcome. Imperative processes map computer memory-to-memory locations whereas functions map typed values to typed values. It has been shown that these two styles of programming are equivalent to each other in what they can do (Church–Turing Thesis: see Stanford Encyclopaedia of Philosophy, 2002). In most programming languages there are elements of both kinds of programming but with a major bias to one or other of the methods.

Figure 1.7 shows the Clarity version and an exact functional replica of the typical diagram shown in Fig. 1.6. Since Fig. 1.6 was constructed unbounded by programming issues in order to provide a teaching aid to explain the workings of a formal functional language and since such schemas have also been independently invented elsewhere by others (e.g. Field and Harrison 1988) it seems reasonable to try to adopt this method of representation as a schematic for a functional programming language. Three examples of using this Clarity version of 'stringcopy' function are

```
QUERY> stringcopy #0 "Fred"
""
QUERY> stringcopy #1 "Fred"
"Fred"
QUERY> stringcopy #3 "Fred"
"FredFredFred"
```

Clarity is really a schematic functional program development environment that has been built to provide all the tools, support and mechanisms the system/program designer needs to have in order to make functional programs creatively. There are lots of ideas or methods about how someone should go about designing creatively and most of them have tried to provide a prescriptive set of steps that take a designer onto good program structures.

An example of the method of design is the top-down approach. This suggests that designers start as though they had a finished design. This is their ultimate goal. Then they consider what the general mechanisms needed to achieve that goal are. The

Fig. 1.7 An exact equivalent
of Reade's function
'stringcopy'

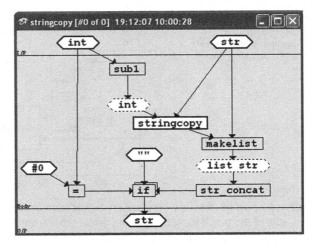

designers then take each of their mechanisms in turn, consider them as sub-goals
and apply the same technique all over again until they reach predefined mechanisms
or computer code. The problem here is that it is not always clear where to start since
a finished product depends upon the available elements from which it is built.

Another popular method is 'object-oriented' where the designers first consider
all the 'objects' they are dealing with and the operations they want to apply to them.
All these methods work very well for some problems but completely fail for others.
In all cases, the chances of getting your design decisions correct or even passable
first time, such as the right choice of mechanisms or objects, are unlikely.

All these approaches are too rigid since ideas and more importantly perspective
of the problem to be solved arise from the activity of design. This in turn will trigger
not just minor adjustments but also major redesigns, redesigns that can be based on
completely new objectives. However, by using functions, such decisions as to what
elements are needed can be made at any time through a process of construction and
this gives the freedom to redesign at any stage. It is the 'problem' that dictates the
route to good design and not some independent notion of 'good practice'.

Experience has shown us that you need at least seven or eight reassessments of
the problem domain before the design is good enough to do the job elegantly. Even
when designers do get their design right, every 'living' program will need to be
modified because life just goes on and things change. Therefore, we built an environment that will allow designers to 'play' and try their ideas out without too much
effort. They can start in the middle and work outwards from many different simultaneous starting points. It is the same way many people solve jigsaw puzzles. They
do what is easy by finding the side edges and some of the major internal features of
the picture. Then they slowly fill in the rest. However, in the programming case a
designer can get the computer to do the work of checking out the designs. If a better
idea occurs or the requirements alter, then the environment will support them for all
their changes.

Different Types of Clarity

There are several kinds of Clarity environments available that are specialised for different purposes. The professional environment (ClarityPro) provides all the facilities for networking at the local level (TCP/IP), file-handling, dynamic link libraries (DLLs), graphics interface functions and some other 300-plus library functions.

Clarity is essentially a development environment that allows a designer to run programs while developing them without the need to commit them. This allows a designer to do a quick test at every step in creating a program since the individual bits can be run at any time. Thus on-the-fly testing can be done since it is the nature of functional programming that every function can be 'run' independently of any programming environment or state. This characteristic is called 'referential transparency' and it relies upon the fact that a function does not depend on external values or flags set up by the program. However, there will be occasions when this is not the case. We will deal with this in chapter 6 page 185.

When a program is finished, it is sometimes useful to disengage all the development support. The schematic program is translated into a functional language called Faith and the freestanding interpreter for Faith is ClarityEye. ClarityEye accepts Clarity-developed programs and runs them without reference to the schema (the Clarity pictures). There is also a version of ClarityEye that can be treated as a DLL. This is FaithDLL and it runs without reference to Windows or other platform-dependent interfaces. The ClarityDLL is written in C and can be compiled to run under many different systems.

We found that all these facilities distracted some beginners from learning the essential elements of functional thinking. It is learning to think about programming in terms of functions that gives a designer the power to create simple solutions. Once such a skill has been learnt, it will give the designer the potential to use this functional thinking in all other programming languages. The result will be much better designs than might have been achieved without this enhanced way of seeing solutions.

So ClarityLite was created to provide a focus for learning functional programming. Some of the facilities found in ClarityPro have been disabled and the library is reduced to about 100 basic functions. We will initially use ClarityLite in this introduction to schematic programming. ClarityPro, ClarityDLL or ClarityEye can run any program developed in ClarityLite.

A Brief History [→ Page 12]

Clarity was first conceived in 1986 on the Sun-Unix workstations before the PC Windows operating systems were generally available. It was created for a project involving Reading University, the General Electric Company (GEC) and Imperial Cancer Research Fund (ICRF). The main purpose of the project was to create a super-fast database engine that could access complex database structures (Addis and Nowell 1990). The concept of Clarity evolved in response to resolving the difficulties in creating complex computer models of genetic structures in terms of a formal logic language (Prolog) working with a large database.

In 1989 the Clarity environment was tested on first-year students to see how they 'took' to it. It was clear from our results that the schematic style of programming could halve the time in model creation and reduces the error rate by a significant factor (approximately one-quarter). This was particularly valuable not because of the speed and error reduction but because functional languages of all kinds are very difficult to teach. Clarity thus proved to be an excellent stepping stone to grasping in practice the subtle ideas behind such languages; it was an excellent teaching tool.

In 1991–1996 Clarity was transferred to the Apple Macintosh OS7 and used in a new project at the University of Bath to explore historical evidence and hence model the science discovery process (Addis et al. 1991). During this time and for a European project on Genetic Algorithms it was also transferred to work on a PC operating system Windows 3.1 (Stender et al. 1993). Further Clarity developments of the PC version under OS Windows XD Professional to date have since been used in several major industrial projects. In particular MPRI Ship Analytics have several products using a Clarity-constructed Expert System for the teaching and the assessment of trainee mariners while they are using different ship simulations (Addis et al. 2005). Other major works include the modelling of discourse (Billinge and Addis 2008) and the explorations of complexity in program structures (Visscher 2005). It is this refined version that is described in this book.

*Getting Going

As described above, Clarity was developed before Windows was established and so many of the assumptions that now generally hold on how to interact with computers do not necessarily hold for Clarity. Although we have moved towards the normal culture of the computer interface there are a few things that are done differently. Usually it is because the nature of schematic programming is better served by different procedures. It is for this reason that the practical descriptions given here make few assumptions and detailed descriptions are given in the early stages. So if many of the initial descriptions seem superfluous or obvious it is because we are ensuring that the instructions are made clear.

The Clarity environment comes as a single program 'Clarity.exe' (we will use Clarity.exe for all variations of Clarity: ClarityLite, ClarityPro, etc.) and is normally recognised by the 'eye of Horus[2]' symbol

clarity.exe .

---

[2]The logo is the mirror image of the Egyptians 'Eye of Horus'. The form is called the Udjat eye representing the eye of the falcon god Horus that was torn from his head by the storm god Seth. It is the combination of the human eye and the markings of the falcon eye. It is used as an amulet against injury and is traditionally used by Egyptian doctors to sign prescriptions or letters. Elements of it are also used to represent fractions. The eye without the markings simply means 'seeing'.

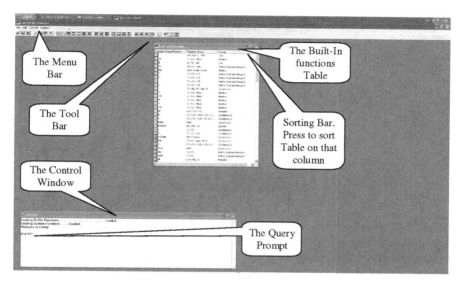

Fig. 1.8 The initial opening of ClarityLite screen

The program should be placed on the main drive in its own folder. Double click on this symbol and the Clarity work environment will open on your screen looking something like Fig. 1.8 .

In Fig. 1.8 there are two Clarity windows (*Control* and *Built-In Functions*), a *menu bar* at the top, which gives access to a range of possible actions, and a *tool bar*. Each of these windows can be made larger or smaller in the normal way. There are several different kinds of windows used by Clarity, some of which can be opened by clicking on the window icons provided in the tool bar. The contents of the menu bar will change depending on which kind of Clarity window has been activated (by clicking once on the window somewhere). Each of the menus in the menu bar will give access to a range of possible actions.

For example, Fig. 1.9 shows the menu 'Window' opened and the range of possible actions relating to the window is displayed. The top item 'Commit...' will translate a drawing (schematic program)[3] into code that can be run. The Ctrl+T indicates that you can have exactly the same effect by pressing the key Ctrl, which should be pressed first and then kept pressed, while pressing T. The 'OK' button in the tool bar also commits. The 'Constructors', 'Function', 'Network' and 'Faith Code' commands are all windows that can be opened and within which a designer can develop, play or see the schema or code.

The window 'User Functions' can be opened once some code is committed and saved on file or a program (referred to as a database in this language) has been

---

[3]This will also 'commit' Faith code put in the Faith Code window. So you can still 'code' if you want to.

Fig. 1.9 The window menu
is opened

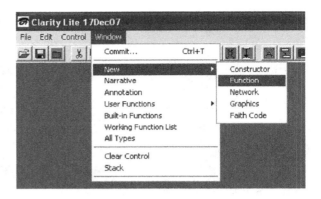

loaded. This will provide a list in one of two forms, 'list view' or ' tree view', of all the functions that are not library or built-in. They are all the other functions that make the program. Double clicking[4] on one of these in the 'User Functions' will open the associated function window. The list can be sorted on function name, date of last modification and output type.

The tool bar provides a useful subset of all these actions given by the menus. These selected actions are all ready to use by simply clicking the icon button required. If the main screen is active the 'arrow' cursor can be placed over a button and then a message will appear showing what that icon button does. Figure 1.10 indicates what some of the icon buttons do.

Note that we have an icon for *open* and *save* a program. Sometimes we will refer to the program as a database. This may seem strange but the reason for this is derived from its history (see Page XX) and that the text version of the schematic language Clarity (Faith) is based on a functional *database* language (Poulovassilis 1988, Poulovassilis & King 1990). This is where a function is considered as a query to a database of functions. The idea comes from extending the concept of a relational

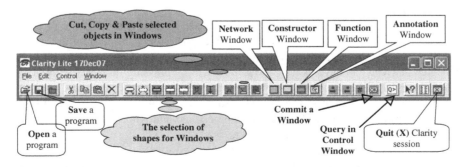

Fig. 1.10 The tool bar commands

---

[4]In some systems (e.g. Windows 95) you require to highlight and press return instead.

database. A 'relation', or a 'set of relations', which form a database (Date 1983) can be extended to include functions because a relation is a particular kind of function. We will explore this idea further in chapter 7.

A Little Bit About Functions[5] [→ Page 17]

Most people are familiar with a mathematical function. The simple notion of adding two numbers together such as 3 and 4 can be represented as

$$3 + 4 = 7$$

where the numbers 3 and 4 are the parameters of the function '+' and the output is the number '7'. Another way of looking at this is as a process '+' that takes two numbers and translates these numbers into another (the answer). This can be shown as a grey box with inputs and outputs (Fig. 1.11).

In this diagram the order of the parameters of '+' is defined clockwise from the output and this will also be the case for Clarity functions. Order is important with some functions such as '−' and '/'. We could have written this in the normal prefix functional notation where the function is always put first and its parameters are listed in a round bracket afterwards. For example, this would become

$$+ (3\ 4) \rightarrow 7$$

where '+' forms a *function* followed by its two *parameters* (3 4). The result is 7. This prefix form can be compared with a typical database relation PARTS (part# : name, quantity) where the part# value is the parameter (key domain) and the result (own domain) is a pair of values (name quantity) (see Fig. 1.5). The advantage of this form is that all functions follow the same structure no matter how many parameters they have, thus

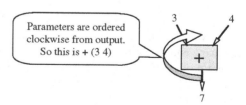

Fig. 1.11 The diagrammatic representation of a function

---

[5]Those readers who are familiar with a strongly typed functional language such as Hope, ML or Miranda may skip the next section. Others may wish to extend their understanding by reading Field and Harrison (1988) or Reade (1989). However, the Faith language that underlies the work in this introduction is a *functional database language* and is described by Poulovassilis and King (1990). The version we are using is defined in Appendix A.

function (parameter1 parameter2 parameter3. ...parameterN)

Since the function is always first, we can move the first bracket so that the brackets encompass the complete expression. This is being done to simplify the way functions are put together. Thus, in the following example of the function 'between' we can present it as

(between 4 7 15) → **True**

where this asks the question "Is 7 between 4 and 15 (in value)" and in this case the result is True. This form has the advantage that we can now nest the functions, thus

(between 4 (+ 3 4) 15) → **True**

where the calculation proceeds from the inner-bracketed expression outwards. Consequently, the value of the function '+' is determined *before* the function '**between**'. We could also draw this expression as shown in Fig. 1.12.

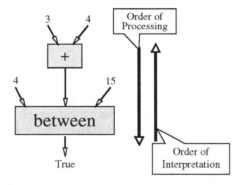

Fig. 1.12 The combination of two functions

Note that this schematic representation changes the description of the processing of imbedded functions to top down rather than inside out. Superficially, the top-down description follows the same form as a normal imperative programming language and might be seen as such in a related 'data flow diagram'. However, the diagram formally remains functional and should *never be confused with a data flow diagram*. This is because the diagram is always first interpreted from bottom to top. In this example there are no ambiguities but in diagrams that contain a function 'if' (see Fig. 1.7) certain branches do not need to be evaluated. This elimination of effort is part of the 'lazy' evaluation nature of the processing.

The 'type' of object the functions process in this case is an 'integer' (or 'int' for short and are just whole numbers). Other objects such as 'strings', 'real numbers' and 'characters' ('str', 'real' and 'char') can be processed. It is also possible to define your own types (see Chapter 3). A function also has a 'type' and this is defined by the kind of object it produces (the output). So '+' is type 'int' and 'between' is type 'bool' (short for 'Boolean').

*"Hello World"

It is traditional in learning to program that the first program to be written is to get the computer to print out "Hello World". We will do the same. This first program will also illustrate that Clarity is principally concerned with problem solving and has only very primitive interface facilities. For the creation of sophisticated interfaces a visual language such as Visual C++ should be used in conjunction with Clarity. How this is done is described later in the book (Chapter 9).

The simplest approach is to use the control window and the built-in function 'print'. So 'print "Hello World"' is typed into the Control Window opposite the prompt QUERY> followed by the return key. Then the result will be "Hello World"True as shown in (Fig. 1.13).

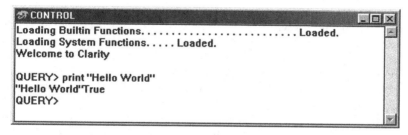

Fig. 1.13 Using the control window

Now this may not be exactly what is expected. The "Hello World" certainly was printed in the control window but then it is immediately followed by 'True'. The reason for this is that the instruction was to print the phrase "Hello World" in the Control Window. However, the *result* of the function 'print' is the Boolean value 'True'. In this case, 'True' means "print operation succeeded" and 'False' means "print operation failed".

It is useful here to make a distinction between the two effects that occur when a function is evaluated. The printing of "Hello World" is an example of a 'side effect'. That is, the function does something in the world that may (or may not) relate to the function name. So the function 'print' could have sounded an alarm, flashed a light or sent a rocket to the moon. The 'primary effect' of function 'print' is to respond to any string with the result 'True' (or 'False'). From the functional programming point of view, the primary effect is the important result. However, sometimes we sneak in a bit of imperative programming, which is the manipulation of side effects. It can be stated that functional programming manipulates mappings and imperative programming focuses on side effects (see Chapter 7).

Exercise 1.1

1. Print out in the control window "Time flies like an arrow".
   Note that in Clarity an integer is always written so it is preceded by a #. Thus, the integer 1 is written as #1 (no space) and the integer 46 is written as #46. Knowing this, and using the built-in library functions '+' and '−', create queries in the control window that do the following:
2. Add the two integers 23 and 48.
3. Add the above result to 32 in a single query (one line of code).
4. Subtract the integer 58 from 125.
5. Subtract the above query from 84 in a single query.
6. Add the three integers 5, 12 and 2 together as a single query (hint see example 'between' and '+').
7. Add the result of adding the two numbers 57 and 32 with that of subtracting the number 43 from 61. Do this as a single query.

An Example Schematic

OXO1A is a program that will learn to play noughts and crosses (OXO or Tic-Tac-Toe) with a player. On opening a database (OXO1A in this case on page 205) a network window may appear showing some of the different functions used in the program and what functions rely on which others. The network window is shown in Fig. 1.14 (left). By double clicking on any of these functions a function window will appear with that function displayed. This is shown in Fig. 1.14 (right). Note that the network does not necessarily show *all* the functions used. To keep the network window uncluttered the designer can choose what functions are shown. You can have a variety of network windows each showing different constructed views of the program. In this case the complete program is shown for OXO.

The inputs of a function are the connecting arrows from either the output of a function or a parameter. The output of a function is a single con-

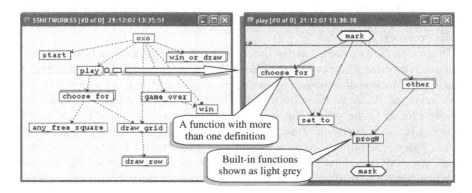

Fig. 1.14   The network window of OXO1A and the function window 'play'

necting arrow directed outwards to another function, constructor or output parameter.

The order of the parameters of a function or a constructor is strictly ordered from the single output arrow (as reference start) in a clockwise direction (see Fig. 1.15). Although a function has only a single output, it can provide many inputs to other functions via a type (or hold) lozenge.

Fig. 1.15 The order of the parameters is important

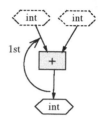

Figure 1.14 shows the function 'play' and this has its 'input' (the 'input parameter') at the top. What is shown is the 'type' of input expected and in this example, it is a 'mark'. A 'mark' is an example of a user-defined type and in this case has been defined elsewhere (not shown here) to have only two possible values: an 'x' or a 'o' in the same way that type **bool** only has the values True or False. Since the 'play' refers to a function that chooses a move in noughts and crosses for a player 'x' or for a player 'o' a different action is required depending upon the input. The function '**choose_for**' does the actual choosing and '**set_to**' places the 'mark' into the noughts and crosses board.

The function '**choose_for**' is a function that has more than one definition. This means, in this example it will do something different to 'x' than for 'o'. The function '**progN**' is displayed slightly grey to show that it is a built-in or library function. This particular function can have many input parameters[6] and will 'evaluate' each parameter in turn in a clockwise order starting with the parameter nearest the output. For '**progN**' the output will always be the same as the last parameter it evaluates. In this case, the output of the function is a value of the user-defined type 'mark'. Now the function 'other' has the job of deciding who plays next and this has more than one definition. Here it takes the input of type 'mark' with a value 'x' and returns the 'mark' value 'o' or takes an input 'o' and returns 'x'. We will look at OXO in more detail in a later chapter.

A First Attempt at a Schematic

Just to make sure the basics are understood we will further develop the idea of "Hello World" using a schematic. The objective is to simply type in the word 'awake' and the response will be "Hello World". Open a function window by click-

---

[6]A very few functions have a variable number of parameters. Another function is 'makelist' that creates a list of all of its inputs. Functions should normally have a fixed number of inputs and a single output. A single output is always the case.

ing on the function window icon button (see Fig. 1.10). This is a 'pink'-coloured window as shown in Fig. 1.16 (left). You will note that there is already an output parameter lozenge placed in the output field at the bottom of the window. This is because all functions must have *one and only one* output. We will deal with this output parameter later.

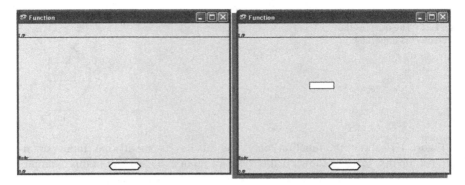

Fig. 1.16 An empty function window and placing a function box in it

Next, select the function window and then go to the shapes for drawing in a function window (see Fig. 1.10) and choose the function box. This is the *middle* of the three box shapes in the tool bar. Bring the cursor back to the window and you will note that the cursor has changed its form (Fig. 1.17). This cursor form reflects in miniature the shape you can expect. Position the cursor where you want the function to be (say in the middle – you can always move it later) and click the left key (Fig. 1.16, right).

Only one function is required now but it is possible to keep clicking and place as many functions as you like anywhere in the function window. If you do put an extra function or two in the window then they can be removed. Items in the window can be removed by selecting them (click to highlight or keep shift depressed as you highlight more than one). Once highlighted then from the edit menu choose 'Clear Selection' at the end or use 'Ctrl+D' on the keyboard.

If you wish, you can always return to the standard cursor (+) by moving the cursor to the bottom section of the function window that contains the output lozenge and left click the mouse. This is also true for other windows of this group even though the bottom section is not always delineated with a line.

Having placed the box, the cursor can then be moved *over* the box. When you type, it will turn into an I-bar, thus indicating that you can continue to type the

Fig. 1.17 Placing a function cursor

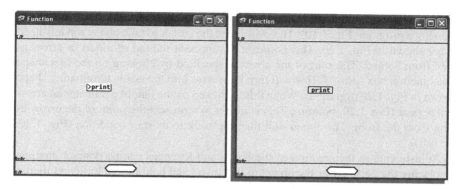

Fig. 1.18 Typing in a function name then return key accepts function

function name. While the typing state is active, the prompt '>' will remain showing (Fig. 1.18, left). After typing, the cursor will return to its previous shape.

Once the typed name is complete the return key will cause the prompt '>' to disappear and only the function name 'print' will remain (Fig. 1.18, right).

If the name is not recognised (say because of a spelling mistake or a function has not been defined) then the name will appear in *italics*. There is only one exception to this and that is the meta-function '*lambda*'. So when it is used the spelling must be checked by human eye. In all other cases the italic mechanism identifies one of the major sources of errors in programming (the typo). The function name can be replaced at anytime by simply typing the name again. It is also possible to edit a name rather than retype it by highlighting the box, move the cursor slightly to the right or left and then click again. This will bring up the contents of the box into a dialogue box that can then be edited.

The function 'print' is then joined onto the output parameter and 'bool' is written in it (Fig. 1.19, left). The 'bool' shows that it will expect to have either True or False as an output. Two objects (boxes or lozenges) are linked together by joining them

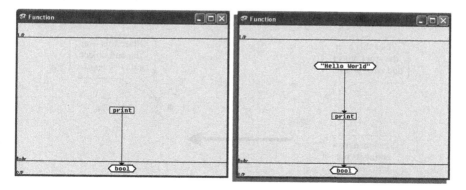

Fig. 1.19 Connecting to the output and the complete function

with an arrow. This linking is done by selecting the arrow (far right of shapes for drawing a program, Fig. 1.10). This will cause the cursor to take on the top left-hand shape shown in Fig. 1.20. This is meant to represent the tail of a dart or arrow as seen from behind. The start of the arrow is specified by clicking on the first shape (the function box 'print'). This will turn the cursor into the arrow terminating shape shown in Fig. 1.20 (top right). When this is clicked on the output parameter an arrow will appear (Fig. 1.20, bottom). This is meant to represent the point of the arrow as seen from the front. The cursor will then flip back to its start condition (Fig. 1.20, top left).

Adjustments to the position of the boxes and lozenges can be done at anytime by placing the cursor over the object to be moved and holding the left-hand mouse button down. An iconic hand appears to show that the object positioning is under your control. All arrows will redraw themselves to maintain the original connectivity *but be careful that the order of the parameters does not change*.

The next step (Fig. 1.19, right) is to place a *parameter* lozenge in the body of the function window (centre field). A parameter lozenge is the same kind as the output lozenge. Of the two lozenge shapes in the tool bar it is the first and has the thickest lines. It is vital that the right kind of lozenge is chosen. There are two lozenges available in the tool bar for you to choose, although there is a third one (plain lines) that is normally inserted by Clarity. All lozenges are to do with indicating types of variables and in principle all arrows should go to or from a lozenge of some kind. In most cases the context is usually sufficient to determine the types but if there is any doubt by the Clarity system on commit it will generate the required lozenge and invite the designer to specify the type.

This *parameter* lozenge will contain the phrase "Hello World". This is equivalent to a local constant in imperative programming. Again note that the lozenge needed for this job is the leftmost one in the tool bar (the thick one). Again, the cursor, when it is moved back into the function window, will have changed shape. This time it will be a small thick lozenge. The lozenge is then placed above the 'print' function as shown in Fig. 1.19 (right). The phrase "Hello World" (including the quotation marks) will be typed into the lozenge. Do not forget to finish by pressing the return key (↵). Finally, the parameter lozenge is linked to 'print' (Fig. 1.19, right).

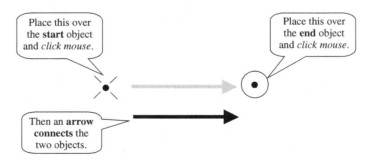

Fig. 1.20 The arrow cursors

Fig. 1.21 What can be done
next

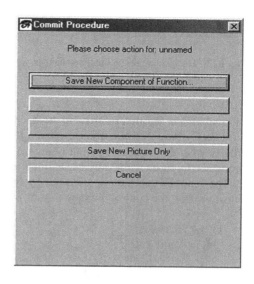

The new function is complete and all that is required to do now is to give it a name. Click the icon 'OK' on the right of the tool bar and up will pop a menu of possible actions (Fig. 1.21). The top bar of this menu is highlighted and is usually the action to be done at this point. Click this bar and a dialogue box (Fig. 1.22, left) will appear. Type in the name of this new function (say) 'awake' (Fig. 1.22, right) and press the OK button on the dialogue box. The following information will be printed in the control window:

```
QUERY> Good! awake declared as a new function
Translated function:
    awake ::= print ("Hello World")
awake Good! A component of function awake defined
Translated OK
```

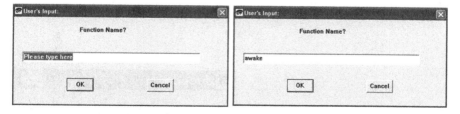

Fig. 1.22 Request to name function and the naming

The window heading (Fig. 1.23) at the top of the function window will change to give the name, the components/definition number 'of' the total number of components/definitions, date and time of commitment. Note that numbering starts at zero (#0). Thus, #0 really means first as is the convention of programming. This process

Fig. 1.23   The heading of the function changes

of *commitment* is often referred to as 'declaring' and/or 'defining' a function. The term *declaration* of a function is reserved to the limited process of simply stating to Clarity what the input and output types are. *Defining* is describing how the input is processed to produce the output. Defining implies declaration.

The function can now be tried out by typing 'awake' (**note** that Clarity is *case* sensitive) into the control window thus:

    QUERY> awake
    "Hello World"True

The function responds by the line "Hello World"True.

Exercise 1.2

As for **Exercise 1.1** but in schematic form.

Changing a Function

This is OK but it would be nice if the primary effect '**True**' was on a different line. What is needed is a 'new line' character to be included as a further side effect of the function 'awake'. It so happens we have a function '**decode**' (and its reverse '**encode**') as a built-in function. Click the sort bar (Fig. 1.8) over the function names

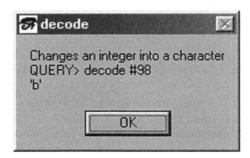

Fig. 1.24   Information about
a built-in function

so you can find it easily. Double click[7] the document icon next to the function 'decode' then a small information window will appear in the middle of your screen (Fig. 1.24).

This tells us that 'decode' will transform an integer into a character. On a PC '#10' is the new line character. The '#' indicates that the characters following represent a whole number (see later). The function 'decode #10' in the control window will confirm the new line by giving a new line.

QUERY> decode #10
'
'

This seems to be what is needed. Note that the character marks ' ' are placed round the new line. The question now is, how should these be combined to work with 'print'? For this, we use the function 'progN' (Fig. 1.25) that will obey a clockwise sequence of functions. Only the last (Nth) function will have its output transferred to the output of 'progN'. The only effect of the other functions will be their side effects. If the 'print' output message is put first followed by a new line character then 'progN' will return a character instead of a 'bool'. The output of the 'awake' function must be changed to 'char' as shown in Fig. 1.25.

So changing the 'awake' function as shown in Fig. 1.25 and clicking 'OK' will cause the action menu (Fig. 1.26) to appear. This is different from the last action menu because the Clarity environment has detected that the declaration of the function has changed. Its output is 'char' not 'bool' and this could affect the functions that use it. As before, the appropriate action is highlighted at the top of the list of possible actions.

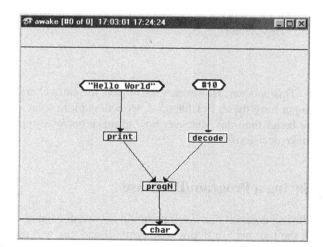

Fig. 1.25 The new 'awake' function after changing

[7]On some PCs the double click option will not work. An alternative method is to highlight the document icon and press return.

Fig. 1.26 List of actions

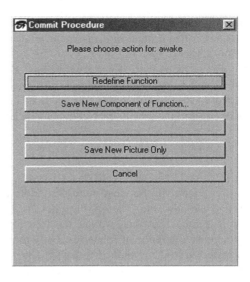

The following report is printed in the control window:

QUERY> Good! awake declared as a new function
Translated function:
    awake ::= progN (print ("Hello World")) (decode (#10))
awake Good! A component of function awake defined
Translated OK

When the function is tried, the following is the result.

QUERY> awake
"Hello World"
`
,

This is better. However, we still have the extra character marks. It would be nice to not have these. In Chapter 2, we will explore some other alternatives that might be better than this, discover how to make our own types and create functions that make decisions.

Saving a Program/Database

Having done all this work it should be saved. Mouse click the second icon button in the tool bar[8] (a floppy disc symbol) and this will open a standard dialogue box

---

[8]This can also be achieved by Ctrl+S.

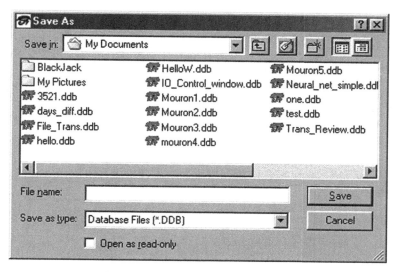

Fig. 1.27 New database dialogue box

(Fig. 1.27) inviting you to give your program/database a name. Type your database name (say HelloW) in the field indicated overwriting the message.

The control window will report what has happened. This shows the two files being written – HelloW.ddb and HelloW.seg. This can be loaded in the next time as shown below with OXO1A.ddb.

QUERY> Created: HelloW.ddb
Created: HelloW.seg
Loading HelloW.ddb. . . Loaded

QUERY> Saving. . . DataBase and Graphs Saved OK

Loading a Program/Database

You will note that a program is stored as two files. One of the files is the Faith code and has the extension '.ddb'. This code is the functional program that has been constructed from the Clarity diagrams. The other file consists of Clarity diagrams. These are coded in a picture language (a schematic) for the Clarity interpreter. This file has the extension '.seg'. The two files together are referred to as the 'database'. Both files can be read as text and edited by a simple text editor. When opening a database, only the .ddb file is shown (see Fig. 1.28) but both will be loaded into the Clarity environment. This operation will be displayed in the control window as follows:

Loading picture segments. . . . . . Loaded
Loading OXO1A.ddb. . . . . Loaded

QUERY>
Faith and Clarity constructors are synchronised.

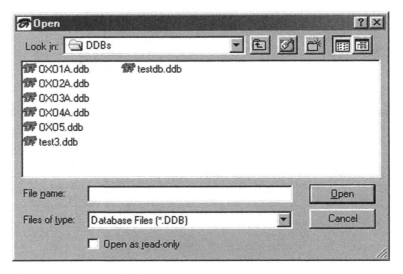

Fig. 1.28 Opening a database (loading a program)

Project: Creating a Simple Clarity Program DICE

We can now go through a step-by-step process of creating a program. This simple program will illustrate several techniques. It is important that the directions are followed while creating this program since the procedure will be used for other exercises.

Dice: Generating a Random Number

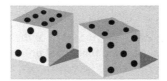

Introduction

This is a simple project which will introduce the reader to one of the basic ideas behind many games, the introduction of chance. The problem with a computer is that it cannot really generate real random numbers. This is because everything is defined and nothing is left to chance. What is done instead is to use a process that has been devised to simulate a sequence of random numbers. The simulation produces a number every time it is called. The sequence of numbers it produces has all the statistical properties of a set of random integers.[9] The problem is that it is always the same sequence. However, we do have the opportunity to start this sequence anywhere and we can do this by *really* choosing a single random number, a number that will select a starting place (say 153rd number from the real start). Since we do not know what this number will be, we cannot predict any number that follows. So each time the process is run the result is just like a 'real' random number. Choosing the initial random number is called 'seeding'.

To Throw Dice

To simulate throwing dice we need to generate a random number between 1 and 6. There is a built-in function **rand** which will generate a random number, but the number will be between 0 and about 30, 000, which is far too large for our purpose. To generate a number no larger than a certain limit, we use a 'modulus', which is the remainder after division by an integer. This is usually written in mathematics as **mod** and is written between two integers (infix notation). For example, **31 mod 4 = 3** because 4 divided into 31 goes 7 times (= 28) and **31 − 28 = 3.** Thus, 3 is the remainder after the division. Other examples are

$$30 \bmod 4 = 2, 29 \bmod 4 = 1, 28 \bmod 4 = 0, 27 \bmod 4 = 3, \text{etc.}$$

In Clarity, the modulus is written '%' and is a built-in function.

In the examples above, when mod 4 was used we got only four remainders – 0, 1, 2 and 3. For a dice, we need six values, so we will use mod 6. Our remainders will be 0, 1, 2, 3, 4 and 5. If we add one, we will get the range 1–6. Look at Diagram 1.1. The diagram should be 'read' from the top down. The number 6 is written **#6** to show it is an **integer**, to distinguish it from the symbol 6 or the character '6'. The parameters to '%' are read clockwise around the output arrow, i.e. **rand** then **#6**. The function **rand** has no parameters.

For example, if **rand** returned #20, **rand** mod **#6** would return **#2.** In Faith, 'rand mod #6' will be written in the form '**% rand #6**', i.e. the function ALWAYS comes first, followed by its parameters. This form is also used in mathematics, e.g. **sin x, log n**, etc.

After obtaining a random number between #0 and #5, we pass it to the built-in function **add1** to have it increased by #1, so it will be in the correct range. The function returns a <u>type **int**</u>, i.e. an integer.

(1) *Define the function **throw in Diagram 1.1**

Test **throw** by calling it in the CONTROL window thus (Diagram 1.2):

---

[9] An integer is a positive whole number such as 3 or 56. No decimals or fractions are allowed. In a set of random integers, between any specified range (say 1–100) means that all the integers in that set have an equal chance of occurring.

Diagram 1.1 throw

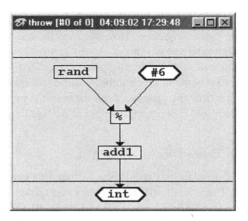

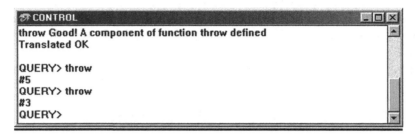

Diagram 1.2 Testing the function 'throw'

Communication

To introduce some communication between the computer and the user and to show
how to use the function **throw** inside another function, look at Diagram 1.3. The
functions **putline**, **getchar** and **progN** are all built-in functions. If we try to read the
diagram from the top down, there seems to be three things going on at once. Moreover, in Clarity, that can be possible. Here, all three things are passed on to **progN**.
Function **progN** ensures that the tasks represented by its parameters are done in a
specified order and the value it returns is the value returned by the last parameter.
All other values are thrown away, which means that, in general, the parameters to
progN have important side effects, such as reading and printing. So, take the parameters clockwise and call **putline**. The function 'putline' prints a string and returns
the value **True**. The side effect is the printing. A string is of type **str** and is a group
of characters enclosed by double quotes, e.g. "Hello". The next parameter to progN
is **getchar**. The function **getchar** waits until the user presses a key. In this case we
are not interested in the value of the character, just the side effect of pressing the
key, so it is OK to 'throw it away'. The last parameter is our new function **throw**.
The function 'throw' will return an integer, type **int**, and therefore so will the function **go** in Diagram 1.3.

Diagram 1.3 The user
interface function 'go'

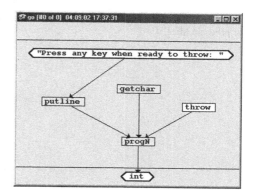

(2) *Define the function **go in Diagram 1.3**

Test **go** in the CONTROL window (Diagram 1.4). You now have a single die to 'throw'.

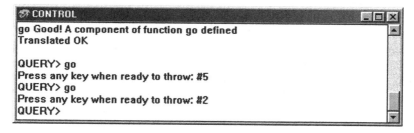

Diagram 1.4 Testing the function 'go'

Note that every time you reload a 'dice' it will start the same sequence all over again from the beginning. This is because the random number generator will simply follow the same calculations. To make it random (in the sense given in the introduction) just call the built-in function '**srand**' (it has no parameters) and this will use the time and date to produce a 'random' seed. You need only call it once per session preferably at the time you first load your database/program 'dice' or the first time you use '**go**'. Alternatively a function could be written that contains '**go**' and this new function is called just once for multiple throws. This function would also do the seeding.

Finally

Save your database and call it 'dice'. Create a network view by opening a network window, go to the find 'menu' and click on 'Create/Update network from database' (Diagram 1.5). This may require a little rearranging to look neat and when you are satisfied with its appearance commit it just like a function window.

Note that a network window uses the stored database. So in order to update a network diagram the database must be saved first.

Diagram 1.5 The network
for program 'dice'

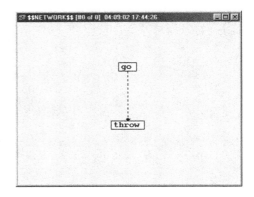

Exercises 1.3

1. Change the dice program so that it <u>always</u> starts a sequence of throws with a random number.
2. Change the above so that the invitation to throw is just "Throw!".
3. Change the invitation to a '>' character without using the function '**putline**'.
4. Change go to go2 so that the string "Your result is" precedes the resulting random number but occurs after the key press. Make sure this answer appears on a new line.
5. Put an extra new line <u>after</u> the resulting random number.
6. Change the program dice to dice2 so that it throws a 12-sided dice.
7. Change dice2 so that the dice only gives even numbers from 2 to 12.

Questions 1.1

1. Given a function $(+ 3 (- 8\ 6))$ what is the result?
2. Given a function $(+ (-3\ 2) (- (+ 5\ 7) (- 7\ 3)))$ what is the result?
3. How many different outputs can a function have?
4. What are the types of #3, 's', and '>'?
5. How do you determine the order of parameters of a function in a function schematic? Illustrate this using subtraction '−' showing the difference between

   a) $- \#10\ \#2$
   b) $- \#2\ \#10$

6. What is meant by 'a function has referential transparency'?
7. Why is referential transparency a 'good' thing to have?
8. What are the differences between a functional and an imperative programming language?

9. How many files are required for a Clarity program?
10. What extensions do these files have?
11. What do they contain?
12. How do you determine the 'type' of a function?
13. What happens if you misspell a function name in a Clarity function box?
14. Why are some boxes shaded?
15. What do the connecting arrows mean in

    (a) A function window?
    (b) A network window?

References

Addis T. R. (1985) *'Designing Knowledge Based Systems'*. Kogan Page/Prentice Hall/Chapman & Hall, London/Englewood Cliffs, NJ/London, published October. Hardback ISBN 0 85038 859 7. Soft back ISBN 1 85091 251 3.

Addis T. R., Addis J. J., Billinge D., Gooding D. and Vissche B-F. (2008) *'The Abductive Loop: Tracking Irrational Sets'* Special Issue Tracking Irrational Sets Science Technology, Ethics. Edited by Magnani L. Journal of Foundations of Science, Vol. 13, No. 1 March pp 5–16, ISSN 1233–1821, Springer.

Addis T. R., Gooding D. C. and Townsend J. J. (1991) *'Modelling Faraday's Discovery of the Electric Motor: An Investigation of the Application of a Functional Database Language'*. Published in the Proceedings of the Fifth European Knowledge Acquisition for Knowledge_Based Systems Workshop, Crieff Hydro, Scotland, 20–24 May.

Addis T. R. and Nowell M. C. C. (1990) *'Scaling Up Knowledge Systems: An Architecture for the GigaKnowledge_base'*. Proceedings of the BCS Specialist Group on Expert Systems, London, September, pp. 238_251.

Addis T. R. and Townsend Addis J. J. (2001) *'Avoiding Knotty Structures in Design: Schematic Functional Programming'*, Journal of Visual Languages and Computing, Vol. 12. pp. 689–715.

Addis T. R., Townsend-Addis J. J. and Gillett, R. (2005), *'Wise Expert: An Expert System for Monitoring Ship Cargo Handling'* SGAI AI 2005 Applications and Innovation in Intelligent Systems XIII, ISBN 10: 1 84628–223 3, pp 137–150.

Billinge D. and Addis T. (2008) *'Seeking Alies: Modelling how Listners Choose their Musical Friends'*, Special Issue of Foundations of Science. Vol 13, No 1. March pp. 53–66, ISSN 1233–1821.

Citrin W. (1996) *'Strategic Directions in Visual Languages Research'*, ACM Computing Surveys, Vol. 28, No. 4. December.

Codd E. F. (1971) *'Further Normalisationof the Database Relational Model'*, IBM Research Report 909, IBM Thomas J. Watson Research Center, Yorktown Heights, New York.

Davis R., Shrobe H. and Szolovitz P. (1993), *'What is a Knowledge Representation'*, AI Magazine, Vol. 14, No. 1, pp. 17–33, Spring.

Field A. J. and Harrison P. G. (1988) *'Functional Programming'*, Addison-Wesley, New York.

Green T. R. G. (1990). *'Programming Languages as Information Structures'*, in Psychology of Programming, edited by Hoc et al., Academic Press, New York, ISBN 0-12-350772-3. pp. 117–137.

Green T. R. G. and Petre M. (1996) *'Usability Analysis of Visual Programming Environments: A 'Cognitive Dimensions' Framework'*, Journal of Visual Languages and Computing Vol. 7, pp. 131–174.

Maier D. (1983) *'The Theory of Relational Databases'*, Computer Science Press, New York. ISBN 0-914894-42-0.

Mead C. and Conway L. (1980), '*Introduction to VLSI Systems*', Addison-Wesley, New York, ISBN 0-201-04358-0.

Poulovassilis A. (1988) '*FDL: An Integration of the Functional Data Model and the Functional Computational Model*', BNCOD6, CUP, Cambridge, pp. 215–236.

Poulovassilis A. and King P. (1990) '*Extending the Functional Data Model to Computational Completeness*'. EDBT-90 (ref. Department of Computer Science, Birkbeck College, University of London).

Reade C. (1989) '*Elements of Functional Programming*', Addison Wesley, New York, ISBN 0-201-12915-9.

Stender J., Addis T. R. and Spenceley S. E. (1993). Principle-Based Engineering and Economic Modelling. '*Parallel Genetic Algorithms*', ed. Stender J., IOS Press, Amsterdam, ISSN: 0922-6389, pp. 117–128.

Stevens W., Myers G. and Constantine L. (1974), '*Structured Design*', IBM Systems Journal Vol. 13, No. 2, pp. 115–139.

Visscher B-V. (2005) '*Exploring Complexity in Software Systems*', PhD Thesis, University of Portsmouth, UK. June.

Wegner P. and Doyle J. (1996) '*Editorial: Strategic Directions in Computing Research*', ACM Computing Surveys, Vol. 28, No. 4. December.

Chapter 2
Making Changes

And though I have the gift of prophecy, and understanding all
mysteries, and all knowledge; and though I have faith, so that
I could remove mountains, and have not charity, I am nothing.
Corinthians 13, 2.

Introduction

One of the criticisms against schematic programming is the issue of 'transparency of the interface '. It was considered that changes and modifications of a visual program are not anywhere near as easy as editing text. In this chapter we will illustrate that this is not an issue and that editing schema is simple and easy; it is certainly as easy as text editing as provided by any program development environment.

In this chapter, we will explore two alternatives in creating a response of "Hello World". In the process of this exploration we will introduce the mechanisms for editing and changing schema . Cutting, copying and pasting schema parts between and within a function, a type and a network window will be described. The equivalent of the spell-check function in document creation has already been described (e.g. an unknown function is given in *italic*). Also in this chapter we will describe annotation. However, during the development of simple projects the environment may warn but it will never stop you from doing what you want, provided it is grammatically correct.

In the first part of this book we will assume that ClarityLite is being used. This has many restrictions and a limited built-in library of functions. In order to prevent clashes when using your program (your functional database) with ClarityPro some of the library functions are recreated with the prefix 'my'.

Problems of Software Design [→ Page 42]

It is worth considering why changes are needed anyway. The problem does not lie in the design process but in the non-conformity of the world being modelled by a simple formal system. It is always beneficial to consider carefully the nature of that

T. Addis, J. Addis, *Drawing Programs: The Theory and Practice of Schematic Functional Programming*, DOI 10.1007/978-1-84882-618-2_2,
© Springer-Verlag London Limited 2010

bit of the world to be modelled and doing a design of the program to be created. It is beneficial because it is easier to correct mistakes and misperceptions while the construct is still fluid and uncommitted simply because it is 'cheaper' in time and effort. Usually, design is considered literally to be a paper exercise but greater flexibility and speed can be achieved through using a suitable computer-aided design tool. However, despite care and consideration problems in design can still occur. One of the useful stepping stones for good design is relational analysis (Codd 1970, Addis 1985). Relational analysis will be considered later (see Chapter 7).

A Typical Example

A typical example of the problems encountered in design is in a company for which we did some work. The company makes specialised automata for industry (e.g. multi-legged robots). The designs require considerable flexibility because their customers wish to run manufacturing systems that are constantly changing to keep pace with the competition and new requirements. The company would like to allow its users to interface easily with their machine systems to facilitate modification to the system during use. However, based on the normal design techniques each bespoke variant is costly to produce. Every item has to be individually programmed for each customer. The programs are non-trivial and in many cases cannot be tested until on the customer's site.

This example is typical of the difficulties with which industry is faced given present approaches to software systems: development, design, maintenance and modification costs. Complex systems are open to continuous modification throughout their lifetime; it is rare to have a final design in any working application.

The Engineering Dimensions of Design

In order to be able to evaluate possible program representations and the design environment in which they are used we propose eight dimensions and four relationships. These describe the potential for change that can be designed into an artefact. They give a language with which to relate important properties of design with a notation or a programming style. They suggest the effects that this potential has on the subsequent quality of the artefact where this quality can be detected through 'indicators'. Indicators are observable characteristics of the program or the environment (see pages 127, 128, 135 to 140).

The first four properties are very similar in that they all have the effect of fragmenting the functions (e.g. sub-routines) into small units:

- **Referential transparency** The advantage of referential transparency is that a function can be tested as an isolated unit.

  Indicators: There will be no side effect programming, e.g. no assignments, no global variables and no sequential (order-dependent) groups of functions.

- *Functional decomposition* of a problem will reduce the design to a set of functions that may be either intensional (composed of other functions) or extensional (in effect a lookup table such as an array or switch statement). Such decomposition should be independent of any particular computer architecture since computer architectures impose a restriction on what can be represented and on how designs are perceived.

  Indicators: There will be a network of user-defined functions that will tend to form a hierarchy. Relatively long path lengths might be expected between top-level functions (i.e. functions with no parents) and basic language functions (i.e. machine code). This is because the problem domain concepts will need to be represented as functional units. These units are likely to be very different from that of the computer; the greater the difference the longer the expected path length.

- *Interoperability* indicates that designs can be responsive to change (O'Reilly, 1999) and in particular it means creating systems of independent working units. Such independent working units can then be used with different systems.

  Indicators: Combines referential transparency with functional decomposition and it is not easily distinguishable from them.

- *System flexibility* refers to the artefact's capacity to be changed or to cope with extensions of its use. It reflects the system's ability to be modified. Flexibility depends on the generality built in to each function. Input parameters should be tested and strategies devised to cope with a range of possible inputs. Thus functions are built to always explore the assumptions about their use. Functions would use functions to analyse the data (e.g. counts on lists, data type testing, conditionals).

  Indicators: Input parameter pattern sensitive (pattern match) extensions could be expected which trigger different strategies. Good referential transparency. Older programs would show traces of change through large numbers of redundant top-level functions.

The next two properties are consequences or give extra benefits that depend on the first four.

- *Reversibility* is the possibility of reconstruction or reverse engineering a design. This ensures that nothing of the basic mechanism is lost in going from design to implementation or from one design representation to another. What losses there are should be easily reinstated or at least detected. Reversibility can also refer to the *inverse* of a function, going from result to the range of parameter values.

  Indicators: In the design case this depends on referential transparency and in the function case this depends on the existence of an 'inverse' function.

- *Design transparency* is the ease of comprehending the overall structure of a system.

  Indicators: Local understanding achieved through simple functions (i.e. functions with few children). This will also result in longer 'call' path lengths since it will involve functional decomposition. The potential for clear overviews of the software through the design environment should also be available. This latter indicator is a representation issue.

The last two properties are concerned with reducing the effort needed by the designer to create an artefact.

- **Environment reactivity** is the immediate responsiveness of the design environment to the designer's decisions and actions.

   Indicators: An interpreter is used.

- **Language extensibility** is how a particular language or representation may be augmented through its own constructions. A measure of this is based on knowing the 'ground state' of the language. The ground state identifies the minimum set of primitives from which all other functions can be derived (see later for further explanation and illustration). The ground state of a functional language[1] has only *three* primitive elements, other than the function itself; these are constructor definitions, parameter pattern match and recursion (Addis and Addis 1998). However, what these three primitives cannot do is provide the side effects that link the abstract functions with the world. This requires engineered code.

   Indicators: The smallest number of elements that provides total control over the machine. Thus the notation should be simple with a minimal grammar involving few symbol types. The machine may be 'virtual' as in the case of the functional language.

Some Definitions for Practical Results

An analysis of program structure in terms of program behaviour using these indicators was done as part of the AMUSE project (EPSRC GR/R11919/01 & GR/R12152/01). Some of them were used as source material for a PhD thesis by Visscher *Exploring Complexity in Software Systems* (Visscher 2005).

Visscher defines *Software Structure* as any component within the software either *composed* or *elementary* that has some definable behaviour. *Elementary* will be procedures such as the programming language's library functions and, at the more primitive level, the machine code. At whatever level you start the task of programming you use these primitives to build new units that perform new behaviours. The range of tasks you can build is in effect infinite since most programming languages are designed to allow primitives and composed procedures to be combined in an infinite number of ways. However, despite this access to an infinite number of behaviours the behaviours are *bounded* by what the primitives provide. So you cannot print with a printer if, for example, it is not attached to the computer or the printer driver is not installed.

A *functional dependency* is the relation between how the mapping of one function influences the mapping of another (see Fig. 2.1). When function A relies on function B for its own functionality, A is then said to be functionally dependent on B.

---

[1] A functional language is derived from lambda calculus. This calculus ensures its coherence as a tool for abstraction and applicability.

Fig. 2.1 An example of a
software structure showing
functional dependencies

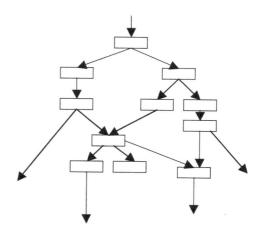

An example of a common functional dependency is where a function A 'calls' a
function B as part of its processing. This will be depicted as

$$A \rightarrow B$$

So we can say, for example, that the function '**sort**' is functionally dependent on
'**greater_than**'; thus

'sort'→ 'greater_than'

since if we were to change '**greater_than**' (or '**>**') to behave like '**less_than**' (or
'**<**') then '**sort**' would do its sorting in a different way and produce the reverse of
what would be expected.

There can be many functions that are dependent on B and A may rely on
many different functions (see Fig. 2.2). However, the functionality (the operational
behaviour) of A will imply the functionality of B but not the other way around; the
existence of A depends on the existence of B. We will call a function A the *dependent* and function B the *enabler* because function B enables function A to have the
desired range of behaviour. The terms 'enabler' and 'dependent' replaces the parent
and child relationship because there is some potential confusion of meaning.[2]

Software structure decomposition is the separation of a function or program into
its constituent or elemental software structure and *a software structure usage* is the
fact of a program constituent or elements being used by some software structure to
build up its new behaviour. In other words the *decomposition* of an element is all
its *enablers* (or the elements of behaviour used to create an element) and the *usage*
of an element is all its *dependents* (or what an element of behaviour is used for).

---

[2] This is because during the activation of a function there is the converse interpretation that the
existence of A depends on the existence of B. This interpretation would imply that the parent is the
child and the child is the parent.

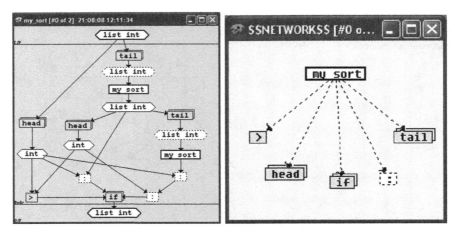

Fig. 2.2 The network window shows the functional dependencies

Given a global interpretation, if there is the possibility of a behaviour changing another element's behaviour, they are called *behaviour dependent* The element whose behaviour is changed is called the *dependent* and the other element is the *enabler*. Two elements are only *behaviour dependent* if the link is direct and not through another element. We can then measure the *decomposition frequency* of an element as the number of elements from which it is composed divided by the total number of *behaviour dependencies* and similarly the *usage frequency* of an element as the number of elements used by it divided by the total number of *behaviour dependencies*.

Choice and Random Selection

There are two distinct forms of rank-frequency distributions that can be observed in human affairs. The first is the well-known Zipf distribution that characterises word usage, peoples' salaries (also called Pareto's law) and city population size. This Zipf distribution implies some kind of constraint in the selection process when people create meaningful structures from a set of items (such as words from characters) and is distinct from the Whitworth distribution that characterises a choice of composing items from a fixed set of items (such as the frequency of characters used in written English).

Visscher created two rank frequency graphs for a range of active commercial programs by first counting the number of dependents that have one, two, etc (n) enablers; this is the distribution for *decomposition*. Then second he counted the number of enablers that have one, two, etc (k) dependents; this is the distribution for *usage*. These numbers are ranked and divided by the total number of elements to obtain their frequency (see Fig. 2.3).

For comparison purposes he also created a structure through a random selection of directed links using the typical frequency of linkages normally found in all the

Fig. 2.3 The distribution difference between enablers (call children) and dependents (call parents)

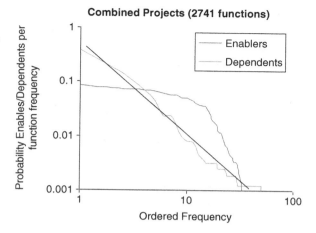

programs examined. This random selection structure shows a Whitworth distribution of the frequency against the rank for the number of distinct elements in *both* decomposition *and* usage. So if there is a difference between these two views of an organisation then it is not because it is a natural consequence of a network.

Over 2.5 K of program elements (e.g. functions) was examined from a range of five commercial programs developed over periods varying from 3 to 20 years by different teams. All these programs were used to simulate different types of cargo ships (such as liquid gas cargo ships). They had all been developed using a mix of languages from FORTRAN, C, C++, and CLARITY. All of these commercial programs show a Zipf distribution for the number of distinct elements in *usage* and a Whitworth distribution for the number of distinct elements in *decomposition* (Fig. 2.3). This suggests that the selection of the dependents is not random. We can infer that *decomposition is arbitrary* while *usage is constrained*. We can assume that designers make the process of understanding more effective by creating new abstractions *from* the behaviour elements. These abstractions are most likely to be useful when they are created by grouping elements together based on their *usage* and not on their *decomposition*.

The key to a good environment is in flexibility of design where changes can be made easily. In some cases a change can have extensive effects requiring many other changes that snowball through the program because of the chains of *behaviour dependencies* The computer-aided design environment should detect the required changes to be done and ensure that these changes are followed through so as to form a consistent system. This will only work sensibly through *usage* by finding the dependent functions rather than through *decomposition* by finding all the enablers. *So functions are not really 'decomposed' but are 'constructed'.* It is also clear that program structure is not symmetrical via its dependency links. So although we will use the term 'functional decomposition' we will take this to mean that functions are composed of selected behaviour elements rather than decomposed into arbitrary sub-functions. This is important because it suggests something valuable about how programs are created and made the choices you should make in the simplification of a complex function. For example, it is only by considering the potential usage of the resulting component parts should one simplify.

*Over Your Shoulder

To continue our practical example we note that so far, the 'Hello World' function is very simple and uncomplicated. If we wish to have a better-printed message, the function 'awake' needs to be adjusted. This adjustment will illustrate how the Clarity system tries to look after you and make sure no mistakes or inconsistent functions are made. This is one of the ways that Clarity supports functional decomposition and system flexibility.

The problem we had with the original method was that we could not explicitly type a new-line anywhere because it is taken as a terminator. Our only chance is to generate a new-line and use that. We can do this using the function 'decode' as shown in Fig. 2.4. This works but it leaves some extra quote marks we would rather not have. So what can be done?

Some useful functions can be found in the built-in functions list. These are '**explode**', '**implode**' and '**reverse**'. To explore what they do, you can double click on them in the built-in list as well as 'interrogate' these functions by trying them out in the query window, thus

QUERY> explode "Hello World"
['H' 'e' 'l' 'l' 'o' 'W' 'o' 'r' 'l' 'd']
QUERY> implode ['H' 'e' 'l' 'l' 'o' ' ' 'W' 'o' 'r' 'l' 'd']
"Hello World"
QUERY> reverse ['H' 'e' 'l' 'l' 'o' ' ' 'W' 'o' 'r' 'l' 'd']
['d' 'l' 'r' 'o' 'W' ' ' 'o' 'l' 'l' 'e' 'H']

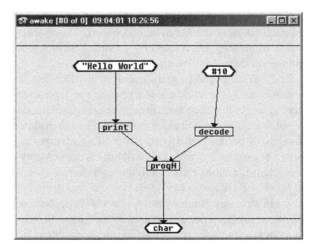

Fig. 2.4 The original 'awake' function'

List Manipulation [→ Page 44]

Before we continue with the process of change, we need to look at the object type 'list'. These types of object have many uses and there is a functional language Lisp (List Processing) that devotes itself to list manipulation. Lisp was the key to Artificial Intelligence in the 1960s (McCarthy et al. 1965). We will use the same functions they used for manipulating lists of things.

There is a 'constructor' symbolised by the colon ':' (called '**cons**') that in effect adds a new item to the front of a list. A constructor is a kind of function that does apparently nothing other than inform the user that a special type of object is being referenced and provides some structure to the object. In this case, the ':' indicates a 'list' type of object so the structure must be designed so that it can represent any length of list. We have already used the special built-in constructor # that shows an integer type. More will be said of constructors later. In the ':' case we note that a list of any length can always be considered to consist of just two objects (except in one particular case, the empty list). The first object is the 'head' of a list, which is the first item in a list, and the second object is a 'tail'. The tail is just the rest of the list and is itself a list. This is a definition of a type and is '*recursive*' since the definition contains a reference to itself. A recursively defined constructor allows lists, in this case, to be 'constructed' of indefinite length. However, lists are normally represented, for both convenient and conventional, with a pair of square brackets, thus

['H' 'e' 'l' 'l' 'o' ' ' 'W' 'o' 'r' 'l' 'd']

But we can represent this list using a ':' as the two objects head and tail

:'H' ['e' 'l' 'l' 'o' ' ' 'W' 'o' 'r' 'l' 'd']

We can try this out in the control window, thus

QUERY> : 'H' ['e' 'l' 'l' 'o' ' ' 'W' 'o' 'r' 'l' 'd']
['H' 'e' 'l' 'l' 'o' ' ' 'W' 'o' 'r' 'l' 'd']

Of course, we can do this again with the tail (because the constructor definition is recursive), thus

QUERY> : 'H' (: 'e' ['l' 'l' 'o' ' ' 'W' 'o' 'r' 'l' 'd'])
['H' 'e' 'l' 'l' 'o' ' ' 'W' 'o' 'r' 'l' 'd']

Note the different uses of square brackets and round brackets. The round bracket delineates a function or constructor whereas the square brackets identify a list. We can continue this process of decomposing a list until we reach the last item. The last item becomes an empty list []. The empty list, the special case of a list that is not two objects, is represented by the constructor '**nil**'. So **nil** ≡ [].

QUERY> 'H' (: 'e'(:'l'(:'l'(:'o'(:' '(:'W'(:'o'(:'r'(:'l'(:'d'nil)))))))))
['H' 'e' 'l' 'l' 'o' ' ' 'W' 'o' 'r' 'l' 'd']

Associated with constructors are functions that manipulate that type of object. The basic pair of functions for list processing is '**head**' and '**tail**'. As you would expect '**head**' will take the head of a list and '**tail**' will return the tail, thus

QUERY> head ['H' 'e' 'l' 'l' 'o' ' ' 'W' 'o' 'r' 'l' 'd']
'H'
QUERY> tail ['H' 'e' 'l' 'l' 'o' ' ' 'W' 'o' 'r' 'l' 'd']
['e' 'l' 'l' 'o' ' ' 'W' 'o' 'r' 'l' 'd']

There are also some complementary functions, which are provided for convenience.

QUERY> front ['H' 'e' 'l' 'l' 'o' ' ' 'W' 'o' 'r' 'l' 'd']
['H' 'e' 'l' 'l' 'o' ' ' 'W' 'o' 'r' 'l']
QUERY> last ['H' 'e' 'l' 'l' 'o' ' ' 'W' 'o' 'r' 'l' 'd']
'd'

The functions 'explode' and 'implode' are symmetrical functions whose sole purpose is to convert a string type into a list-of-chars and back again. Functions that change the type of an object into another are called '*casting*' functions.

*Improving 'Awake'

Figure 2.5 uses list manipulation and casting functions. Here we reasoned that if we could put the new-line character, which is only obtainable through '**decode**', at the end of the string "Hello World" then this would get rid of the new-line appearing as a single character. The function 'explode' will convert the single string into a list of characters. Unfortunately, the constructor ':' will only add a character to the front of a list. We need a function called '**tag**' that will add a character to the end of list. This is an example of decomposing a function into useful sub-functions. The '**tag**' function is available in ClarityPro. So, if we reverse the list, add the new-line and reverse again then the new-line will, in effect, be added to the end of the list of characters. We can then 'implode' the character list into a single string with the new-line as part of it and 'print'.

We can edit the original awake by deleting the function 'progN' and the arrow connecting the string "Hello World" to the function 'print'. To delete a line or icon we can first highlight it by clicking on it and then from the pull down menu Edit we select 'Clear Selection'. Several items can be selected by selecting with the shift key down (as for files in Windows – see later). We can then move the 'decode' and #10 to the other side. Both can be moved together by clicking on one and with the shift key down click on the other. Then hold (depress left-hand mouse button but do not release) one of them and move to the new position. This is similar to moving files in windows. Create the function as shown in Fig. 2.5. There is a mistake – can you spot it?

Fig. 2.5 An edited version of 'awake' with an error

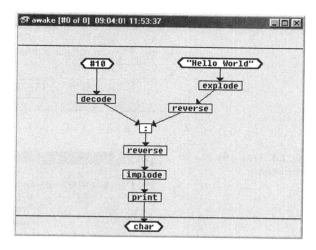

Click 'OK' on the tool bar (commit window) and the pop-up menu, as shown in Fig. 2.6, will appear. Click on the top bar 'Replace Component'.

Fig. 2.6 The choice of actions

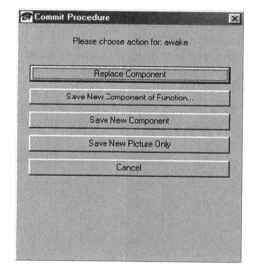

Figure 2.7 shows the warning message that appears indicating that the output of the defined function 'awake' is not what it says in the output lozenge. It should be 'bool' not 'char', as it was originally. It will still work (that is why it is just a warning) but it should be kept consistent. Note that its output type defines the function 'type'. So we will need to change this function type from 'char' to 'bool'. Click the 'OK' button on the warning box.

Another 'warning' message immediately 'pops up' showing that you ought to be more specific about the type of object going into the function 'implode' (Fig. 2.8).

Fig. 2.7 The error detected

Fig. 2.8 Testing for a specific type

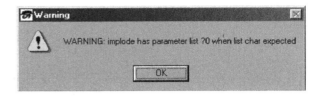

Click 'OK'. The following appears in the control window, which is a reminder of what you should check out and change:

QUERY> WARNING: print has output char when bool expected
WARNING: implode has parameter list ?0 when list char expected
Translated function:
    awake ::= print (implode (reverse (: (decode(#10)) (reverse (explode ("Hello World"))))))
awake Good! A component of function awake defined
Translated OK

The function window has also been changed and a 'type' lozenge is inserted for you to alter to 'list char' (see Fig. 2.9). As before, you will still have to shift the

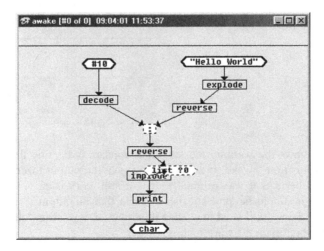

Fig. 2.9 The result of first commitment

function boxes around to get it looking neat and fit in the new lozenge. **Note** that ?0 (or ?1, etc.) is used here to denote a general type of object (int or str or char, etc.). The meanings of these '? variables' are dependent on the context in which they are used.

So the two changes should be made are first to alter the output lozenge from 'char' to 'bool' and then, after adjusting the function boxes and type lozenge to look neater, the new output of reverse should be changed to 'list char'. The result is shown in Fig. 2.10.

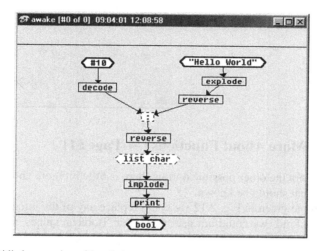

Fig. 2.10 A tidied up version of 'awake'

Click 'OK' to commit the function and Fig. 2.11 will appear giving you a choice of actions. Click the top one 'Redefine Function'.

The control window will report the following:

QUERY> Good! Function awake re-declared
Translated function:
awake ::= print (implode (reverse (: (decode(#10)) (reverse (explode ("Hello World"))))))
awake Good! A component of function awake defined
Translated OK

It is now possible to try the function 'awake' again.

QUERY> awake
"Hello World
"True

This is better, but we still have the double quotes. We can do even better than this.

Fig. 2.11 A set of possible
actions

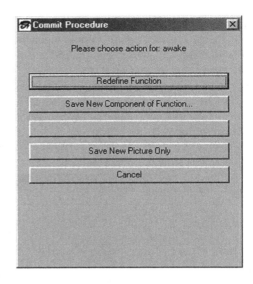

A Little Bit More About Functions [→ Page 51]

Before we explore the other possible option, there is little bit more about functional
programming that should be known.

In the example given in Fig. 2.12 we could replace any of the integers with others of the same kind (we could not use 'words' or 'Boolean values' for example).
A function is said to *map* from a domain consisting of all possible combinations
of the input parameter values (i.e. cross product of the domains) to values of the
output parameter (called the co-domain of the function). So if we were to define the
function '+', for example, we would have to specify what sort of input parameters it
has and what kind of output it produces. In a functional language this might be done
as follows:

> **fdec**
>   + ::= integer **X** integer → integer ;
> ;

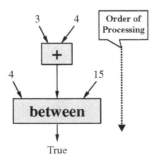

Fig. 2.12 The combination
of two functions

where **X** represents the cross product. That is, every example of one type is paired with every example of the other type. In the above example, it means every possible pairing of integers. However, we can also make an '**add 3**' function by leaving the last parameter blank so it may be used as follows:

$$(+3)(4) \rightarrow 7$$

or

$$(+3)(5) \rightarrow 8$$

The functions (that are kind of incomplete functions) are called *Curried* functions (after the mathematician H. B. Curry). Because we can place the second bracket anywhere, it means that we can make a mapping occur anywhere. Thus, we can write the above declaration as follows:

> **fdec**
>> + ::= integer → integer → integer ;
>
> ;

Built-In Library and Function Types [→ Page 51]

Figure 2.13 shows the built-in library function window in Clarity that gives this kind of information about the built-in functions. For example, the maths function '%' means the 'mod' of a number. That is, the remainder after an integer has been divided into another a whole number of times (see Chapter 1, dice project). So 3 divides into 7 two times with a remainder of one, thus

QUERY> % #7 #3
#1

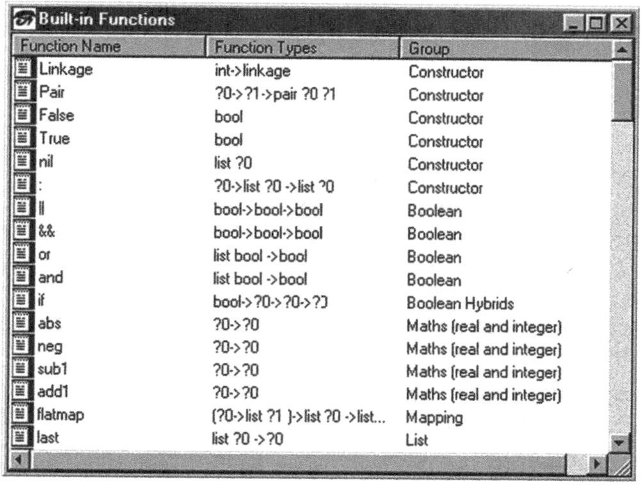

Built-in Functions		
Function Name	**Function Types**	**Group**
Linkage	int->linkage	Constructor
Pair	?0->?1->pair ?0 ?1	Constructor
False	bool	Constructor
True	bool	Constructor
nil	list ?0	Constructor
:	?0->list ?0 ->list ?0	Constructor
ll	bool->bool->bool	Boolean
&&	bool->bool->bool	Boolean
or	list bool ->bool	Boolean
and	list bool ->bool	Boolean
if	bool->?0->?0->?)	Boolean Hybrids
abs	?0->?0	Maths (real and integer)
neg	?0->?0	Maths (real and integer)
sub1	?0->?0	Maths (real and integer)
add1	?0->?0	Maths (real and integer)
flatmap	(?0->list ?1)->list ?0 ->list...	Mapping
last	list ?0 ->?0	List

Fig. 2.13 The built-in library function window

The declaration of the function '%' is

% ::= int → int → int

This tells us that the function '%' takes just two integers as its parameters and will return an integer. This is straightforward but there are some more complicated descriptions, such as the function 'filter', thus

filter ::= (?0 → bool) → list ?0 → list ?0

The first parameter of 'filter' is a function of the form '?0 → bool', such as 'odd', 'even' or the 'curried' function '(> #34)'. Another example of a function that takes a function as a parameter is **'map'**. This function takes a function that has a single parameter and applies it one at a time to each item in a list. Map is declared as

map ::= (?0 → ?1) → (list ?0) → (list ?1)

and is used for example, thus

QUERY> map add1 [#1 #3 #2]
[#2 #4 #3]

The functions that use other functions for their parameters are called '*higher-order functions*'.

The second parameter of 'filter' is the list of items ('list ?0') required to be filtered and the result will be yet another list of similar items ('list ?0'). If you double click on a built-in function in the built-in window, a window will pop up with an example of how that function is used.

Note that we are using a *naming convention* such that all functions start with a lower case character and all constructors (a function that does no mapping) starts with an upper case letter. This is the case except for some built-in constructors such as 'nil'.

Exercise 2.1

1. Write queries that will:

    a) give the first item of the list ['a' 'b' 'c' 'd']
    b) give the last three items of list ['a' 'b' 'c' 'd']
    c) give the second item of the list ['a' 'b' 'c' 'd']
    d) give the first item list [[#1 #2 #3] ['a' 'b' 'c' 'd'] ["Fred" "Jack" "Bob"]]
    e) give the first item of the first list of the list [[#1 #2 #3] ['a' 'b' 'c' 'd'] ["Fred" "Jack" "Bob"]]
    f) give the first item of the second list of the list [[#1 #2 #3] ['a' 'b' 'c' 'd'] ["Fred" "Jack" "Bob"]]
    g) give the second item of the second list of the list [[#1 #2 #3] ['a' 'b' 'c' 'd'] ["Fred" "Jack" "Bob"]]

2. Write queries that will:

    a) put 'a' at the beginning of the list ['b' 'c' 'd']
    b) put 'e' at the end of the list ['a' 'b' 'c' 'd']

c) put the list [#1 #2 #3] as an item at the beginning of the list [['a' 'b' 'c' 'd'] ["Fred" "Jack" "Bob"]]

d) put the list ["Fred" "Jack" "Bob"] as an item at the end of the list [[#1 #2 #3] ['a' 'b' 'c' 'd']]

3. Change the new version of 'awake' (Fig. 2.10) so that there is a new line at the beginning of "Hello World" rather than at the end.

4. Change the 'awake' so that there is a new line at both the beginning and end of "Hello World".

5. Create a function (schematic) called '**mytag**' that adds a single item to the end of a list. The declaration (fdec) of '**mytag**' should be:

$$\text{mytag} ::= (\text{list ?0}) \rightarrow \text{?0} \rightarrow (\text{list ?0})$$

Questions 2.1

1. Put the following into normal list form:

a) : 'a' nil

b) : 'x' (: 'y' nil)

c) : (: #2 (: #4 nil)) (: (: #1 (: #3 nil)) nil)

2. Put the following into 'cons' form:

a) [#2 #3]

b) [['a' 'b']]

c) [[['x']]]

d) [[#3 #6]["Fred" "Jack" "Bob"]]

e) ['a' [#2 #1] [["Bob"]]]

3. What does 'casting ' mean? Give an example.

4. What is the difference between the functions '**prog1**' and '**progN**'?

5. What is a 'Curried' function?

6. What is a 'higher-order' function?

7. What is the ' naming convention ' in Clarity?

*Great Functions Have Little Functions

It would be nice if we could dispense with the double quotes representing the string. Unfortunately, the current 'print' function insists on showing that strings are strings and characters are characters. It will also precede numbers with # or **#r** depending on whether they are integers or real numbers (**Note #r** uses two symbols together to show a real/floating point/decimal number, e.g. #r34.67). This problem is overcome in ClarityPro by having a special output 'narrative' window, which has several output functions with names prefixed by 'nar_'. However, the problem is a useful exercise in ClarityLite.

The library function '**putchar**' has the side effect of putting a single character in the control window. The function returns 'True'. So if we try it in the control window we will get

> QUERY> putchar 'a'
> aTrue

This time there are no single quote marks. The function '**putchar**' really does put out a single character. The 'True' afterwards, of course, is the result of the '**putchar**' function. This result will be hidden if called by another function and only the side effect , the printing of a single unadorned character, will be in the control window. It looks good.

Figure 2.14 shows the initial construction before commitment ('OK') of the function '**myprint**'. This function will accept a list of characters and the function 'map' will apply '**putchar**' to every character in the list. Each character is replaced in the list by a 'True'. In the end, we will have a list of 'True's such as

[True True True True True True True True]

Fig. 2.14 The initial version of '**myprint**'

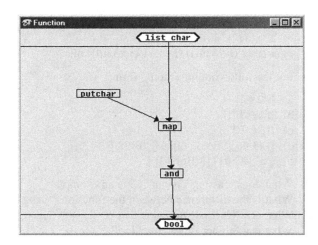

The function '**and**' will simple 'and' the list together to form a single 'True'. This last bit is done for tidiness. It is not necessary but it is good practice .

On committing the function '**myprint**' two warnings will appear.

The first one (Fig. 2.15) will require us to use a type (dotted) lozenge as found on the tool bar. This is needed to reassure Clarity that we do know there is a missing parameter on '**putchar**' and we know what it is.

It is missing, of course, because the function 'map' is going to supply the character and will do so as many times as there are items in the list. In this case, '**putchar**' is just a type of object to be passed on to '**map**'. This 'object' is then used, internally, by the function '**map**'. The function '**putchar**' cannot be interpreted before

Fig. 2.15 A warning about
absent types

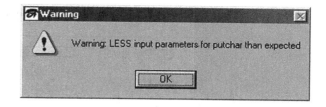

'**map**' can use it and this will be when '**putchar**' has its parameter fulfilled by a
character (only one parameter in this case).

Figure 2.16 shows another warning message that comes next. This is similar
to the one we have had before where you are required to make the type lozenge
'list ?1' more specific, that is 'list bool'. It could be left, since 'list ?1' means a list
of anything we like.

Fig. 2.16 A check for type
correctness

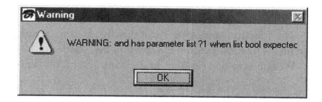

Figure 2.17 shows the final form of '**myprint**' after all our corrections and
adjustments.

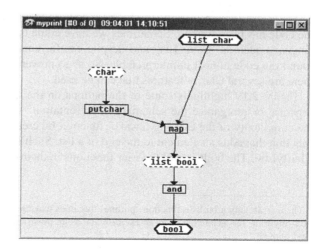

Fig. 2.17 The final form of
'**myprint**'

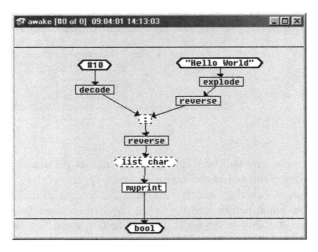

Fig. 2.18 Using '**myprint**' for better output

The function '**myprint**'[3] can now be used in '**awake**' instead of '**implode**' and '**print**'. The modification is shown in Fig. 2.18.

We can now test 'awake' in the control window with a much superior result.

    QUERY> awake
    Hello World
    True

More Schema Editing Features

There are other improvements we can make that is nothing to do with the final result. These are to do with maintaining a representation that is understandable long after the code has been written. Sometimes we have come back to code written in some language such as 'C' or Lisp and despite careful annotation and layout we have found the code almost uninterpretable. So as to prevent such situations happening there are several Clarity features that can be used.

Figure 2.19 highlights some of the buttons on the tool bar that can be used to organise or reorganise the schematic representation. We can use these to reduce the complexity of the existing 'awake' function by creating a variation of the 'tag' function that adds an element to the end of a list. Such a function is not available in ClarityLite. The built-in and the user functions in their list form can be highlighted

---

[3] There is already a built-in function 'putline' that does exactly what 'myprint' does. The function 'myprint' has been created as an exercise and as an illustration of the features of the Clarity environment.

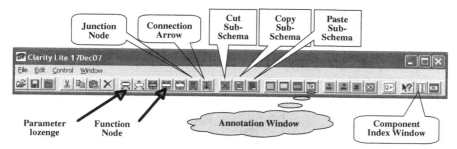

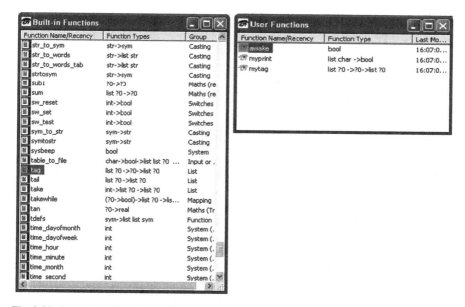

Fig. 2.19 Another look at the tool bar

Fig. 2.20 Part of the ClarityPro built-in functions and user functions windows

(see ClarityPro Fig. 2.20) and then dropped into either a function window to appear as nodes or the control window to appear as text.

We will produce our own tag function to show how a sub-schema (part of the schema) can be extracted from a function window and copied to another window in order to make it a separate function. This is the creation of a sub-schema into a function in its own right and it is done because often many structures are repeated in code within a particular application and, as such, take on the role of a language extension of the problem domain . We know that 'tag' is useful in many domains and it has become a library function. So it is worthwhile making it a function if it is not already available.

Figure 2.21 shows the function 'awake' with the sub-schema that performs the action of 'tag' selected by forming a 'square' around the elements. This is done by

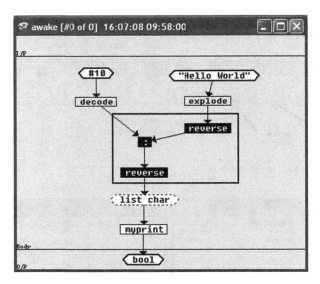

Fig. 2.21   Selecting a sub- schema

putting the normal cursor on the background of the function window and holding
the left key down and pulling out a square. When the button is released the captured
functions will be highlighted for creating a new function in a new window, deletion,
copying or moving.

The selection can now be transferred to a new window by going to the menu item
'edit' and selecting 'Copy Selection to New Window'. Alternatively, a new function
window can be opened by the tool bar and then using the tool bar buttons copy from
one window and paste into the other. If you wish to delete the selected items in the
old window then click 'cut' for that window. The combined process can be achieved
by simply dragging the selected items from one window to the new window.

The function '**mytag**' requires the list parameter to be first (Fig. 2.22) if it is to
conform to the library function '**tag**'. This will result in the crossing of the linking arrows that can too often lead to some very confusing schemas. To avoid such
crossings we draw upon mechanism of a labelled junction as used in electrical circuit diagrams. The source circle is automatically filled and the sink is an open circle.
The label is made similarly to a function in that it can be named, copied, pasted and
cut. More is said about the junction later.

All functions should be annotated to explain what they do (see Fig. 2.22). As
good practice the annotation should contain at least one test with an expected result.
This is so that if a function is replaced or extended then the original functionality
can be tested. It is also a quick way of explaining what is done since normal cut
and paste can be used between the control and annotation windows. We can test a
function by copying the query from the annotation window and pasting it as a Query
into the control window followed by 'return'.

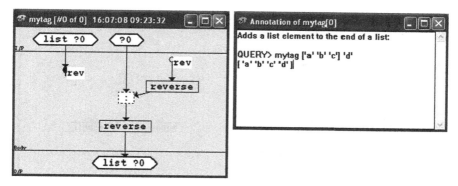

Fig. 2.22 Using the sub- schema and the junction 'rev'

It is possible that a function may have been given the wrong name or there turns out to be a better name. Any name of a symbol such as a function or type can be globally edited. Clicking on the control window then pulling down the edit menu can do this. In the last two items in the list are 'Rename Symbol ...' and 'Remove Symbol ...'. This has been done with 'awake' becoming 'hi' (Fig. 2.23). Note also that this change is automatically extended to all schemas (Fig. 2.24)

Fig. 2.23 The function 'awake' renamed 'hi' globally

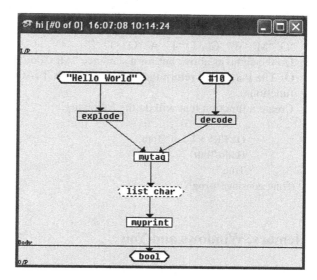

The purpose of these examples was to illustrate how schema can be edited as easily as text. Clarity has the desired transparency of the interface required to make it more acceptable (see criticism by Citrin 1996 given in Chapter 1).

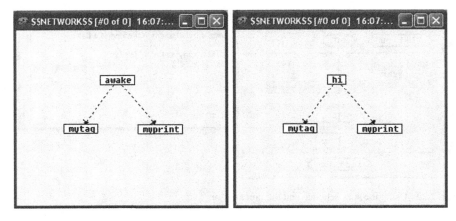

Fig. 2.24 The global rename is reflected in all windows such as the network

Exercise 2.2

1. Create a function that will subtract #1 (see function '**sub1**') from each number in a list of numbers.
2. Create a function that will add #2 to each number in a list of numbers.
3. Create a function that will return a list of all the first items of a list of lists.
4. Create a function that will return the first letter of a list of words (e.g. ["All" "Good" "Men" "Will" "Come" "To" "The" "Aid" "Of" "The" "Party"] → ['A' 'G' 'M' 'W' 'C' 'T' 'T' 'A' 'O' 'T' 'P'].
5. Do the same as above but for a sentence "All Good Men Will Come To The Aid Of The Party" but return the string "AGMWCTTAOTP" (Hint: look at 'casting' functions).
6. Create a function that will do the following:

> QUERY> I_am "Tom"
> Hello Tom
> True

(Hint: consider '**progN**')

Memory, Windows and You

So far, we have *committed* functions and *saved* databases (or programs). These actions are to do with the change of level at which a function or constructor definition or Faith code is stored.

We can consider that the Clarity environment consists of *three levels of memory*. To understand what is happening when a change of commitment level occurs we need to keep these three levels of memory in mind. The program or database is normally stored in main memory during its development. However, in between development stages, the current stage can be saved in a folder. What are saved are two descriptions of the same database, the Faith code with the modifier .ddb and the Clarity schema with the modifier .seg. Both of these are text files and can be read and changed by any text editor. Note that the previous version of the .ddb and the .seg files are saved in .dbk and .sbk respectively. The current database can be replaced (see File menu) by this back-up database.

The advantage of having two different forms of the same thing is that it provides a secure store for your work. If one or other of the files becomes corrupted then it is possible to regenerate a version of the corrupt file from the uncorrupted file. So Faith code can be regenerated from a Clarity schema and a Clarity schema can, in a very limited sense, be regenerated from Faith code (the latter cannot be done with ClarityLite). What is lost in the last transformation is that the internal representation of the 'hold' function is used instead of the line lozenge and both the layout of the diagrams and the annotation are lost.

The initial stage of creating a program is to construct it in one or more of the windows in which the different types of schema are formed: Faith, Declarations, Function and/or Network. The information placed in these *windows* is temporary and not linked with the program at this stage other than through consistency checks. The 'running' program is kept in main memory (Fig. 2.25). To include a function or constructor created in one of the windows in main memory so that it connects to the program is the act of *commitment* (tool bar 'OK'). This action will translate the Faith code and the Clarity schema into the main memory and integrate them into the model. However, even this is not permanent and to ensure that the model is not lost it has to be 'saved' to the database. Once this is done, the model is secure.

The Network window is unusual in that it is principally concerned with describing the state of the model as expressed in the *database* rather than in the *main memory*.[4] The Faith window describes each function in Faith code and its state in

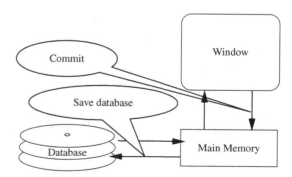

Fig. 2.25 The three types of memory

---

[4] However, it can be used in reverse to place function frames into main memory.

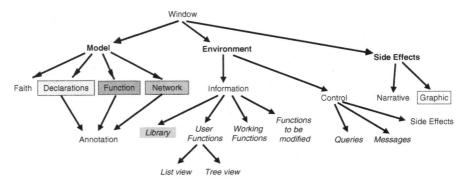

Fig. 2.26 Windows and their role

the *main memory*. So if changes have occurred through program side effects then these changes will be shown for each function in the Faith window.

For the creation of a program or model there are three classes of windows that can be identified (see Fig. 2.26):

1. *Model* – Includes all those windows that incorporate mechanisms for creating a program. They are referred to as the class *model* because a program is considered a model of something.
2. *Environment* – The control window informs us about the design environment and provides the input to the program and some primitive output of the program. The information windows provide details about the library functions (built-ins) and the user's program functions. The latter allows two possible views: List and Tree.
3. *Side Effects* – The windows that provide output for the program. This class of windows is not available in ClarityLite. A 'side effect' is any world event that occurs when a function is applied. In general, this includes some of the physical events of the computer, such as the change of states of memory.

Figure 2.26 shows the complete set of windows separated by their roles. The boxes indicate graphical windows and the others are text. The program is normally formed in the declarations and function windows although the Network and Faith windows will accept program structure and code respectively.

An *annotation window* contains text that is tied to a specific window as well as the tokens in that window. This provides a means of keeping detailed comments, descriptions and explanations about the program. In particular, these annotations should link each function to its role in the program and what the function means in the world it represents. The annotation window can be found under the menu *Features* since it is considered a feature of a function. Names of functions should be chosen with great care. *There is a fourth memory, and that is yours*. Today the function all seems simple but tomorrow, next week or in a year, it will not be so obvious. These annotations are little messages in a bottle that you write to your future self. Be kind to yourself and make the messages useful and clear.

There are currently four *information windows*. The *library* window contains 100 (ClarityLite) or 300+ (ClarityPro) built-in functions. The *user functions* window contains all the functions committed by the user. The *working functions* window provides a means of keeping useful *library* and *user functions* together in one short list. This allows the user to have available frequently used functions that can be clicked on and then clicked into (copied to in the right form) either the *control* window or one of the *model* windows.

The final *information* window is a list of *functions to be modified*. This is a list generated by ClarityPro in response to redefining a function. All the functions that are enabled by the redefined function are listed. These are deleted from the user program except for the associated function window, which allows the user to recommit the dependent functions with the changes required to maintain functional constancy. The list is a 'to be modified' list that must be used from bottom to top. This is because as changes take place this list may grow through additions of functions to the end of the list as more dependencies are discovered. Only when all these functions have been dealt with and the modification list is empty will ClarityPro allow the user to continue. Saving the database before the list is completed will create an inconstant program and this program is liable to crash if reloaded.

Exercises 2.3

1. Construct a function called 'hi' such that the computer responds with 'what is your name?'

2. Construct another function so that if you type in

   QUERY my_name_is *"your name"*

   Then the computer responds with 'Hello *your name*'. How are you?

   For which another reply is needed from the user. For which the response will be 'Tell me why you are *your reply*'.

3. Construct a function that will print any message to the user but will include his name. The user's name is given as a parameter so the 'function' will be declared as

   a) 'function' ::= str → str → str

4. Construct a function using the above so that you type 'hi', it asks your name, you give it your name and the function responds "Thank you *your name*".

Questions 2.2

1. What is a 'side effect'?
2. When you 'commit' a function what memories hold the function?
3. What is the 'fourth' memory?
4. Under what menu can you find the Annotation Window?
5. How many files does the database have?

6. Where are the last modified back-up database kept and how do you recover them.

7. What is lost if you regenerate a schematic from Faith?

Project: A Simple Interactive Program

Guess: Finding Your Number with Least Questions

Introduction

In this project we are going to use all that we have covered so far and introduce three more techniques. The *first* will be the use of 'pattern match' with multiple component functions. The *second* will be a 'hold' lozenge that allows you to have local variables. The *third* is 'mutual recursion' where two functions call each other. We will introduce these techniques through the process of writing a program that will try to guess the number you are thinking.

The problem of determining a number that someone has chosen between some fixed range of numbers (say between 0 and 100) with the minimum number of questions is quite easy. You just ask is it between 0 and 50 (say), if 'yes' is it between 0 and 25 and then if 'no', is it between 24 and 36 and so on. Each time we split the remaining unknown set of numbers into half. We know that identifying a number between 0 and 128 only requires at most six questions. This is interesting because a similar question/answering approach could be used for anything (other than a number) if the features, characteristics or categories of that object are sufficient to identify it. In the game of 20 questions we are told that the unknown object or concept is Animal, Vegetable or Mineral. This information starts the identifying process.

In this project, we simply consider the easy case of 'figure out the number I have chosen'. This is a special case of the more interesting question 'figure out the object/concept I have chosen'. The features of the numbers used are its value but we could have asked questions such as 'is it primary?' or 'is it odd?'.

One wonders why web-search engines do not use this technique (see Chapter 10).

You will be given instructions that are preceded by a bracketed step number, and an * as well as <u>underlined</u>. For example,

(2) *<u>Define the function</u> ' **think_of_number** ' in Diagram 2.1 .

This means that in step 2 you should create the function '**think_of_number**' (**note** the underscores).

Diagram 2.1
'think_of_number'

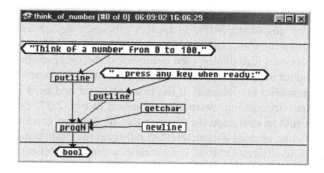

Guess a Number

You think of a number between 0 and 100 and the computer will ask you questions until it knows your number. In this program, there is an example of a mutually *recursive* pair of functions 'find' and 'find_again', i.e. ones that keep calling each other, as the gap between the possibilities narrows. These two functions also use the idea of a *function with more than one definition* (see Chapter 1, Fig. 1.14 'choose_for'). Each definition of a function is called a '*component*' and is distinguished from the other components by the *pattern of input parameter values*. This mechanism (called '*pattern match*') allows you to do some elegant programming. This will be discussed further in Chapter 3.

An example of such a function is the function 'if'. Now you may never have thought of 'if' as a function since it is normally considered as a *process controlling operation*. Since we only have functions in Clarity we have to simulate this control process as an explicit 'mapping'. An example of an explicit mapping is an array (say int A[5]). This is an explicit mapping of the index into the values contained in the array (say A[3] → 253 where the integer 253 was stored at some time). We can do this in Clarity with the mechanism of 'pattern match' by declaring and defining a function with more than one definition where each definition has a unique pattern of input parameters. So we can define 'if' as follows:

```
fdec
    if ::= bool → ?0 → ?0 → ?0;
;
fdef
    if False ?0 ?1 ::= ?1;
    if True ?0 ?1 ::= ?0;
;
```

This function works by matching the pattern such that if the first parameter has the value 'True' then it will result in the second parameter, otherwise for everything else it will result in the third parameter. It is a bit like a two-way switch but works 'upside down' compared to the normal imperative programming 'if'. The reason why this works is due to another efficiency device used in functional interpreters called '*lazy evaluation*'. As you might expect, 'lazy evaluation' means that only the necessary calculations are done. So, if the first parameter of 'if' is True then only the set of functions required for the output of 'if' is needed and thus only the second parameter is evaluated. If the first parameter had been False (or anything else other than True in our alternative definition in Fig. 2.27) then only the third parameter would be evaluated. In this way the 'if' function can switch between evaluating the second or third parameters depending on the truth-value of the first parameter.

To illustrate this as a schematic we have to define a function '_if' because we are not allowed to declare and/or define a library function. However, this does show how you can create your own control functions in Clarity. Figure 2.27 shows the general case and Fig. 2.28 the special case when the first parameter is True. The mechanism of 'best' match does the selection of a component where 'best' will be explained in more detail in Chapter 3. Simply (but not completely), parameters are matched from left to right, left-most taking precedence.

First, look at (do not do anything yet) the function '**think_of_number**' in Diagram 2.1.

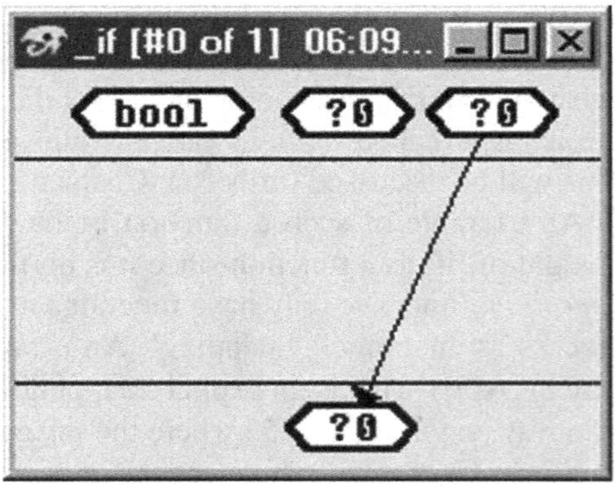

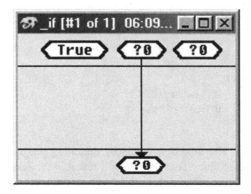

Fig. 2.27 Declaration of '**_if**' definition for 'False' condition. First (#0) component of '**_if**'

Fig. 2.28 Declaration of '**_if**' definition of second (#1) component for 'True' condition

The parameters to the built-in 'progN' are evaluated in a clockwise order. The function 'putline' is a built-in function to output a string (characters enclosed by double quotes). The function 'getchar' is a built-in function. This function waits for a keyboard input, but in this case we are not interested in what the key is, just the fact that it has been pressed (for an example of a side effect, see Chapter 1). The function 'newline' is the function in Diagram 2.2 to output a new-line character (see Chapter 1).

Diagram 2.2 'newline'

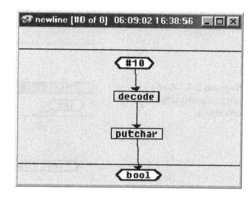

Now do the following:

(1) *Define the function ' **newline**' in Diagram 2.2.
(2) *Define the function ' **think_of_number**' in Diagram 2.1.

Look at the function '**find**' in **Diagrams 2.4 to 2.6** . The function '**find**' is another example of a function with more than one definition. It has three parameters like, but not the same types as, '**if**'. The first parameter is the lowest number in the guessing range, the second is the highest, and the third is the difference between them. There are three *components* to '**find**'. Each component represents a condition we wish to identify in order to do something special. In this example, the first component, component #0, is the general case. The general case is the default pattern if none of the specified patterns fit. However, there are occasions when a general case is not defined. We will explore that issue later. Here we find the '**middle**' of the range (e.g. #50, for #0 to #100). The function interrogates the user through the function '**question**' (see Diagram 2.6) to see if their number is "less than" this one. The process continues with the next guess in '**find_again**' until it is found (the termination condition).

Before we look at '**find_again**', consider the special cases of '**find**' when the difference is #0 or #1. If the difference between the numbers is #0 both numbers are the same, and we have found the answer. If the difference is #1, then the answer must be one or the other. We '**question**' the user to see if their number is "equal to" the first parameter. The result will be True or False, which is the first parameter to

Diagram 2.3 'find'
component #0 <u>before</u>
committing

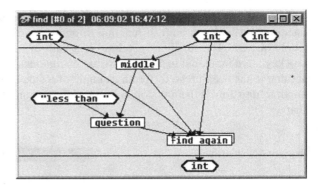

Diagram 2.4 'find'
component #0 <u>after</u>
committing

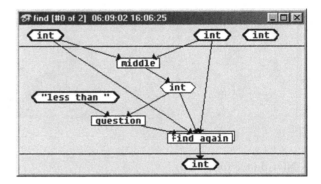

the built-in function '**if**'. If the answer is True, the result is the second parameter of '**if**', i.e. it is the first number or else it is the second number (third parameter of '**if**').

You will note when you commit '**find**' (Diagram 2.3) something strange happens. A new kind of lozenge (with ordinary lines) appears after the function '**middle**' (Diagram 2.4). This is called a 'hold' lozenge and it serves two purposes. The *first* purpose is simply representational in that we need to ensure that every function has one and only one output. If this were not the case then the order of parameters would become ambiguous since there would be more than one reference point. The *second* purpose is that the 'hold' lozenge also reduces the amount of processing by evaluating the function, to which it is attached, once only. In other words, the lozenge acts like a local variable and stores the result. It works such that the first time the function is called (in this case the function '**middle**') the result will be stored. Any subsequent use of this value during the activation of the parent function ('**find**' in this case) will use the stored value rather than recalculate the result. However, if a recalculation is necessary then the *hold* lozenge can manually be replaced by a *type* (dotted) lozenge. In both cases, you may be asked to specify the type of value that is being stored or used at this point. You are expected to type it in replacing whatever is there (usually a ?0).

Diagram 2.5 'find'
component #1

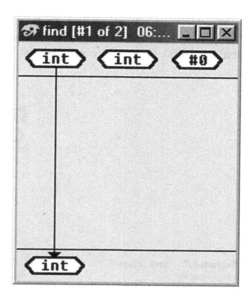

Diagram 2.6   'find'
component #2

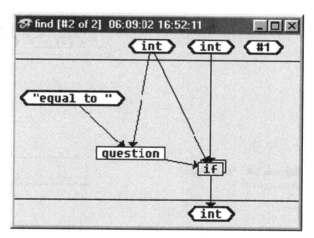

The first parameter to '**find_again**' will be the result of the '**question**' in '**find**'. If the result is True, the general case, component #0, of '**find_again**' will be called and if False the special case, component #1. Suppose the answer is 'yes' then the number (in our example) will be less than #50 and we must guess again between #0 and #49.

The built-in '**sub1**' subtracts #1 from the 'middle' parameter, and the function '**find**' is called again. If however the result of '(**question** "**less than**")' is False, and the number is not less than, say, #50, we must guess again between #50 and #100. The function '**find**' is called again with these new limits.

Now look at the function '**find_again**' in Diagrams 2.7 and 2.8.

Before we can define '**find**' and '**find_again**' we will look at '**middle**', '**question**' and '**diff**'. First look at '**middle**' and '**diff**' Diagrams 2.9 and 2.10.

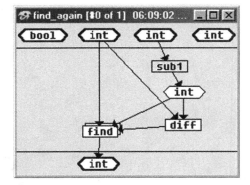

Diagram 2.7   'find_again'
Component #0

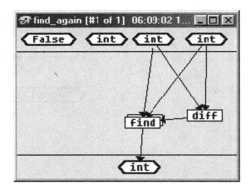

Diagram 2.8   'find_again'
Component #1

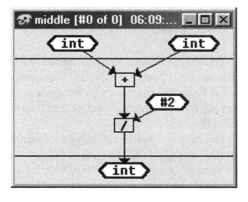

Diagram 2.9   'middle'

Diagram 2.10 'diff'

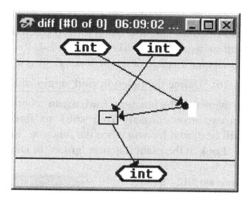

The function '**middle**' finds the integer nearest to the middle of two given integers. '**diff**' finds the difference between the lowest and highest integers. Note that '**diff**' in Diagram 2.10 has a new kind of symbol called a '*junction*'. A *junction* does many things but in this case it allows us to put a bend in the link between the input lozenge and the '-' function. We have to do this because we want the first parameter taken away from the second parameter. The junction is found under the menu 'features' or the tool bar symbol ✗.

(3) *Define the functions ' **middle**' and '**diff**' in Diagrams 2.9 and 2.10.

Now look at **question** in Diagram 2.11.

Diagram 2.11 'question'

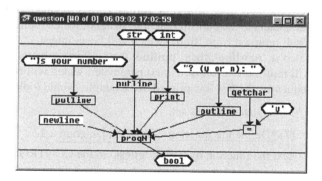

Again, the parameters to **progN** are read in a clockwise order.

If the first parameter to question type str (string) is for example "equal to", and the second is, say, #50, then the whole message after the new line would be

Is your number equal to #50? (y or n):

The function '**getchar**' waits for input, then '=' compares that with 'y' and returns the result.

(4) *Define the function' **question**' in Diagram 2.11 .

(5) *Define the function 'find' in Diagrams 2.4 , 2.5 and 2.6 .

However, note that you create the component #0 of the function '**find**' to look like Diagram 2.3. You will find, as predicted, that on committing the function, it will redraw itself to look like Diagram 2.4. Remember that the lozenge drawn is *not* a parameter lozenge or a *type* lozenge; it is a '*hold*' lozenge.

(6) *Define the function '**find_again**' in Diagrams 2.7 and 2.8.

Note that the function '**find_again**' contains underscores. *Note* also that you draw the two arrows directly from '**sub1**' to '**find**' and '**diff**'. As before, the *hold* lozenge will be drawn for you when the function '**find_again**' is committed.

Look at the main function '**guess**' in Diagram 2.12.

Diagram 2.12 'guess'

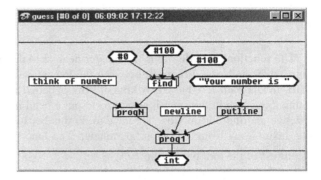

Reading this function from the top down and clockwise around each function box, the function '**think_of_number**' is evaluated first, then '**find**'. These are parameters to the built-in function '**progN**', which returns the last parameter, i.e. the result returned from '**find**' (which will be an integer). The next function to be evaluated is '**newline**', then '**putline**' that will print the message. The built-in '**prog1**' will return the result of its *first* parameter, which will be the integer guessed. Consequently, the last line printed, for example, would look something like this:

Your number is #88

(7) *Define the function '**guess**' in Diagram 2.12.

Test the function by typing '**guess**' in the CONTROL window.

Finally

Save your database and call it '**guess**'. And then create a network view by opening a network window, go to the find 'menu' and click on 'Create/Update network from database'. This may require a little rearranging to look neat and when you are satisfied with its appearance commit it just like a function window.

Diagram 2.13 shows a summary of the complete program in terms of functional dependences. Thus the arrows indicate the called function (resources) needed by a function. Note that a double-headed arrow shows the mutual recursion (and also mutual dependency). Because neither function has precedence we chose to arrange

Diagram 2.13 The network for **'guess'**

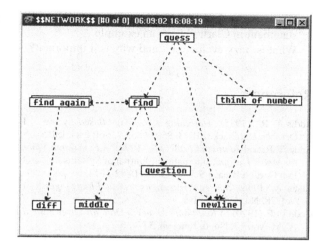

them at the same level. It is very important to draw schematics (function, constructor and network) according to some simple rules. All arrows should point downwards and, where possible, not cross or pass through other icons.

Exercise 2.4

1. Define a function **'ans'** (as a schematic of course) that will switch (like **'if'**) according to three possible strings "Yes", "No" and "Do not know", where

   ans ::= str → ?0 → ?0 → ?0 → ?0;

2. Define a function **'rand_one'** that will generate a list that contains the pair of a random number and a two times that random number. The range of the number does not matter.

3. Define a function **'rand_two'** that will generate a list of just two random numbers. (Hint: consider a 'type' lozenge).

4. Change the function **'guess'**, and any other functions used by 'guess', so that it will work for any number between 0 and 250.

Questions 2.3

1. What is meant by 'mutual recursion'?

2. For what two reasons was the 'hold' lozenge introduced into Clarity?

3. What mechanism would you use to simulate an array with a function in Clarity? Give an example.

4. What mechanism would you use to simulate a 'control' operation or 'case' statement in Clarity? Give an example.
5. What is 'lazy evaluation' and why is it important?

References

Addis T. R., (1985) *'Designing Knowledge-Based Systems'*, Kogan Page. Published, London, October. Hardback ISBN 0 85038 859 7. Soft back ISBN 1 85091 251 3.

Addis T. R. and Townsend Addis J. J. (1998) *'A Functional Schematic Interpreter: An Environment for Model Design'*, International Journal of Systems Research and Information Science, Vol. 7, Pub Gordon Breach Science, ISSN 0882-3014, pp. 263–299.

Citrin W. (1996) *'Strategic Directions in Visual Languages Research'*, ACM Computing surveys, Vol. 28, No. 4. December.

Codd E. F. (1970) *'A Relational Model of Data for Large Shared Data Banks'* Communications of ACM. Vol. 13, No. 6, June, pp. 377–387.

McCarthy J., Abrahams P. W., Edwards D. J., Hart T. P. and Levin M. I. (1965) *'LISP 1.5 Programmer's Manual'*, MIT Press, Cambridge, MA, Twelfth printing 1980. ISBN 0 262 13011 4.

O'Reilly T. (1999) *'Lessons from Open-Source Software Development'*, Communications of ACM, Vol. 42, No. 4. pp. 33–37.

Visscher B-F. (2005) *'Exploring Complexity in Software Systems'*, Ph.D. Thesis University of Portsmouth. Available from: http://www.clarity-support.com/research/papers or The AMUSE project: http://userweb.port.ac.uk/~addist/amuse.html

Chapter 3
In Pursuit of Elegance

And though I bestow all my goods to feed the poor, and though I give my body to be burned and have not charity, it profiteth me nothing.

Corinthians 13, 3.

Introduction

Functional languages were designed to represent the formal operations required to compute in a way that could be made elegant by a designer. There is a beauty in a representation that can capture an idea in both its form and its expressiveness. An example of such elegance is the familiar relationship between energy (E) and mass (M):

$$E = MC^2$$

This equation is elegant because it is so simple and yet expresses a truth that is remarkable. Computation, in its most general form, is also more than just arithmetic calculations; it involves everything we know about the mechanics of thinking. If we can capture the complexity of thought processes elegantly then we will have captured it simply.

The interactions between a computer and a person or a computer and an operational mechanism are awkward processes that do not match well within the functional representation. In this chapter, we will explore some simple ways of interacting with the world in real time that can be achieved by ClarityLite. The intention behind Clarity is for a designer to focus on the creation of functionality and modelling in the first instance rather than providing nice interfaces. ClarityPro has more sophisticated ways of linking with the world that can involve your favourite 'visual' interface language, which we shall not deal with in this chapter. Get the functionality right and the rest will follow.

T. Addis, J. Addis, *Drawing Programs: The Theory and Practice of Schematic Functional Programming*, DOI 10.1007/978-1-84882-618-2_3,

Inferring Internal Experience [→ Page 81]

When preparing to design a program it often starts from the designer talking to the expected users of the program so as to understand their problem in terms that they will comprehend. That part of the world in which their problem exists is known as the 'problem domain'. This task of understanding and translation often comes under the heading of 'Systems Analysis' or 'Object Analysis'. The users' views of their problem domain are often inconsistent simply because each person has their own notion of what exactly the shared world they have in common is like. It is then up to the designer to find a representation of their problem that is acceptable to all the users and also one that is formally consistent with a computer program.

Classical linguistic philosophy suggests that language understanding arrives from denotational (referential) semantics. If we examine what people talk about we find that many of the conversations are descriptions of their own internal life. Since nobody can have direct access to another's internal experiences, the only way in which such experiences can be understood is indirectly through inference and external reference. We can infer each other's experience because we share the state of being a person, in a culture, using a language and sharing external experiences (such as a musical performance; see Billinge and Addis 2003). It is hence possible through conversation to build an internal model of another person's view of the world. The only requirement for this model is to be able to make predictions from conversations about such things as:

- one's own possible future experiences,
- the way one should respond to another person,
- an interpretation of what is said in terms of your own actions,
- new ideas and ways of looking at the world.

For example, if the non-technical music literature is examined,[1] it becomes evident that the common experience does not have to be even the music itself in order for one person to describe an experience to another. The rich and extensive use of metaphor suggests that emotional resonance and association with a commonly understood situation can be employed to trigger what, to the author of the description, is his 'accurate' emotional response to a piece of music (Billinge and Addis 2003, Lakoff and Johnson 1980, Lakoff 1986). Communication, in this case, will depend mostly on our shared humanity, sometimes on our personal experiences but unlike computers, little on any referential semantics (Wittgenstain 1953). This identifies a problem of how we can relate a natural language description, whose nature we do not fully understand, to a formal model, a model that can only depend on reference to provide meaning.

---

[1] Examples are record reviews, concert reports, descriptive, as opposed to analytical, music histories and biographies.

A Philosophical View of Computing [→ Page 81]

The implications of such observations on the communication of internal experience are radical. We can take the step that predicate calculus and its philosophical bases (Wittgenstein 1921) is a complete model of computing and further, a complete system for any formal description. We can take this step because the Church–Turing Thesis shows that the Turing Machine (the classical computer) is equivalent to Lambda calculus involving recursive functions (Kleene 1967). Lambda calculus and recursive functions together form the description of a functional programming language (e.g. ML, Hope and Faith). As with all formal systems the descriptive form is based on denotational (or referential) semantics. That is, the meaning of a word is the object it represents in the world. However, if you look carefully at the requirements to be an object that can cope with the role of being a referent for a formal system it must have some logically very strange properties. Objects must be

- *independent* in that they can freely combine to form 'states of affairs' that can be described. You need this independence so that every object can participate freely as a referent in any predicate calculus statement. So if we state that 'for all A, A implies B and we know that an example of A exists' then we want to be able to *always* infer that there will be an associated example of B. We do not want to have to start making exceptions. If we do allow exceptions than how do we know that the list of exceptions is either complete or finite.
- *atomic* in that there are no smaller constituents. If a referent is not atomic then it can be decomposed and reconstructed into a different kind of object. This produces the possibility that any inferences made that include this object could become invalid under its reconstruction. All the statements that use this object will change their meaning or if the object is destroyed the statements will become meaningless. They become meaningless simply because the object is no longer there to refer to. OK, it might exist in the past but formal systems only exist in the present unless a time dimension is explicitly stated.
- *in all possible worlds*. This is required because you want your formal system to describe all possible situations that might occur in all potentially describable worlds; if you can think of it you should be able to describe it.
- *immaterial*. A material object is not always accessible and suffers from not being atomic. An example of two non-material objects that describes the material world is the Newtonian physicist's view of force and mass. Both of these are suitable candidates to be objects (see below) but neither of them can exist on their own in isolation. So in this sense they must be:
- *indescribable* except by their behaviour (form). To be describable means that they have constituent parts that are in a relationship, they form a statement built from other elements and will thus be non- atomic.
- *self governed* in that they have their own internal rules of behaviour. So 'Mass' and 'Force' are *only* understood through their relative behaviour with each other as a measurable and observable acceleration; thus

$$\text{Force} = \text{Mass} * \text{Acceleration}$$

Function (with Constructor) and Type are also understood in the same way through the process of transformation.

These referents (objects) are intended to be more than just elements of description; they form the real world. They provide the underlying constraints that make us acknowledge 'reality' and 'truth' (of a statement). From these referents, the full force of logic, predicate and propositional calculus retains stability of meaning and sense. Such a stance results in the position that everything is potentially unambiguously describable provided we can always categorise the world in a way that is unambiguous. There must always be a method of determining if an object or observation belongs to a named set since without that possibility we cannot apply deductive logic or make any certain inferences about the world.

We now introduce here the idea of a 'rational' set.[2]

> A *'rational' set* is a set where there is a finite set of rules that can include unambiguously any member of that set and unambiguously excludes any non-member of that set.

It should be noted that all the sets used by formal systems are assumed to be rational where set membership is always specifiable and context independent or has an explicit context that is also rational. If we cannot do this then there will be no atomic objects and no description of compound objects expressible that makes any sense. There is the notion of 'fuzzy' sets but these are also rational in that membership for a particular 'fuzzy' distinction is defined (see Gegov 2007).

It might be argued that all sets are really rational; it is just that we do not yet know all the rules. This may be the case but, from a practical point of view, if we do not have access to the rules that define membership of an element to a set then it is impossible for us to determine when a statement is applicable. Such a statement remains meaningless or at best has a very limited and constrained sense.

You might also say, "but what about 'Unicorns'?" The Unicorn is a mythical animal and does not exist and yet we can describe it and talk about it. The fact that we can describe it is a clue that it is not an object but 'a description'. The argument is that names (in practice signs, the visible part of an expression or name) in

---

[2] Jan Addis proposed the term of rational and irrational sets (private communication February 2004). She related the irrational sets to Cantor's (1845–1918) irrational numbers. In the case of rational numbers the rule was a member number could be expressed as a ratio of integers and they are countable. Irrational numbers are not countable. Examples of irrational numbers are $\sqrt{2}$ and π. There are infinitely more irrational numbers than rational numbers. However, as for irrational numbers an irrational set can always be approximately represented by a rational set.

propositions do not always refer to primitive objects but are themselves referencing propositions.

These propositions, often referred to as objects, in computer programs, in turn, are complexes that finally end up as compound statements whose ultimate referent is the bit. For example, in computer languages we have seven bits of the ASCII code identifying 1000001 as the character A and 1000010 as the character B and so on. There are also special characters that relate to actions such as 'delete' 1111111 and 'start' 0000001. Here the bit is the mechanical equivalent of a referent object. The bit, if taken as a detectable distinction, has all the strange properties of an object.[3] For example, a world cannot exist (or at least be detectable) unless it contains at least one distinction. It so happens that a 'bit' is a concept that can only be embodied in a distinction. A distinction is immaterial since although physical phenomena may be used (voltage for example) it is the relationship between the physical phenomena that captures the 'bit'. Further, it is at the bit level that the program links to the world and has meaning; in normal practice they are voltage levels in silicon. It is this meaning that allows the program to have "sense" with respect to the computer. Thus formal semantics and the ability for programmers to create procedures and sub-routines (sub-propositions or expressions) are the primary characteristic of all high level and assembler programming languages.[4]

The consequence of such a formal model is that any set of names can be used in a program to represent a proposition. All that is necessary is that there is a formal definition that gives the name meaning within the program in terms of the proposition it represents. Since a proposition can take on an infinite number of forms through the use of tautologies and other formal equivalences there is an infinite but bounded set of possible organisations that can be adopted for a program. One would expect that there would be some minimum organisation or representation for any given program. However, the additional adopted structure is also represented, in the end, by bits on a computer. This will appear as a program overhead that is used to support a chosen program organisation or structure and in this sense only the program interpretation has changed.

Note that we have introduced the option of choosing 'names' and 'organisation' in a program. A program is a formal statement and this means that a program has 'meaning' with reference to the atomic object 'the bit'. We then might ask the question: If the 'meaning' of the program is the same for different names and organisations then why should we be bothered to make anything other than an arbitrary choice of these names and organisation? The answer is that such a choice has consequences.

---

[3] For Wittgenstein a particular 'bit' is an argument place (Tractates paragraph 2.0131).

[4] The original high level programming language COBOL in its initial form did not provide procedures and sub-routines except those that were pre-constructed in assembler as library routines.

Dual Semantics [→ Page 81]

The choice of names and organisation in a program is not arbitrary but is a link
to the fact that computer languages have a *dual semantics* (Stepney et al 2005).
Dual semantics in that the program signs (e.g. the names/labels given to data items,
procedures and sub-routines) at the highest level also have referents in the problem
domain (Fig. 3.1) as well as bits in a computer. This set of referents is drawn from
the analysis of the problem domain in terms of records (as in database and program
structures), relations (as in normalised data structures) and objects (as in object-
orientation where the objects are usually propositions defined in terms of examples).
It is this analysis that identifies constructs in the world that are meant to be stable and
unchanging to which names can be given and meaning assigned. It is the purpose
of the analyst that the compound objects chosen to represent the problem domain
will be stable enough, and for long enough, to behave like atomic objects during
the lifetime of the program. In practice this purpose is rarely achieved.

Now it is acceptable that propositions can represent material properties, relationships, and any complex model of the world *but a proposition can have one and only
one complete analysis*. If it has more than one analysis in the sense of an alternative
interpretation then it would be impossible to compute or to know what meaning to
give it. Meaning in this case means a predetermined and single result. So even such
functions as (sqrt #1), which have two possible answers #1 and #-1, is required to
give a single answer. This can either be #1 (as it is in Clarity) or the pair [#1 #-1].
The function 'rand' (generates a pseudo random number) is also specific and each
time it is called it will step through a predefined sequence of numbers. It is for this
reason that there is an additional related function '**srand**' which starts the sequence
at different points so that a random element can be added. In Clarity the starting
position is chosen from the time and date. Even this random element has a single
analysis.

The analysis of a proposition or program is dependent on only the *essential* features of the proposition or program that links it to the referent objects, which is the
bit in our case (Fig. 3.2). The essential features are those that identify the proposition
for what it is. In our case the uniqueness of the names we have used within the program for our variables, relations and operations. How we have made the component
parts unique is not important other than its uniqueness is recognised. *Accidental* features are all those other properties of the proposition that we can identify but have
not been used to identify it. So 'colour' of the characters may be *accidental* but the
choice and sequence of the letters may be an essential characteristic.

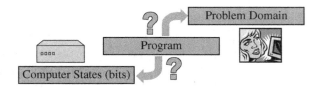

Fig. 3.1 The problem of dual
semantics

Fig. 3.2 The only rational interpretation of a computer program

A computer program, as we have already seen, has such an analysis with respect to the computational engine (Fig. 3.2), where the meaning of the program in terms of its propositions maps eventually to the pattern of bits in store. But we can have an *alternative* interpretation of a program provided we use only the remaining accidental features. We can use other features such as colour, capital and italic letters. We can use layout, the organisation (decomposition) and the alternative tautologies of the logic to reflect the domain. In particular:

We can use the concept of constructor and 'type' in a functional program to be functions interpreted by the user whereas we use the concept of extensional (lookup table) and intensional (composed) functions to be left to the computer to interpret.

This necessity for a dual semantics develops a peculiar tension in program design that is hard to keep stable, particularly with respect to the informal, and often undefined, mechanism which links the program names with the user's domain. It is undefined because it relies on people to invoke meaning from these accidental characteristics. To make matters worse, the 'objects' that are usually chosen to be referenced in the informal analysis of the problem domain are not normally rational sets. They are propositions posing as atomic objects (rational sets). The reason for this is that most practical programs would require an unacceptable level of complexity and computation to fulfil the ideal to be only referencing objects in the sense we have just described.

So we have computer programs with a semantics based on computer bits but we create programs that cannot rationally be assigned meaning for the very problem domain for which they have been written. Programs must remain in the domain of rational sets if they are to be implemented on a machine (Addis et al 2008). However, we do have the freedom to use the program's accidental properties without affecting the program's meaning with respect to the computer. We can choose the names we use and select the computer organisation from the possibilities bounded by the essential program. The tension caused by the dual semantics that pivots on the essential and accidental meaning of the signs used in programs is the underlying stimulus for the continued search for new languages, new program structuring and new systems design methods (e.g. Java, conceptual modelling and object orientation).

More on Functions [→ Page 81]

In the description of functions, so far, we have not outlined any *functional* mechanism of carrying out arithmetic operations, such as addition, other than the built-in functions '+' and '**add1**'. For these built-in functions, we use the computer machinery; often special high-speed arithmetic units. In this case, the arithmetic operations are side effects in that the process is done as a world event. Such operations are not functional in *principle* though in *practice* they have the same outcome. This is fine, but the functional language, in its pure form (i.e. not using side effects), does not assume that there is a computer handy. If we did not have a computer to do this arithmetic (i.e. adding) the best we could do is simply list all the possible combinations (pairs of integers), thus

> **fdef**
> $+ 1\ 1 ::= 2 ;$
> $+ 1\ 2 ::= 3 ;$
> $+ 2\ 5 ::= 7 ;$
> $+ 3\ 4 ::= 7 ;$
>
> ;

and so on. Then all we do is look up the pattern of parameters in the table. As we stated earlier each pattern is referred to as a *component* of the function '+' and is a set of pattern-sensitive definitions of the function. The set of components that are specifically defined with constants (as in this case) is called the *extension* of the function. If a pattern cannot be found then the function is returned, thus

$$(+\ 3\ 5) \rightarrow (+\ 3\ 5)$$

So if a function cannot be evaluated it is simply returned unevaluated (it is not an error[5]). There is a way round this particular problem of defining addition by using the idea behind the Curried function (+1):

$$(+\ 1)\ \text{number} \rightarrow \text{next number}$$

We would have to define a mechanism for generating the next number in a series of infinite numbers. As we have seen, the computer system already has this function

---

[5] In fact, such an unevaluated function can be used just like a constructor; it may be used to package information and may be accessed in the same way.

'**add1**' as one of the built-in library functions. In this case we have to use the integers provided by the computer and we indicate these types of integers by preceding them with the symbol # (an example of a basic constructor with a single parameter). We have to interpret what an integer means in the problem domain ourselves.

$$(+ \text{ \#3 \#4}) \rightarrow \text{\#7}$$

The computer's arithmetic unit carries out the calculation and the result returned. This calculation is also considered a 'side effect' because it is triggered by the calling of the function '**+**' (in this case) and as we have suggested, the calculation is done 'on the side'. Remember that side effects happen in the world and are beyond the range of defining events within a functional language.

However, if we wanted to define *our own numbers* we can do so by introducing *our own type* where each integer is a *'constructor'* with no parameters. These constructors define what is called an *'enumerated'* type.

> **cdec**
> 0 ::= digit
> 1 ::= digit
> 2 ::= digit
> 3 ::= digit
> .
>
> ;

We would then have to define the way in which numbers are concatenated to form new numbers in an infinite series followed by the arithmetic functions (see Chapter 4 for a complete implementation of integer arithmetic). However, we have a perfectly good set of mathematical (side effect) mechanisms associated with the computer. What we have shown, and this is important, is that the functional language is capable of defining from first principles any kind of mathematics or calculus. It is important because it proves, by induction, that the functional language can express any formal system in its minimum form of just the three mechanisms of pattern match, function definition[6] and recursion .

*Creating Components

We have already created functions with more than one component (Chapter 2). However, it is worth noting that in many cases you can define a component by using

---

[6] Function definition is really the use of 'lambda' that will be covered later. The term 'function' also includes the term 'constructor'.

the first component as a template (or form). In the example, for explicitly defining '+' we can define a '_+' using ClarityLite ('underscore' to distinguish it from the built in +). Figures 3.3, 3.4, 3.5, 3.6, 3.7, 3.8, 3.9, 3.10 and 3.11 illustrate the steps you go through.

First (Fig. 3.3),[7] we open a function window (pink) and then second, we place two parameter lozenges (thick line) in the input field. The types are then typed into these lozenges and the output lozenge. In these cases, they are all 'int'. This is then

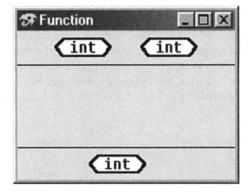

Fig. 3.3 Input/output types

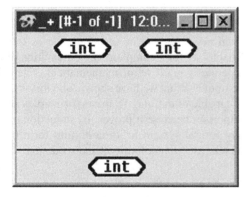

Fig. 3.4 Declare function 'OK'

---

[7] In most cases the windows have been reduced in size via the edit menu. This reduced size can then be stored and allows many more windows to be on the desk top at the same time. It is 'good practice' to not expand the size of a window larger than the pre-set size. This encourages keeping functions simple. Functions that are getting complicated (more than seven to nine different functions) should be decomposed into simpler functions.

Fig. 3.5 Put input/output values

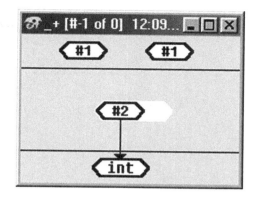

Fig. 3.6 Commit new component

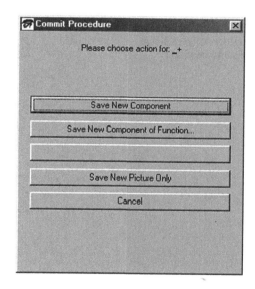

Fig. 3.7 First component accepted

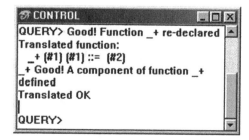

Fig. 3.8 First component

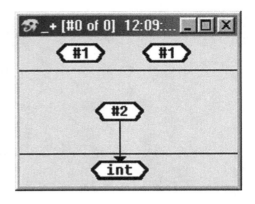

Fig. 3.9 Change first to
second component

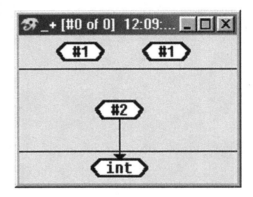

Fig. 3.10 Second component
accepted

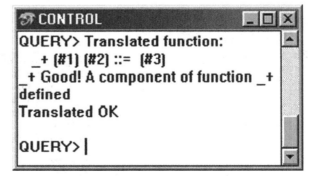

Fig. 3.11 Second component

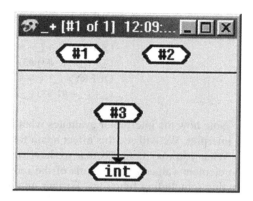

committed so as to register the declaration of the function '_+'. We do this because we do *not* want a general case. Anything not explicitly defined must fail by simply returning the unevaluated function (e.g. (_+ #7 #5)). The control window responds with 'Good! Function _+ declared' (see Fig. 3.7) and the function window changes to show that a declaration only has been made either with '_+ [#-1 of -1]' or '_+ [#-1 of 0]' in the banner (Fig. 3.4). The difference depends on the opportunity the function window has to update itself.

Second (Fig. 3.5) the first explicit component can now use the declaration as a template for the first component. However, we need to explicitly give an output value for the function and using a parameter lozenge to feed the output does this. Figure 3.5 shows how we alter the input lozenges and add the explicit value we require to the output. This is then committed (Fig. 3.6). Note that Clarity detects the change in the input parameters and infers that you are defining a new component. The function is then translated (next line in Fig. 3.7) and the new component is marked by a change in the banner of the function window to '_+ [#0 of 0]. This is the first actual component of the function.

Another component can then be created from this first component by simply altering the values in the lozenges (Fig. 3.9) and committing it (Fig. 3.10) giving you a new component (Fig. 3.11). The second component is marked '_+ [#1 of 1]' in the banner.

There are several combinations worth trying. These will help you understand the behaviour of such a description that does not have a general case. Consider

```
QUERY> _+ #1 #2
#3
QUERY> _+ #1 #1
#2
QUERY> _+ #2 #3
( _+ #2 #3)
```

QUERY> (_+ (_+ #1 #1) (_+ #1 #2))
(_+ #2 #3)
QUERY> (_+ (_+ #1 #3) (_+ #1 #2))
(_+ (_+ #1 #3) #3)
QUERY> (_+ (_+ #1 #3) (_+ #1 #5))
(_+ (_+ #1 #3) (_+ #1 #5))

Note how the interpreter evaluates what it can and simply leaves the rest for you to interpret. We will see this effect again for constructors.

What you may notice is that we have, in effect, a two-dimensional array where the element values are the sums of the indices. These values, of course, could be anything, including functions. Further, the indexing does not have to be limited to integers but can be 'strings', 'characters', 'lists', 'reals', 'own data types' and even 'structures'. One advantage of using a function as an array is that you can store sparse arrays very efficiently. Sparse arrays are arrays with few elements that are scattered over large range of index values. This is because you do not have to store those elements of no value. The general-case (i.e. any index combination not specified) can be used for all 'no values'. It will return a null value. Assignment to arrays will be considered in Chapter 4. The accessing of such functions is quick. The limitation (if you can call it that) is that an array of this kind is restricted to 250 dimensions (i.e. 250 parameters).

Constructors: The Packaging of Data

Constructors are a valuable mechanism for creating our own types of objects. They wrap up into a single package a collection of data that has some fixed and humanly understood relationship.

In Clarity, we declare a new type of object normally through a *constructor window* (see Figs. 3.12, 3.13 and 3.14). This must first be opened (yellow background). An empty output lozenge will appear in the output field of the window. The new type name (e.g. '**co_ord**') should be placed in this single output (dotted) lozenge at the bottom of the constructor window (Fig. 3.12). The associated constructor (e.g. '**Co_Ord**') is placed in a dotted box in the body of the window. New types (all lower case, e.g. '**x**' and '**y**') with their constructors (that start with a capitol letter, e.g. '**X**' and '**Y**') can then also be declared in the body of the window using dotted lozenges and boxes respectively. New constructors and types will appear italic at this point showing that they are not known to the system.

There is no need of a new window for related new constructors and types provided they are connected to the final output type (Fig. 3.12). The boxes and lozenges are joined to create a structured 'package' that is used both for passing information from function to function. You must make a careful choice of names for these types and constructors, for self-documentation purposes. It is normal to give the same name to the constructor and its output type. The only difference is that the constructor should start with a capital letter. This is done as 'good practice' but it is

Fig. 3.12 Defining
constructors

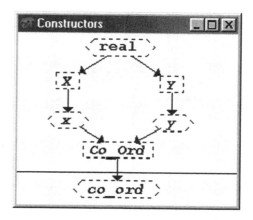

Fig. 3.13 Commit the
constructors

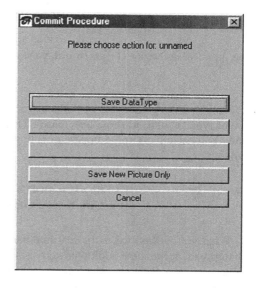

not an essential requirement. It is 'good practice' because it helps us to distinguish the role of a symbol (e.g. as a function name) and helps avoid clashes of names (Clarity is case sensitive). However, all names for any symbol whether it is a type, constructor or function must be distinct. Also, note that in this window both the boxes and lozenges are dotted. An annotation window can be used for both describing the complete window and any of the icons (boxes, arrows, etc.).

Figures 3.12, 3.13 and 3.14 show how we may, for example, define a co-ordinate vector. A co-ordinate is a package of data that identifies the single idea of a position. In this definition, we can send a single package of data of a co-ordinate by using the constructors as follows:

$$(\textbf{Co\_Ord} \; (\textbf{X} \; \#r4.2) \; (\textbf{Y} \; \#r3.6))$$

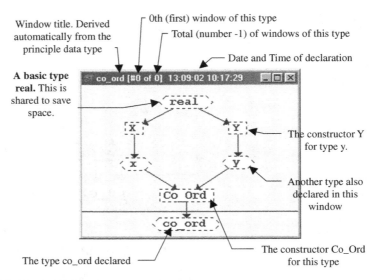

Window title. Derived automatically from the principle data type

0th (first) window of this type

Total (number -1) of windows of this type

Date and Time of declaration

A basic type **real.** This is shared to save space.

The constructor Y for type y.

Another type also declared in this window

The constructor Co_Ord for this type

The type co_ord declared

Fig. 3.14   The declaration of types **co_ord, x** and **y.**

Note that the parameters of the constructor '**Co_Ord**' are also constructed and are of type '**x**' and '**y**' (note lowercase). These types then use the constructors '**X**' and '**Y**' respectively (note uppercase). If you type this in at the query level, you will get

QUERY> (**Co_Ord** (**X** #r4.2) (**Y** #r3.6))
(**Co_Ord** (**X** #r4.200000) (**Y** #r3.600000))

What you will notice is the real numbers that are interpreted but do not really change except for some additional zeros. The rest of the expression responds in the same way as a *function*, which has a set of inputs that do not match any of the predefined cases, and has no general case (see above). As we have suggested earlier this is because the interpretation or the meaning of a constructor depends on the user whereas a function has its meaning defined in terms of the computer. This makes a nice distinction between what is modelled and what is not.

Positions in space may be defined in many different ways, such as using angle and distance, as well as the normal x and y distances from a fixed origin. So we could have the alternative structure

(**Radial** (**Radius** #r42.3) (**Angle** #r3.2))

If we are constructing something complicated with positions, and we do not really want to worry about the details of how that position is defined, we can use either or both forms in our processing and then, using pattern match, recognise the construction form to know how to handle it. We will show how this is done in the next section.

We can also use different constructors to define the different types of co-ordinate. We can then create some functions that combine positions or extract the information from them no matter in what form they are. Here position is used as though it was a single idea, which it is really. New forms can be added without changing the structure of the program that uses them. This is a very useful freedom to have and it is why the idea of 'objects' was originally proposed for programming. Position or co-ordinate, along with its set of conversion and extraction functions, is a generic object. It is a generic object because it represents the structure of an infinite number of actual positions (specific objects).

Another example where the same data type may have more than one constructor associated with it is the type 'date'. This may have both UK and USA form. To avoid an overcrowded diagram each variant of a type can be placed in a different constructor window (constructor component).

Looking Through the Function Window

We can imagine the function window as a palette on which a function can be declared, defined and modified. The generic type (e.g. ?0) input and output parameters, we have used before, declare what the function takes as input and what it will deliver as output. The body (the middle part of the window) of the function is its definition and expresses how it will deliver its output from the inputs. All functions have to be declared but it is also possible to declare a function without commitment to its generic form. That is, you can insist that the function will only do things with particular examples of the input types.

What we mean by the generic form of a function is the particular component of a function (if it exists) that has all its input parameters specified as a type (e.g. as int or str or ?0, etc.). So there are no actual values such as #3 or "Fred" specified in the input parameters. The output parameter can only be specified as a type in all cases.

To recap we have:

1. A *generic object,* which is the general class of a set of objects that is related to object-oriented programming.
2. A *generic type* (e.g. ?0), which is the general class of all types including user defined types.
3. A *generic function,* which is the general case of a function definition.

Once a function has been declared or defined, it may then be used actively in the declaration or definition of other functions. In practice, it is possible to use functions before they have been declared or defined but only as placeholders.

There are other tokens or aids that can be used to make a function or type declaration and definition clear in the problem domain . These do not provide any further functionality but they do provide a means of assigning the informal semantics (the problem domain meaning) to the schema (the graphs that represent a program). These include labelled join nodes (junctions) and colour.

When a function is declared without a body (a definition), as in Fig. 3.15, then it adopts the segment number −1. The reason for making an isolated declaration of this kind is to establish the input and output types when the intended finally declared function will rely only on specific 'patterns' of input (i.e. no general case). In this case we need a function that will allow us to 'unpack' the constructor so that we can use its contents. We will need a set of functions whose job is to extract specific items from the constructor. We do this by being very explicit about the item we want returning by showing the system where it is through the use of generic values/variables (e.g. ?0 , ?1, etc.). Note that it is possible to name each component with an individual heading. This facility is particularly useful if there are a large number of components . An index of component headings will be displayed if you double click on the background.

In the function '**x_co_ord**', shown in Fig. 3.16, we only use this function component for the specific pattern shown. Other components of this function can be used for alternative patterns. Here we identify the real value of x that is 'wrapped-up' in the constructor formation of '**Co_Ord**' and pluck it out as a returned result of this function. Other pattern sensitive components can do different things but they must all return the same output type (i.e. 'real' in this case). Figure 3.17 shows an alternative measure for position using a Radial definition. Figure 3.18 shows how the second component of '**x_co_ord**' can be used for both types of vectors.

So applying this we can see from the following that we get whatever result we need without worrying what kind of vector is involved. This extension of functionality over different objects is referred to as 'overloading'.

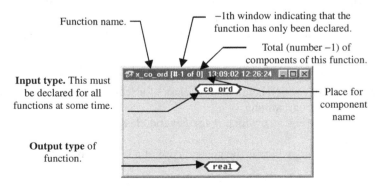

Fig. 3.15   The initial declaration of a function

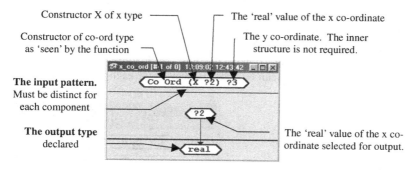

Constructor X of x type ⎯⎯⎯⎯

Constructor of co-ord type
as 'seen' by the function ⎯⎯⎯

The 'real' value of the x co-ordinate

The y co-ordinate. The inner
structure is not required.

The input pattern.
Must be distinct for
each component

The output type
declared

The 'real' value of the x co-
ordinate selected for output.

Fig. 3.16 A specific function for extracting the real value of an x co-ordinate

Fig. 3.17 Defining
constructors

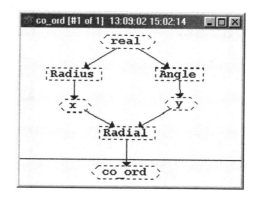

Fig. 3.18 Commit the
constructors

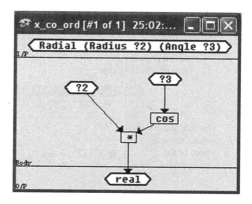

QUERY> x_co_ord (Co_Ord (X #r4.2) (Y #r3.6))
#r4.200000
QUERY> x_co_ord (Radial (Radius #r4.2) (Angle #r3.6))
#r4.191712

We also need to create a function that will do the same kind of task for the other value in the vector. The function '**y_co_ord**' will extract the second value from a co-ordinate system (Figs. 3.19, 3.20 and 3.21).

Another common use of an 'object' needing overloading is 'date' since there are many different forms that can be used. However, for each vector we build a set

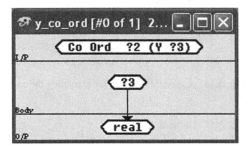

Fig. 3.19 'y_co_ord' for
Co_Ord vector

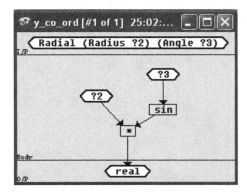

Fig. 3.20 'y_co_ord' for
Radial vector

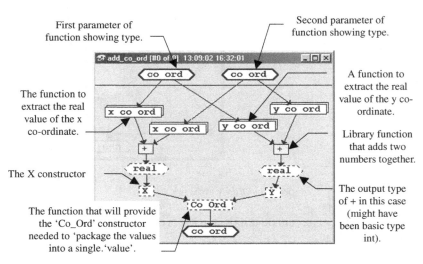

Fig. 3.21 The declaration and definition of a function

of manipulation functions. For example, we will need to add two vectors together. We may also require at some point a function that will take two elements and put them together to construct a vector. At one level we have the pre-decision that certain elements can be put together. So X can only go with Y to form a Co_Ord and Radius can only go with Angle to form Radial. However, there is no mechanism that can choose for us the co-ordinate systems. Only we can do that and that is why we have to use constructor sensitive decisions at this point.

The function in Fig. 3.21 is an example of a generic function declaration (saying what the input and output types are) and the definition (what to do with the input and what to return as a value). The function's purpose is to add two co-ordinates together (i.e. vector addition). Note that we have to 'construct' the output so that it is packaged into a single (but complex) value. The function can also be made to respond specifically to other forms of co-ordinate provided we use the constructor to create pattern-match parameters instead of the generic input shown in Fig. 3.21. This works because specific patterns are always favoured against the generic form.

The function '**add_co_ord**' can be tested by 'calling' it with some example input in the control window as follows:

QUERY> add_co_ord (Co_Ord (X #r3.7) (Y #r5.6)) (Co_Ord (X #r4.2) (Y #r9.6))
(Co_Ord (X #r7.900000) (Y #r15.200001))

QUERY> add_co_ord (Radial (Radius #r3.7) (Angle #r5.6)) (Radial (Radius #r4.2) (Angle #r9.6))
(Radial (Radius #r7.895206) (Angle #r7.726620))

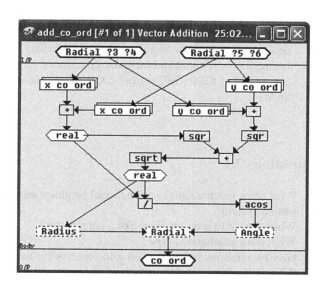

Fig. 3.22 The specific case
for '**add_co_ord**'

Note that in Fig. 3.22 we have introduced another kind of lozenge which is generated by Clarity when it detects two outputs from a function. More of this will described later. The function '**acos**' may not be available in ClarityLite.

Exercises 3.1

Do the following in schematic form unless otherwise stated.

1. Declare a type <month> that enumerates all the months of the year: January, February, etc.
2. Declare a type <day> that enumerates all the days of the week.
3. Define a function that translates an integer into a month so that #1 returns January.
4. Define a function that translates an integer into a day so that #1 is Sunday.
5. Declare a <date> type and a constructor <Date> so that (Date <day> <month> <year>) is its structure. Note: It is 'good practice' to have an '**Unknown_date**' constructor to deal with errors.
6. Define a function that returns <day> given <date>.
7. Define a function that returns <month> given <date>.
8. Define a function that returns <year> given <date>.
9. Extend the declaration <type> date to have an alternative form of (Int_Date <integer> <integer> <integer>).
10. Define a function that translates an Int_Date to a Date.
11. Define a function that translates a Date to an Int_Date.
12. Define a function that will always return Date for either Date or Int_Date.
13. Define a function that will always return Int_Date for either Date or Int_Date.
14. Define a function that changes a Month or Day to a string. So that January becomes "January" or Monday becomes "Monday".
15. Define a function that takes a given year from *a limited set of years* and returns a string. Thus #2001 will return "2001". Any years outside the set will be undefined.

Questions 3.1

1. What three mechanisms in a functional language ensure that it can represent any formal system?
2. When does a function behave like a constructor?
3. What is an enumerated type?
4. Give two reasons why you need a constructor for function output?
5. What is the theoretical limit to the number of constructors for a given type?
6. What are the three uses of the word 'generic' in programming?
7. When do you need to declare a function without a definition?

The Notion of Casting

We have already considered a mechanism for printing a string of characters by creating the function 'myprint' in Chapter 2. This works well for characters but we may want to print out a number. This is a problem because the internal representation is *not* *characters* or *strings*, it is a *number*. A further complication is that there are two kinds of numbers: *integers* and *reals*. The integers are marked by a preceding '#' and a real by a preceding '#r'. So 34 can be represented in Faith/Clarity by

A string "34"
A list of characters ['3' '4']
An integer #34
A real #r34

What we need is a function that will transform an integer or real to a string and the inverse transformation of a string representation of a number to an integer or real. This process of changing the type of data is called *'casting'*. Such *'casting'* functions are available as built-in functions in ClarityPro. However, we are able do number transformations, in principle, without special library functions for three good reasons:

1. All numbers are based on a finite set of primitives (e.g. the numerals 0–9) that can be used together to create any number.
2. The rules of creating a number from these primitives are very simple.
3. A function can be made *extensional* to represent any finite mapping of any type (composite or simple) to any type.

We know from our experience with printing a string that the trick was to represent the string as a list of characters (using the built-in function 'explode') and then print the characters to the control window. If we can convert an integer into a list of characters then we could use the same technique. But how do we do that?

A Structure Process Diagram (SPD)

We need to break down an integer into a *list of numerals* (i.e. the numbers 0–9) and then convert each numeral by an extensional function into its character equivalent. The problem is then solved. To capture the process just described we can draw Structure Process Diagram (SPD).

Figure 3.23(a) shows a solution to the printing of a number as a SPD. Such diagrams might be usable for an initial design but here we are using it as an alternative to Clarity for describing the process. SPD, in a way, combine the objectives of annotation (to explain in English) with the objectives of a program (to describe

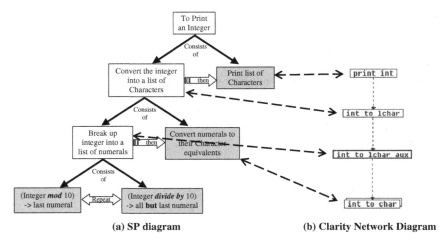

(a) SP diagram   **(b) Clarity Network Diagram**

Fig. 3.23 The process of printing an integer

as instructions). We interpret the diagram from the top. To print an integer we need
two processes. The first process converts an integer into a list of characters and then
each character in the list is printed (in the correct order).

The process of converting an integer into a list of characters is done by converting
an integer into a list of numerals and then using an extensional function to translate
each numeral into a character (see Fig. 3.24). That is, we just look each number up
in a table and output its character equivalent.

Finally, the process of converting an integer into a list of numerals comes from
the built-in functions '%' (modulus or mod) and '/' (divide by).

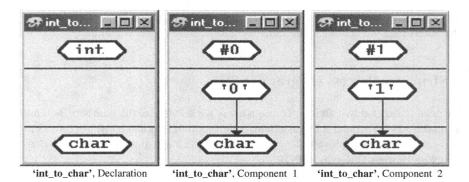

'int_to_char', Declaration   'int_to_char', Component 1   'int_to_char', Component 2

Fig. 3.24 An extensional function 'int_to_char'

This breakdown (deconstruction) of operations into simpler operations can continue until we reach the built-in functions or functions we have already defined. These are marked in grey.

Note that a SPD can only be constructed if you already know what primitives you are going to use. Many alternative solutions would use different primitives (see Chapter 6). SPDs are a useful summary of a solution once it is known. SP diagrams should not be relied on as a design method but may be helpful on occasions.

Starting our implementation halfway up the SPD (see Fig. 3.23), we can construct the extensional function '**int_to_char**'. So we first do

> Convert numerals to
> their Character
> equivalents

Since we are not interested in a general case because all numerals must have a character equivalent then we start by making a declaration only. This can be done by creating a function window that has only input and output parameter information, as shown in Fig. 3.24. By pressing 'OK' the system will respond with a list of actions (see Chapter 1) the first of which will be 'Save Declaration Only'. This is the action you choose. You will then be asked to provide a name as before (see Chapter 1).

As we have described previously the function window '**int_to_char**' can be altered to provide the first component and committed (press OK again). Clarity will then respond with a list of actions with 'Save New Component' at the top; this you chose. The window we showed can be used as a kind of form, where the lozenges and functions are fields to be changed. This allows you to repeat the process to produce the remaining set of components. [8] The following Faith code will be generated:

```
fdec
  int_to_char ::= int->char ;          int_to_char #4 ::= '4' ;
  ;                                     int_to_char #5 ::= '5' ;
fdef                                    int_to_char #6 ::= '6' ;
  int_to_char #0 ::= '0' ;             int_to_char #7 ::= '7' ;
  int_to_char #1 ::= '1' ;             int_to_char #8 ::= '8' ;
  int_to_char #2 ::= '2' ;             int_to_char #9 ::= '9' ;
  int_to_char #3 ::= '3' ;             ;
```

The next mechanism to construct is the function that will convert a number into a list of numerals. Therefore, from Fig. 3.23 we have Fig. 3.25.

---

[8] An alternative method is to type in an empty Faith window the code as shown and then commit the faith window (i.e. press OK).

Fig. 3.25 Converting a
number into a list of numerals

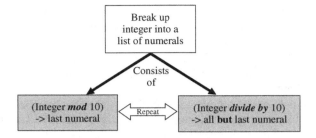

This is going to be a loop in that the same process is going to be repeated on
the result of the previous application of the process. This requires that we have to
consider three distinct phases of this process:

1. An initial phase at the start of the process where the first result is generated.
2. The process itself.
3. The terminating conditions .

Beginning with the process, we can assume that we have a list of characters; it
will be characters rather than numerals because we will do the simple conversion
while new numerals are generated. We can also assume that we have an integer
to work on and finally (and remarkably) *we will assume that we already have the
function that will do this process.*

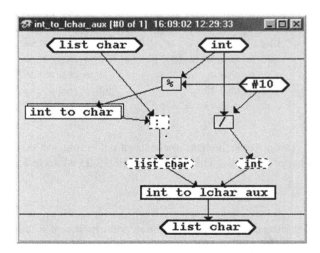

Fig. 3.26 The general
condition of
'**int_to_lchar_aux**'

The '**int_to_lchar_aux**'[9] in Fig. 3.26 shows what we then do. We take the integer in the second parameter and find the modulus 10. Modulus gives the remainder after an integer division. For example, 10 goes into 34 three times and the remainder is 4. So we have for example

$$\% \ \#34 \ \#10 \rightarrow \#4$$
$$\% \ \#567 \ \#10 \rightarrow \#7$$

On the other hand if we integer-divide the same numbers by 10 we get

$$/ \ \#34 \ \#10 \rightarrow \#3$$
$$/ \ \#567 \ \#10 \rightarrow \#56$$

These two operations together have the effect of separating the last numeral from the number. We thus go on to the next application of this operation by transferring the new reduced number (#3 or #56) to the second parameter. We also attach the new numeral (#4 or #7), converted to a character, to a growing list of characters. For example, the function will transform #256 into the character equivalent of the following list of numerals, given in mathematical form, thus

$$\#256 \rightarrow [((\#256\,/100) \ mod \ 10) \ ((\#256/10) \ mod \ 10) \ (\#256/1 \ mod \ 10)]$$

When implementing this function you choose the function box with the *thickest* line to represent the function you assume to exist (which is the function you are creating). As we have shown before a function that calls itself in this way is a '*recursive*' function. There is no need to name a recursive function within the definition since Clarity will insert the name into the thick lined box when you finally commit the function and give it a name.

The next thing to consider, *and must never be forgotten*, are the *terminating conditions* (see Figs. 3.27 and 3.28). In this case, there are two:

1. A situation where the original integer is #0.
2. The condition when the integer reaches #0 because it consists of no more numerals (Fig. 3.29).

Figure 3.28 shows the first situation; the list is empty because this is the first time the function has been called and the integer is #0. Here, the character '0' is required. Figure 3.27 shows the more general situation where there is a list of characters but

---

[9] It is called '**int_to_lchar_aux**' because it is an auxiliary function to '**int_to_lchar**'. An auxiliary function performs the process on behalf of the function that calls it. Auxiliary functions are usually unique to one function and are never called by another.

Fig. 3.27 The *first*
terminating condition. of
'**int_to_lchar_aux**'

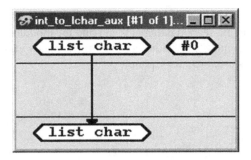

Fig. 3.28 The *second*
terminating condition of
'**int_to_lchar_aux**'

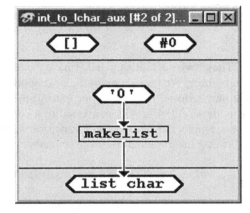

Fig. 3.29 Starting conditions

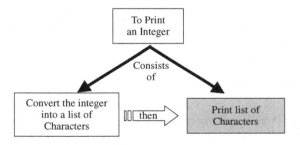

the integer given to the function is now #0. In the second case, we do not want '0' to
be placed at the beginning of our number; here we just output the numbers we have.

Next, we consider the starting conditions:

One of the primitives we have not yet included was the negative sign ('-'). If
the integer is negative then the resulting string is to start with a negative character.
Otherwise, nothing else is required. In '**int_to_lchar**' (Fig. 3.30) we assume that the
function '**int_to_lchar_aux**' has finished its job and will return the list of characters
correctly. To this list, we add a negative character provided ('**if**') the original integer

Fig. 3.30 The function
'int_to_lchar'

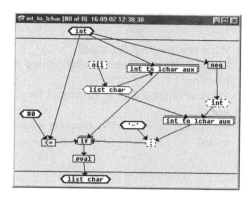

is negative. We then present a positive integer to '**int_to_lchar_aux**' by negating
the negative number. In both cases, the function '**int_to_lchar_aux**' must start with
an empty list.

Finally, the function '**print_int**' follows the same structure as in Chapter 2 for
'**myprint**'. The difference being that the integer to be printed is processed by
'**int_to_lchar**' first in order to generate the required list of characters. Note the function '**eval**'. This function gives the output of '**if**' in this case another run through the
interpreter. This is not necessary but we do it here just so that you get the final list
in a more readable form. If you do not put the extra evaluation in then the list will
appear in 'cons' form. The function '**eval**' should be replaced by '**print_int**'.

Exercise 3.2

1. Write a recursive function that adds a number to every element in a list of
   integers.
2. Write a recursive function that counts the number of items in a list.
3. Write a recursive function that returns 'True' if a particular given integer is in a
   list of numbers.
4. Modify '3' so that it will work with any list of objects (i.e. strings, characters,
   reals, integers, etc.).
5. Write a recursive function that will add up a list of integers.
6. Write a function that will divide two integers and will return a list where the
   first item is the number of times the second integer goes into the first a whole
   number of times. The second item in the list is the remainder. The third item is
   a real number that represents the real division of first by the second. Note that
   you will have to use the casting functions '**float**' and '**fix**'.
7. Write a function that will find the average of a list of numbers (see 2 and 5).
8. Write a function that will find the largest number in a list of numbers.
9. Finish the process of printing out an integer.
10. Change the printing process so that it can print a real number. Note that you
    will have to introduce the decimal point into the list of numbers.

Questions 3.2

1. What is a 'casting' function?
2. What are the three reasons why casting numerals does not require special library functions?
3. What advantage does a Structured Process diagram have over other representations?
4. When making a recursive function what is the most important thing to remember to do?

Project: Playing a Simple Game

Paper: Out Guess the Computer

Introduction

We will now illustrate some of these techniques at work in a simple playground guessing game. There is something odd about playing a computer at a guessing game. This game of 'out guessing' your opponent is very simple. It is normally played by two people. The people hold their hands behind their backs and on the command 'go!' each person puts their hand in front of them to form one of the signs 'paper' – a flat hand, 'scissors' – two extended figures or 'stone' – a fist. 'Paper' beats 'stone' because paper can wrap around stone. 'Stone' beats 'scissors' because stone will blunt scissors. Scissors beats 'paper' because scissors can cut paper. It is a simple way of deciding between two options if you do not have a coin to toss. It is a draw if each opponent shows the same sign.

It is odd playing with a computer because a person will have some idea about how a person might make a 'random' choice since you really do have to *decide* what you are going to display. Playing with someone will give you some insight as

Diagram 3.1 'item'

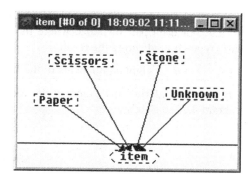

to how they might make the choice given the history of the game and their insights as to how you might be thinking.[10]

Since the computer does not really think but just chooses at 'random' (however, see project 'Dice') then such an out-guessing game cannot really be played. Still building it does illustrate some valuable techniques.

Paper, Scissors and Stone

First, we must define the three items Paper, Scissors, and Stone. Look at Diagram 3.1. The diagram defines the new type '**item**'. Here we define four new values (actually constructors) of that type (an enumerated type), '**Paper**', '**Scissors**', '**Stone**' and '**Unknown**' (it is often useful to have an '**Unknown**'). Do not forget that it is good practice to always start a constructor with a capital letter and a type or function with a lower case letter.

(1) *Define the type **item** as shown by **Diagram 3.1** in a *constructors window*.

Now, we need a function to play the game.

First, look at the function '**choose**' in **Diagram 3.10**. The simplest way to read this is from the top and the inputs of the functions in clockwise order around the output. The built-in function '**rand**' is the first function to be called. This function will return an integer, which is the basic type '**int**'. The built-in function '**%**' (modulus) takes this integer and the integer #3, and will return an integer in the range 0 to 2. The function '**!**' (Shriek) is a built-in function that returns the nth item of a list, where n begins at 0, so one of the list **[Paper Scissors Stone]** will be selected at random. The computer will choose this way (see project Dice).

(2) *Define the function '**choose**' in a function window.

Remember that the function components start at #0 as is a convention with Clarity for the general case. The special cases start at #1.

---

[10] It is possible that people actually do display the fallacious 'law of averages' when forced to make random decisions.

Now look at the function 'outcome' in Diagrams 3.2, 3.3, 3.4, 3.5, 3.6, 3.7, 3.8 and 3.9. For each pair of items, where the computer is the first, there is a string (basic type **str**) indicating the result.

(3) *Define all eight components of the function 'outcome'.

Before considering the game itself, look at the function 'char_to_item' in Diagram 3.12, e.g. 'x'.

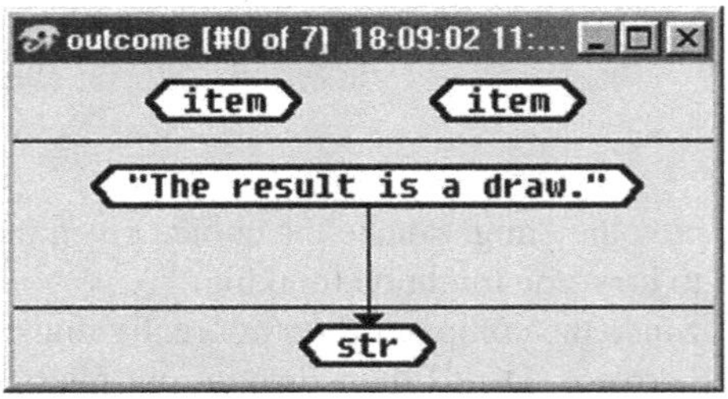

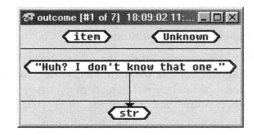

Diagram 3.2 'outcome'
component #0

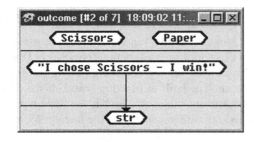

Diagram 3.3 'outcome'
component #1

Diagram 3.4 'outcome'
component #2

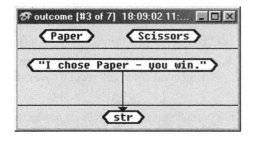

Diagram 3.5 'outcome'
component #3

Diagram 3.6 'outcome'
component #4

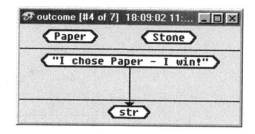

Diagram 3.7 'outcome'
component #5

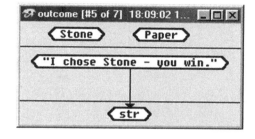

Diagram 3.8 'outcome'
component #6

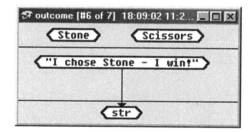

Diagram 3.9 'outcome'
component #7

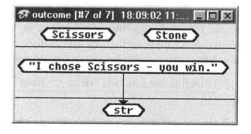

Diagram 3.10 'choose'

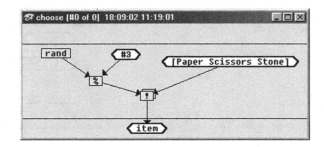

Diagram 3.11
'char_to_item'

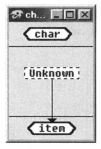

Diagram 3.12
'char_to_item'

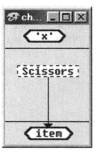

The function '**char_to_item**' takes a '**char**' and returns an '**item**'. Now we can see the reason for having an '**item**' value called 'Unknown'. The purpose of this casting function is so that the user will be able to select from the list [**Paper, Scissors, Stone**] by simply keying in one character.

(4) *Define the function '**char_to_item**' as shown in Diagram 3.11, 3.12, 3.13, and 3.14.

Note the underscores in the function '**char_to_item**'.

Now look at function '**call**' in Diagram 3.15. The function '**outcome**' will input the '**items**' chosen by the computer and by the user and return a message indicating the result. The second parameter for '**outcome**' is the result of '**progN**'.

Diagram 3.13
'char_to_item'

Diagram 3.14
'char_to_item'

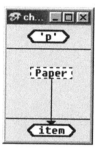

Diagram 3.15 'call'

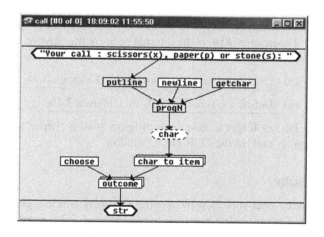

There are three functions driven by '**progN**'. These are '**putline**', '**newline**' and '**getchar**'. The function '**progN**' evaluates its parameters in order such that '**putline**' is done first, then '**newline**' and finally '**getchar**'. The function '**progN**' returns the result of the last function. In this example it is the '**char**' returned from '**getchar**' and is whatever the user/player chooses.

The function '**putline**' is a built-in function, which prints out its parameter of type '**str**', i.e. a string, which is a group of characters enclosed by double quotes

Diagram 3.16 'newline'

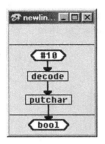

Diagram 3.17 Network for
Paper

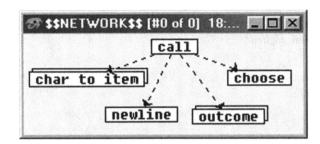

(e.g. "Hello"). The function '**getchar**' is a built-in function that waits for keyboard input.

The function '**newline**' is the function shown in Diagram 3.16.

The integer '**#10**' is the internal code for the newline character. The built-in function '**decode**' returns a newline character for output by '**putchar**'.

(5) *Define the function '**newline**' in Diagram 3.16.

(6) *Define the function '**call**' in Diagram 3.15.

Do not forget to save your program (call it 'Paper'). You can play the game by typing '**call**' in the CONTROL window.

Finally

Create a network view by opening a network window, go to the find 'menu' and click on 'Create/Update network from database'. This may require a little rearranging to look neat and when you are satisfied with its appearance commit it just like a function window. Again, save your program (Diagram 3.17).

Exercise 3.3

1. Create two functions, and any supporting functions if needed, for the castings from an American style date to a UK date '**usa_to_uk**' and its reverse '**uk_to_usa**'. Hint: use pattern component extraction.

2. Create two functions, and any supporting functions if needed, for the castings from radial to x, y co-ordinate systems '**rad_to_coord**' and its reverse '**coord_to_rad**'. Hint: use trigonometric functions.

3. Create a function, and any further supporting functions if needed, to convert '**print_int**' (see end of section 'A structure Process Diagram') to '**print_hex**'. That is an integer to the base 16 rather than 10 where the numbers are [0 to 9 A B C D E F].

4. Change the game 'Paper' to 'Man' so that it works for Man, Fox, Goose and Corn. Where Man beats Fox, Fox beats Goose, Goose beats Corn and Corn beats Man (do not ask why).

5. Change the game 'Paper' so that two people and the computer can play it. A score for a player is the number of wins minus the number of loses.

6. Add an accumulating score to 'Paper' for the two people and the computer.

7. Change 'Paper' so that it can work for any number of people at any time.

Questions 3.3

1. What important extra constructor is usually needed in an enumerated type?
2. Describe one situation where you need a general case for a function.
3. Describe one situation where you should *not* have a general case for a function.

References

Addis T. R., Townsend-Addis J. J., Billinge D., Gooding, D. C. and Vissher, B. (2008) '*The Abductive Loop: Tracking Irrational Sets*', Special issue on Tracking Irrational Sets, Science, Technology, Ethics, Volume 13, No. 1, March, ISSN 1233-1821, edited by Lorenzo Magnani.

Billinge D. and Addis T. (2003) '*The Functioning of Tropic Communication: A Mechanism for Consistent Figurative Descriptions of Artistic Effect*', AISB'03 Symposium on AI and Creativity in Arts and Science, University of Wales at Aberystwyth.

Gegov A. (2007) '*Complex Management in Fuzzy Systems: A Rule Base Compression Approach*', Springer, New York, ISBN-10 3-540-38883-4.

Kleene, S. C. (1967). '*Journal of Mathematical Logic*', Wily, New York.

Lakoff G. (1986) '*Women, Fire, and Dangerous Things*', University of Chicago Press, Chicago, IL.

Lakoff G. and Johnson M. (1980) '*Metaphors We Live By*', University of Chicago Press, Chicago, IL.

Stepney S., Braunstein S. L., Clark J, A., Tyrrell A., Adamatzky A., Smith R. E., Addis T R., Johnson C., Timmis J., Welcj P., Milner R. and Partridge D. (2005) '*Journeys in Non-classical Computation I: A Grand Challenge for Computing Research*', International Journal of Parallel, Emergent and Distributed Systems, Vol. 20, No. 1, April ISSN 1744-5760, Taylor & Francis pp. 5–19, March.

Wittgenstein L. (1921) '*Tractatus Logico-Philosophicus*' edition 1961, Routledge and Kegan Paul, London.

Wittgenstein L. (1953) '*Philosophical Investigations*', Blackwell, Oxford.

Chapter 4
Mind Maps™ and Mechanisms

Charity suffereth long and is kind; charity envieth not; charity vaunteth not itself, is not puffed up;

Doth not behave itself unseemly, seeketh not her own, is not easily provoked, thinketh no evil;

Corinthians 13,4-5

Introduction

Mind Maps are diagrams that show how ideas and concepts are linked together. The idea was first proposed by Tony Buzen (1993) in order to provide a different way of making notes other than through just writing. He points out that the problems[1] with standard notes are:

1. They obscure key words and this prevents you from making appropriate associations between the important concepts.
2. They make it difficult to remember. In particular, notes are boring and are unstructured; they look like lists.
3. They waste time since you have to search for what you want to know. All concepts are uniformly represented (see point 1).
4. They fail to stimulate creatively. Linear presentations prevent you from making associations, thus counteracting creativity and memory. Specifically, reading a list implies an 'end' or 'finish' whereas a mind map encourages you to build on existing thoughts and ideas.

The diagrams start with a central idea and branch outward through links (lines) that indicate associated ideas. The types of associations can be coded by using different kinds of line (e.g. dotted or simply labelled). The value of the Mind Maps is through the organisation of the way the map is laid out showing grouping of ideas.

---

[1] Information obtained from internet sites on mind maps.

T. Addis, J. Addis, *Drawing Programs: The Theory and Practice of Schematic Functional Programming*, DOI 10.1007/978-1-84882-618-2_4,
© Springer-Verlag London Limited 2010

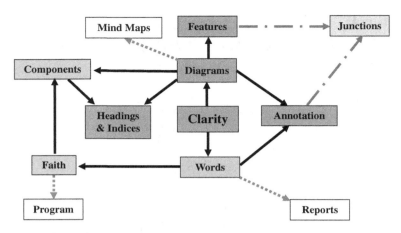

Fig. 4.1 Part of a mind map centred upon Clarity

Further, the act of creating the diagrams also helps in remembering its content and structure. They are particularly useful for groups to be creative through the construction of such maps. Figure 4.1 is an example of a Mind Map centred upon Clarity. The arrows indicate simple connectivity relationships (such as belongs to) and colours can suggest grouping of ideas (such as generic concept). Any relationship can be labelled next to the arrow.

The Clarity diagrams (and in particular the Network diagrams) can be used in a similar way to that of Mind Maps except instead of growing outwards we constrain the Clarity diagrams to always flow downwards. *This is so that we use the up/down direction to show the order of processing or functional dependency.* In this chapter, we will examine some of the ways in which a Clarity diagram can be enhanced to display more than just the program mechanism. We will be deliberately expanding the secondary semantic links between the accidental (not formally significant) features of the program representation and the problem domain. We will also show some alternative semi-formal ways of representing ideas that are related to the program but are distinct from it.

Junctions, Colour and Organisation

The junction was introduced in the Guess project in Chapter 2, Diagram 2. 10. In this case, the junction was used to simply provide a bend in the line. More importantly, the bend in the line was necessary to ensure that the first parameter of the function '**diff**' arrived at the right place of the function '−'. The function '**diff**' is the same as '−' except the parameters are swapped around.

Figures 4.2, 4.3 and 4.4 show three ways in which the junction can be used to change direction. Figures 4.3 and 4.4 use two junctions. The first junction is a

Fig. 4.2 Using a junction to 'bend' a line

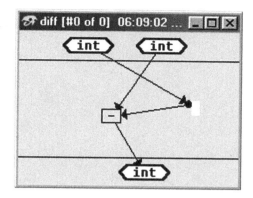

Fig. 4.3 Using a junction to 'jump' a line

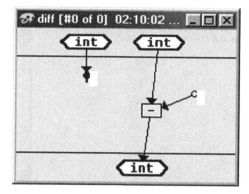

Fig. 4.4 Using a junction to 'bridge' a line

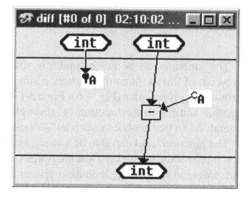

'*source*' and to show this, the system retains its filled colour. It is called a '*source*' because this is where the 'signal' is coming from. The second junction is the '*sink*' and the system does not fill the junction with any colour. A '*sink*' receives the signal.

Fig. 4.5 'Multiple sinks'

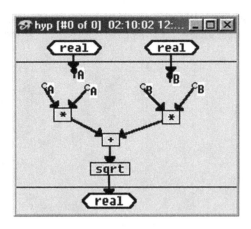

Fig. 4.6 'Bunching' inputs

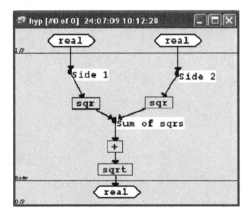

The junction can be given 'multiple sinks' by repeating a label (Fig. 4.5). The converse of this is 'bunching' where a single arrow (link) can represent a bunch of arrows in a given order (Fig. 4.6). Figure 4.7 is an example of the two sums coming together and fed to the function '+' through a single arrow. The order of the inputs is retained so that functions such as '−' would work as expected.

The junction label can also be a string including spaces. Junctions can be inserted as a mechanism for making simple notes (see Fig. 4.6). Since these are also labels and provided the string, including spaces, is the same then these notes can also bridge bunches with both single and multiple sinks (Fig. 4.7). These particular examples do not really improve the presentation a great deal but there are cases where this can be very effective.

Colour can also be used effectively to show up paths and groups (Fig. 4.8). Every icon can be coloured from a limited list of colours selected from the menu 'colour'. These colours remain permanent in that they will be saved when the function, con-

Fig. 4.7 'Bunching' and
'Bridging'

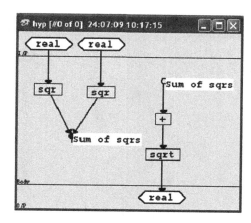

Fig. 4.8 Colouring groups

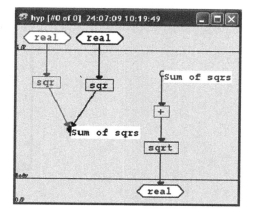

structor or network is committed (toolbar 'OK'). It is also possible to change the
colour of all function or network or constructor windows (Fig. 4.9). This, however,
will only remain for the session and it is currently not saved but can be useful to copy
into documents. The background colour can be chosen from a very wide selection.

Annotation

Annotation is very important. It is important because, as we have shown, a computer language has two meanings. We have referred to the different interpretations as formal and informal. The formal meaning of a statement in a computer
language is what happens in the computer when it is obeyed and the reference
objects are the bits. The informal meaning is what the program means to the

Fig. 4.9 Changing
background

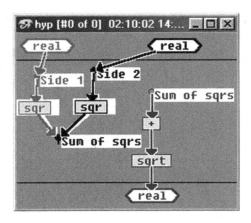

Fig. 4.10 General labels

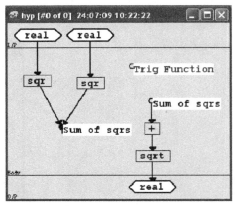

programmer in terms of what it represents in the world (the problem domain).
Thus the simple machine code

add 2 146

formally means to increase register 2 in the computer by the contents of word 146
or it could informally mean (say) a car is changing its acceleration by a prefixed
amount. The formal semantics is always clear but the informal semantics could
mean anything. It is because it could 'mean' anything that a good choice of names
and annotation is the only way the program can be 'understood'. That is, what it
means to the programmer or users in its role within the problem domain.

Junctions give a simple upfront method of annotation but it is very limited in what
it can do. Figure 4.10 shows a coloured junction not attached to anything being used
as general label in a function. An alternative to this is a function heading. Such a

Fig. 4.11 General annotation

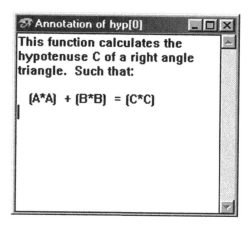

Fig. 4.12 I/O arrow
annotation

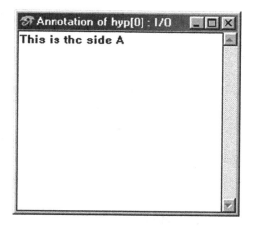

heading is particularly useful when there are a large number of function components. Each component can be briefly described and the list of these headings with component number is obtained on double clicking the function background. The annotation window can also be used to indicate much more description (Fig. 4.11). Only a single annotation window can be opened at any one time. To view other annotations you need to either click on a function window or a function box in a window. Arrows, lozenges and even junctions can have their own individual annotation (Fig. 4.12).

The annotation is picked up when you choose a function box in a window (see Fig. 4.13) by 'see-through'. Such 'see-through' can be locally adjusted or changed without affecting the original. 'See-through' is marked by two parallel lines (see Fig. 4.14).

Fig. 4.13 The function 'distance'

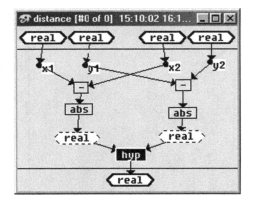

Fig. 4.14 'See-through' annotation

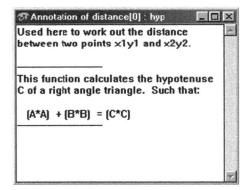

List Processing and Constructors

We introduced list manipulation in Chapter 2. We described the effect of the constructor ':' (in a dotted box) to do what appears to be the function of placing an item at the start of a list. Lists are one of the most important types of objects since they can represent so many things. Lists are used to represent any collection of things from the contents of a bag to groups of people. A list can also be used, by having lists of lists, to represent structures such as the componentsof a bicycle or a family tree or even a collection of family trees. It is even possible to describe electronic circuits or maps by using lists. In these cases, the lists are collections of lists where each of the sub-lists represents junctions. An example of this description of connectivity is given in Fig. 4.15.

We showed that lists in Clarity and Faith are represented in one of two ways. The usual way is as a list of items between open and closed square brackets. Therefore, a list of characters would be

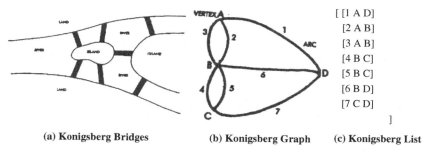

| (a) Konigsberg Bridges | (b) Konigsberg Graph | (c) Konigsberg List |

Fig. 4.15 Three different representations of the Konigsberg bridges[2]

$$['A' \; ' ' \; 'n' \; 'i' \; 'c' \; 'e']$$

We also showed that an alternative way is in its **basic constructor** form, thus

$$(:'A'(:' '(:'n'(:'i'(:'c'(:'e' nil))))))$$

We noted that this latter form is because a list is really a construction made with the repeated use of the special **cons** constructor ':'. If the constructor ':' was not already part of the language it might have been defined in Clarity/Faith as shown in Fig. 4.16 (a) and (b) respectively.

The constructor window shown in Fig. 4.16(a) shows how the type list (dotted lozenge at the bottom) can be two alternative constructors: the '_:' or '_nil'.The '_:' takes two parameters: the first of type generic[3](?0) and the second is a type 'list'.

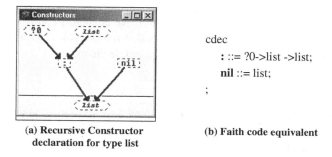

cdec

: ::= ?0->list ->list;

nil ::= list;

;

| (a) Recursive Constructor declaration for type list | (b) Faith code equivalent |

Fig. 4.16 An imaginary constructor declaration for object type '**list**'

---

[2]The Konigsberg bridges cross over the river Pregel in Germany. The question arose as to how you might plan a walk so as to cross all seven bridges but only cross each bridge once. It can be proved that it cannot be done unless the graph contains 2n odd vertices where n is any integer. The addition of a bridge AC or the removal of BD would provide a solution (Kasner and Newman 1949).

[3]Generic because you can have a list of anything.

The '**_nil**' has no parameters since it defines an empty list. In this way, a list can be constructed from embedded list constructors.

This explains why '**:**' is not a function in the operational sense of the word. It does the more passive job of *binding information/data/objects together into a single package*, called a list, which can be dealt with as a single item. Such an object relies upon the user and programmer to interpret.

We showed in Chapter 3 how information can be read from a constructed 'package' such as '**Co_Ord**' and we have also shown how different componentsof a function can be created and selected through pattern match. We can also use these techniques on lists in both its forms

(:?0 ?1) can be used to select the head or tail of a list.

[?0 ?1] can be used to identify a list of exactly two elements.

Dealing with Input

ClarityLite is limited to single character input to the control window. ClarityPro can handle all the normal kinds of input that you might expect from any programming language (e.g. files, other programs and the graphic interface). For understanding the principles behind schematic functional programming such complications are not necessary and can just be distracting. However, more can be done with such a primitive input just as for the single character. The art is to build up useful primitives in terms of functions that, in effect, make a special language designed for your own needs.

Since we are reversing the process of printing, we can look upon creating the reverse processes for some of the other functions we created. In particular, we can consider the problem of reading an integer typed in the control window. First let us try the primitive function '**getchar**' that reads a single character.

QUERY>getchar

'k'

When you type the function '**getchar**' followed by the return key, the Clarity environment will hang and wait (listening) for your next character to be typed. On typing (say) 'k' Clarity stops hanging and returns the character you typed. We will use this function to convert a string of characters typed in from the control window into an integer that can be used by a program.

The SP diagram in Fig. 4.17 (a) can be compared with the SP diagram Fig. 3.26 in Chapter 3. As can be seen one process is almost an inversion of the other. This illustrates the important rule that for every casting (conversion from one type of object to another) there should be an inverse. In mathematics, division is the inverse of multiplication and subtraction is the inverse of addition. We nearly have this inverse relationship with the last two operations of the diagrams. The reason that

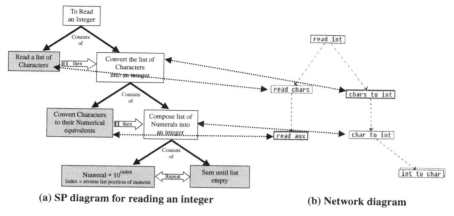

(a) SP diagram for reading an integer   (b) Network diagram

Fig. 4.17   Reading an integer from the control window

there is not an exact conversion is to do with simplicity of implementation; you go with the language. In most cases, the process order has been swapped and the sentence describing the process has swapped its object with its subject.

The network diagram is also changed in response to the SP diagram. You will note that the initial process refers to the parent of the second process in some cases and not in others (see Fig. 3.26(a), Chapter 3). However, the inverse of 'print_int' ('read_chars') becomes a secondary process, the inverse of **'int_to_lchar'** ('**read_int**') becomes a parent and the inverse of **'int_to_lchar_aux'** ('**chars_to_int**') becomes a child.

Figure 4.18 (a) shows another inverse that is made explicit by the built-in function 'inverse'. This is a function whose first parameter is the name of a function and the second parameter is a result or value of that function. Provided the function is an *extensional* function then this can look up the parameters that would give the result in its second parameter. In general, there can be zero or more possible answers so the result of 'inverse' is a list and that is why we take the 'head'. This is a useful function in that it saves you having two conversions of 'int' to 'char' and back again. It also avoids the possibility of error in constructing the inverse. Here we use it to find the inverse of numeral to character; only one answer is expected in this case. A function, such as 'inverse', that requires a function as a parameter is called a *higher-order function*.

Another higher order function 'map' is introduced later. The function 'map' applies a function (its first parameter) to every item in a given list (its second parameter). It is a very useful function and it can be used as an alternative to some recursive definitions; in these cases it is quicker and uses less memory.

Figure 4.18 (b) shows how each character in the list is converted to a numeral. This is an example of a *recursive* function in that it refers to itself. More will be said about how to design recursive functions. Then each character is multiplied by

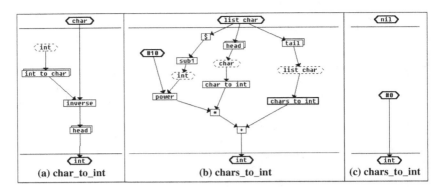

Fig. 4.18 Casting a list of characters to an integer

10^{index} where the 'index' of the list is counted in reverse. This is so that the most significant figure of the number is multiplied by the power of its index.[4] For example, the function will convert

$$['2'\ '5'\ '6'] \to [\#2 * 100 + \#5 * 10 + \#6 * 1] \to \#256$$

Figure 4.19 (a) shows the two elements of the process come together. The reading of the characters follows the pattern of reading recursively (a loop), adding each new

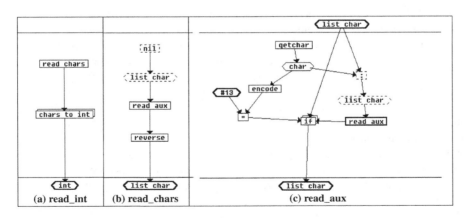

Fig. 4.19 Reading an integer from the control window

---

[4]An 'index' of a list is another list of numbers starting at #0 and increasing by #1 until the list terminates. The 'index' of an item in that list is the corresponding number.

character to the head of a growing list until a new-line character (decode[5] #13) is reached. Note that there is no check to see if these characters are in fact numerals.

Functions as Global Variables

Figure 3.27 shows an extensional function '**int_to_char**'. This maps the numerals onto their character equivalent. Another way of looking at this function is as a global character array called '**int_to_char**' that is indexed from #0 to #9. Instead of calling the process a *mapping* of the function '**int_to_char**' we can call it an *access* to an array of the global array '**int_to_char**'. In each case, the result is the same and the process is the same; it is just a question of how you wish to describe it.

However, we do have a big advantage over a normal array access because the indexing can be on any type or pattern we like *provided* it is unique and identifies only one result. The usefulness of this flexibility of indexing will become apparent later.

We do have a *higher-order* function 'setq' that behaves like an assignment. In functional terms, it simply maps a specified function component to a Boolean value. In practice and as a *side effect,* it will change the extensional result of the specified component. It alters the definition of a function by changing the mapping of an index to a result. This is very non-functional but necessary to keep programming easier than it might be otherwise. In an array-like view, we have in the control window the following sequence:

```
QUERY> int_to_char #3
'3'
QUERY> setq (int_to_char #3) 'A'
True
QUERY> int_to_char #3
_ 'A'
```

Such 'arrays' are global variables in that they are accessible at any place in the program. There is a range of *function and constructor creators* that make these alterations: '**set**', '**setq**', '**deny**', '**denyall**', '**forget**' and '**remember**'. We will describe these in more detail later. There are still others in ClarityPro.

As a rule, global variables of this kind should be limited to information associated with the *world model* and not used for processes. Too many global variables will lead to programs that are difficult to debug or test. You lose the independence of a function when you rely too much on global information (see side-effect programming later).

So what does this exercise in creating input and output functions tell us about elegance? Each of our functions is simple and easy to understand. What is also rather nice is that we have been able to construct the reading of an integer through

---

[5] 'decode' is the inverse of 'encode'.

the simple process of inverting the functions of printing an integer. This was not just by chance because we chose a particular approach; *it was because of our choice in the solution structure*. Later, we will show other ways of achieving elegance and efficiency.

Excercises 4.1

1. Write a function 'read_string' that reads characters from the control window and returns a string.
2. Write a function 'print_string' that takes a string and prints it to the control window as a sequence of characters.
3. Alter the function '**read_int**' so that it can accept negative numbers.
4. Alter the function '**read_int**' so that it will also accept numbers beginning with '#' and #r (i.e. real).
5. Write a function 'read_float' which reads a decimal number from the control window (hint: numbers are symmetrical about the decimal point). It should be able to accept negative numbers and number variations (such as beginning with # or #r).
6. Write a function 'print_float' which will print a decimal number to the control window (hint: numbers are symmetrical about the decimal point).
7. Write a function 'print_it' which will recognise the different requirements to print data to the control window.
8. Write a function 'read_it' which will automatically interpret data from the input correctly.
9. Extend the function 'read_it' so that it prints the information as it is read.
10. Extend the function 'read_it' so that wrong characters can be deleted.

Questions 4.1

1. What direction should the 'flow' of Clarity diagrams be where possible?
2. What three ways can a 'junction' be used to change the direction of a connecting arrow?
3. What are the two junctions called that form a 'jump'?
4. What is the difference between a 'jump' and a 'bridge' junction pairing?
5. What does 'bunching' mean and how would you implement it?
6. What are permanently coloured and what are only coloured for a session?
7. What are the two kinds of meaning that are associated with computer code?
8. What semantics is being referenced by the annotation window?
9. What does 'see through' mean and how is it marked?
10. What do you use to 'package' different information so that it can be used as single item?
11. How is an 'array' represented in Faith/Clarity?
12. How do you assign a new value to an 'array' element?
13. Are there any limitations on what you use for an 'array' index?

Details of Pattern-Matching [→ Page 140]

This is a good place to expand the rules regarding *pattern matching*, which, in any but the simplest cases, can seem quite complicated. Moreover, this example is not a simple case. The basic rule is that the function will take the 'best' match to the parameter list. However, the parameter *order* is more important than the *number of matches*. In fact, matching the first parameter **only** would override all the other parameters taken together.

One way to reason about this is to convert the matches to a binary number. The example we choose is the function used in a Snakes and Ladders game (Chapter 5) called '**mark_str**' (see Figs. 4.20 and 4.21 below). In this function there are four parameters that define a square's status and in the game there are six possible outcomes (pictorial representations) for this function. The outcomes are identified by parameter matches for components #0 to #6, where a match for a parameter is designated by a 1 and no match is designated by a 0, are as follows:

component #0 0000 (no matches)   [The generic case]
component #1 1100 (2 matches)   [Only the first two parameters are fixed]
component #2 1101 (3 matches)   [Only the first two and last parameters]
component #3 1110 (3 matches)   [Only the first three parameters]
component #4 1111 (4 matches)   [All the parameters are fixed]
component #5 0100 (1 match)   [Only the second parameter]
component #6 1000 (1 match)   [Only the first parameter]

If we order these matches as binary numbers we have 1111, 1110, 1101, 1100, 1000, 0100, 0000. Therefore, the component order in which the function '**mark_str**' will try to match is #4 (highest binary number), #3, #2, #1, #6, #5, #0 (lowest binary number). Component #0 is usually the default. Nevertheless, the important thing to remember is that the match sequence 1000, which has only one match, would override the match sequence 0111 which has three matches. So matching the first parameter **only** will override all the other parameters despite the case where they all matched perfectly. This is a programming trap that can cause some worries in that all seems correct but only if the concept of 'best' match is assumed to be 'most' match. But in Clarity/Faith it is not.

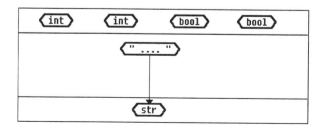

Fig. 4.20 '**mark_str**',
component #0. General case

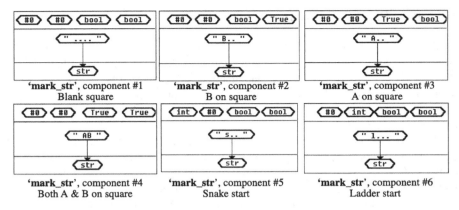

Fig. 4.21 All the extensional components of '**mark_str**'

Dealing with Conditionals (Ifs) [→ Page 140]

As we introduced in the first chapter, the psychologists Petre and Green (1993) have investigated schematic programming for imperative languages such as Basic or C. In particular they have studied the use of conditionals (if) using a standard test (see Fig. 4.22) over a range of notations. The ability of people (the subjects) to understand these different notations of imperative programs was tested. They were asked questions about a program written in these different notations and then their performance assessed in terms of speed and errors. The results were used to assess each of the notations as a means of describing the given process clearly to other people.

The task for the subject when faced with such a program was to determine what it does and what given results might be implied about a given input condition. A further task was to compare programs in the same and different notations. The questions are then to do with explaining how the programs differ. Every attempt was made to layout each notation at its best. Experts in each notation were used to design the test programs. It was a good experiment, fair and well designed. As we stated in Chapter 1 they concluded that:

- Overall, graphics was significantly slower than text to interpret.
- Moreover, graphics was slower than text in all conditions and the effect was uniform.
- The intrinsic difficulty of the graphics modes was the strongest effect observed.

But why are Mind Maps , for example, so successful as a way of recording ideas? Perhaps it is because Mind Maps are not describing processes as a sequence of

Fig. 4.22 One of the problems in Nest-INE notation from Petre and Green (1993)

```
if high:
  if wide:
    if deep: weep
    not deep:
        if tall: weep
        not tall: click
        end tall
    end deep
  not wide
    if long:
        if thick: gasp
        not thick: roar
        end thick
    not long
        if thick: sigh
        not thick: gasp
        end thick
    end long
  end wide
not high
  if tall: burp
  not tall: hiccup
  end tall
end high
```

instructions. Further, it should be noted that these experiments are only concerned with imperative programming and functional programming was never explored or even discussed. It is worth considering what differences there are between these two forms of programming. Before we do this we need to understand the notion of coherence as related to design.

The Engineering Coherences of Design [→ Page 140]

Coherences describe the similarity relationship between a programming language and elements of design. There are four elements of design where the coherence or lack of it (incoherence) has practical consequences (the observable effects are given as 'indicators' described in Chapter 2 page 36):

- *Operation:* This relates language with the engine it controls.
  Indicators: The language reflects the actual operations being done by the machine. The further away the language is from these operations the less a designer is able to predict the performance of the machine from the sequence of instructions given.
- *Semantic:* There are two kinds of semantics. The *formal semantics* and the *informal semantics.*
  Indicators: The semantic coherencebetween the two semantics can be achieved by the introduction of one or more abstracting layers in the program. These layers

are translations that reform the formal instruction set into recognisable actions and objects in the problem domain. This will be indicated in a similar way to decomposition. The formal semantic are assumed to be different to the informal semantics and that this is overcome to some extent by the introduction of mediating functions and extensive use of the accidental properties of the languages that provide this translation. New concepts would be introduced through constructors that are used to create new types of variables and objects. Also, there will also be extensive use of annotation, variable and function naming with program restructuring.

- **Representation:** This coherence occurs with computers, which are primarily sequential, and a sequential programming language is used. However, time-ordered tasks, in general, are both sequential and parallel and as such a two-dimensional representation would be more consistent. Representational coherence is related to the match–mismatch hypothesis (Gilmore and Green 1984).

  Indicators: If there is good coherence then the degrees of freedom of the representation are the same as its functionality. Thus the notation will be used to represent only the functionality. For example, in the incoherent case of text notation there are variables used to make links; links that do not, in themselves, take part in the processing except to pass information. These variables may cause unwanted side effects.

- **Design:** *Design coherence* ensures a well-formed representation at the formal level through the structure of the language and support of the design environment.

  Indicators: An indication of design incoherence is when there are type mismatches or redundant code. With good coherence there will be a reduction of errors during implementation and we would expect simple functions with few children.

Functional vs. Imperative Programming [→ Page 140]

Essentially, we have only two major choices in programming styles: functional or imperative. Logic programming has the functional style and OO has functional properties embedded in an imperative style.

A pure functional approach has advantages over a pure imperative approach in having *referential transparency*. This makes for clear design structures and thus it does not require very sophisticated error tracing facilities. However, a strictly correct (pure) functional language has two disadvantages:

1. It requires that the links to real world operations (such as 'read' or 'print') are side effects. That is the inputs from the world to a function, and the outputs to the world from a function are not definable within the formal structure of a pure

functional language. These side effects are events that are not expressible within the formal semantics.

2. The problem domain states must be passed/copied between functions (also see *interoperability*). That is, if many functions process the data then each function can have access only through one of its input parameters.

Imperative languages have good *operation coherence* in that they reflect the computer processes in their syntax and semantics. Thus machine code maps directly into the computer device and describes exactly what is done within the machinery. Operation coherence begins to be reduced as higher-level languages are introduced. Unfortunately, because the state of such an imperative program depends on its history and because communication is done through side effects, problems arise when errors occur or changes have to be made. Consequently, the cause of an error may be many thousands of operations distant from its observed symptoms. In particular, changes can have effects that are not traceable until a problem arises, and that may be measured in years.

Creating a Schematic Language [→ Page 140]

When we started to consider alternative ways of programming we asked ourselves the question 'Given complete freedom of choice on a representation, unbounded by physical constraints, what would it be?' One puzzle was that if there are good reasons for choosing a functional language then why are we not all using such a language style now? We concluded that some of the problem lies in the history of computing rather than based on any real current cause.

The Problems of a Functional Language

Notwithstanding the lack of take-up of functional languages to date, we will argue that in principle, they offer many of the desired attributes we need for design and are a good starting place to resolve many of the difficulties encountered. However, we must consider why functional languages have failed, thus far, to find acceptance.

The three major problems with a functional language are the three incoherence classes of operation, semantics and representation. The three problems are:

1. *Functional languages do not match the computer architectures* on which they run. This can lead to unexpected massive processes, sequential changes of operations and heavy main memory demands. Links with the real world are indirect and have the reduced status of being just 'side effects'. The need, from an engineering point of view, for operational coherence soon becomes apparent if you try to run the program Digits (see later) with any large number. In this example,

the performance for any calculation is dependent upon the size of the number; a very peculiar behaviour that does not correspond to the normal computer.

2. The formal assumption behind a pure functional language is that *the informal world for which a program is to be implemented is completely known and definable*. Although this gives a language in which all formal concepts may be represented (a powerful property) it creates a barrier to many practical applications where not everything can ever be known. So even processes that depend on time, a basic assumption with imperative languages, require a laborious and explicit description of time itself. The representation becomes unwieldy as soon as the complexities of the world are included.

3. *The mathematical parentage of a pure functional language makes it obscure* to many people. Processes are described as relationships and although in many cases the representation is the same there are some important differences (e.g. the use of recursion instead of iteration).

Solving the Problems

We will consider the three <u>in</u>coherence classes of operation, semantic and representation together with the possible options of ameliorating their difficulties and then explore the effect of these choices on design and design support.

Operation Incoherence

This will be exaggerated through the use of an interpreter but an interpreter needs to be used in order to retain the *reactivity* and the *flexibility* of the design environment. Experience has shown that there is an ideal engineering balance between imperative and functional specifications that optimise the advantages of both styles of expression (e.g. LISP). If we can take a small step away from a pure functional language and invoke 'side effect' programming as a clear and distinct activity then we can support *operation coherence* when and where required. Such a decision should remain under the designer's control. However, to retain the *semantic coherence* such a step would still have to operate through an interpreter.

In many cases, and with advances in technology, the performance overhead of an interpreter is not as significant as it was (say) 20 years ago. However, in cases where the real time performance becomes critical and because of *referential transparency, interoperability* and *decomposition* then any function on the critical path could be translated into its imperative form without much loss of *design transparency*. Such a modification would neither alter the original design nor interfere with the *design coherence*. It would also allow the natural integration of already existing software.

Informal-Semantic Incoherence

This is mainly caused by the need to refer to a world that is continually changing. If an extensional function is allowed to have its extension changed dynamically (using the function 'setq', as in Lisp or 'assertq' as in Prolog (see Bramer 2005)) then this function can act as a global variable. The parameters of such a function would then behave like an array index with the additional advantage that this index can be any conceivable type.[6] In this way real world data can be represented without the need to pass it around as parameters. If this is combined with both 'side effect' programming and the functional notation then this combination will increase the *extensibility* of the representation into another dimension and still retain *semantic coherence* in both.

Representation Incoherence

This can be alleviated by representing the two dimensions of a process as a set of diagrams. To aid the transfer of design skills of engineers and imperative pro-grammers graphical equivalent representations have been used (Reade 1989). These graphs have three characteristics: *first* it makes clear the relationship between the component parts of a user-constructed function, *second* the directed graphs are at their most transparent when they have few elements connected together and *finally* functions are best constructed from only a few component functions. Given this match and the observation that many designers choose to use a graphical representa-tion to explore design options a functional language that can be directly interpreted through a graphical representation seems to provide the optimum design environ-ment (Larkin and Simon 1995). In this way we have good *representational coher-ence*, *design coherence* and *transparency*.

Exploring Possibilities

We originally considered combining and extending SQL and its pictorial form (Elleby and Addis 1987, Addis and Bull 1988) but the problem with this is that the range of constraints to be imposed by the language had to be preset to cope with what amounted to an infinite range of constraints between and normalisations of data (Codd 1971, Maier 1983). A further disadvantage is that very few people were able to comprehend the extended normalisation process required to use such a language. The real breakthrough was the adoption of an alternative perception of a database as a set of extensional functions rather than just relations (a relation may be considered as an extensional function) as proposed by Carol Small, who joined our team and was a PhD student of Poulovassilis (1988) (see Addis and Nowell 1990). It was Carol Small who constructed the first Faith interpreter. This view left open

---

[6] We can see an example of this in the function 'respond' (Fig. 4.26) which behaves as an array indexed on the type 'list feature', feature being a user defined enumerated type. Functions can also be used as an index either evaluated to a type or unevaluated. In the latter case, the function behaves like a constructor. The 'best-fit' pattern match allows variables to be used. In the rare instances of ambiguity, the 'best-fit' rule makes a selection based upon a well-defined criterion.

the possibility of extending constraints between data as functions provided the data was represented also as functions.

We thus chose, in the form of Clarity, an approach that will combine graphical (schematic) and functional representation. Taking our lead from those in VLSI design (Mead and Conway 1980, also compare Crowther et al. 1995, and Davis et al. 1993) we have given the designer the option to select and mix any combination of the two representation schemes (graphical or text). We should also ask, to ensure that Clarity in its current form is still the best we can do, 'what kind of diagrams should we use?'

Doing Without 'Ifs' [→Page 140]

As engineers and designers, our first instinct is to abandon all the schematic forms investigated for the problem posed by Petre and Green (e.g. Fig. 4.22) (Petre and Green 1993, Green and Petre 1996, Green 1990). They are all difficult to use for this problem and the given graphical representations they used are particularly so. Instead we chose to produce a decision tree/network (Fig. 4.23) as our common interpretation of each notation.[7] This matches the problem nicely. It shows that there are two types of variables: *features* and *actions*. 'Not' may also be considered a feature. In Clarity, these features can be represented by *constructors* that belong to the types '**feature**' and '**action**'. Under this representation choice '**Not**' becomes a

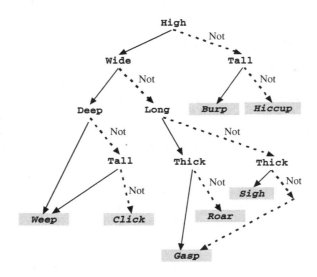

Fig. 4.23 A decision tree/network that describes the test problem

---

[7]Some designers may prefer a decision table. This really is a matter of choice and the designer's habits rather than any fundamental issue.

Fig. 4.24 The set of type 'feature'

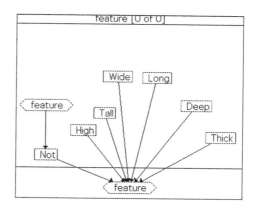

Fig. 4.25 The set of type 'action'

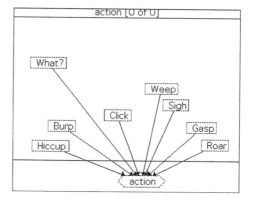

unique feature in that it takes a feature as a parameter. This is shown in Figs. 4.24 and 4.25.

Going down all the paths of the decision tree (Fig. 4.23) it is possible to list the features that lead to a particular action. These lists of features can be used to index an extensional function 'respond' the output of which is an action.[8] This function is equivalent to a look-up table. All non-specified sequences of features are caught by the general case (Fig. 4.26a) that will respond 'What?'. Such a nicety is optional.

Within the Clarity environment it is possible to look at the Faith code generated from the schema (Fig. 4.27), flick through the extensions of 'respond' sequentially or display all the extensions at the same time. It is also possible to 'query' the function in the control window.

QUERY> respond [High Wide Deep]
Weep

---

[8] Each schema extension can be used as a pro forma to produce the next extension.

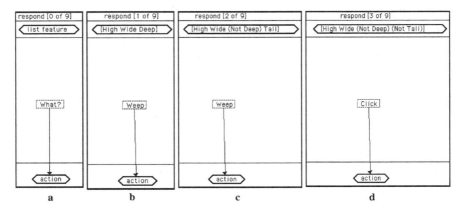

Fig. 4.26   A sample of the extensions of the function 'respond'

```
fdec
     respond ::= list feature->action ; ;
fdef
  respond ?0   ::= What?  ;
  respond (: High (: Wide (: Deep nil)))   ::= Weep  ;
  respond (: High (: Wide (: (Not Deep) (: Tall nil))))   ::= Weep  ;
  respond (: High (: Wide (: (Not Deep) (: (Not Tall) nil))))   ::=  Click  ;
  respond (: High (: (Not Wide) (: Long (: Thick nil))))   ::= Gasp  ;
  respond (: High (: (Not Wide) (: Long (: (Not Thick) nil))))   ::= Roar  ;
  respond (: High (: (Not Wide) (: (Not Long) (: Thick nil))))   ::=  Sigh  ;
```

Fig. 4.27   The complete Faith code generated by Clarity

QUERY> respond [High (Not Wide) Long (Not Thick)]
Roar
We can also 'query' the function in reverse

QUERY> inverse respond Weep
[[High Wide Deep]
  [High Wide (Not Deep) Tall]]

The current arrangement requires that the features be listed in a particular order, so the function 'go' was written to overcome this problem (see Fig. 4.28). The function 'go' can be used thus

QUERY> go [Tall (Not High)]
Burp
QUERY> go [Deep Thick]
What?

Note that this program has been written without a single 'if'. It relies upon two useful characteristics of a functional language: *pattern match* and *constructors*. We doubt if any fingers will be required to answer questions on the behaviour of this program other than to use the keyboard. The overall nature of the function 'respond'

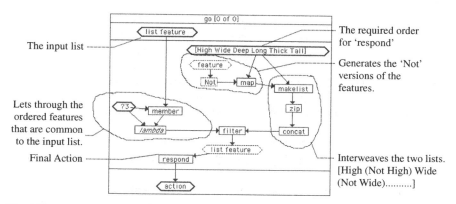

The required order for 'respond'

Generates the 'Not' versions of the features.

Interweaves the two lists.
[High (Not High) Wide (Not Wide).........]

The input list

Lets through the ordered features that are common to the input list.

Final Action

Fig. 4.28 A simple function 'go' to avoid feature sequence. It also shows the potential for further decomposition

is that it *responds* to patterns, the details of which can be ignored or changed when used within a larger context such as 'go' (Fig. 4.28).

The Digits project will further illustrate the extraordinary power of the trio of pattern match, constructors and recursion.

Exploring 'Real' Programs [→ Page 140]

The Approach, Results and Interpretation

Our objective in this section is to see if some of the indicators described in Chapter 2 and in this chapter (coherence) are observable in 'real' programs. In particular, we will be looking for the differences of these indicators between functional and imperative programs. With such a comparison, we hope to demonstrate that functional programs encourage design properties that make a schematic representation a viable form of representation.

All the programs we have chosen to examine are 'real' in the sense that they were created to perform a job. In most cases they are programs paid for by business and written by professional programmers. 'Novice' refers to inexperienced (months rather than years) programmers in the language referenced. A further requirement is that they are all non-trivial programs. We have selected a range of authors from expert to novice.

The three programs X, Y, Z and Q have been written in Clarity. The lines of code refer to the generated Faith. Approximately, 17 K of the lines of code of X are related to the Expert System rule set and these have been discounted from the analysis since they are not really part of the program design; they are data. These rules are stored as the extensions of three functions. X was created in 1 year (Addis et al. 2005). Y is non-commercial and is an ongoing and ever changing tool for exploring 'agent' group behaviour (Addis and Gooding 2008). At the time of these measurements Y is about 7 years old but 'cleaned' by the removal of redundant functions from time to time. Z is a new industrial control system that has been created in Clarity and written by a novice in 2 months. Q is a program used to modify bridge designs through Genetic Algorithms and written by a competent programmer over 2 years (Addis et al. 1994). Four different authors have written the four C programs. They have not been dealt with individually. Initially, they will be taken as a single source and used as our standard (Fig. 4.29). Figures 4.30 and 4.31 are headed with the dimensions for which the containing data are indicators. These dimensions and their indicators are described in Chapter 2 and in this chapter, the Engineering Dimensions and coherence of Design.

The natural unit for a functional program is the 'function'. The composition of a function consists of a selection of pre-defined library functions and a set of user defined functions. What we need to show, in order to make a comparison between programming styles, is that these user functions are equivalent to the functions in a C program. We will assume that a designer has a completely free choice in the size and content of a function within the constraints of the problem. The designers will thus choose a 'unit' of design (the function) with which they are comfortable and which can be handled easily. However, the aberrations of a particular problem to be solved by a designer may demand a larger unit size than might be considered 'comfortable'. Nevertheless, we would expect that the units should tend towards a norm. The units, by their nature, will be defined in terms of other units and it is the number of *different*[9] units per function that we will use as our measure (Fig. 4.30). This is the dimension of *functional decomposition* that can be measured by the statistics of the children of a function (see Fig. 4.30).

By considering the number of parents of a function we can assess the nature of the functional composition; this is the function's deployment. If there is more than one parent then we are detecting the existence of an intermediate conceptual layer. Such a layer suggests that there is a tension between the formal and informal semantics and that, in effect, a new set of concepts needs to be constructed to better match the

	X 'Clarity'	Y 'Clarity'	Z 'Clarity'	Q 'Clarity'	C 'C'
Job	Expert System Rules (No Rules)	Agents Model	Industrial Control	Engineering Genetic Algorithms	Interpreter, Statistics, 2 translators
Total Size Kb	946 (372)	58	65	72	139
Programmer	Expert	Expert	Novice	Competent	4 Programs
Code (lines)	31961 (15354)	2033	1838	413	5444
Tot Functions	194	176	90	52	125
Code/Function	80	12	20	8	44

Fig. 4.29 Summary of programs used for the analysis

---

[9]Rather than the total number.

Functional decomposition, interoperability, design transparency, semantic coherence, design coherence					
	X	Y	Z	Q	C
Number of children					4 Programs
Average All (Ω)	6.3	6.0	8.5	4.9	$3.8 + 3.7^{10} = 7.5$
Sigma σ_a All	4.2	3.6	7.6	2.7	4.0
Standard Err ε_a All	0.30	0.27	0.80	0.37	0.36
Expected# User (μ_c)	2.0	2.0	4.0	1.2	1.9
Sigma σ_c User	2.0	1.9	4.9	1.4	2.2
Standard Er ε_c User	0.14	0.14	0.51	0.19	0.20
Expected# Library (μ_l)	(4.3)	(4.0)	(4.5)	(3.6)	5.6
Sigma σ_l Library[11]	(5.6)	(4.7)	(9.5)	(3.5)	(5.2)
Standard Err ε_c Library	(0.40)	(0.35)	(1.00)	(0.49)	(0.47)

Fig. 4.30 The sets of children functions used to define a function

flexibility, functional composition, semantic coherence,					
	X	Y	Z	Q	C
Number of parents					4 Programs
Approximate age (years)	1.0	7.0	0.2	2.0	?
Zero (α)	19%	24%	6%	34%	14%
One (β)	50%	44%	61%	47%	42%
Expected# (μ_p)	1.5	1.8	2.2	1.1	1.9
Sigma σ_p	1.5	2.6	2.4	1.5	2.3
Standard Err ε_p	0.11	0.14	0.25	0.20	0.20

Fig. 4.31 The sets of parent functions per function (usage)

problem domain. Many functions with zero parents indicate either that the program itself is a kit of tools or that the functions have been created, replaced or abandoned. This percentage of zero parents will be one of the indicators of System Flexibility (Chapter 2) and should be positively correlated to usage and time. Therefore, if flexibility is an issue then the number of the latter type of function should grow with age.

Functions with a single parent suggest that complex functions have been simplified. The simplification is by the removal of a set of functions within a function to form a new single unit. For example, extracting one or more of the operations circled in the function 'go' (see Fig. 4.28) could have done this. The results show that the expected number of library children remains reasonably constant in all cases in that they overlap within the standard error. This supports the hypothesis that the composition comes primarily from the user functions. Where there are a small number of expected user children per function then this implies that either the library functions are used more effectively or there is a better match of the notation with the problem.

---

[10] These are the language library functions such as '==', 'while' and 'for'.

[11] Use equation $\sigma_1 = \sqrt{[2\sigma_a^2(n-1)/n - \sigma_c^2]}$

Design transparency, system flexibility		
	XYZQ	**C**
Progs (Authors)	4 (4)	18 (10)
Ifs/Fun μ_p	Average [0.17 0.17 0.26 0.38] = **0.25**	3.38
Sigma σ_p (crctd)	0.086 (0.099)	2.04 (2.10)
Standard Err ε_p	**0.05**	**0.49**

Fig. 4.32   The number of ifs per function

The high value of expected children for Z suggests that the problem domain is not well matched to a functional approach. In an informal support, the programmer and his colleagues confirmed this observation.

The expected 'ifs' per function for C were determined by counting the number of 'if's used per program for 18 different programs (Fig. 4.32). The population is now based on programs rather than functions. These include the four programs used in the function equivalence study (Fig. 4.29, 4.30, and 4.31), financial, utilities and textbook C. The Snedecor's F test for the difference between the variances = 450 which gives a significance better than 0.1% (1 in 1000 of the result happening by chance). The difference between the two populations is greater than six standard errors, a very significant difference.

Discussion on Results

We have shown for experienced programmers through these experiments that the functional unit tends to consist of about six different child units. The expected number of library programs per unit for all programmers, problems and notations is about four units. The observed variation in the number of user functions per unit could be explained by differences in experience and the problem domain. In the latter case, the relevance of library functions becomes less, as more user functions are developed to overcome the semantic tension experienced between the problem and the resources of the language.

We have shown that the expected frequency of 'if's in a C program is an order of magnitude higher than in a functional language. This seems to be the case for both Expert and Novice programmer. Generally novice programmers will use more 'ifs' than experienced programmers. Even so, a novice Clarity programmer will still use about eight times less 'ifs' than a C programmer.

Consequences of the Experiments

We can now respond to the deliberations in Chapter 1 given by Citrin, Green, Petre et al. Consider the issue of 'appropriateness of mapping'. So long as the formal semantics of a range of notations are the same then the choice of notation is not relevant to the structure and size of a function. This we have demonstrated above with our experiments. The choice of notation, whether it be schema or script, is an independent matter; a matter of preference. Considering the potential to use the informal features of the Clarity notation to some advantage we can make such a choice. In the case of Clarity, the schema provides a useful transformation on the layout of a functional language.

One of the difficulties with a functional programming language is that the functions are imbedded in each other, the interpreter works from the outside in and it evaluates from the inside out.[12] Imperative languages are more straightforward in that they evaluate in the order they are written unless explicitly commanded otherwise. This is much more easily understood. Clarity, however, provides the option to arrange the schema to place the inside of functions at the top and the outside of the functions at the bottom. In this way the display of the functions has all the benefits of the imperative ordering of functions and yet it also has all the formal equivalence and the advantages of a functional language.

The issue of 'scalability' has been resolved partly through the use of a functional language, partly through a good supporting environment that gives views of children and parent functions and partly due to the reactivity of an interpreter. The responsive environment of a functional database interpreter supports a designer by allowing questions to be asked of the program during development. We have shown that sizeable commercial programs are not only feasible but also quick to design and create. Our current example (Program X), with a small team of three, took an idea to a product in less than 18 months.

The issue of 'transparency of the interface' has also been resolved in that the schema has the positive advantage of representing a form where the text in the function boxes and parameter lozenges can be easily edited to produce functional extensions or used to construct new functions. The manipulation and editing of the schema, with modern GUI, is as simple as editing text. Move a function box and the arrows change to follow, highlight a box to edit or delete (as in text), press a key and any icon can be placed. The transmission of diagrams is now easy but the text code representing the diagrams can also be transmitted where there might be problems and regenerated by the Clarity interpreter at the receiver end.

The difficulty of 'interpreting graphics' depends on the graphics. The examples used by Petre and Green were grossly mismatched to the problems they addressed. Figure 4.23 shows that better diagrams do exist and may be used in preference to a text representation.

Although we have not explored the issue of the speed in creating diagrams, our experience supports the observations made by Green et al. Oddly, the expert users tend to be slower than novices because the experts spend a lot of time doing minor adjustments to the diagram, adjustments such as getting the lines straight or

---

[12]It is the case that not all evaluations may conform strictly to the process. Lazy evaluation is designed to avoid unnecessary work. However, evaluation of any kind for any function cannot go to completion unless all the parameters of that function have been evaluated to completion.

rearranging for minimum line cross-over or where that is not possible using labelled junctions to span the schema (as used in engineering drawings of circuits). This is an indication that 'interpretation' and long-term 'understanding' is a concern for the experienced designer. Experienced users, thus confirming the concern for clear interpretation, usually also add extensive annotation.

The source of the difficulties in the visual programming languages explored was that they were derived from designing fixed physical devices whereas programming in general is different. This was fully discussed in Chapter 1.

Finally, the major problem of 'knots' in program structures is created by an excessive use of 'ifs'. We have shown that using a functional programming language through a graphical representation naturally reduces the number of 'ifs' used by an order of magnitude. We have argued that this effect is a property of the functional language rather than the visual interface. Despite the excellent design properties of functional languages they have tended to be ignored for commercial program development because of the operational incoherence. We have shown that the real advantage of the graphical notation is that it makes a functional language easier to use by reducing operational and the semantic incoherence. It is this marriage between a functional language and its diagrammatic representation that unifies them into a viable program development tool for industrial-sized applications.

*PROJECT: A Minimalist Program

Digits: Doing Without the Built-In Library

Introduction

The question addressed here is 'what are the minimum set of mechanisms that are required of a pure functional language so that it retains its full expressiveness?' By a 'pure functional language' we mean one that has no (useful) side effects. We will illustrate this by using Clarity and through the creation of simple integer arithmetic from which any calculus can be constructed using only the two basic mechanisms of *exact pattern match* and *recursion*.[13] These two mechanisms act on the notion of a *function* and *constructed types*. We will illustrate the power of these two mechanisms to express any calculus by constructing primitive objects (enumerated types)

---

[13] The significance and value of these two mechanisms for program creation is illustrated by Glaser et al. (2000).

and the operations on those primitive objects and thus showing that it leads, in our example, to a complete integer arithmetic. By induction, we will argue that this process will also lead to any formal system that has the same framework as integer arithmetic.

The approach is based upon the three primitive ideas of Peano. These ideas were the inspiration from which Whitehead and Russell (1910) constructed the first stages of Principia Mathematica (see Russell 1919). These ideas are the zero (0), number and successor. The function 'successor' refers to the next number in the natural order such that 0 maps to 1 and 1 maps to 2 and so on. There are five primitive propositions assumed by Peano:

1. Zero is a number.
2. The successor of any number is a number.
3. No two numbers have the same successor.
4. Zero is not the successor of any number.
5. All numbers inherit the properties of zero and the properties of the successors of zero.

In addition, we wish to employ the Arabic representation of a number such that all the numbers can be represented by concatenating the ten elementary symbols 0–9.

The Digits

'Digits' is a Clarity/Faith program that uses no computer based or library functions. However, we will use the notion of lists and the operations on lists for the sake of brevity. We have shown that 'lists' and their associated operations can be defined using just the two primitive mechanisms *exact pattern match*[14] and *recursion* and they are the only mechanisms we will allow ourselves to employ in this program. Although a computer is used to perform the operations, integer arithmetic can be specified independently of the computer's in-built computational potential.[15]

The initial task is to form the basic 'objects/symbols' of manipulation by integer arithmetic. These are the digits 0–9 and are specified as enumerated constructors (Diagram 4.1).

The next stage is to introduce a simple extensional function '**next_digit**'; this is the basic 'successor' function for 'single' digits. This function maps digits onto their successors (Diagram 4.2). The odd one out in this sequence is 9 which maps back to 0 (zero). The reason for this becomes clear in the '**next_digits**' function (note the '**s**') which is the successor function for combined digits (lists of digits). Here

---

[14]In practice, we invoke '*best fit*' pattern match and '*lazy evaluation*'.

[15]The final program can be very slow and expensive on memory. This illustrates the effect of '*operational incoherence*' that exists between the computer and the functional language. Creating library functions in a language that is '*operationally coherent*' (such as C) makes functional programming fast and practical.

Diagram 4.1 Initial
definition of digits

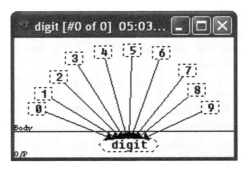

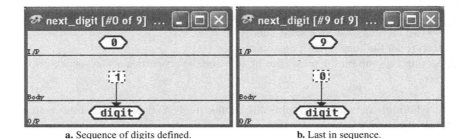

a. Sequence of digits defined.   b. Last in sequence.

Diagram 4.2 'next_digit' gets the next digit

we depart slightly from Peano's approach in order to take advantage of the Arabic number representation.

The function '**next**' (Diagram 4.3) splits the least significant digit (last in list) from the rest of the number (front of digit list) and passes the two components to '**next_digits**' (Diagram 4.4). This will then use '**next_digit**' (Diagram 4.2) on the lone digit and then tag the result to the list thus increasing the whole number by one. However, in the special cases of the digit 9 this is dealt with through an exact pattern match rather than a generic match. Note that '**next**' and '**next_digits**' are *mutually recursive* in that they call each other in a loop. Recursion will be considered in detail in Chapter 5.

A number is thus defined as a list of digits so that number 326 will be represented by [3 2 6]. The in-built representation of a list is used for convenience but we do know that it can be defined within the limitations we have imposed on ourselves. We could have produced a *recursively* defined 'Number' constructor that would link the digits together to form numbers in exactly the same way as a 'list'. However, we would lose the simplicity and clarity of the in-built syntax of the square bracketed list.

The '**previous**' function uses the '**inverse**' of '**next_digit**' in a similar way in order to achieve a count down rather than a count up. The two together can then be used to make the arithmetic operation '**+**' ('**add_digits**' – Diagram 4.5). The '**–**' ('**subtract_digits**') is obtained by simply counting down and down simultaneously

Diagram 4.3 'Next'
Numbers as list of digits

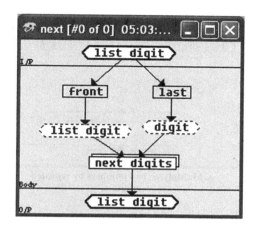

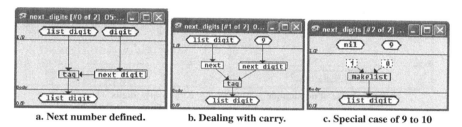

a. Next number defined.   b. Dealing with carry.   c. Special case of 9 to 10

Diagram 4.4 'next_digits' creates next number

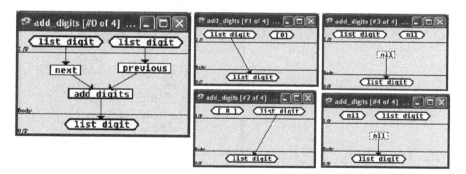

Diagram 4.5 'add_digits' adding two numbers

until one list is empty. We use the built-in '**inverse**' for convenience. Otherwise, we could have simply created an inverse of digits as separate function.

Multiplication is simply repeated addition and division is repeated subtraction. From here all integer arithmetic can be defined (Diagram 4.6). The network diagram (Diagram 4.8) shows the overall Digits program in terms of the 'uses' relationships

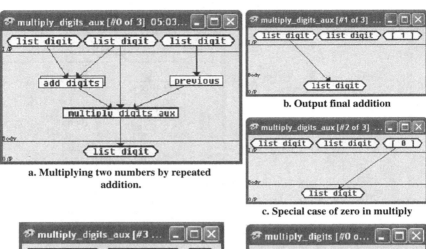

a. Multiplying two numbers by repeated addition.

b. Output final addition

c. Special case of zero in multiply

d. Special case of no number.

e. 'multiply_digits' The interface of multiply: initial conditions

Diagram 4.6 Multiplying two numbers

Diagram 4.7 'previous' last number

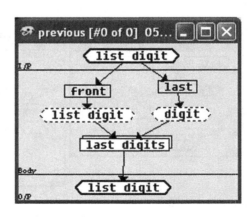

(dotted arrows). Note the symmetry of the functions. The following tests show the expected results but it is bounded by stack depth using this technique.

    QUERY> factorial_digits [5]
    [1 2 0]

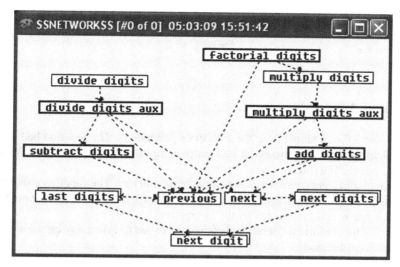

Diagram 4.8 Overview of complete 'digits' program

```
QUERY>factorial_digits [6]
[ 7 2 0 ]
QUERY>factorial_digits [7]
[ 5 0 4 0 ]
```

The method can be extended to include arithmetic for negative numbers and floating point arithmetic by extending the digits to include the negation sign and the decimal point. Boolean algebra can also be specified using the same technique and combining with arithmetic such tests as '<' and '>' can be formed. This allows different comparisons other than exact match to be done. It requires only a few more steps to produce 'predicate calculus ' or any other formal system of this kind.

Exercises 4.2

1. Make a function 'xxx' with three character parameters that will respond "yes" for three character 'x's, "maybe" for any two 'x's and "possible" for any one 'x' and "no" for no 'x's.
2. Make a function 'choice' that will respond to:
   (Thin or Fat) and (Blond or Dark) but not Old -> Star
   (Green or Blue) and (Thin or Fat) -> Alien
   Thin and Blond and not Old -> Model
   Old and Fat and not Green -> Actor
3. Make a simple Roman Numeral calculator that can add and subtract Roman numbers for the numbers 1–9. (**Hint**: do all the calculations using the primitive i.) For

reasons of the internal workings of Clarity do not use the capital letters C B S K and I. These are reserved characters called *combinators* and are used by the interpreter.

Questions 4.2

1. Consider an extensional function with three parameters. The function had either a match for the first parameter or two matches for the last two parameters. Which is the one the interpreter would select?
2. Consider an extensional function with three parameters. The function either had a match for the first parameter or had matches for the first and last parameters. Which one would be selected by the interpreter?
3. What are the minimum operational elements needed to define any calculus using a functional language?

References

Addis T. R., Gooding D. C. (2008) *'Simulation Methods for an Abductive System in Science'*, Special issue called TRACKING IRRATIONAL SETS: Science, Technology, Ethics in Foundations of Science (2008) The official Journal of the Association for *Foundations of Science, Language and Cognition*, ISSN: 1233–1821 (print version), Springer Netherlands: Electronic versions already published.

Addis T. R. and Bull S. P. (1988) *'A Concept Language for Knowledge Elicitation'*, Proceedings of the Second European Workshop on Knowledge Acquisition. Bonn, pp. 1/1–1/11. June.

Addis T. R. and Nowell M. C. C. (1990) *'Scaling Up Knowledge Systems: An Architecture for the GigaKnowledge-base'*, Proceedings of the BCS Specialist Group on Expert Systems, London, September, ISBN 0-521-40403-7, pp. 238–251.

Addis T. R., Townsend Addis J. J. and Gillett, R. (2005), *'Wise Expert: An Expert System for Monitoring Ship Cargo Handling'* SGAI AI 2005 Applications and Innovation in Intelligent Systems XIII, ISBN 10: 1 84628-223 3, pp. 137–150.

Addis T. R., Pretlove, A. J. and Townsend, J. J. (1994). *'A Functional Approach to Creating Evolutionary Models for Engineering Design Illustrated by a Bridge Design'*, Proceedings of the 14th Annual Conference of the British Computer Specialists Group on Expert Systems (ES94), ISBN 1-899621-01-6, pp. 275–284.

Bramer M. (2005) *'Logic Programming with Prolog'*, Springer, New York, ISBN 10: 1-85233-938-1.

Buzen T. (1993) *'The Mind Map Book: How to Use Radiant Thinking to Maximize Your Brain's Untapped Potential'*, Penguin Group, Dutton, ISBN 0-525-93904-0.

Citrin W. (1996) *'Strategic Directions in Visual Languages Research'*, ACM Computing Surveys, Vol. 28, No. 4, December.

Codd E. F. (1971) *'Further Normalisation of the Database Relational Model'* , IBM Research Report 909, IBM Thomas J. Watson Research Center, Yorktown Heights. New York.

Crowther W. J. et al. (1995). *'Knowledge Acquisition for Engineering Systems using Bond Graphs'*, Research and Development in Expert Systems XII. Proceedings of Expert Systems 95, Cambridge, December, pp. 41–56.

Davis R., Shrobe h. and Szolovitz P. (1993), *'What is a Knowledge Representation'*, AI Magazine, Vol. 14, No. 1, pp. 17–33, Spring.

Elleby P. and Addis T. R., (1987) 'A Conceptual Model for Transaction Integrity', Proceedings of MILCOMP 87, Microwave Publishers, pp. 381–386, October.

Gilmore D. J. and Green T. R. G., (1984) 'Comprehension and Recall of Miniature Programs' International Journal of Man-Machine Studies, Vol. 21, pp. 31–48.

Glaser H., Hartel P. H. and Garrett P. W., (2000), 'Programming by Numbers', The Computer Journal, Vol 43, No 4. pp. 252–265.

Green T. R. G. and Petre M. (1996) 'Usability Analysis of Visual Programming Environments: A 'Cognitive Dimensions' Framework', Journal of Visual Languagesand Computing, Vol. 7, pp. 131–174.

Green T. R. (1990) 'Programming Languages as Information Structures' in Psychology of Programming, edited by Hoc et al, pub Academic Press, ISBN 0-12-350772-3.pp. 117–137.

Kasner E. and Newman J. (1949) 'Mathematics and the Imagination' Bell G & Sons Ltd, London, 6th edition (1961).

Larkin J. H. and Simon H. A. (1995) 'Why a Diagram is (Sometimes) Worth Ten Thousand Words' in Diagrammatic Reasoning: Cognitive and Computational Perspectives. eds. Chandrasekaran B, Glasgow J. and Narayanan H. N. AAAI Press/ The MIT Press, Washington, DC/Cambridge, MA, pp. 69–109

Maier D. (1983) 'The Theory of Relational Databases', Computer Science Press, Rockville, MD, ISBN 0-914894-42-0.

Mead C. and Conway L. (1980) 'Introduction to VLSI Systems', Addison-Wesley, New York, ISBN 0-201-04358-0.

Petre M. and Green T. R. G. (1993). 'Learning to Read Graphics: Some Evidence that 'Seeing' an Information Display is an Acquired Skill'. Journal of Visual Languages and Computing, Vol. 4, pp. 55–70.

Poulovassilis A. (1988), 'FDL: An Integration of the Functional Data Model and the Functional Computational Model', BNCOD6, Cambridge University Press, Cambridge, pp. 215–236.

Reade C. (1989) 'Elements of Functional Programming', Addison Wesley, Boston, MA, ISBN 0-201-12915-9.

Russell B. (1919) 'Introduction to Mathematical Philosophy', George Allen & Unwin, London.

Whitehead A. N. and Russell B. (1910) 'Principia Mathematica', Vol. 1, Cambridge University Press, Cambridge.

Chapter 5
Functional Thinking

Rejoiceth not in iniquity but rejoiceth in the truth;
Beareth all things, believeth all things, hopeth all things,
endureth all things.

Corinthians 13,6 to 7.

Introduction

We have shown how a simple function that adds two vectors together may be defined and used. We have also shown that programming depends on much more involved processes that require, in imperative terms, loops, iteration and jumps. Such operations tend to lead to very complex and obscure code. Such code is obscure because the processes cause changes in flow of the program and thus radically alter the behaviour of the processes themselves. Further, a change in the value of a stored item can make many different functions that use that value to perform differently from before it was changed. This, of course, may be what is required but the link back to some global variable may be difficult to trace. Also, if an error or unexpected result occurs it can require the tracing of instructions, which may be many millions, to find out exactly when an erroneous jump or change occurred.

We have already seen that a functional language relies upon recursion and higher-order functions to support loops, iteration and jumps. These techniques avoid the above difficulties by hiding the processes that cause the problems to the user. Jumps (gotos), where there is a change of control from one part of the program to another, are definitely not allowed in functional programming. Jumps are well known to cause problems in tracing the history of program instruction events and they cause even more obscurity than many other imperative processes. Jumps make debugging extremely difficult.

In functional programming recursion is the most important technique of all. It might be said that to think recursively is to think functionally and we might add that to think functionally is the way to good program design. We have also implied earlier (Chapters 3 and 4) that there is more than one elegant solution to a problem. We will

T. Addis, J. Addis, *Drawing Programs: The Theory and Practice of Schematic
Functional Programming*, DOI 10.1007/978-1-84882-618-2_5,
© Springer-Verlag London Limited 2010

demonstrate this by producing a range of solutions for calculating the mathematical function factorial. Factorial of N (sometimes written as N! – c.f. N^2 for square of N) is a function that multiplies together all the numbers from 1 to N. The function factorial is chosen because despite its simplicity it has many of the characteristics that might be found in the design of complex systems, such as control systems, that requires feedback. Since such systems may be working for any length of time then, from a functional point of view, we have to deal with the potential of an indeterminate number of calculation cycles. This means using an indefinite amount of computational resources. This will be dealt with in Chapter 6.

We will show that, although Clarity is essentially functional in form, there are many ways of obtaining the same efficiencies or the same kind of operations that make imperative languages useful under these time-extended or time-dependent circumstances. However, what these studies will not show is the value of the Clarity representation for exploring designs, controlling complexity and working closely with others.

Let us first look at recursion and higher order functions in more detail.

Loops and Recursion

As we have seen, one of the many mechanisms for implementing a loop is recursion. Recursion can be considered as a means of re-entering a function from the beginning but with different parameter values. Just as with (say) a 'for' loop there needs to be some kind of stopping condition. A simple example of recursion is the calculation of 'factorial'. Factorial is used in the statistics of combinations where, for example, one might want to know how many ways there are of ordering a set of items. In particular, there may be a three-letter code for opening a lock consisting of the letters A, B and C. The question might arise as to how secure such a lock would be? There are 3 ways of selecting the first letter, 2 ways of selecting the second letter and only 1 way of selecting the last letter. So there are 3* 2* 1 = 3! = 6 possible arrangements of these letters. So there is a one in six chance of getting the order correct on the first try. If we were to do this imperatively, we might write

```
define factorial (N);
begin
        X : = 1 ;
        If N = 1 then (return N) else
                        for i := 1 step 1 until N do
                                X := X * i ;
        return X ;
end ;
```

In the functional language, the approach is slightly different. We need to have three kinds of insight that is usually the case for all recursive solutions. First, it is useful to note that 3! = 3* 2! and in the general case N! = N* (N–1)! Second, we can 'pretend' in a functional language that 'factorial' is **assumed to work** *before it is* *defined* so that the output of 'factorial' is certain. Then the third and fourth requires us to figure out *how factorial changes from one* **step** *to the next* in the loop and *how it might* **terminate**. It was observed from the nature of factorial that

factorial (N) = N *factorial* (N - 1);{The generic case or the **step**}

and

factorial (0) = 1; {The **terminating** condition or simple case}

This latter condition must hold otherwise all factorials would be 0. Since the above is a true relationship that holds for all N we can define it as shown in Fig. 5.1[1].

The second component in Fig. 5.1b expresses the termination condition (N = #0 where, of course, # is used to mark an integer) whence it returns #1. The *dotted lozenge* can be used to show the type of value being passed between functions.

If you were to trace out the actual order of processing you will find that this suspends the calculations until the terminating condition is reached by running the loop backwards (from N) until factorial (0). We thus have to arrange the calculation so that the input condition to 'factorial' is stepped towards the specific case (i.e. the terminating condition). At this point, it then returns up the loop completing the calculations until the final answer is calculated at the point of starting.

Figure 5.2 illustrates this *head recursion* showing how each factorial is called by subtracting #1 from each call until #0, the termination condition, is reached (Fig. 1b). The answer to this termination condition is predefined and so the path can now be retraced carrying out the multiplication as shown in Fig. 5.1a.

This technique of 'holding' an evaluation while continuing the evaluation process, which may also require further 'holding', is called a 'stack'. It is a 'stack' in

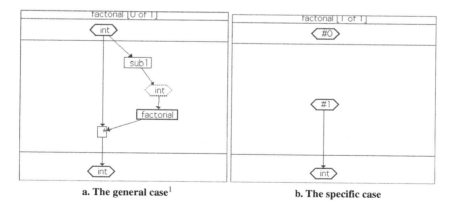

a. The general case[1]   b. The specific case

Fig. 5.1 Defining 'Factorial'

---

[1] The line drawing versions of the function and network windows are created from Menu/File/Save Win as PICT.... rather than using the system print screen.

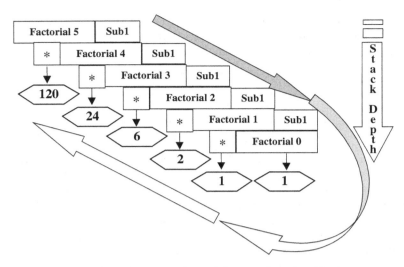

Fig. 5.2 An illustration of *Head recursive factorial*. Max. stack depth = N + 1

the sense that the evaluation is 'stacked up' and then dealt with from the last in first out. This process of stacking is usually hidden from the programmer in a functional language and is automatically invoked when required. Some imperative languages such as C or C++ also provide such a service. Consider the query

> **QUERY>** factorial #5
> #120

This query will test the function factorial, which will work for all positive integers, or until the computer's upper limit of an integer is reached. A little experiment will show you what this limit is as follows:

> QUERY> power #2 #30
> #1073741824
> QUERY> power #2 #31
> #-2147483648

The number of bits allocated to an integer, in this case, is only 32 but that also includes a negative 'flag' in the most significant (highest binary position) bit place. This bit is just reached by the power of 31 as can be shown by

> QUERY> sub1(power #2 #31)
> #2147483647

Therefore, this will be the highest positive integer. When #2 is raised to the power #32 the negative flag is 'carried' into a place where there are no bits to support the number (i.e. position 33). This can be confirmed by

QUERY> power #2 #32

#0

This recursive process of the function factorial is called *head recursion*. It can be viewed in a different way to that shown in Fig. 5.2 by illustrating the process as an extending Curried function as follows:

factorial #5 = * #5(factorial (sub1 #5)) = * #5 (factorial #4)

           = * #5 (* #4 (factorial (sub1 #4))) = *#5 (* #4 (factorial #3))

           = * #5 (* #4 (* #3 (factorial (sub1 #3)))) = * #5 (* #4 (* #3 (factorial #2)))

           = * #5 (* #4 (* #3 (* #2 (factorial (sub1 #2)))))

               = * #5 (* #4 (* #3 (* #2 (factorial #1))))

           = *#5 (* #4 (* #3 (* #2 (* #1 (factorial (sub1 #1))))))

               = * #5 (* #4 (* #3 (* #2 (* #1 (**factorial #0**))))) **Termination condition**

           = * #5 (* #4 (* #3 (* #2 (* #1 #1))))

           = * #5 (* #4 (* #3 (* #2 #1)))

           = * #5 (* #4 (* #3 #2))

           = * #5 (* #4 #6)

           = * #5 #24

           = #120

This is known as *'expanding'* the evaluation. Notice that a step down the stack only occurs when the function calls itself. The **'sub1'** process occurs at the same level. This process will always complete an evaluation of a function at a level in a stack if (and only if) the function has *all* its parameters evaluated.

Recursion can be used whenever there is at least one clear termination condition that can be guaranteed to be reached. This does not have to be numeric as can be seen from the next example (Fig. 5.3). Here we are finding the difference in length between two lists by pairing each item in one list with the other. When there is no more pairings possible (i.e. one of the lists is empty), the remainder of the list, which is not empty, is returned. In this function, the library function 'tail' is used which removes the first item from the list and returns what is left.

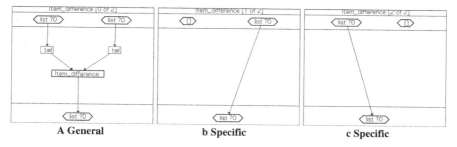

| A General | b Specific | c Specific |

Fig. 5.3 The function showing more than one terminating case

The queries

> QUERY> item_difference['a' 'a' 'a']['b' 'b']
> ['a']
> QUERY> item_difference['a']['b' 'b']
> ['b']
> QUERY> item_difference[ ][ ]
> nil

test the definition. On an aside, it is tests like these that should be cut and pasted into the function's annotation so that there is a ready way it can be described and tested. This form of 'looping' has the disadvantage of depending on the stack to process the answer and thus the number of cycles is limited because the stack size is limited.[2]

As we have seen earlier, these examples also demonstrate the pattern matching properties of the underlying functional language in that processes can be triggered by a specific pattern of parameter values. As we have also noted before, another way of looking at this is as a function that can be considered a potentially multidimensional array of processes or values. This means it can be used as an array that can have a generic index value for all those elements that are not part of a specified collection of predetermined indices; such array elements do not have to be explicitly saved as in normal arrays.

Therefore, the first component of '**factorial**' is a generic response to all numbers except #0 where #0 triggers the specific response. Of course, we could have a specific response (which could include a process) for other numbers as well.[3] The function '**item_difference**' is an example of a *two*-dimensional array that uses this facility. Thus, sparse arrays can be represented without resulting in large amounts of empty storage. Further, the array can be indexed on any kind of type (e.g. integer, string, lists) and if there is more than one dimension (more than one parameter) a generic undefined dimension can also be declared.

Tail Recursion and Auxiliary Functions

A slightly more efficient process than *head* recursion is *tail* recursion. The idea behind *tail recursion* is to avoid the reverse process of the stack by doing the calculation as you proceed. We can redesign 'factorial' so that it works as a tail recursive

---

[2]It is limited to about 120 cycles.

[3]There is a library function '**remember**' that will automatically convert any generic function that is used with a specific number into a component of that function. Thus every example gets added to the (growing) list of specific cases. The process then changes to a simple table lookup. This is particularly useful where the generic component of the function is expensive on computer resources and it is used for only a narrow range of values at any one time. There is a reciprocal function 'forget' that deletes all the extensional components.

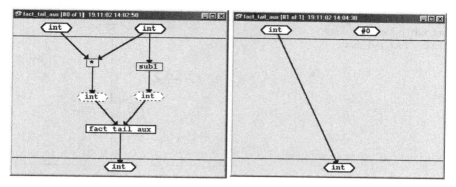

Fig. 5.4 Tail recursive factorial. Max. stack depth = N or = 2

function. The first component of the function '**fact_tail_aux**' in Fig. 5.4 uses a parameter to hold the accumulating value (the first parameter in this case). Note that we use the post fix '_aux' to indicate that this will become an auxiliary function. The reason why it is 'auxiliary' is that it has an extra parameter that is not really of interest to the user; it is only a local requirement for tail recursion. Therefore, we will be wrapping this function up in another function to hide this extra parameter.

The advantage of tail recursion is that the stack will exit from the function at termination instead of having to 'bubble' all the way back to the top (c.f. Fig. 5.2). This roughly halves the processing time. The function can be tested in the Clarity control window, thus

QUERY>fact_tail_aux#1#5

#120

The function can be used as a Curried function by combining its first parameter in a bracketed expression, thus (**fact_tail_aux** #1). Otherwise, this Curried function can be made into a single parameter function by defining the Curried combination as an *auxiliary function* as shown in Fig. 5.5. Expanding the evaluation of '**fact_tail_aux**' we have

fact_tail_aux #1 #5 = fact_tail_aux (* #1 #5) (sub1 #5) = fact_tail_aux #5 #4
$\qquad$ = fact_tail_aux (* #5 #4) (sub1 #4) = fact_tail_aux #20 #3
$\qquad$ = fact_tail_aux (* #20 #3) (sub1 #3) = fact_tail_aux #60 #2
$\qquad$ = fact_tail_aux (* #60 #2) (sub1 #2) = fact_tail_aux #120 #1
$\qquad$ = fact_tail_aux (* #120 #1) (sub1 #1) = fact_tail_aux #120 #0
$\hfill$ **Termination Condition**
$\qquad$ = #120

Note that in the auxiliary function '**fact_tail_aux**' the **termination condition** uses the generic dimension of the first parameter and the specific dimension of the second parameter to terminate. The first parameter is returned as the result with the final calculation.

Fig. 5.5 The function
'**fact_tail**' using an auxiliary
function '**fact_tail_aux**'

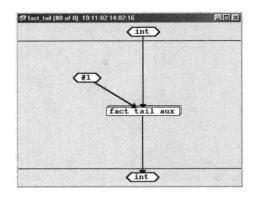

Exercise 5.1

1. Expand the function item_difference ['a'] ['b' 'b']
2. Expand the function item_difference ['a' 'a' 'a'] ['b' 'b']

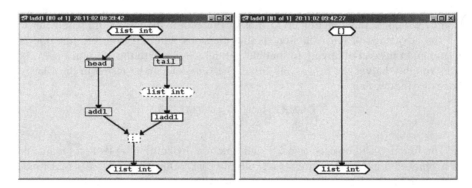

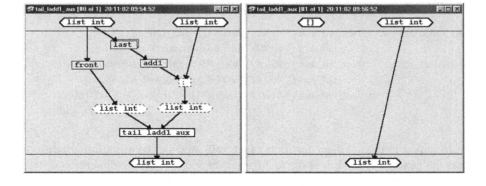

3. Expand the following Clarity head recursive definition of the function 'ladd1'
4. Expand the following Clarity tail recursive definition of the function 'tail_ladd1_aux'

Questions 5.1

1 Why does imperative programming make code obscure?
2 How does a functional language avoid the obscurity normally found in imperative languages?
3 What is the imperative equivalent of recursion ?
4 What three insights are required for recursive solutions?
5 What advantage does tail recursion have over head recursion?
6 What is a stack?
7 How would you test for maximum integer possible for a particular computer?
8 Why do large integers go negative when increased beyond their maximum size?
9 What is meant by expanding a function?
10 Why should you need an auxiliary function ?

Functions as Mappings [→ Page 160]

There are some concepts we have used already that ought to be understood more deeply before we go much further. In general, a function is considered a *'mapping'* of one type of thing onto (or into) another. A *'mapping'* is any mechanism that relates a set of values to another set. A typical example is, not surprisingly, a map. A map *'maps'* a point on a piece of paper to a point on the earth. Another example of *'mapping'* is the relationship between people, which *'maps'* a person to another person. So if we had a set of people, we may propose a function (a lookup table really) that shows who is married to whom. The function would simply answer a question like

Is Tom *married to* Deborah?

We might expect the answer 'Yes' or 'No' or more formally 'True' or 'False'.
The function (shown as a table in this case) could be constructed by taking every man you know with every woman you know (the cross product of men and women) and then assigning True (if married) and False (if not married). This cross product is called the ***domain*** of the function 'married_to'. The pair of possible resulting values {Yes, No} or {True, False} is called the *range* of the function 'married_to'. An example of the table you get if you only know three men (Tom, Steve, Keith) and only three women (Anna, Jan, Deborah) is given in Table 5.1.

Table 5.1 '*married_t o*'

Parameter ?0, type person	Parameter ?1, type person	married_to, type Boolean
Tom	Anna	False
Tom	Jan	True
Tom	Deborah	False
Steve	Anna	True
Steve	Jan	False
Steve	Deborah	False
Keith	Anna	False
Keith	Jan	False
Keith	Deborah	True

Another way of looking at this is as an array of Boolean values (True or False) that are indexed on a pair of names. It so happens that True and False are built as constructors (enumerated). We could have made our own constructors Yes and No by bringing up a constructors window and creating a new type (say type 'answer') that has these two values (Fig. 5.6).

We can visualise an array of data as equivalent to a mapping of an index (usually given as integers) to a value. The flexibility we have by using functions is that we can use other types than integers to index values and we can have values that are structured data by using constructors that have arguments. In this case, Yes and No do not have arguments.

The names of the people can also be defined in the same way (Fig. 5.7). In this case we ignore the distinction between male and female since this distinction should be made as a single argument function 'male' that returns 'Yes or 'No'.

Describing a mapping in such an exhaustive way, as '*married_to*' above, can be very inefficient and in most cases impossible. A simpler way would be to only keep a table of married people and leave the other cases to return False or No. This uses the property of a function that it can be defined for any value (the generic case) and

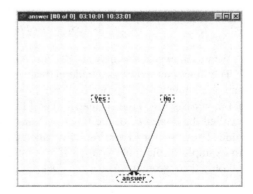

Fig. 5.6 Creating your own answers

Fig. 5.7 Creating people
(type person)

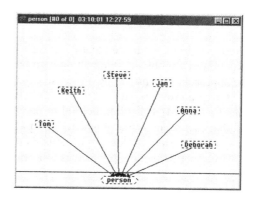

that particular cases will be chosen before a generic case. So putting these two ideas together, the function '*married-to*' can be represented as in Table 5.2.

Table 5.2 ' *married_t o* '

Parameter ?0, type person	Parameter ?1, type person	married_to, type answer
?0	?1	No
Tom	Jan	Yes
Steve	Anna	Yes
Keith	Deborah	Yes

So using best fit pattern match we could ask

$$(married\_to \text{ Tom Jan}) \rightarrow \text{Yes}$$

$$(married\_to \text{ Tom Deborah}) \rightarrow \text{No}$$

We thus have the set of pairs {(Tom Jan)(Steve Anna) (Keith Deborah)} that map to Yes and all the other pairs that map to No (e.g. (Steve Deborah)). The **generic case** is

$$married\_to \text{ ?0 ?1} \rightarrow \text{No}$$

where '?0' or ?1 matches anything that is <u>not</u> already in the table. The **simple cases** are the rest of the table. This also illustrates the principle of a 'functional' database used as a simple 'relational' database. A relation is an extensional function and relational operations can be defined as higher-order functions.

*Programming by Numbers

We have already indicated that there are three insights needed to create a recursive solution to a problem[4]. We will now go into more detail on how recursion should be approached by providing 10 steps.

Given a problem, such as the need to create the function 'factorial', how should this be tackled? It is often helpful to proceed with problems in a methodical way so that each step is clearly made (Glaser et al. 2000). This means that the valuable mental ability to have 'design insights' is stimulated by the process.

To create a function, proceed as follows:

1. *Bring up a function window:* We are defining a function so we need a function window (Fig. 5.8).
2. *Insert the input parameters and their types:* To know what you are dealing with is important. A function is to do with a transformation of 'something' into 'something'. *'What is it that you are transforming?'* is the first question. In the case of 'factorial' it is a single integer because that is sufficient to define the list of numbers. So #5 is represent by the list [#1 #2 #3 #4 #5]. In this case, the numbers always start from #1 and step through, in units of #1, to #n. Thus, we have:

There is *one* **input** parameter that is an *integer*. The integer describes the list of numbers to be multiplied together.

$$int \rightarrow ????$$

Fig. 5.8 A function window

---

[4]Programming by numbers was proposed by H Glaser et al (Programming by Numbers: A Programming Method for Novices – The Computer Journal Vol 43, No4, 2000, pp252 – 265). We have modified this to conform with Clarity.

Fig. 5.9 Defining the input
type

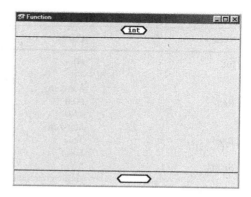

So we select a parameter lozenge (bold lozenge), place it in the input (parameter or argument field) and type in 'int' into the lozenge (Fig. 5.9).

3. *Insert the single output type:* This describes what you are transforming the input parameter(s) into. In the case of 'factorial' we are transforming it to a single integer:

> The **output** parameter is an *integer*
> int → *int*

Therefore, we type into the single output parameter lozenge 'int' (Fig. 5.10).

4. *Consider all cases:* For **any parameter type** there is **a set number of cases** that should be considered. There may be others but this will depend on the function. For the type integer we have to consider the case of #0 and #n (where #n is any integer). Thus, we need to consider the following transformations:

> factorial #0 → ???? – The simple case.
> factorial #n → ???? – The generic case.

Examples of cases for the built-in types are shown in Table 5.3.

5. *Insert possible functions that might be useful in the generic case:* Not all these functions will be required (Fig. 5.11) and there may be some not initially

Fig. 5.10 Defining the
output type

Table 5.3 Cases for built-in types

Type	Cases	Step
Int	#0	sub1/add1
	#1	
	non-zero	
Real	#0.0	sub1/add1
	#1.0	
	non-zero	
Bool	True	&/ ||
	False	
String	""	explode/implode
	single character	(treat as list)
	non-empty	
List	nil	head/tail
	single element	last/front
	non-empty	
Pair	(Pair case)	first/second
'User defined'	See Constructor Window	

Fig. 5.11 Selection of possible functions needed to define generic case

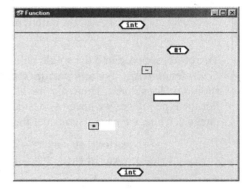

considered. Sorting the built-in functions in the library window into types will list all those likely to be needed together. Possible 'ingredients' for 'factorial' are:

- the function itself ('factorial') given as an empty thick lined box,
- the parameter #n,
- constants of the same type as the domain and range of the function (e.g. #1),
- built-in functions over those types (e.g. '∗' and '−').

Figure 5.11 shows the potentially required functions to construct the generic case of 'factorial'.

6. *Use the functions to 'solve' the generic case:* Either there is a relatively easy solution (Fig. 5.12) or the solution may be found by dividing the problem into simpler sub-problems. A reference to the initial problem may provide a clue as to how sub-problems can be determined.

Fig. 5.12 The functions are joined up into a process

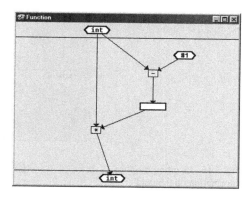

A frequent sub-problem form that a function can take is where there are starting conditions that are always the same. An example is the function '**fact_tail_aux**' (see Fig. 5.4) where the first parameter always begins as #1. This parameter is not really of interest in the final form of the function so we may define '**fact_tail_aux**' as the function '**factorial_aux**'. Then call '(factorial_aux #1)', a Curried function, by the function '**factorial**' where '**factorial**' has only the single integer parameter needed (Fig. 5.13). This gives the function the same external form has the head recursive approach. We will now continue with this head recursive approach.

7. *Name the function:* Naming the function is important (Fig. 5.14). A set of good names will make the use of the functions read almost like an explanation of the program. The name is a vital link between the formal program and the domain to which it relates. As we keep saying, it is the informal strand that indicates what the formal program means.

8. *Correct type descriptions and insert missing information:* Clarity does a type check. Where there are inconsistencies, a request for user intervention is called for. This intervention is requested by explicitly showing the types proposed or by messages in the control window prefixed by 'WARNING'.

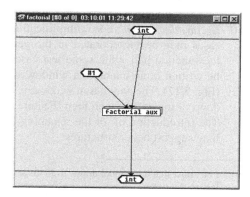

Fig. 5.13 Factorial defined with a 'tail recursive' auxiliary function

Fig. 5.14 Naming the function

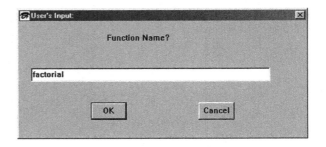

Fig. 5.15 Inserting missing information on demand

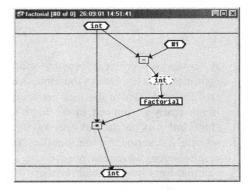

These should never be ignored. It is important that the function is internally consistent. In this case there is a clash between the input of factorial with the output of '−' (Fig. 5.15). The function '−' can be used for both integer and real numbers. This flexibility is expressed by the generic variable ?0.[5] In this case, ?0 should be replaced by 'int'.

9. *'Solve' the simple case(s):* As a rule, the simple cases are usually one or more terminating conditions for the cycle created by recursion (see table above). Simple solutions should be limited to the case under consideration. So for the simple idea of 'factorial' #0 the only result required is #1 (Fig. 5.16). All other cases should be ignored at this point. Other cases may have to be considered but these should be dealt with separately.

10. *Reconsider the solution:* Simplification may be possible. Some of the special cases may be incorporated in the generic case. Recheck the output type of the function and write some test cases. A description of the function should be written in an annotation window with at least one test case with its result (Fig. 5.17). The annotation window is found in the tool bar with the other windows or under the menu item 'Features'.

The introduction of, or the renaming to, an 'auxiliary' or other sub-functions may suggest better structures.

---

[5]or ?1 etc. **note** that the symbol drawn from the set ?0 to ?n can represent any type **or** is a variable **or** refers to the parameter/argument position of the function. Context determines how it will be interpreted by Clarity/Faith.

Fig. 5.16 The simple case
for factorial

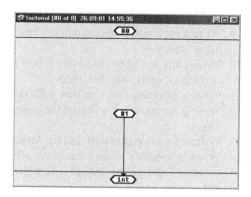

Fig. 5.17 Annotate the
function

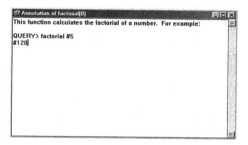

Exercises[6] 5.2

The following exercises have been ordered according to difficulty. Some of the early exercises will be very simple but are useful to do. See how far you can get. There is no unique 'correct' answer. Some 'correct' solutions are better than others. Look for simplification. Do not forget many of the solutions will require the specification of more than one function.

1 Write a function that provides the logical negation of its argument.
2 Write a function to provide the arithmetic negation of its argument.
3 Write a function to return a string that has a number of copies (first argument) of (its second argument) a string.
4 Write the function '*married_to*' as described earlier.
5 Extend the function '*married_to*' so that the two people concerned can be put in any order. Thus, 'married_to Tom Jan' will be the same as 'married_to Jan Tom'.
6 Write a function to return the last element of a list.
7 Write a recursive function that adds a number to each item of a list of integers.

---

[6]Examples drawn from Glaser et al (2000) 'Programming by Numbers' The computer Journal Vol 43 No 4.

8 Write a recursive function that counts the number of items in a list.
9 Write a recursive function that returns 'True' if a particular given integer is in a list of numbers.
10 Modify the last exercise so that it will work with any list of objects (i.e. strings, characters, reals, integers, etc.).
11 Write a recursive function that will add up a list of integers.
12 Write a function that will find the average of a list of numbers (see points 8 and 11).
13 Write a function that will find the largest number in a list of numbers.
14 Write a function to add the elements of two lists together, for example, the results of adding the lists [#1 #2 #3] and [#4 #5 #6] should be the list [#5 #7 #9].
15 Write a function to return a list that has an element (first argument) inserted into the nth position (second argument) of a list (third argument).
16 Write a function to return the sorted version of its argument list (we will consider integers in this example).
17 Write a function to sum the leaves of a tree.
18 Write a function to increment each element of a list.
19 Write a function to compute the nth element from the Fibonacci sequence #0, #1, #1, #2, #3, #5, #8, . . ., in which each number is the sum of the previous two.
20 Write a function to compute an ascending sequence of integers n, n + #1, . . ., m.

Questions 5.2

1 What is a mapping?
2 Name the ten steps in order that should be followed to create a recursive function.

Project: Using Pattern Matching

Snake1: Snakes and Ladders

Introduction

The odd thing about this game is that it is fun despite the fact that the computer, in effect, does both players. Somehow, when you are identified with a token that befalls all sorts of fate, it gives you feeling of involvement. In the same way, you might get involved with a horse that is in a race. It is all very basic.

We will do this in two stages. Recursion is not used in the first stage but will be used in a minor way in the second. A lot depends on pattern match , 'progN' and 'map'.

Keeping Score and Making Snakes (and Ladders)

This is a simple version of the game of snakes and ladders. There are two players: 'A' and 'B'. Their score is kept by the function **score** in Diagram 5.1.

The functions **score 'A'** and **score 'B'** will be updated as the game progresses.

(1) *Define the function score in Diagram 5.1.

The 'snakes' and 'ladders' are set up using functions called '**snake**' and '**ladder**'. For example, if '**snake #83**' returns **#21**, that means a player landing on square 83 will go 'down the snake' to square 21. A similar rule applies to the function '**ladder**'. In this game, we have defined five snakes and six ladders. Part of the definition is seen in Diagrams 5.2 and 5.3.

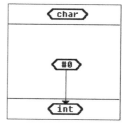

Diagram 5.1   score

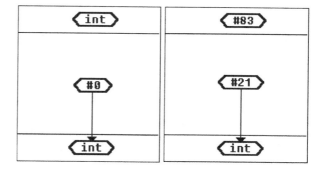

Diagram 5.2   snake

Diagram 5.3 'ladder'

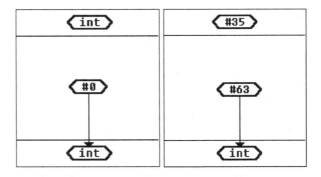

There are two components of '**snake**' illustrated in Diagram 5.2. The others are defined in a similar way

> snake #73 returns #5
> snake #59 returns #14
> snake #24 returns #3
> snake #90 returns #6

(2) *Define the function '**snake**' in Diagram 5.2 plus the additional definitions.

(3) *Define the function '**ladder**' in Diagram 5.3 plus the additional definitions.

> ladder #10 returns #70
> ladder #75 returns #82
> ladder #55 returns #79
> ladder #92 returns #94
> ladder #4 returns #23

Drawing the Board

Since we only have a very primitive interface the best we can do is create a board from characters. This will look like this:

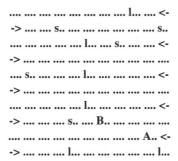

The start of the game is at the bottom left-hand side and a little arrow is printed to show the direction of movement of the tokens. In this example, Token A is at the beginning of the second line from the bottom. B is ahead and half way through line 3 going from left to right. Each of these lines are made up of squares where each square has to show empty or A, B and l or s.

Therefore, the next function to create will draw a given square. This function is '**draw_square**' in Diagram 5.4 and will be part of the drawing of the board on which the game is played. Note that '**putline**' is a built-in function that outputs a string to the control window.

Diagram 5.4
'draw_square'

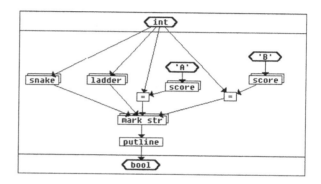

Moving a Token

The input parameter to this function is an integer and is the number of the square. The function will respond with the following side effects:

- If a snake starts on that square, we will mark it 's..'.
- If a ladder starts on the square, we will mark it 'l...'.

Note that a snake and a ladder cannot both start on the same square.

- If player 'A' and/or player 'B' is on the square, we will mark it 'A..', 'B..' or 'AB'..

Note that a player will not be found on a square where a snake or ladder starts.

- A blank square will be marked '....'.

Keeping all the above points in mind, look at the function '**mark_str**' in Diagram 5.5. There is a general component, #0, which returns the default mark. The other six components correspond to the different combinations detailed above.

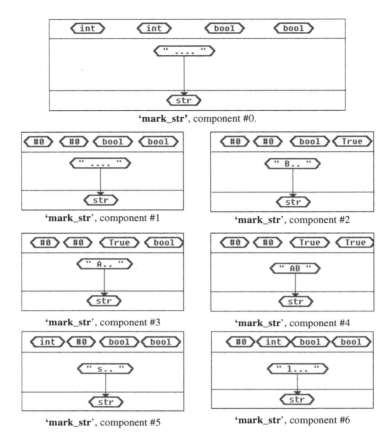

'**mark_str**', component #0.

'**mark_str**', component #1

'**mark_str**', component #2

'**mark_str**', component #3

'**mark_str**', component #4

'**mark_str**', component #5

'**mark_str**', component #6

Diagram 5.5 'mark_str'

In '**mark_str**', component #1 would correspond to a blank square. Components #2 to #4 are the cases where there are no snake or ladder starting squares, but the squares have A and/or B on them. Components #5 and #6 would correspond to a square being a snake/ladder starting point. Component #0 is simply the default case.

As components #0 and #1 return the same result, it is tempting to think we can do without one of them. However, if we leave out component #1, the combination of parameters '**#0, #0, False, False**' would match most closely to component #6, thus all the blank squares would be marked '1. . .'. The only component we could do without is component #0, but it is always a good idea to have a default case, even if it is never expected to match.

(4) *Define the function '**mark_str**' in Diagram 5.5.

(5) *Define the function '**draw_square**' in Diagram 5.4.

Now let us move on with the rest of the drawing of the board. In a snakes and ladders game the players move along 100 squares from bottom left to top left, like this:

```
100 99 98 97 96 95 94 93 92 91
 81 82 83 84 85 86 87 88 89 90

        ....................
        ....................
 20 19 18 17 16 15 14 13 12 11
  1  2  3  4  5  6  7  8  9  10
```

There are 10 rows of 10 numbers each. If this is to be printed in the usual way, from top to bottom, left to right, we will print row 10 down to row 1. If we are printing an odd row then the numbers are increasing, if we are printing an even row then the numbers are decreasing.

Look at function '**draw_board**' in Diagram 5.6. The function '**prog1**' calls the function '**newline**' first, which simply prints a newline character (see '**Getting Started**', Chapter 1). The function '**list_of_int**' is a built-in function that creates a list of integers, in this case starting at #10, ending at #1, and going down in steps of #1. These are the row numbers. The built-in '**map**' will apply '**draw_row**' to each of these row numbers in turn.

(6) *Define the function '**newline**' in Diagram 5.7.

Look at function '**draw_row**' in Diagram 5.8. If we consider a particular row, say 2, then this row will end (as far as the player is concerned) in 20, and it will be an even row.

The function '**even_row**' will return '**True**' or '**False**'. It does this by calculating the remainder on division by #2 (mod #2, which is the built-in '**%**') of the number and compares this with #0.

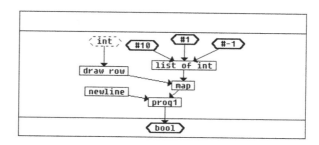

Diagram 5.6 'draw_board'

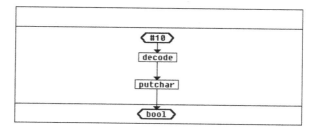

Diagram 5.7 'newline'

Diagram 5.8 'draw_row'

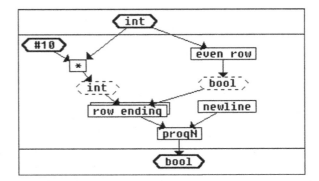

Diagram 5.9 'even_row'

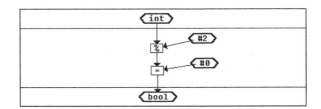

(7) *Define the function '**even_row**' in Diagram 5.9.

The function '**row_ending**' draws the squares in the row ending with the given integer, and will have two components , one for an even row and one for an odd row. The default case is the odd row.

The function '**row_ending**' calls the simple function **minus9**.

(8) *Define the function '**minus9**' in Diagram 5.11.

(9) *Define the function '**row_ending**' in Diagram 5.10.

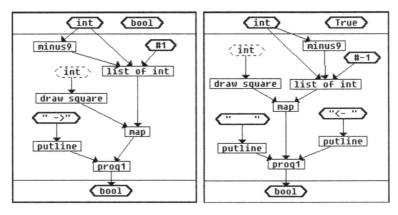

Diagram 5.10 'row_ending'

Diagram 5.11 'minus9'

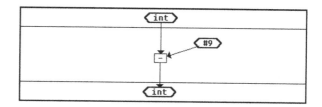

Diagram 5.12 'start'

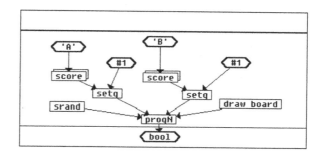

(10) *Define the function **'draw_row'** in Diagram 5.8.

(11) *Define the function **'draw_board'** in Diagram 5.6.

At the start of the game the players will begin on square 1. The random number generator **'rand'** will be used later to simulate throwing the dice, so to seed the generator we need to call the built-in **'srand'**.

(12) *Define the function **'start'** in Diagram 5.12

After the game has been started, each player will throw a dice and move that number of squares. If a player lands on a snake, they will go down the snake. For example, if a player lands on square 83, they will immediately go to square 21. The function 'snake #3' returns #21. For any 'non-snake' square N, 'snake N' will return #0. A similar rule applies to **'ladder'**.

So to update a player's score when they land on square N:

- **if** 'snake N' and 'ladder N' both return #0, the player's new score is simply N,
- **otherwise** it is the value of 'snake N' + 'ladder N', as only one can be non-zero.

Look at function **'update_score'** in Diagram 5.13.

The input parameters to this function **'update_score'** are the value of the dice throw, and the name of the player, A or B. The throw value is added to the existing score and tested against 100, as we have to throw the exact value to win. There is a new score for the player only if the test returns **True**.

Diagram 5.13
'update_score'

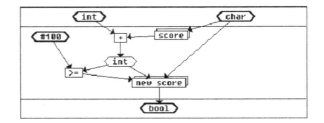

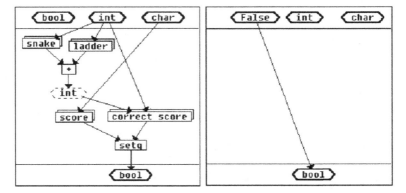

Diagram 5.14 'new_score'

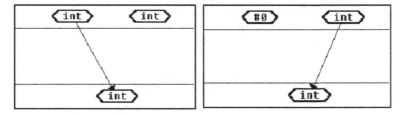

Diagram 5.15 'correct_score'

Now look at '**new_score**' in Diagram 5.14. Here the new score for the player is set to the correct score, depending on the values of '**snake**' and '**ladder**' for this square.

(13) *Define the function '**correct_score**' in Diagram 5.15

(14) *Define the function '**new_score**' in Diagram 5.14.

(15) *Define the function '**update_score**' in Diagram 5.13.

Diagram 5.16 'go'

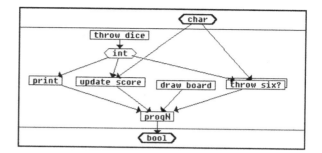

Diagram 5.17 'throw_dice'

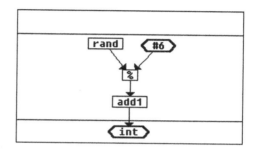

Diagram 5.18   throw_six?

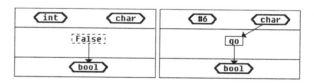

To play the game, we call the function 'go' in Diagram 5.16. The input parameter to this function is the player 'A' or 'B'. The function throws the dice, updates the score, draws the board and then has another go if a six was thrown. The function **'throw_dice'** in Diagram 5.17 is a function to generate a random number between 1 and 6, using '%' (modulus).

(16) *Define function **'throw_dice'** in Diagram 5.17.

The function **'throw_six?'** will call **'go'** again if the integer input parameter is #6.

(17) *Define **'throw_six?'** in Diagram 5.18.

The function **'go'** will be declared at this stage but not defined yet.

(18) *Define the function **'go'** in Diagram 5.16.

Diagram 5.19 Network of selected functions for 'snake1'

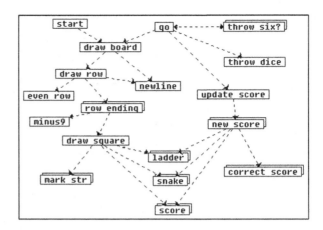

Now you can play the game. First, type '**start**' in the CONTROL window, followed by **go** 'A', then **go** 'B', and so on.

QUERY> go 'A'
#4

```
.... .... .... .... .... .... .... .... l... ....
<- -> .... .... s.. .... .... .... .... .... s..
.... .... .... .... .... l... .... s.. .... .... <-
-> .... .... .... .... .... .... .... .... .... ....
.... s.. .... .... .... l... .... .... .... .... <-
-> .... .... .... .... .... .... .... .... .... ....
.... .... .... .... .... l... .... .... .... .... <-
-> .... .... .... s.. .... B.. .... .... .... ....
.... .... .... .... .... .... .... .... .... A.. <-
-> .... .... .... l... .... .... .... .... .... l...
```

Finally, for Stage 1

Save your database and call it '**snake1**'. Create a network view by opening a network window, go to the 'find' 'menu' and click on 'Create/Update network from database' Diagram 5.19. This may require a little rearranging and the deletion of some functions to look neat. A proposed arrangement is shown in Diagram 5.19. When you are satisfied with its appearance, commit it just like a function window. Other views of the network, showing different functionality, can be created in separate network windows.

Snake2: Snakes and Ladders

Introduction

It is tedious to type **start**, followed by **go 'A'**, **go 'B'** and so on until the game is over. Just hitting a key would be nice. So some kind of 'loop' is needed.

Controlling the Cycle

This cycling is achieved by the function **play** in Diagram 5.20.

The function '**progN**' calls the function '**start**', followed by '**next_go**' which will call itself, as long as the user selects the '**go_ahead**' key 'y' (see Diagram 5.22). The function start has changed slightly to add information for the user.

(1) *Make the changes to '**start**' as in Diagram 5.21.

The function '**go_ahead?**' in Diagram 5.22 simply asks the user for confirmation to carry on with the game.

(2) *Define the function '**go_ahead**' in Diagram 5.22.

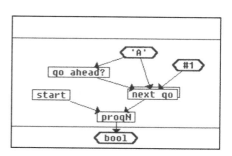

Diagram 5.20 'play'

Diagram 5.21 'start'

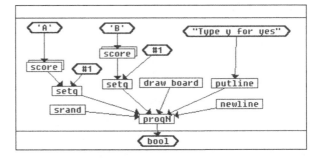

Diagram 5.22 'go_ahead?'

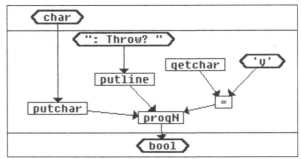

The function '**next_go**' in Diagram 5.23 has three input parameters. The first determines whether it carries on with the game, the second is the player for the next go, and the third is the score of the opponent.

If the result of '**go_ahead?**' is False, the game stops. If the score of the opponent is 100 a message is printed and the game stops. Otherwise, the function '**go**' is called for the current player, then '**next_go**' is called for the other player, along with the '**score**' for the current player.

(3)*Define the simple function '**other_player**' in Diagram 5.24.

(4) *Define the function '**next_go**' in Diagram 5.23.

(5) *Define the function '**play**' in Diagram 5.20.

The other modification to this version is a clearer picture of the board. Instead of this

```
.... .... .... .... .... .... .... .... l... .... <-
-> .... .... s.. .... .... .... .... .... s..
.... .... .... .... .... l... .... s.. .... .... <-
-> .... .... .... .... .... .... .... .... .... ....
.... s.. .... .... .... l... .... .... .... .... <-
-> .... .... .... .... .... .... .... .... .... ....
.... .... .... .... .... l... .... .... .... .... <-
-> .... .... .... s.. .... B.. .... .... .... ....
.... .... .... .... .... .... .... .... .... A.. <-
-> .... .... .... l... .... .... .... .... .... l...
```

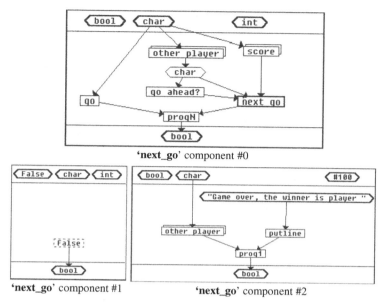

'next_go' component #0

'next_go' component #1   **'next_go'** component #2

Diagram 5.23 'next_go'

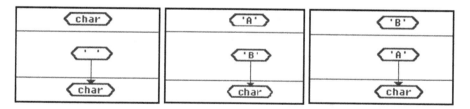

Diagram 5.24   other_player

we will print this:

```
.... .... .... .... .... .... .... .... 94 .... <- 91
81 -> .... .... 21 .... .... .... .... .... .... ..6
.... .... .... .... .... 82 .... ..5 .... .... <- 71
61 -> .... .... .... .... .... .... .... .... .... ....
.... 14 .... .... .... 79 .... .... .... .... <- 51
41 -> .... .... .... .... .... .... .... .... .... ....
.... .... .... .... .... 63 .... .... .... .... <- 31
21 -> .... .... .... ..3 .... B... .... .... .... ....
.... .... .... .... .... .... .... .... .... A.. <- 11
01 -> .... .... .... 23 .... .... .... .... .... 70
```

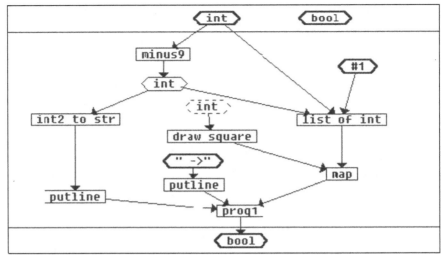

'**row_ending**', component #0

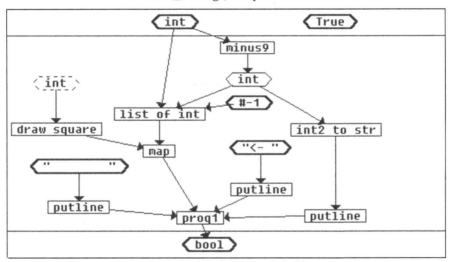

'**row_ending**', component #1

Diagram 5.25   row_ending

Instead of 's' denoting the start of a snake we print the number of the square at the end of the snake. We do the same for a ladder. The function '**draw_row**' has an extra **newline**. There are also changes for function '**row_ending**' in Diagram 5.25.

We have added a new function here, called '**int2_to_str**' in Diagram 5.27. This function converts a 2-digit integer into a string for printing. It makes use of a function called '**int_to_char**' defined in Diagram 5.26. ClarityPro has this as a built-in function so this will not be required to be defined. This function simply converts a single-digit integer into its character equivalent. So if running under ClarityLite:

Diagram 5.26
'int_to_char'

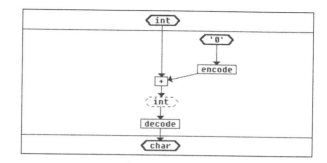

Diagram 5.27 'int2_to_str'

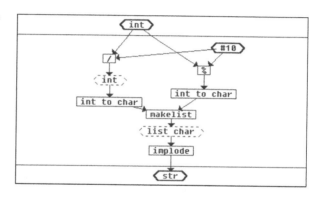

(6) *Define function ' **int_to_char**' in* Diagram 5.26.

(7) *Define function ' **int2_to_str**' in* Diagram 5.27.

(8) *Make the changes to ' **row_ending**' in* Diagram 5.25.

   The function '**mark_str**' has changed too. There are now only five components. Components #1 to #4 are unchanged. The other two components can now be deleted. So remove the old components #5 and #6. Go to the 'Find' menu and click on 'Remove . . .' then chose Remove picture and Faith code. Look at component #0 in Diagram 5.28 and edit the existing component #0 to look like that.

   This component alone will deal with all the squares that are the starting points of a snake or a ladder. The '**snake**' and '**ladder**' functions are added together, because only one of them is non-zero, and the result converted to a string. This is then converted to two characters by the built-in function '**explode**'. The function '**chars_to_mark**' in Diagram 5.29 converts these to the string to be printed.

(9) *Define the function '**chars2_to_mark**' in* Diagram 5.29.

(10) *Make the changes to '**mark_str**' in* Diagram 5.28.

Diagram 5.28 'mark_str' component #0

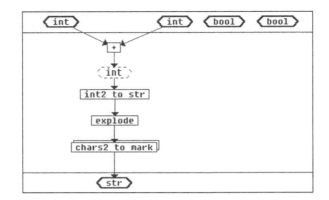

Diagram 5.29 'chars2_to_mark'

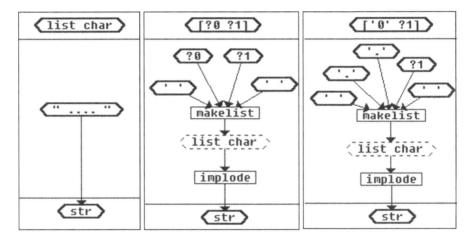

Diagram 5.30 Network of selected functions for 'snake2'

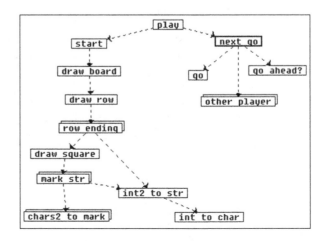

Finally, for Stage 2

Save your database (chose 'Save as ..') and call it '**snake2**'.

As before create a network view. A proposed arrangement is shown in Diagram 5.30. When you are satisfied with its appearance, commit it. Other views of the network, showing different functionality, can be created in separate network windows.

Exercise 5.3

1 Change Snake 3 players instead of two.
2 Change Snake for N players where N is a parameter of '**play**'. Do not worry about the board layout.
3 Use a number to indicate more than one person on a position.
4 Indicate on the far right of the board the players on that line. Mark the position number for each player.
5 Create a new hazard 'trap' which holds a player for n throws where n can vary between 1 to 3.
6 Create a new advantage where a position will allow a player to leave a trap for other players.
7 Create a 'guard' which allows a player to escape a 'trap' or at least reduce the penalty a trap imposes.

Reference

Glaser H., Hartel P. H. and Garratt P. W. (2000) '*Programming by Numbers*', The Computer Journal, Vol. 43, No. 4. pp. 252–265

Chapter 6
Thinking Practically

*Charity never faileth: but whether there be prophecies, they
shall fail; whether there be tongues they shall cease; whether
there be knowledge it shall vanish away.*

Corinthians 13, 8.

Introduction

So far, we have mostly ignored how the machine interprets the functional
representation generated by Clarity. We have discussed the stack and noted that
this uses up different amounts of memory depending on what you do. We also note
that despite the efforts of the technologists to provide machines of infinite speed and
infinite memory computers are still limited. We will need to consider the practical
limitations of these computers by designing our solutions to minimise the use of the
computer's resources.

We have also considered 'elegance' as a valuable concept that addresses our own
limitations as Homo sapiens. An elegant representation is also a simple one as well
as providing greater generality. The skill we have to achieve is to retain both elegance and computational efficiency in program design.

Experience has shown us that there is a neat balance that can be retained between
the functional representation, as expressed in any functional language, and an imperative representation, as might be expressed through an imperative language. For this
reason, we include functions that are really imperative procedures. We will introduce some of these 'imperative' functions here and give some advice on how to
retain representational elegance.

Conditional Control

The flow of processing in a program needs conditional control that depends upon a
test so that some data items are treated differently to others. One of the kinds of test
often required is where a particular data item is equal to some form or structure.

T. Addis, J. Addis, *Drawing Programs: The Theory and Practice of Schematic
Functional Programming*, DOI 10.1007/978-1-84882-618-2_6,
© Springer-Verlag London Limited 2010

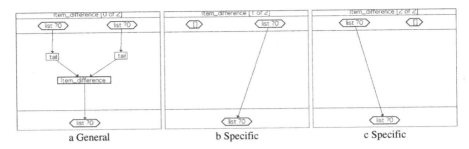

Fig. 6.1 Pattern match

This can be dealt with by using the in-built pattern matching as in recursion (Fig. 6.1).

In the example shown in Fig. 6.1 (Pattern Match) we have it such that when the left-hand list is empty we stop the processing and return the right-hand list and vice versa. This pattern match approach to control is by far the best because it is both representationally neat and it is computationally efficient; it should be used wherever possible. However, the tests for some situations do not conform to such a simple pattern match.

Consider the problem of deciding when to round a number up or down. The normal assumption is that any number whose decimal part is greater than or equal to 0.5 should be rounded up. However, such a decision does *not* rely upon any exact match. To resolve this explicitly (there is a better way of doing the same job by adding 0.5 to the number and 'fix'ing the result) we introduce an intermediate function that transforms the test ($>= 0.5$ in this case) to a category expressed in terms of (say) an enumerated constructor (a constructor without arguments). The library function 'if' is the simplest and most basic of this type of approach. The use of the function 'if' to make the rounding decision by converting the test to a Boolean is shown in Fig. 6.2. The function 'if' is defined in Faith such that

fdec
    if::=Bool→?0→?0→?0;
  ;

fdef
    if True?1?2::=?1;
    if False ?1?2::=?2;
  ;

This definition converts the inexact match into an exact match through the Boolean values '**True**' and '**False**'

The use of the function '**round**' (see Fig. 6.2) can be shown by the following example:

    QUERY> round #r3.6
    #4
    QUERY> round #r3.4
    #3

Fig. 6.2 Conditional control

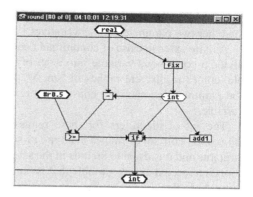

Another example of the use of the function 'if' is in the situation where we have two objects on a plane each of a different size. Now suppose one of the objects was to move to a new co-ordinate position. The question arises can we provide a function that will show if the two circular objects collide if the move were to take place? A collision in this case is considered where the two objects are within 0.1 cm of each other (see Fig. 6.3a).

Figure 6.3b shows a solution using the user-defined co-ordinate operation '**distance**'. The function '**distance**' gives the measure between the two centres of the circular objects. If the distance is less than the sum of the two sizes (given as radii) + 0.1 then the constructor '**Hit**' is returned otherwise '**Miss**'. The constructors '**Hit**' and '**Miss**' could be any pair of functions. The function '**if**' can be considered to be

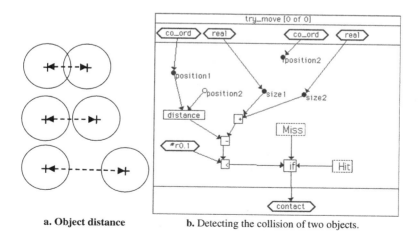

a. Object distance   b. Detecting the collision of two objects.

Fig. 6.3 Colliding objects

equivalent to a Boolean controlled switch where the first parameter is the toggle and the other two parameters the alternatives.[1]

A more extensive use of conditional control is where we need a function that will divide a continuous variable into a set of discrete ranges. Clothes size, for example, comes in discrete ranges of **Sm, M, L, XL** and **XXL**. This may depend on, for example, the size of a chest measurement for jackets, which is a continuous variable.[2]

The set of identifiers for these ranges is expressed as a set of constructors (Fig. 6.4). This set of ranges is a type of scale.[3] Scales normally form sets of constructors and it is usual to include in the set a name for the empty set. Here the empty set is interpreted as any variable that is outside the range considered; so we add the term '**Not_Size**'.

The most natural approach to the problem is to start using the function '**if**' in such a way that it is triggered by a test that compares the input value with the different ranges. If it fails one range then the value is passed onto the next test until it passes and then the range name is given as a result. The problem with this is that the function soon becomes cluttered with all the required tests. Further, most of the tests are the same process repeated with different values.

It is always worth asking the question *'Is there any way in which a pattern of repeated operations can be written only once?'* The answer in this case is 'yes' and Fig. 6.5 is an example of a single element of the repeated pattern of functions.

Observe how in Figs. 6.3 and 6.5 the 'junctions' have been used to annotate the parameters of the function as well as being used to link across the function 'by

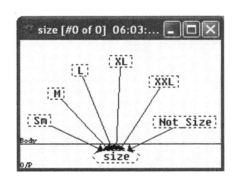

Fig. 6.4 The set of ranges for clothes size

---

[1]**Note** that '**if**' works in reverse (or upside down) to the normal flow diagram equivalent but is similar to that found in spreadsheets.

[2]**Note** that the constructor '**Sm**' is chosen rather than '**S**' because '**S** ' is already a special built-in function referred to as a combinator (see Chapter 9).

[3]The naming of items is called a 'nominal' scale and if these names have a special order (as they do here) then it is called an 'ordinal' scale. Other scales are 'interval' which have no absolute zero (such as 'date') and 'ratio' which has an absolute zero (such as volume or time interval).

Fig. 6.5 The function
'**chest_size**' that compares

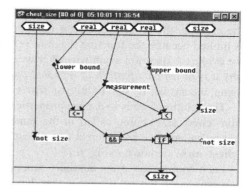

name' (e.g. 'not size') rather than by an arrow. This helps keep the function diagram well laid out by:

- avoiding crossed arrows,
- ensuring that no arrows point up the diagram,
- *not* being restricted in the placement of function icons because of the order of their input parameters.

Figure 6.6 shows how this test function is used in a cascade of the same function '**chest_size**'. The initial condition is '**Not_Size**' and the entry into the lowest range is #r35–#r38. If the measurement fits into this first range, then '**Sm**' is passed forward otherwise '**Not_Size**' is passed on. This continues until the final stage whence the identifier of what range fits is the result. If no range fits then '**Not_Size**' will be the result.

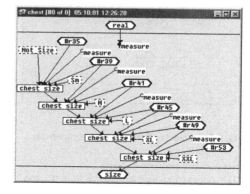

Fig. 6.6 A cascade of tests

The advantage of the function '**chest**' (Fig. 6.6) is that it shows very clearly the cascade, the ranges[4] and their identifiers. However, the length of the cascade is limited because the function diagram very quickly becomes cluttered. Therefore, we evoke the question again whenever we see a repeated set of operations '*Is there any way in which a pattern of repeated operations can be written only once?*' Yet again, the answer is 'yes' or at least *nearly* 'yes'.

The solution here is to use the properties of 'pattern match'. Instead of the function '**chest_size**' being called in the same component of the function '**chest**', it can be called once by different components. We do this via the auxiliary function '**chest_aux**' as shown in Fig. 6.7.

Each component of the auxiliary function is devoted to a particular range. It is a constraint on this set of ranges that they must be contiguous. This is ensured by the way in which the recursive call uses the upper bound of the current range to be the lower bound of the next range. In this way, a cascade through the components is achieved until either a range is found to satisfy the input value or the final component

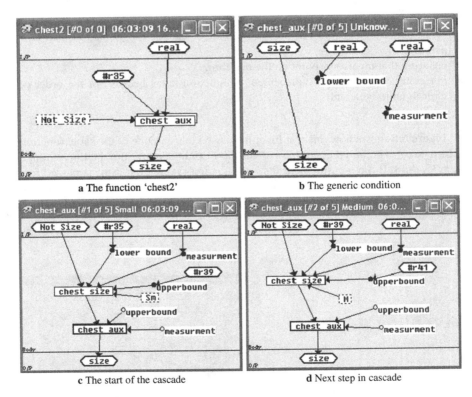

a The function 'chest2'   b The generic condition

c The start of the cascade   d Next step in cascade

Fig. 6.7 Replacing the cascade bycomponents

---

[4]The ranges given have been taken from 'Cotton Traders' catalogue.

is reached. The final component, in the linked set of components, is where there is no component that has the lower bound given by the last recursive call. This triggers the generic component (Fig. 6.7b) that returns the answer. Note that the order of parameters has been chosen to ensure that the pattern matching works primarily with the lower bound measure rather than size.

This approach has the advantages of providing a simple and single representation of each range. This single template can be reused to generate new components by simply changing the values in the icons and re-committing the component as a new. It allows many extensions of the set of ranges at any time without any further complexity. It is also a very efficient process in that it will drop out of the cascade as soon as a satisfied test is reached. Some test queries are

```
QUERY> chest2 #42
L
QUERY> chest2 #37
Sm
QUERY> chest2 #30
Not_Size
QUERY> chest2 #50
XXL
QUERY> chest2 #55
Not_Size
```

However, such a mechanism relies heavily upon the properties of 'best pattern match'.

Higher-Order Functions

A *higher-order function* is simply one that has at least one parameter (argument) that is a function. Higher-order functions give us another solution to overcoming the problem of repeated program structures. For example, in Chapter 3 we defined a function for adding two co-ordinates and this function forms a pattern of connections that is almost identical for many other functions of the same kind. In this case, we note that the addition and subtraction of two co-ordinates only differ by a single function (i.e. the function '+' is replaced by '−', see Fig. 6.8). Therefore, we could reason that if the function can be transferred across as a parameter then we will only need to construct a single function that will perform a set of related operations.

Thanks to the ability to create our own higher-order functions it is possible to design a function that will accept a function as one of its parameter values. All we need do is design a single function that will take a function from a range of potential functions and apply it within itself to produce a unique result. However, a guard is required to be placed on the type of function that can be passed over as a parameter

First parameter of
function showing type.

Second parameter of
function showing type.

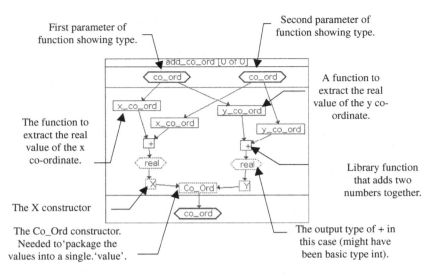

A function to
extract the real
value of the y co-
ordinate.

The function to
extract the real
value of the x
co-ordinate.

Library function
that adds two
numbers together.

The X constructor

The Co_Ord constructor.
Needed to 'package the
values into a single. 'value'.

The output type of + in
this case (might have
been basic type int).

Fig. 6.8 The addition of two co-ordinates

value. So an extension of the type checking is needed to ensure that the correct form of function (function type) is deployed.

The key to creating a higher-order function is the function '@'. This is usually called the '*apply*' function since it takes as its first parameter a function and applies it to its second argument. At the query level, we note that

```
QUERY> add1 #5
#6
QUERY> @add1 #5
#6
```

At this level the function '@' looks a waste of time but it is necessary if you wish to express the function as a variable within the context of a function definition. In certain special cases it is possible to get the same effect without the use of an '@'. If the function and its parameters are, in their turn, parameters of the function within which this operation is required we can reference the parameter by its position in a parameter lozenge. Note that parameter positions always start at ?0. Thus because the positions are reference by a variable ?N and when we wish to use a local variable for purposes of pattern match of *lambda* functions we tend to always use a number greater than the number of parameters. This is shown by the function 'example' in Fig. 6.9. It is queried, thus

```
QUERY> example + #3 #5
#8
```

Fig. 6.9 Using parameter
position as a reference

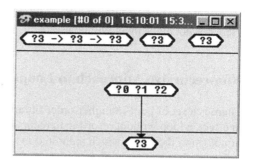

Figure 6.10 illustrates a generalised vector operation ('**vop**') where any function
of the type (real → real → real) can be used to combine two co-ordinates to produce
a co-ordinate result. We have then

QUERY> vop − (Co_Ord (X #r3.7)(Y #r5.2)) (Co_Ord (X #r2.4)(Y #r3.71))
(Co_Ord (X #r1.300000)(Y #r1.490000))
QUERY> vop + (Co_Ord (X #r3.7)(Y #r5.2)) (Co_Ord (X #r2.4)(Y #r3.71))
(Co_Ord (X #r6.100000) (Y #r8.910000))
QUERY> vop / (Co_Ord (X #r3.7)(Y #r5.2)) (Co_Ord (X #r2.4)(Y #r3.71))
(Co_Ord (X #r1.541667)(Y #r1.401617))
QUERY> vop * (Co_Ord (X #r3.7)(Y #r5.2)) (Co_Ord (X #r2.4)(Y #r3.71))
(Co_Ord (X #r8.880000)(Y #r19.292000))

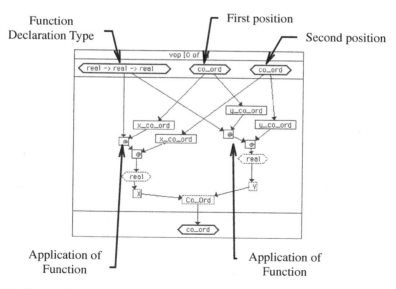

Fig. 6.10 The creation of a higher order function

Any function that takes on two real numbers and returns a real number can be used, but not all of them will be useful.

Non-recursive Approach to Loops

There is a set of built-in higher-order library functions that help to perform what is, in effect, a loop without resorting to recursion. This has the advantage in most cases of not using the stack, which is limited in size. Consider '**factorial**' again. Another way of defining factorial is as

$$\text{factorial (N)} = [1 * 2 * 3 * \ldots \ldots * N]$$

In Clarity/Faith we have a library function ('**list_of_int**') that will generate a list of integers from any number to any greater number in a specified step. What we need is a means of multiplying these generated numbers together as per definition above. For this, we have to call upon the higher-order function '**foldr**'. The name '**foldr**' stands for the concept of '*fold right*'. It applies a two-argument function, given as its first parameter, and to a list of arguments, given as its second argument. Because it is applying a two-argument function, this function requires an initial second parameter. This initial second parameter is provided by the second argument of '**foldr**' (e.g. #1 in Fig. 6.11). The first argument of the applying function is taken as the last item of the list. Once started, the result of the applied function is used to supply its second argument for the next item on the list as it continues to repeatedly apply itself all the way to the start of the list (N). The definition describes the mapping thus

foldr :: = (?0 → ?1 → ?1) → ?1→list?0 → ?1

An example of its application at the query level is

QUERY> foldr append ['A'][['b' 'c']['d' 'e']]
['b' 'c' 'd' 'e' 'A']

In Fig. 6.11, it can be seen to move down the list (N–1) applying the result of the operation to be folded ('*' in this case) to each number until there are no more numbers in the list. The final result is returned as the answer to the completed process. Fold left ('foldl') starts at the beginning of the list. In the example of Fig. 6.11, it makes no difference but in some case, it might. For example,

foldl ::= (?0→?1→?1)→?1→list?0→?1

QUERY> foldl append ['A'][['b' 'c']['d' 'e']]
['d' 'e' 'b' 'c' 'A']

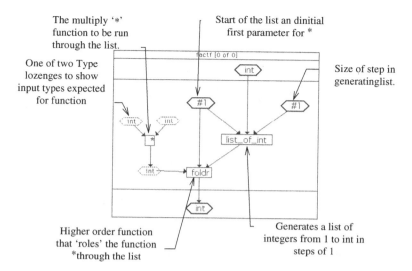

The multiply '*' function to be run through the list.

Start of the list an dinitial first parameter for *

One of two Type lozenges to show input types expected for function

Size of step in generatinglist.

Higher order function that 'roles' the function *through the list

Generates a list of integers from 1 to int in steps of 1

Fig. 6.11 Pre-generation factorial, max. stack depth = 2 and list int = N + 1

A range of higher-order functions is available (written in C) that helps avoid recursion and thus are not stack limited. As we have seen Fig. 6.11 is an alternative method to calculate factorial as a list of integers from #1 to N in steps of #1 where they are all multiplied together (**'foldr'**). Here the function **'foldr'** has as its first parameter the function '*' that is used to calculate the result by applying this function to the list of numbers. There is no use of the stack but there is the need to generate the list of numbers. This method places an upper limit on the operational potential in that the list will be limited by memory.

A way of dealing with an unlimited number of cycles is to take charge of any cumulating values. However, this can only be done in principle in the case of factorial. This is because we are bounded by the maximum integer value within the machine unless we define an alternative to the integer as a list of integers. Then the maximum length of the list that can be stored would set limits.

We introduce a simple 'data structure' or 'object' by using the built-in constructor **'Pair'** (we can define our own constructor if we wish). This constructor can take on two specified types to make a completed object. To this end, we define a terminating test (**'first_is_one'**) which tests the operations done by the function **'until'** to see if the first of the pair is equal to unity (#1).

Note, in Fig. 6.12 (third picture), how the element ?1 of the pattern (Pair ?1 ?2) in the specified input parameter can be accessed by direct reference by name (i.e. ?1). The same technique is used in the function **'reduce'** that not only multiplies the second value by the first but also reduces the first value by #1 and replaces the second value by the increasing result.

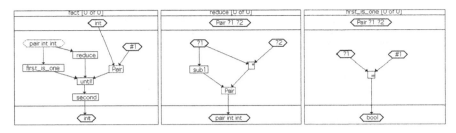

Fig. 6.12 Carry-forward factorial. Max. stack depth = 3

Factorial is finally calculated by the higher-order function '**until**' which accepts these two functions to test for termination, what to do each time and from where to start. The definition

$$\text{until} ::= (?0 \rightarrow \text{bool}) \rightarrow (?0 \rightarrow ?0) \rightarrow ?0 \rightarrow ?0$$

For example,

> QUERY> until (<=#5) add1#1
> #5

There is no expanding demand of computational resources with this version of factorial since function 'until' does not call upon the use of the stack. A test of its operation is

> **QUERY>** fact #0   **QUERY>** fact #5
> #1   #120
> **QUERY>** fact #1   **QUERY>** fact #9
> #1   #362880

Creating Two Useful Functions

ClarityLite has had the range of library functions much reduced. The main reason for this is that it was found that a large library distracts from the principles of learning Schematic Functional Programming. Further, many of the extended library functions can be recreated using functions from the reduced range of ClarityLite. So in one restricted sense, we are not limited (see Chapter 5). What cannot be created is access to computer facilities such as file operations, graphics and links into other languages. However, there are two useful functions that we can create: '**combine**' and '**zip**'.

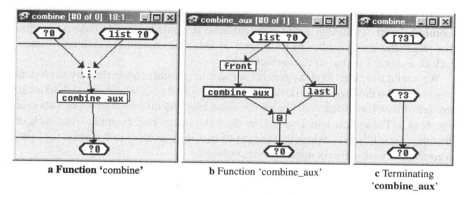

a Function 'combine'   b Function 'combine_aux'   c Terminating 'combine_aux'

Fig. 6.13 The **function** 'combine'

There are times when the parameter values we wish to apply a function to are ordered in a list. The function '**combine**' performs this task. Figure 6.13a defines the function '**combine**' in terms of '**combine_aux**'. However, we would recommend that if you wish to use this combine with ClarityPro then you should give it another name such as '**my_combine**'. The function '**combine_aux**' takes a function description in terms of a list, thus

QUERY> combine_aux [+ #3 #5]
#8
QUERY> combine_aux [− #3 #5]
#-2

In effect, it converts square brackets into round brackets (it does not really; at least not straight away, that is just its effect). Note that '**combine_aux**' has to be applied *backwards* because the process is reversed due to the way in which the stack is used for recursion (see also Chapter 4). Thus, expanding the process we have

combine_aux [+ #3 #5]
(@(combine_aux [+ #3]) #5)
(@(@(combine_aux [+]) #3) #5)
(@(@+ #3) #5)
(@(+ #3) #5)
(+ #3 #5)
#8

Note how the pattern match is used to define a list that contains a single element. Such structure recognition is another very valuable tool derived directly from pattern match. We use this technique again in defining the function '**zip**' but in a slightly modified form. Again, we advise you to use another name, such as '**my_zip**', if you wish to transfer your work to ClarityPro.

There are also many occasions when all the different values you wish to 'combine' with a function are in different lists. It would be nice to have a function that 'zips' the lists together to form a set of lists that contain the different values, each in a single list, and in the correct order.

We would like 'zip' to be as general purpose as possible (often the way to elegant programs). We thus consider the most general case of its use where we wish to make any set of lists (provided they are all the same lengths) into another set of lists (see Fig. 6.14.). These new lists contain, in the same order, one example from each of the other lists. If you consider that the set of lists is equivalent to a matrix, the 'zip' is equivalent to the matrix operation 'transpose'.

QUERY> zip[['a''b''c'][#1 #2 #3]['X''Y''Z']]
[['a'#1'X']['b'#2'Y']['c'#3'Z']][5]

The function 'zip' uses the built-in higher order function 'map'. The function 'map' is a very valuable function since it will apply a function (its first parameter) to a list of values (its second parameter). In this example we have

QUERY> map head [['a''b''c'][#1 #2 #3]['X''Y''Z']]
['a'#1'X']
QUERY> map tail [['a''b''c'][#1 #2 #3]['X''Y''Z']]
[['b''c'][#2 #3]['Y''Z']]

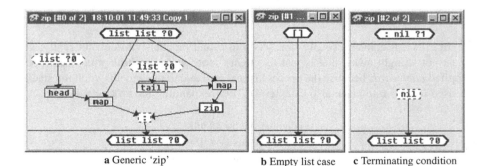

a Generic 'zip'   b Empty list case   c Terminating condition

Fig. 6.14 The function 'zip'

---

[5]It is likely that the output will look like the following:
(:['a' #1'X'](:['b' #2 'Y'](:['c' #3 'Z']nil)))
To get it in a readable form you have to query it again, thus
QUERY>(:['a' #1 'X'](:['b' #2 'Y'](:['c' #3 'Z']nil)))
[['a' #1 'X']['b' #2 'Y']['c' #3 'Z']]
A permanent solution for any particular function is to use the interpreter function 'eval' just before the output.

and of course

> QUERY> zip[['b''c'][#2#3]['Y''Z']]
> [['b'#2'Y']['c'#3'Z']]

where

> QUERY> : ['a'#1'X'][['b'#2'Y']['c'#3'Z']]
> [['a'#1'X']['b'#2'Y']['c'#3'Z']]

which, of course, is the result. The terminating case is where we have a list of empty lists. Since we do not know how many lists this is likely to be we cannot just put [nil nil nil . . .]. However, we can represent the list as a head and a tail, thus

> :head tail

Now since all lists will become empty (nil) at the same time a list of indefinite length can be represented as

> :nil ?1

where '?1' represents anything including a list or nil.

Non-recursive Approach to Iteration

There is a higher-order function called '**iterate**' that captures all the essential elements of normal iteration. However, it is not often used since many of the desired results can be done more directly with the higher-order function '**map**'. The function '**map**', as we have seen, is used to apply a function to a list of items; items which may be complex. For example, taking a list of paired integers and characters by using the built-in constructor '**Pair**'. Then we can apply the built-in operation '**first**' to each item giving us a list of integers, thus

QUERY> map first [(Pair #1 'a')(Pair #2 'b')(Pair #3 'c')(Pair #4 'd')]
[#1 #2 #3 #4]

Alternatively, we could have applied the function '**second**' to each item to get a list of characters.

QUERY> map second [(Pair #1 'a')(Pair #2 'b')(Pair #3 'c')(Pair #4 'd')]
['a''b''c''d']

On the other hand, we may want a list of integer and character pairs but only have lists of the items separately. The first step is to '*pair*' the two lists together. This can be done for two lists of the same length with the function '**zip**'. Zip takes any number of lists as a list of lists and generates pairs, triples, or n-tuples depending on how many lists there are. Therefore, we can get our sets of two items together as follows:

> **QUERY>** zip [[#1 #2 #3 #4]['a' 'b' 'c' 'd']]
> [[#1 'a'][#2 'b'][#3 'c'][#4 'd']]

However, this is not a constructed pair. To bind the set of items to a function or constructor we need the function '**combine**'. This will convert a list of items into the parameters of a function to create an expression. For example,

> **QUERY>** combine + [#3 #2]
> #5
> **QUERY>** combine Pair [#3 'c']
> (Pair #3 'c')

So we can '**map**' the Curried function '(**combine Pair**)' over the list of pairs to produce the structure we need.

> **QUERY>** map (combine Pair) [[#1 'a'][#2 'b'][#3 'c'][#4 'd']]
> [(Pair #1 'a')(Pair #2 'b')(Pair #3 'c')(Pair #4 'd')]

'Lambda': Controlling the Parameter Assignment

Now suppose we wanted to divide a number (#3 say) successively with a range of numbers then we could use the notion of the Curried function and write

> **QUERY>** map (/#r3) [#1 #2 #3 #4]
> [#r3.000000 #r1.500000 #r1.000000 #r0.750000]

On the other hand, suppose we wanted to divide each integer in a list by a number (say #3 again). We would have to somehow inform the interpreter that each number to which the function is applied must be placed in the first parameter position of divide ('/') and not the second as was done above. For this operation, we need the 'interpreter instruction' (it is not a function) '*lambda*'. Note, that in Clarity, '*lambda*' always appears in italic since it is not recognised as a function or constructor. In the 'control window' we can write the function we need, thus

> **QUERY>** map (lambda ?7 (/?7 #r3))[#1 #2 #3 #4]
> [#r0.333333 #r0.666667 #r1.000000 #r1.333333]

The use of all these functions (i.e. 'try_move', 'combine' and 'zip') and the type 'co_ord' can now be drawn together to produce the function 'check_move'. This function takes a list of 'objects' each of which is represented by a position and size pair. 'Check_move' assesses if a move to a particular position is going to cause a 'Hit' with any of the objects and if so which one.

Figure 6.15 shows the final version in Clarity of the function we started to produce that determines if a set of objects will collide while trying to move one of them. The list of objects is given in the second parameter and each of these is tested with 'try_move' to see if there is a Hit or a Miss. Since 'try_move' was defined with the position and size of each object as separate parameters then each object has to be 'unpacked' to get at the individual values. Since this is a one-off function *lambda* is used to provide the parameter identification in a temporary function. This temporary (and unnamed) function is applied to each object in the list returning, for each object, a Hit or a Miss.

The list of Hits and Misses are combined with a list of positions obtained by applying the function 'first' to each of the pairs. The two lists then form a list of lists through the function 'makelist'. The function 'makelist' is one of the few functions (e.g. progN) that can take on any number of parameters. It is unique to Clarity/Faith because it services the diagrammatic representation and allows 'lists' to be expressed.

The function 'zip' pairs each item of each list in order returning another list of lists, this time of position and contact sub-lists. Each sub-list is converted to a position and contact pair using 'combine'. An example of 'check_move' in use where 'realtoc' is described in Chapter 7, Fig. 7.2:

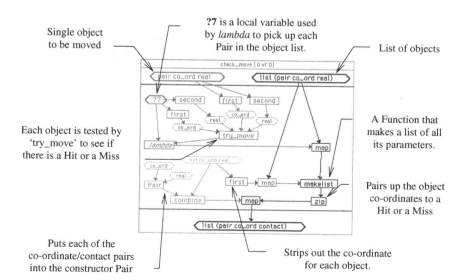

Fig. 6.15 A function to check over a range of objects for a **Hit** or a **Miss**

QUERY> check_move (Pair (realtoc #r3.7 #r5.2) #r1.5) [(Pair (realtoc #r2.3 #r4.6)
#r2.3)(Pair (realtoc #r7.3 #r8.1) #r0.5)]
[(Pair (Co_Ord (X #r2.300000)(Y #r4.600000)) Hit)(Pair (Co_Ord(X #r7.300000)(Y
#r8.100000)) Miss)]

Much more can be done in keeping this diagram simple. It is also always important that function names are chosen to be meaningful. Both these strategies can be
applied to '**check_move**' by replacing the *lambda* expression by a single function.
This function tests to see if there is a '**hit_or_miss**' and will return '**Hit**' if there is
contact with another object and '**Miss**' otherwise.

Editing out Sub-functions to a New Function Window

The replacement process is made easy in Clarity. To save a sub-function we can
either highlight the collection of functions we wish to use by holding down shift
and clicking on each function or we can lasso the functions. If we highlight, then
we can then go to the edit window as in Fig. 6.16 otherwise we go straight to the
edit window and lasso the functions we want (Fig. 6.17a).

Fig. 6.16 Pull down Edit
menu

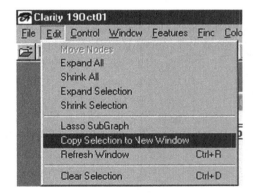

In either case, we end up with the functions and their connecting arrows in a new
window. These we can rearrange and add to in the normal way to create the sub-
function we want. Figure 6.17b shows the result and Fig. 6.18 shows the final form
of the function '**check_move**'.

The Annotation Window

The annotation window we have introduced before. We have shown examples where
it can be associated with a diagram and any token within the diagram. As we have
emphasised, the purpose of the annotation is to help keep a record of the informal

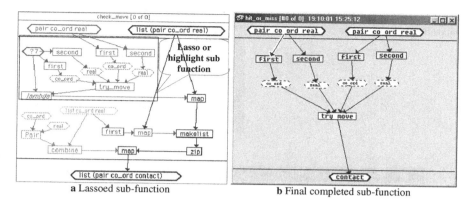

| a Lassoed sub-function | b Final completed sub-function |

Fig. 6.17 The function '**check_move**'

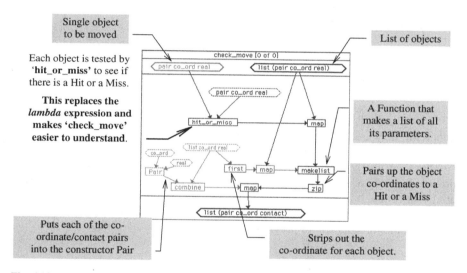

Fig. 6.18 Replace lambda expression by a single function

semantics of the function. Figure 6.19 shows where to find the call to opening an annotation window. It is not in the list of windows, as one might expect, but under the menu item 'features'. This is because it is a feature of a window rather than a stand-alone window (Fig. 6.20).

The annotation window can be filled with text. Again as we have suggested it is always a good idea to include in the annotation an actual example (cut and pasted from the control window) of the function. This provides a ready-made test if the function needs to be debugged at some future occasion. When the annotation is completed, the function is recommitted to link it with the annotation. Annotation is

Fig. 6.19 Calling an
annotation Window

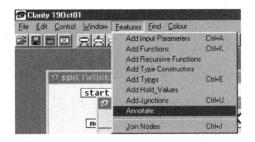

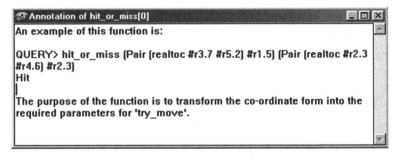

Fig. 6.20 An annotation window associated with the function 'hit_or_miss'

important; they are little messages to your future self when you may have to come back to this code. Remember that living programs never remain the same.

There are nearly 400 library functions in ClarityPro, many of them created to provide freedom of expression. There are also mechanisms for creating and generating Faith code. It is worthwhile to simply browse through the manual of functions during periods of low activity such as watching television. In this way, you can get a grasp of the full capacity of programming in Clarity.

Exercises 6.1

The following questions *must not include recursion*. However, sometimes it is useful to create a recursive version first as a means of getting clear what has to be functionally done. Make sure all functions are well annotated and referenced (using junctions where applicable). Network diagrams should also be created where required.

1. Write a function that will find the larger, smaller or any alternative comparative property of two numbers in a list.
2. Write a function that will find the biggest, smallest or any alternative comparative property. Do this first as a recursive function then without using recursion.
3. Do 2 another way that is also not recursive.

4. Write a function to return a string that has a number of copies (first argument) of its (second argument) a string.
5. Write a function to return a list that has an element (first argument) inserted into the nth position (second argument) of a list (third argument).
6. Write a function that will return a sorted version of its argument list (second argument) according to a comparator function (first argument).
7. Construct a single comparison function that extends the notion of '>' and '<' to include strings and clothes sizes. Use this function to sort lists of all strings and clothes sizes as well as numbers of any kind and characters.

Questions 6.1

1. What two benefits would you expect from 'elegant' programming?
2. What important question should you ask yourself in order to produce an elegant definition of a function?
3. In what three ways does a junction help provide elegance?
4. In pattern match, for multi-parameter functions what is the most important feature of the matching process?
5. How do you represent a function as a parameter when declaring a higher-order function. Why is this representation important?
6. What is the single most important reason for avoiding recursion?
7. When declaring functions in ClarityLite that may have equivalent functions already in ClarityPro library why should you make sure the names are distinct?

Project: A Simple Learning Strategy

Oxo: The Game Player That Learns

The Basic Game

In this project, we will take you through five stages. At the end of each stage, you will have a working learning program, a program that will play you "noughts and crosses" (sometimes called "TicTacToe") and it will also learn from its (and your) mistakes. The first stage will not be very clever and will not learn from its mistakes.

Each further stage you complete will make the program smarter so that at in the end it will learn how to play at least as well as you.

The first stage is rather long because so many little bits have to be built to make it work. However, once done it is done and you can use these bits again for your own and future projects. Each stage makes a big difference in how smart the program becomes but strangely enough, gets less and less difficult for you to do.

If you are working with ClarityPro rather than ClarityLite it is worth checking such things as the casting functions to ensure that they are not already defined in the library.

The Game: The First Version

We have called this game "oxo" because of the noughts and crosses used to play the game. It is a game for two players, one is 'x' and the other is 'o'. They start with an empty square grid of nine squares. The two players take it in turns to put their mark on an empty square on the grid. The first to complete a horizontal, vertical or diagonal row wins.

Building Your Stage 1 Program

When we build the first simple (and dumb) Clarity version of 'oxo', we will make the program oxo be 'x', the player will be 'o', and we will allow the program oxo to go first.

We have to do the following:

- Define the marks 'x', 'o' and for an empty square we will use '.' So we have your move, oxo's move and empty place.
- Make a function that will say who has won.
- Make a function that will output a message to you.
- Identify what is a winning arrangement of xs or os and detect when that occurs.
- Make a function that can output a grid so that the game can be played. In practice, we will put out two grids. One gives the numbers that represent the grid positions that are free for you to use and one to show the game.
- Make a function that shows oxo what moves it can make in response to your move.

You will be given instructions that are preceded by a bracketed step number and an * and underlined. For example,

(8) *Define the function '**win_this**', Diagram 8b.

This instruction means that at this step 8 in the construction you should create the function **win_this**. This is done by recreating the associated diagram 8b that shows the function **win_this** as it should be drawn in a Clarity function window. The instructions are not always given in the order in which the diagrams appear.

In the end, it will not matter in what order you create your functions but you may not be able to test them as you go along. *It is always a good idea to try out each function in the control window to make sure it works before you proceed.* Also, do not forget that many functions consist of more than one component. That is, it has more than one definition.

There is a lot to be done on the drawing of the grid and other ways the program must communicate with you. Once done the fun of how the program makes a decision to play with you can be worked on. In the first stage the decision is made simply at random. It will be very easy to beat. In stage 2 we will show you how to change this first Oxo so that it can learn from its successes.

The First Step: Making Your Mark

First, we define the marks 'x' and 'o' that go on the grid. Look at Diagram 6.1. Here we define the <u>type</u> **mark**. Notice the two extra marks, '.' and 'Unknown'. There are two reasons for these:

(1) squares 1–9 on the grid can also be empty, and that has been defined as '.', and
(2) square n, where n is less than 1 or n is greater than 9 does not have meaning, so square n is Unknown.

Diagram 6.1   mark

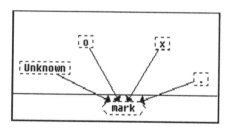

(1) *Define the type **mark** Diagram 6.1.

This is done in a <u>Constructor window</u> as shown in Diagram 1 above.

Overview of the Program Oxo

Now look at the function **oxo** in Diagram 6.2. This function **starts** the game, **plays until** the **game** is **over, draws** the **grid** and displays a message to say who won. These four activities must be performed in the correct sequence, and we make sure of that by using **progN**.

The function **progN** performs all the functions in a clockwise order (left to right), and the result is the result of the last function, in this case **bool**. The term **bool** references another basic <u>type</u> and it only takes two values, **True** and **False**.

Diagram 6.2 oxo

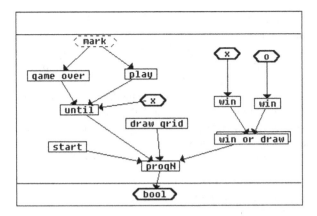

The reason for such a result is that **win_or_draw** returns **True** if the message is printed successfully. Many functions return the simple type **bool**.

Now look at **win_or_draw** in Diagram 6.3. There are four versions of it, called components. If you look at Diagram 6.2 you will see that **win_or_draw** is called with two values. These are called input parameters. In this case, the parameters are the results of the function calls 'win x' and 'win o'. The function **win** returns the value **True** or **False**. There are three possible outcomes: x wins, o wins, or there is a draw. But, there are four combinations of **True** and **False**. We always make sure we deal with all cases, and that is why we have four versions of **win_or_draw**.

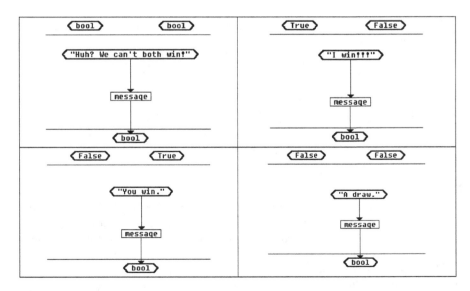

Diagram 6.3 win_or_draw

These four components will be numbered #0–#3 of 3. This may seem odd, but it is usual practice in Clarity programs for the general case to be component #0, and special cases to start at #1. Having different versions of a function is an example of 'pattern-matching', that is, you will get the version of the function that best matches your input parameters. In the case of **win_or_draw** the matches will be exact.

Setting up Communications with Oxo

(2) *Define function **newline** Diagram 6.4.

The built-in functions **decode** and **putchar** will be described shortly.

Diagram 6.4 newline

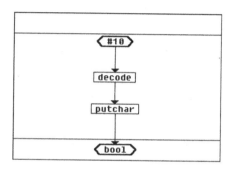

(3) *Define the function **message** Diagram 6.5.

The type **str** is a string, i.e. characters enclosed by double quotes. **putline** is a built-in function that prints a string. As you complete each function, try it out in the CONTROL window to make sure that it works.

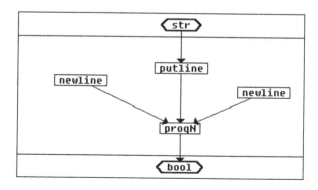

Diagram 6.5   message

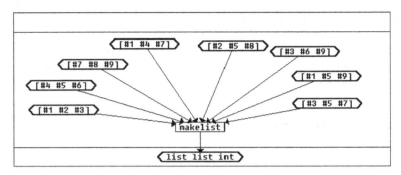

Diagram 6.6 winnings

Detecting a Win

(4) *Define the function **win_or_draw** Diagram 6.3.

To complete this part of the program, we will look at the function **win**.

But first of all look at **winnings** in Diagram 6.6. This function returns a **list** of **list**s of **integer**s. An **integer** is another type. It represents positive and negative whole numbers, and to distinguish it from a simple character it is preceded by '#'. **winnings** makes a list of lists of the numbers of the squares in the grid that would constitute a win, for example [#1 #2 #3] is the list of integers #1, #2 and #3 in the top row. **makelist** is a 'built-in' function that makes a list for us, and will take any number of input parameters. It is unusual in this, as the majority of built-in functions and ALL the user-defined functions have a fixed number of input parameters.

(5) *Define the function **winnings** Diagram 6.6.

Remember to check it out by calling it in the <u>control window</u>.

Laying Out the Board

The next function to consider is **square** in Diagram 6.7. It takes an **integer** as an input parameter and returns a type **mark**. **Unknown** is one of the marks. The function **square** is going to represent a square on the grid, for example, at some point in the game, 'square #3' may be defined as 'x'. Here we define the general case only, as the other values for **square** will be changed as the game proceeds. More on that later.

(6) *Define the function **square** Diagram 6.7.

Look at the function **on_square** in Diagram 6.8a. If its input parameters are **x** and **#1**, for example, it will return **True** if 'square #1' returns **x**.

Diagram 6.7 square

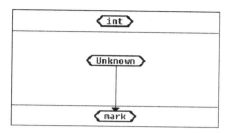

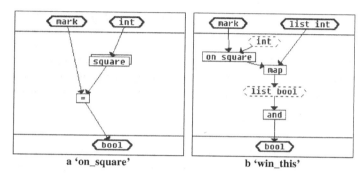

a 'on_square'   b 'win_this'

Diagram 6.8 'on_square' and 'win_this' functions

Look at **win_this** in Diagram 6.8b. This function is defined as having **mark** and **list int** as input parameters and returns **bool** (True or False). Suppose the input parameter **mark** is **x**. **map** is a built-in function which applies 'on_square x' to each of the integers in the list. For example if the list were [#1 #2 #3], the first application would be 'on_square x # 1'. The built-in **and** will return **True** if all the elements in the **list bool** are **True**. So if all three squares have the same mark then **win_this** returns the value **True**.

(7) *Define the function **on_square** Diagram 6.8a.

More About Winning

(8) *Define the function **win_this** Diagram 6.8b.

Look at function **win** in Diagram 6.9. The input parameter is **mark** (which will be x or o), and the return value will be True or False. Suppose mark is x. 'win x' will tell us if x has won. **map** applies 'win_this x' to all the lists of integers in **winnings**. For example, 'win_this x [#1 #2 #3]' returns True if x is on squares #1, #2 and #3

Diagram 6.9 win

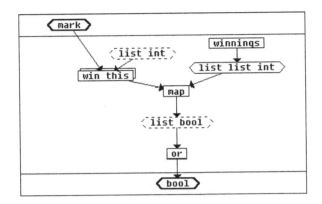

of the grid. **map** goes through all the winning lists and returns a list of **bool**. The function **or** is a built-in that determines if one of the list is True, i.e. x has won.

(9) *Define the function **win** Diagram 6.9.

We cannot get very far with this game unless we draw the grid in some way. There are some very basic built-in functions to input characters and output characters and strings. These are **putchar**, **putline** and **print**. These are used to draw the grid in two simple ways. For example,

```
x  o  3        x   o   .
4  5  o         .   .   o
7  x  9         .   x   .
```

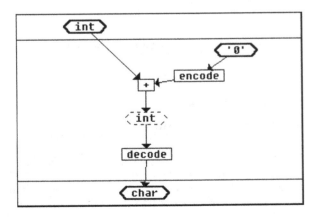

Diagram 6.10 int_to_char

Firstly, look at function **int_to_char** in Diagram 6.10. This function takes an integer and converts it into the corresponding character, ready for output. **char** is another type, for example 'a'. The built-in function **encode** gives the internal code for a character, for example, the internal code for 'a' is the number 97. The function **decode** does the opposite and returns the character that an internal code represents, for example, 'decode #100' returns 'd'. The codes for the number characters run in sequence, so we find the code for '0', add our integer (say #3) and decode to give the corresponding character (say '3').

Handling the Opponent's Moves

(10) *Define the function **int_to_char** Diagram 6.10.

Another example of **decode** is in the function **newline** in Diagram 6.4. The internal code for a new line character is the number 10. We **decode** that to output a new line character. The new line is known as a 'side effect'. **newline** actually returns a **bool**, True. This is usually the case with side effect functions.

Next, look at the function **print_square** in Diagram 6.11. This function will **print** the mark on the square if it is x or o, but otherwise will print the number of the square. **if** is a built-in that takes three input parameters. The first is a bool, which is usually the result of some function, in this case !=. The second is the return value if the bool is True and the third is the return value if the bool is False. The return values here will be the same in both cases (**True**), but the side effects are different. **print** is used for the mark, as it can handle any type, but **putchar** is used for the **char** to avoid **print**'s single quote marks. It is usually clearer to avoid the use of **if**, by using pattern matching instead.

Diagram 6.11   print_square

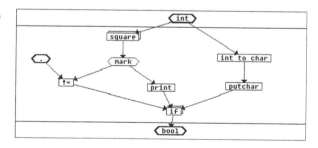

(11) *Define the function **print_square** Diagram 6.11.

Look at **draw_row** in Diagram 12. Again the general definition is not interesting but is there for completeness. Components #1–#6 draw rows 1–3 (LHS) and 4–6 (RHS) as illustrated in the above example of the picture of the grid.

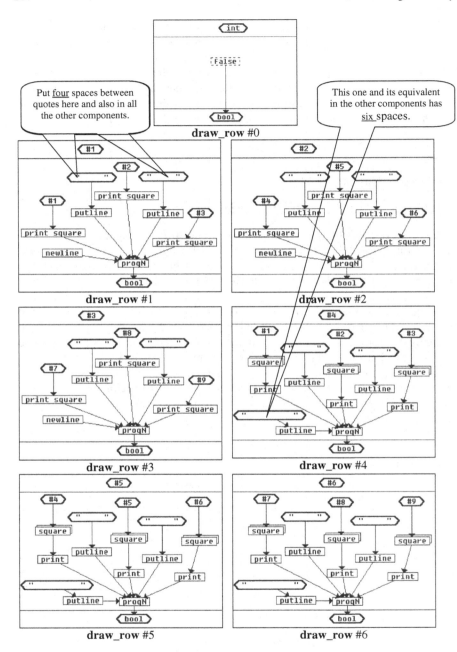

Diagram 6.12 All the components of the function '**draw_row**'

(12) *Define the function **draw_row** Diagram 6.12.

Do not forget you need to draw all seven components. This is the general case and the six special cases.

(13) *Define the function '**draw_grid**' Diagram 6.13.

The function **draw_grid** in Diagram 6.13 is the last function in this group. The built in function **map** is used to apply the function **draw_row** to each of the numbers in the list. This is done in the order they are given, i.e. 1, 4, 2, 5, 3, 6, and it will generate two pictures of the grid, as illustrated above. The function **newline** is added for neatness.

Diagram 6.13 'draw_grid'

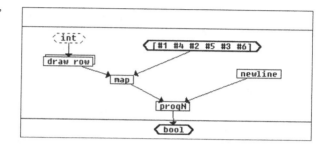

Starting the Game

Look at '**start**' in Diagram 6.14. It has three things to do: clear the grid, something called '**srand**', and print a message for the user. During the playing of the game itself, random numbers will be used to select a square to mark. The built-in random number generator '**rand**' will generate these, but needs to be 'seeded' by calling the built-in '**srand**'.

To clear the grid, '**clear_square**' is applied to all the integers 1–9. Look at '**clear_square**' in Diagram 6.15. '**setq**' is a built-in which takes two parameters: the first is another function (with its parameters if there are any) and the second is

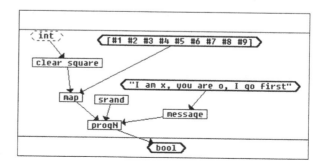

Diagram 6.14 'start'

Diagram 6.15
'clear_square'

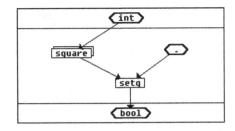

a value that the function is set to. So here, if the input parameter is #1, square #1 is set to '.', i.e. it is cleared.

(14) *Define the function '**clear_square**' Diagram 6.15.

Test it by calling 'clear_square #1', followed by 'square #1'.

(15) *Define the function **start** Diagram 6.14.

Now let us look at the game itself. Look at Diagram 6.2 again. The built-in function '**until**' takes three parameters, but processes ONE value only, in this case a value of type '**mark**'. The first parameter, '**game_over**', is a test on '**mark**' to determine if the function should stop. The second, '**play**', is a function which inputs '**mark**' and returns '**mark**'. In fact, if it inputs x, it returns o, and vice versa, so the game can continue until it is over. The third parameter to '**until**' is the starting value of mark, i.e. x. As we said, x goes first.

Finishing the Game and Knowing Where to Move

Look at '**game_over**' in Diagram 6.16. Supposing o was to go next. The game would be over if either x had won, or there were no empty squares. The built-in function || is 'or' as in 'either ... or'.

The function, '**other**', in Diagram 6.17 has three components, and simply means the other mark.

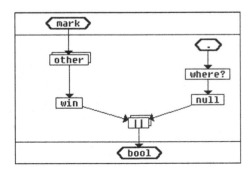

Diagram 6.16 'game_over'

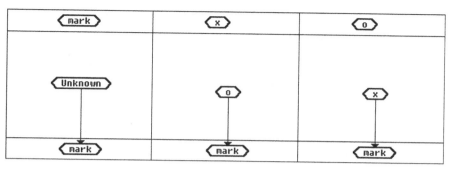

Diagram 6.17 'other'

Diagram 6.18 'where?'

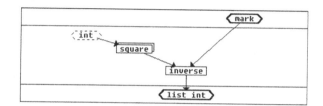

Look at function **'where?'** in Diagram 6.18

It uses the built-in **'inverse'** function which in this case will tell us which squares have the mark '.', i.e. empty. In **'game_over'**, the built-in **'null'** is a test which returns True for an empty list.

(16) *Define the functions **'other'** Diagram 6.17.

(17) *Define the function **'where'** Diagram 6.18.

(18) *Define the function **'game_over'** Diagram 6.16.

Now look at **'play'** in Diagram 6.19. There are three tasks here in order. **'Choose** a square _ **for'** x or o, **'set** that square _ **to'** x or o, and return the **'other'** mark for the next play. The function **'set_to'**, in Diagram 6.20, is very similar to **'clear_square'**. It sets a given square to x or o.

(19) *Define the function **set_to** Diagram 6.20.

Look at **'choose_for'** in Diagram 6.21. This is a simple version of the game, and so choosing a square for x, the computer, is just a matter of taking any free square.

The function **'any_free_square'** in Diagram 6.22 needs some explanation. The built-in $ returns the number of items in a list. The built-in % returns the remainder

Diagram 6.19 'play'

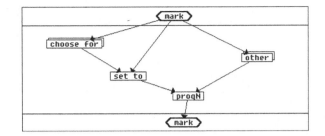

Diagram 6.20 'set_to'

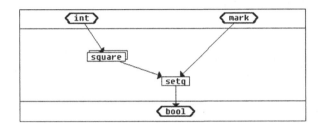

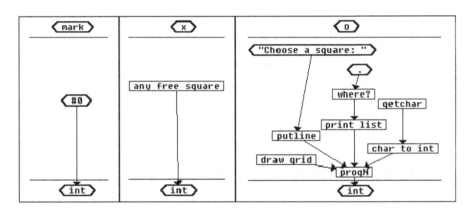

Diagram 6.21 'choose_for'

after integer division, e.g. '% #12 #5' returns #2. This is to get a random number within certain limits. The built-in **!** selects an item in a list by order, beginning at 0, e.g. '! #1 [#2 #4 #6]' returns #4. Starting at the top and working down, supposing 'where? .' returns [#1 #3 #4 #8] as the free squares. '$ [#1 #3 #4 #8]' will return #4, and '% rand #4' will return an integer between #0 and #3, say #2. '! #2 [#1 #3 #4 #8]' will return #4, so **square** #4 will be chosen for x.

Diagram 6.22
'any_free_square'

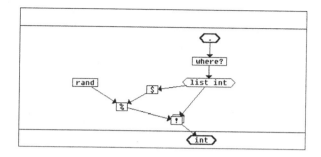

(20) *Define the function **'any_free_square'** Diagram 6.22.

The user has the mark 'o', and can choose a free square. **'choose_for'** 'o' draws the grid in two ways, with **'draw_grid'** and then invites the user to choose from a **printed list** of free squares. Look at **'print_list'** in Diagram 6.23.

Diagram 6.23 'print_list'

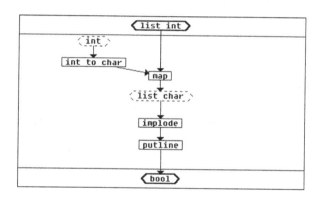

The function **'int_to_char'** turns an integer into its character equivalent (see Diagram 6.10 again), and **'map'** applies this to the list of free squares. The built-in **'implode'** takes a list of characters and returns a string, e.g. 'implode ['1' '3' '4' '8']' returns "1348". This is printed for the user.

(21) *Define the function **'print_list'** Diagram 6.23.

The function **'char_to_int'** in Diagram 6.24 does the opposite of **'int_to_char'**.

(22) *Define **char_to_int** Diagram 6.24.

The built-in **'getchar'** waits for a character input from the user and the returns it as a result.

Diagram 6.24
'char_to_int'

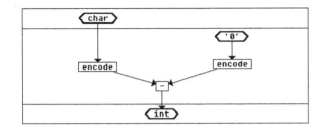

The Final Steps

(23) *Define the functions '**choose_for**' Diagram 6.21.

(24) *Define the functions '**play**' Diagram 6.19.

(25) *Define, finally, '**oxo**' Diagram 6.2.

To play the game, type in '**oxo**' in the CONTROL window and follow the instructions.

Finally

Save your database and call it 'OXO1A'.

Create a network view by opening a network window, go to the find 'menu' and click on 'Create/Update network from database'. This may require a little rearranging and the deletion of some functions to look neat (see Diagram 6.25). A proposed

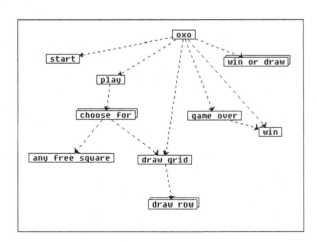

Diagram 6.25 Network of selected functions for '**OXO1A**'

arrangement is shown in Diagram 6.25. When you are satisfied with its appearance, commit it just like a function window. Other views of the network, showing different functionality, can be created in separate network windows.

You have finished stage 1. The next stages will be much easier in Chapter 7.

Chapter 7
Side Effect Programming and Schematic Design

For we know in part, and we prophesy in part.
But when that which is perfect is come, then that which is in part
shall be done away.

Corinthians 13, 9 & 10.

Introduction

Functional programming does not normally concern itself with the order in which processes are executed; just that if a process can be completed it is done before those that are still waiting for all their parameter values to be accessible. Thus, parallel operations that are complete may be carried out in any order. In some cases, the specific order of doing operations must be forced. Order is important in the case where a program is controlling a process in real time. As you might expect, all because it is possible (say) to steer left before right does not mean that it should be done in that order.

One of the advantages of a functional language is that it avoids many of the problems of imperative languages. In particular, the pure functional language gains its advantage through the idea that a function will always respond exactly the same way no matter when or how it is called. This characteristic of stable and predictable results is *referential transparency*. The problem with imperative languages is that they rely upon referencing stored data and this data may be changed anywhere and at any time in a program. In many cases, this will result in a procedure (equivalent to a function) responding differently at different times to the same input. Thus we can note that *imperative programs will perform differently depending upon their history*. This characteristic is fundamental to imperative programming since such programming depends totally on side effects.

For this reason, much work has gone into debugging tools for imperative programming that allows the programmer to trace the history of a process in order to 'see' at what point an 'error' occurs. Such tracing forms a major part of the activities of a programmer. As we pointed out earlier, often the consequence of an error does

T. Addis, J. Addis, *Drawing Programs: The Theory and Practice of Schematic Functional Programming*, DOI 10.1007/978-1-84882-618-2_7,
© Springer-Verlag London Limited 2010

not occur until many thousands of operations after the event. This entails that an imperative programmer has to examine these steps in order to determine where an error has manifested itself. One necessary skill an imperative programmer requires is the ability to spot a wrong or changed pattern in masses of text. An interpreted and pure functional language needs no such debugging tool since a function will always behave in exactly the same way at all times unless one deliberately evokes side effect programming. In pure functional programming an error is always only one step away and thus errors are easy to find.

Functions as Data

There is a price to pay for *referential transparency* in that *there seems to be no place to 'store' data*. All data that represents the 'state' of the world has to be passed on from function to function through the parameters. In the simple case, this does not matter but where the 'state' of the world is complex then there is one major side effect that is present all the time that will catch the functional programmer out and that is a *stack overflow*. This is because the computer is inherently a real and limited imperative machine. The computer is not a functional machine even though it is theoretically equivalent in potential. Further, the functions become very 'busy' as each function has to 'handle' and pass on the 'state' of the world in order to access or update the data. The problems involved in handling such states can cause the function definitions to be clumsy, unwieldy and inefficient. It is not surprising that imperative programming was favoured in the early days of computing where resources were limited. They had to be managed with care for even the simplest programs. Despite the vast improvements of computer power the demand to ask for almost infinite resources for what seems a simple task is easily and often done.

As we have shown earlier, we can define a function with no parameters such that when it is called it will return a value. We can then use this function as a global constant that is accessible anywhere in the programme. For example 'constant1' in Fig. 7.1 can be used as a global constant.

As we have also demonstrated earlier, it is possible to change this constant at any time by using the function '**setq**', thus

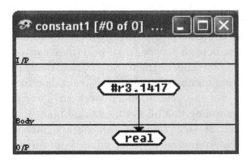

Fig. 7.1 A function of constant value

QUERY> constant1
#r3.141700
QUERY> setq constant1 #r5.622
True
QUERY> constant1
#r5.622000

Functions can have parameters and as such each component of a function can respond with a value. As we have used before in this way, a function becomes an array with the option of having indices of any kind (integer, string, real or any user-defined type). This gives considerable power to the expressiveness of the language. Further, it allows the existence of sparse arrays without any overheads. To make such an assignment the function 'setq' takes on two parameters[1] such that the first parameter is not evaluated[2]:

setq (<function> {<index>}) <body>

is its general form. So not only values but also expressions and constructed values can be assigned to a function component within the program. For example, suppose we wanted to model the behaviour of bacteria on a Petri dish and we need to keep track of each individual bug such as its current position and size. Figure 7.2 shows a component of the function '**bug**' with a constructed set of information.

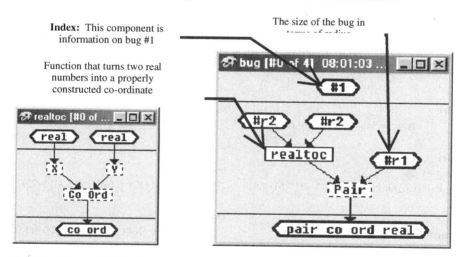

Fig. 7.2 A bug and its details

---

[1] But not its alternatives '**assertq**' (and other variants) which can take on a variable number of parameters.

[2] Note that 'q' stands for '**quote**'. There is also '**set**' that does evaluate the first parameter.

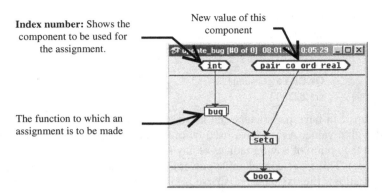

Fig. 7.3 'update_bug' is a function for changing a '**bug**' position

A function can now be constructed which will assign a new value to a '**bug**' where this value is some complex construct. Figure 7.3 is such a function.

Functions as Relations

If it is possible to use functions as arrays to store data then this opens the possibility of considering a set of extensional functions as a relational database. Consider the Faith code of the '**bugs**' function described above. In the Faith window the function would look like this:

fdec
    bug ::= int->pair co_ord real ;
;
fdef
 bug #1 ::=
   Pair (Co_Ord (X #r22.1)(Y #r17.6)) #r1.0
;

bug#2 ::=
   Pair (Co_Ord (X #r16.4)(Y #r19.9)) #r1.5
;

bug #3 ::=
   Pair (Co_Ord (X #r11.4)(Y #r10.6)) #r2.5
;

bug #4 ::=
   Pair (Co_Ord (X #r6.6)(Y #r12.1)) #r2.0 ;

bug#5 ::=
   Pair (Co_Ord (X #r13.5)(Y #r14.2)) #r1.0
;

where **Pair** *<position>* *<radius>* describes the body of the relation. These are the non-key properties of the relation and sometimes referred to as *own* domains.

Now it is possible to convert this function into a list of lists by using the library function '**list_fdefs**'. This function creates a list which is a special kind of relational form that can be manipulated by all the list operations such as '**head**', '**tail**' and '**:**'. The function '**list_fdefs**' will convert 'bug' as follows:

```
QUERY>list_fdefs bug
[
        [bug #1 (Pair (Co_Ord (X #r22.1) (Y #r17.6)) #r1.0)]
        [bug #2 (Pair (Co_Ord (X #r16.4) (Y #r19.9)) #r1.5)]
        [bug #3 (Pair (Co_Ord (X #r11.4) (Y #r10.6)) #r2.5)]
        [bug #4 (Pair (Co_Ord (X #r6.6) (Y #r12.1)) #r2.0)]
        [bug #5 (Pair (Co_Ord (X #r13.5) (Y #r14.2)) #r1.0)]
]
```

If '**bug**' had been defined with a general case then this would normally be the first n-tuple of this relation.

Stages of System Design

We can thus put forward an approach that supports the designing of all systems using a functional schematic environment.

Computer systems design has been well served by relational analysis (Date 1995), an approach that can be harnessed from an object orientated perspective. The notion of normalised objects (see Fig. 7.4), always in the context of activities and the objects that are recognised, provides the key to the construction of a model. In particular such a set of normalised objects with a set of dependency constraints is referred to as a *conceptual* model (Addis 1985). A normalised object is characterised by having a set of attributes that identify it from any other object of its type. These attributes are usually assigned and artificially created by the analyst to be unique.

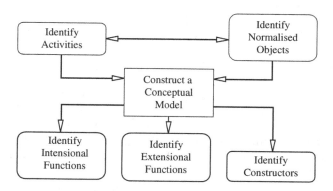

Fig. 7.4 Approaches to analysis

The most convenient means of assigning unique identifiers is to use numbers – such as **'part-number'** and **'bug-number'**. The other attributes, if they exist, are specific to the description of the object and are expected to be 'simple' values. However, an attribute may be an identifying attribute to another object. It is through these *foreign* identifiers that the dependency constraints between objects can be identified.

Such an approach leads to coherent system design. A less common approach, and one that is not well documented, is through the analysis of activities. These activities require a description of what they act upon and what the actions produce. Such an analysis also leads to the emergence of normalised objects.

The analysis provides a framework in the form of this conceptual model, this conceptual model can be translated into a functional language Faith, and in our case this is generated via the schematic interpreter Clarity. The important decisions in a functional representation of such a model are what elements of this model are functions or constructors. Some of these functions will naturally form extensional functions that may or may not have a general component (see Fig. 7.4).

Fig. 7.5 A conceptual model of a purchasing system (An Sfd graph)

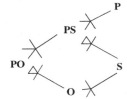

Figure 7.5 is an example of a conceptual model where **P, S, PS, O** and **PO** are normalised objects (i.e. conform to normalised relations). The conceptual model shows a set of dependency constraints that exist between the elements of the object sets. Thus, in this example **P** represents a set of parts where each part p_i consists of a set of attributes that describe that part and **S** represents a set of suppliers in the same way. So we can say that $p_i \, \varepsilon \, P$ and $s_k \, \varepsilon \, S$ where **PS** is the link between parts and suppliers such that $p_i \, s_k \, \varepsilon \, PS$ recording which parts are obtainable from which supplier. This link can also be taken as a normalised object in its own right and as such is likely to have attributes specific to the linking. In this case, it might be the attribute 'price' so that **PS** can be considered as a merged set of price lists for all suppliers **S**. **O** are the orders to suppliers such that $o_j \, \varepsilon \, O$ for the parts given in **PO**. Thus $p_i \, o_j \rightarrow o_j$. Note that an order **O** needs to have at least one part; the order has to be for something.

The symbols that connect them show the mappings zero/many to one ⊁⎯ and the one/many to one ⋈⎯ . Thus an order (o_i) uniquely identifies a supplier (s_i)

although a supplier may have zero, one or many orders. This implies that an order has to refer to at least one part, otherwise it is not an order.

As we have described (but see Appendices A and B) Faith is a direct derivative of lambda calculus and can be represented (formally) as a set of diagrams that are a form of schematic BNF which have a rich informal interpretation potential. This potential can be used to aid understanding and hence improve the design or help support more complicated systems. The relationship between the diagrams supported by Clarity and the formal language Faith is exact. Further, the diagrams command the creation of a multi-layered abstraction of virtual mechanisms and because diagrams encourage simplicity (since too many items can confuse but a simple drawing is insightful) each mechanism is easy to understand.

Consider a the normalised object

Part [PNo : Description, Size]

that represents parts in a database and records the parts available in store. It is normalised because it has the simple set of functional dependencies **PNo** → *description* and **PNo** → *size*. **PNo** is the identifier attribute (indicated by being to the left of the colon :) and is an *integer*. This relation can be represented as a function '**part**'. Given in Faith, the extensional component of a functional description[3] of a set containing only two parts would appear as

part #45672 ::= **Part_Own** (**Description** "Nut") (**Size** #32);
part #3214 ::= **Part_Own** (**Description** "Screw") (**Size** #24);

and this could be stored as a **part** relation with the value as shown in Table 7.1.

In this table **bold** and all lower case represents a function, **Bold** with initial upper case a constructor and ***bold*** italic a type. Values are signified in normal case and are type marked with # for type integer and " " for type string. Note that any 'constructor' can be replaced in this extensional form by a 'function'. However, if such a replacement was made it will need to be 'normalised' yet again to make the description into its most atomic relational description. The decision to terminate the detailed description at a type depends on the information needed

Table 7.1 A 'Part' relation or function

part_no	*part_own*
#45672	**Part_Own** (**Description** "Nut") (**Size** #32)
#3214	**Part_Own** (**Description** "Screw") (**Size** #24)

---

[3] The language used here is FAITH which is similar to HOPE.

by the program and the user requirements. As we have seen before ?0 represents a variable. This representation is consistent with representing an intensional function that has an extensional component (the terminating condition) such as 'factorial':

> **factorial** ?0 ::= **multiply** ?0 (**factorial** (**sub1** ?0));
> **factorial** (#1) ::= (#1);

It is thus possible to have many pattern sensitive components of a function that override the general case. The patterns are chosen by a 'best' fit algorithm that we have already described. Moreover, since a functional language is used, it is possible to model at any level of abstraction, combining different levels of complexity in the same representation.

We can now see that a function in extension can be considered as a relation. For extensional functions the equivalencies are shown in the Table 7.2.

Table 7.2   Function and Relation equivalences

Functional data language	Relational database
Function name	Relation name
Parameters (domain)	Key domain
Output (co- domain)	Own domain
Constructor or function	Domain or domain group (e.g. own) generator

A function can be tested with examples by querying, thus

> **QUERY>** part #3214
>   (Part_Own (Description "Screw") (Size #24))
> **QUERY>** part #4444
>   (Unknown_Part #4444)

The complete Faith code for our example will be as shown in Table 7.3:

So a good approach to design is to *analyse the problem in terms of its normalised relations.* Make these normalised relations extensional functions and then tie up *the update constraints as a set of additional functions* linked to the relations that form the states of the model or domain being considered.

Sequences

Unless you are going to keep an explicit track of time or the ordering of events a functional language will, as we stated before, apply functions in any order

Table 7.3 A Faith code relational model

tdec	fdec
part_no ::= typeop #0 ;	part ::= part_no → part_own ;
size ::= typeop#0 ;	;
description ::= typeop #0 ;	**fdef**
part_own ::= typeop #0 ;	part ?0 ::= Unknown_Part?0 ;
;	part #45672 ::= Part_Own(Description "Nut") (Size #32) ;
cdec	part #3214 ::= Part_Own(Description "Screw") (Size #24);
Size ::= int->size ;	;
Description ::= str->description ;	
Part_No ::= int->part_no ;	
Unknown_Part ::= part_no->part_own ;	
Part_Own ::= description->size->part_own ;	
;	

provided the function is complete (has all the parameter values). Some control can be achieved through the nesting of the 'if' function which can be arranged like dominoes; the completion of one set of functions triggering off the next. However, all this is very clumsy and as we have shown makes the tracing of a program difficult. It would be better to provide a set of functions whose sole job is to order events. One of the most useful is the function '**progN**' and its variants.

The function '**progN**' can take on any number of parameters and will evaluate them in strict sequence starting from the first parameter and finishing on the last. In this case the evaluation of '**progN**' is the evaluation of the last parameter. All the other evaluations are ignored. This means that the other evaluations do not exist as far as the functional program is concerned. The only results will be through side effects.

Figure 7.6 is an illustration of side effect programming for displaying the movement of a bug on the screen. Most of the operations are benign and this limits the risk involved in evoking side effect functions. In this example, it is vital that the correct order of events happen. The moving of a '**bug**' must involve the sequence of eliminating its appearance in the old position. Then redrawing it in the new position and at the same time updating its new position in the function '**bug**' (potentially malignant – see later – Benign and Malignant Side Effects).

Another example of using a global is with '**factorial**'. Here we can declare a function with no parameters to act as a global working store to carry the intermediate results during calculation. This is equivalent to the second value of Pair in the 'carry-forward' method that uses a constructor to carry forward these calculations. In the example we show here (see Fig. 7.7), the initial value of this working store ('**working_value**') is set at the primary factorial parameter. The next operation is to do the 'until' which continues until the factorial parameter is reduced to #1 or less. At this point, the 'working_value' is returned (last parameter value).

The key to this is shown in Fig. 7.7 where the function '**fact_step**' re-asserts the value of '**working_value**' by multiplying its current value by the incoming integer less #1. The result of this function is the equivalent to just 'sub1' but it

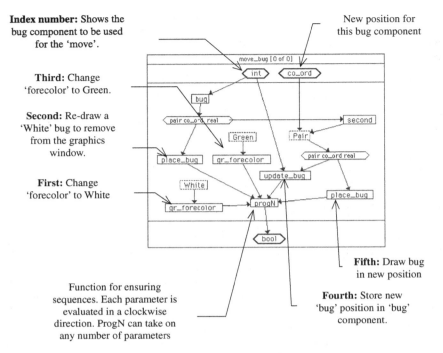

Index number: Shows the bug component to be used for the 'move'.

New position for this bug component

Third: Change 'forecolor' to Green.

Second: Re-draw a 'White' bug to remove from the graphics window.

First: Change 'forecolor' to White

Fifth: Draw bug in new position

Function for ensuring sequences. Each parameter is evaluated in a clockwise direction. ProgN can take on any number of parameters

Fourth: Store new 'bug' position in 'bug' component.

Fig. 7.6 The ultimate in side effect programming **'move_bug'**

has the additional operation of producing a side effect by changing the value of **'working_value'**.

Note that the full-line lozenge indicates a 'HOLDN' operation. As we described earlier, 'HOLDN' is a mechanism that combines the notion of a local variable and a

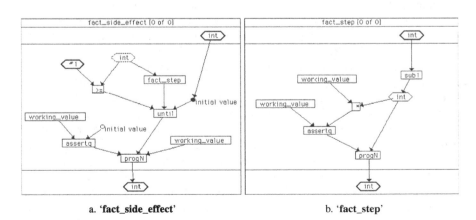

a. **'fact_side_effect'**   b. **'fact_step'**

Fig. 7.7 Side effect factorial. Max. stack depth = 6 for any N

local assignment. You can consider that the full-line lozenge contains the evaluated result of the output function. However, unlike 'let' which does this job in most functional languages the 'HOLDN' only comes into action when needed. In this example, the subtraction of #1 from the incoming integer is done only once. The result is stored as a local variable with no name. The advantage here is that this holding of a value will occur only once no matter which order an operation is called through 'HOLDN'. This efficiency (and sometimes a logical necessity) is automatically applied unless overridden by the user.[4] It is a unique mechanism to Clarity and is only practical because of the diagrammatic representation.

There may be many other ways of implementing factorial but the importance of this study is that many valuable characteristics of 'programming' in Clarity have been demonstrated with a very simple problem.[5] We can infer from the examples that the functional form gives Clarity its representational power. However, the schematics give its capability to keep complexity in check and support free form design.

Evaluation Control

There are four functions that can be used in controlling the order of the evaluation of functions. However, evaluation deferral is discussed in Chapter 8 under the heading of Casting and Code Generation. The first function '**progN**' and its variants is an obvious candidate for controlling a fixed sequence of operations. Here lazy evaluation is suspended and each task is done in a clockwise direction. The actual value returned can be the first task with '**prog1**', the last with '**progN**' and any with '**prog**'. In Fig. 7.7b the second evaluation controlling function 'HOLDN' forces a return of the new integer value *after* the assignment. However, it is also possible to force an evaluation *before* it is required in the same way.

The third evaluation controlling function is '**quote**' which suspends one evaluation step. A simple example is in the case of a zero parameter function such as the constant shown in Fig. 7.1. This is required to be quoted by '**setq**' so it could be addressed and assigned a new value. Likewise, if a constant is to be a parameter for a higher-order function then it will have to be quoted otherwise it will be evaluated before it can be used. It is worth noting that at the query level an extra step of evaluation is done before a function result is displayed. This means that you do not always observe in the control window exactly what is used internally.

---

[4] To override the HoldN you replace the HoldN lozenge by a (dotted) type lozenge.

[5] In ClarityPro links to the outside world are done through special 'user_functions' that will provide values (such as Boolean or integer) in real time. In the case of software that is used for process control, such 'user_functions' provide the external links to the Clarity 'program' from other processes.

The final evaluation controlling function is 'eval'. This function does exactly the reverse of 'quote' by applying an extra level of evaluation. It is worth noting that functions that have a variable number of parameters such as 'makelist' evoke a full evaluation on all its parameters. It can be useful to use instead the constructor ':' to minimise processing.

Benign and Malignant Side Effects

A functional program in its pure sense exists in the abstract world of mathematics. In practice, it has effects on the world and in particular the states of a computation engine. Benign side effects of a function do not interfere with the normal flow of a functional program; the call of a function merely triggers events in the world. In principle, these events could be anything and they may not have a sensible relationship to the meaning of a function in a program. For example, an evaluation of the function 'add1' might (but does not in our case) have a side effect of setting a kettle to boil or causing an alarm to be sounded. However, most side effects do have some sensible events attached to them. Examples are 'print', 'setq', 'sysbeep' and 'trace'.

- *The main issue of 'malignant side effects' is that they cause the mapping of a function to be indeterminate.*

Figure 7.8 illustrates the ultimate example of an indeterminate function. This one calls the library function 'rand' that generates a random integer (needs to be seeded by the function 'srand'). This integer can be contained by the modulus function '%'. The function '%' does an integer division and returns the remainder. In this case, it integer divides the random number by #26 and therefore the remainder is always going to be less than #26. #13 is subtracted so that we can obtain both positive and negative numbers. This function is called twice even though it is represented only once, once for the x and once for the y co-ordinate position. This function is used to move the bug in a random direction. The distance moved will vary between 0 and $\sqrt{(13^2 + 13^2)}/10$ for each cycle.

Figure 7.8 is also an example of a line of Faith code being used within the schematic. In this case, the random number generator is so simple it is clearer to use a bit of program text. However, the danger is that anything in a parameter lozenge and used in the body of a function definition is *not type checked*.

Associated with Clarity is a method of analysis that depends on determining the *functional dependencies* that exist in the problem domain and this is the major process in finding the conceptual model. Next we will look at an emergent design technique that works with the Clarity representation.

Fig. 7.8 A function that
generates a random
co-ordinate change

A line of **Faith** code that
generates a number between
−1.2 and +1.2

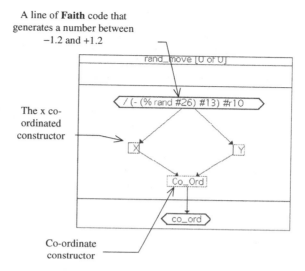

The x co-
ordinated
constructor

Co-ordinate
constructor

What we have shown here is that there is considerable advantage to be gained in balancing the functional and imperative approaches provided the functional language element dominates.

Schematic Design

An Emergent Design Technique

An emergent design technique is an interactive process between the designer, the problem domain and the implementation language. In our case the implementation language is ClarityPro. As we have suggested, one of the valuable techniques of bridging the gap between the problem domain and the implementation language is the process of normalisation. Normalisation has been more fully covered elsewhere [Addis 1985, Date 1995] but in essence it is a way of looking at the world in terms of functional dependency and then reconstructing what is observed into the simplest functional dependency units, units that contain no further functions and only a single functional dependency. In addition to this normalisation is the requirement to reconstruct the constraints between these simple units, again, in terms of functional dependency. These constraints are usually in the form of zero- or one-to-many existence dependency (an A can only exist if there is a B).

In practice there are potentially an infinite number of different types of constraints across all possible databases. For example, it may be a requirement that an even number of elements (such as a ballroom dancing class) is necessary. It was because of this potentially infinite number of constraints that we abandoned the relational view and moved to the functional view of which the relation is a subset. Further, the design process requires some inventive insights into how best to categorise the problem domain in the light of the implementation requirements. The design process is analogous to scientific discovery in that the final set of categories of objects that make up the problem domain is always open to change; change that will provide the greatest generalisation and the simplest implementation. The simple zero/one-to-many type of functional dependencies covers an important set of constraints that is still worth considering in the initial design stages.

We will illustrate the design process by giving a description derived from the log of ourselves designing a General Problem Solver. This will involve several attempts at getting the abstraction of the formal description general enough to tackle possible variants of the problem domains that might occur but still retaining a schematic description that is elegant. But first we should look briefly at where the General Problem Solver came from and what it does.

Artificial Intelligence

Traditional artificial intelligence has been primarily expressed as symbol processing as described by the work of Newell and Simon (Newell and Simon 1963). This was derived from their analysis of the statements made by people when asked to give a running assessment of their thinking while solving a range of problems. It was possible to 'explain' these subjective assessments as state transformations that acted directly on the symbol strings representing the problem. What was more impressive was that in the late 1950s using primitive computers they were able to make a Logic Theory (LT) machine (Newell et al. 1963) using this technique. This machine eventually evolved into the General Problem Solver (GPS) (Newell et al. 1963). At the heart of the GPS is the mechanism for applying transformations to symbol strings where the symbol strings represent the initial statement of the problem. These symbols that represent the starting conditions of the problem are transformed into different and meaningful symbol strings that give a potential route to a solution. Each transformation is linked to an acceptable step of reasoning about a problem. The purpose of the mechanism was to find a sequence of transformations that led to a 'solution' (i.e. a symbol string recognised to be the goal conditions of the problem).

The important issue, from the system-engineering point of view, is that the factual knowledge represented in the computer is complemented by some method of reasoning. The method of reasoning should be justified, accepted and expressible in a mechanistic form. It ought to make no appeal to 'understanding' but exist upon its own foundation. Further, it must be expressive enough to model successfully human performance in problem solving. The task of the knowledge engineer is to create a competence model that will give an acceptable response to a given state of affairs: a response that can be equated with expert and rational activity. It is the competence model in that it ultimately provides a service to people employed in a particular task domain.

Behind the skill, intellect and committed artistry of the AI programmers there is a sound collection of techniques. The 'hard' school created a core method from which most artificial intelligence programs are eventually shaped. This core consists of production systems, graph search, rule-based inference (based on the Resolution Principle) and heuristic control. These are all embodied in the General Problem Solver.

The General Problem Solver

A General problem solver is formed from three distinct elements: the global database, transformation rules (or production rules) and a control strategy (Nilson 1998). The global database represents the problem states, the transformation rules express how a database may change to conform with the problem, and the control strategy decides from all the applicable transformations which one should be applied next to achieve the solution (goal state). All the rules can have access to the global database at all times, but they must not act upon themselves or the control strategy.

Each rule has a precondition that relates to the global database and describes when the rule can be used. If the precondition is satisfied, then the rule can be applied to the database to transform it into a new state. The control strategy chooses the rule by drawing upon some heuristic knowledge about the nature of the problem and its solution. It is called 'heuristic' because it is 'an aid to discovery' (i.e. helps find the goal). It does not necessarily have any analytic foundation but calls upon a deeper understanding of the problem than that apparent in the representation alone. The control strategy ceases computation when it reaches a termination condition; a condition where the objectives are satisfied.

The principle of the production system can be illustrated by the problem of navigating a car through the centre of a town in a foreign country, whose language is unknown to the driver. The goal is to travel through the town from south to north making as few wrong turnings as possible. Unfortunately, the town is old, large and rambling with no regular structure. There is no map of the town available, but there is a compass in the car that gives an approximate indication of north.

The global database represents the current junction giving the number of turnings, the density of houses and a history of such junctions ordered according to their encounter. The transformation rules are marked by the choice of turnings at each junction. The transformation is the effect of taking a road from the current junction to the next junction. The intermediate road connecting the junctions is the mapping function from state to state. When the mapping function is (initially) unknown, it is called 'implicit'. The act of taking a route makes it 'explicit'. The heuristic for the control strategy is to make a choice that is governed by some crude generalisation of this mapping. The heuristic control strategy could be, for example, 'take the turning that is nearest the northern route'. This heuristic does not guarantee a correct choice, since that route may change direction and even double back on itself. The heuristic can be further enhanced by taking into account the distribution of houses encountered at each junction on the basis that the density of houses usually increases towards the centre of town. The goal is reached when all the houses are in the south and the density of houses at the junction is zero. There may be several such goals since there may be more than one road out of north end of the town.

There are two kinds of heuristics proposed to help find a solution to these problems. The compass provides a clue to the possibility of a particular transformation being a good one to try (the pre-emptive heuristic), and the density of houses indicates the effectiveness of a transformation once it has been tried. The second kind of heuristic (density of houses) illustrates the 'generate-and-test' approach to problem solving where a possibility is explored and then matched against a requirement. There is also the driver's memory of the roads traversed so that going in a circle can be avoided.

Graph Search

A problem space can be represented as a directed graph (see Fig. 7.9) where each node is a particular state of the global database. Each directed arc that connects the nodes is a transformation applied to one state and converts it into another. In the case of the town, the problem space is topologically equivalent to the road map of the town; the junctions are the states and the connecting roads are the transformations. The arcs and nodes of the problem space are then set within the three-dimensional reference space of the compass points, the distance and the house density.

One of the most used examples is the tiles problem space which consists of nodes showing the distribution of tiles within the grid, and arcs indicating the moves that take one pattern of tiles to the next. One of the tiles is missing so that the remaining tiles can slide within a frame into that space. The tiles have to remain in the frame so rearrangement of the tiles has to be done by using the space. Each tile has some

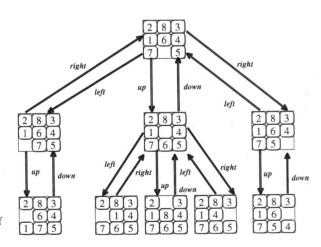

Fig. 7.9 A segment of the tiles problem space. Direct of 'space' given

pattern on, in this case numbers, and the purpose is to reorganise the tiles so that a specified goal pattern is achieved. Figure 7.9 shows a small segment of the tiles problem space, and an examination of symmetries of such a problem spaces may also imply some elegant solutions.

In practice, most complete problem spaces are too large to store within a computer, and it is not necessary to have all the problem space since the solution is only concerned with a small part. Itineraries given for holiday travel only plot 'the solution' ignoring most of the surrounding terrain, and it is desirable, in the 'town problem', to find the shortest route with minimum effort. What would be better is some surety that the route is the shortest. One result from graph search theory is that such an assurance is given provided certain conditions are met. These conditions are that the heuristic rules must be 'optimistic' in that they should always underestimate the number of actual steps needed to solve the problem. The more accurate this estimate the less 'trial' transformations are needed to find the shortest path.

The 'And/Or' Graph

The And/Or graph is a familiar procedure in many AI systems and it forms the backbone to Expert Systems and Knowledge Based Systems in general. However, the And/Or process, as described above, is complex enough to represent a design challenge. If a design method introduces new mechanisms of achieving at least the same result as others, it can suggest improvements and it proves to be useful then that method is worth keeping as an approach.

The And/Or graph is already an abstraction of the process of problem solving. The assumption is that the problem domain (task domain or World) can be expressed as a set of groups of 'facts'. These groups of facts describe different situations that might occur in the task domain if the process of problem solving is actually carried out. The problem is described in terms of an initial state and a goal situation. There is also a set of actions that are dependent on the situation under consideration and these actions change the facts so as to change the situation. These are referred to as transformation rules. Consider a very simple illustration:

A boy collects stamps (M).

He has a:

- winning conker (C),
- bat (B),
- small toy animal (A).

We can describe the situation in problem space terms as
Initial State of Database = (C, B, A)
Transformation rules (value of different swaps he can make):

- *IF C THEN* (D, S)
- *IF C THEN* (B, M)

Fig. 7.10 Swapping toys

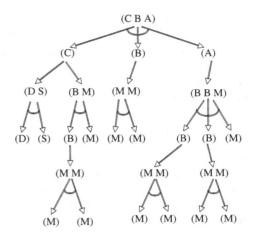

- *IF B THEN* (M, M)
- *IF A THEN* (B, B, M)

Goal: to be left with only stamps M

How can he get all stamps M by swapping the toys he does not want?

Figure 7.10 shows the route to a solution where the boy accumulates a different range of toys each of which can be further swapped.

This example is also a puzzle that can be deconstructed into smaller parallel puzzles each of which has to be solved before a complete solution is obtained.

Emergent Analysis Stage

Figure 7.11 is an illustration of a problem solving activities of these kind showing different possibilities (it is not the given example). Each node in the graph represents a situation and each arrow an action that leads to a new situation. The ties between the arrows indicate that the problem has been decomposed so that each of the tied paths has to lead to a solution. In the illustration given in Fig. 7.11 the top node (initial situation) has two possible decompositions. Other situations generated from the first can also be decomposed. The tied arrows are referred to as 'k-connectors' and are considered to behave like a single multi-headed arrow (k number of heads).

If we now consider the And/Or Graph as an object in its own right irrespective of its interpretation then there are clearly two kinds of objects that form the graph; these are Nodes and K-Connectors. The initial Conceptual Model of the graph is shown in Fig. 7.12. The cardinality relationship between the two objects is 'many-to-many'

Fig. 7.11 And/Or Graph

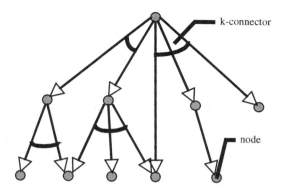

Fig. 7.12 First attempt at a conceptual model (see Fig. 7.13)

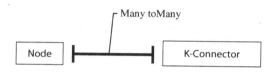

in that a node can be associated with (connected to) many k-connectors and a k-connector may be associated with (bound by) many nodes.

It is known that such a model where a many-to-many constraint is included that this is likely to lead to difficulties; it does not lead to a good structure. However, the data types can be defined for a functional specification and these are shown as Clarity diagrams in Fig. 7.13.

Figure 7.13 defines a node as consisting of a value (a description of the situation that may be complex) and a list of k-connectors associated with each node. The list may be empty. A k-connector consists of a list of nodes. Each description is bounded by a constructor (the dotted box) that packages (constructs) the objects; these are 'Node' and 'K_Connector' in this example.

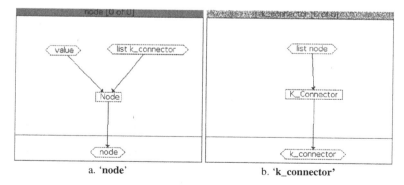

a. 'node'   b. 'k_connector'

Fig. 7.13 First attempt at a model

These data types, which are defined in Clarity, suggest a simple and obvious structure, a structure that is mutually recursive. However, we know from experience that functions, which manipulate this structure, become very complex and difficult to define unless the functions are only concerned with local information. Thus, the control and use of such a structure where global information is required for local decisions is awkward to achieve. Since in the And/Or graph the cumulative costs of actions is used to make local decisions as to the viability of a particular solution path and these costs also depend upon parallel paths that have evolved from decomposition elsewhere in the graph, this structure is not recommended.

The design problem we now have is how do we remove the many-to-many constraint. This can be done by reconsidering the And/Or graph by viewing it differently; do a further abstraction. Figure 7.14 shows how this new abstraction may be visualised in that by encircling the k-connector it suggests a k-connector node joining all nodes with a simple arrows. Thus if the objects are simplified to normal binary arrows but incorporate the idea of the k-connector as another kind of node (thus two types of node are now involved) then we will eliminate the mutual recursive structure. However, to compensate we will need a structural grammar to ensure that the two types of node alternate.

This new abstraction makes it possible to see a more general extension of the concept of a k-connector to a jk-connector as shown in Fig. 7.15. A possible

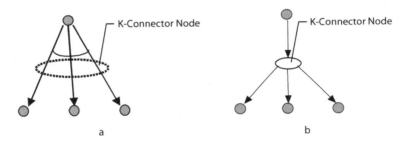

Fig. 7.14 Introduce K-connector node

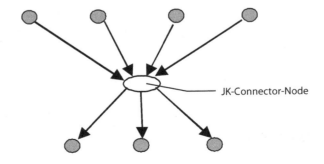

Fig. 7.15 A generalisation: JK-connector node

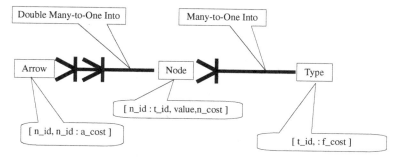

Fig. 7.16 Conceptual model of JK-And/Or Graph

interpretation of this extension is that an action may depend on several situations to be merged before it can be decomposed into an alternative set of situations.

Figure 7.16 shows an alternative conceptual model to that of Fig. 7.12 where no distinction is made between the two types of node except through the attribute t_id (indicates type). The arrow is identified by its start node (arrow tail) and its terminating node (arrow head). These nodes are distinguished by a number <n_id> and so an arrow is distinguished by a unique pair of nodes. Each arrow also has a cost associated with the transformation <a_cost>. The node contains a foreign key that identifies its type (normal or jk node). It will have a value and a cost. The type of node may also incur further costs <f_cost>. The Clarity description of this new abstraction is given in Fig. 7.17.

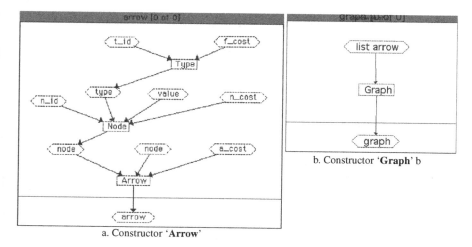

Fig. 7.17 Second attempt at model

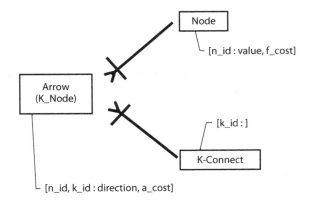

Fig. 7.18 Third attempt at
the conceptual model

This particular specification allows two nodes of the same type to be connected and this can lead to the wrong structure being formed unless special construction functions inhibit this possibility. However, this potential for error suggests a modification on the original conceptual model. Figure 7.18 separates out the two different kinds of node into two different classes of object. This then encourages different descriptions of these objects and allows these descriptions to be expressed.

Figure 7.19 shows the Clarity description of these objects as constructor type definitions. However, the structure of k_node types can be simplified by deconstructing the diagrams in Fig. 7.19 to the diagrams in Fig. 7.20. The 'flattening' of the types into simple types is equivalent to the normalisation of relations. Graph now has to carry all three lists of structures to describe all situations created by the process of stepping through the And/Or graph.

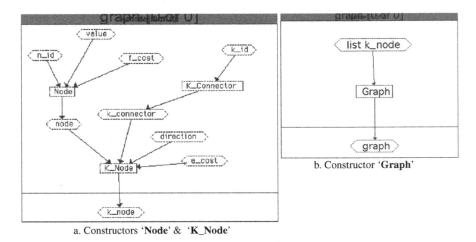

a. Constructors 'Node' & 'K_Node'

b. Constructor 'Graph'

Fig. 7.19 Third attempt at model

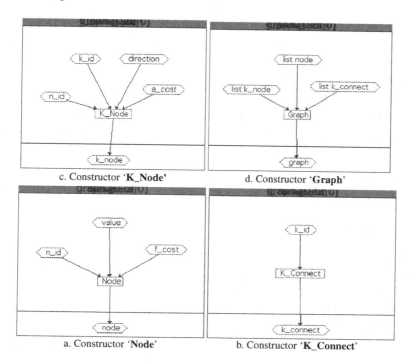

c. Constructor '**K_Node**'   d. Constructor '**Graph**'

a. Constructor '**Node**'   b. Constructor '**K_Connect**'

Fig. 7.20 Data types for And/Or Graph

The final form of the data types for the And/Or graph are shown in Fig. 7.21. Adding additional structures to cope with other details that emerged during implementation required the modification of the types proposed in Fig. 7.20. However,

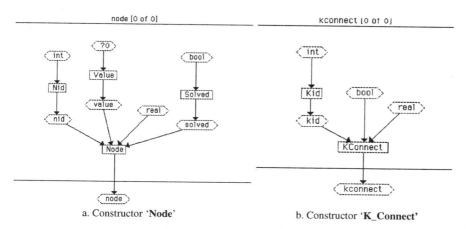

a. Constructor '**Node**'   b. Constructor '**K_Connect**'

Fig. 7.21 Data schema for And/Or Graph

they are both essentially the same. The final form of the objects is then represented as a set of normalised relations:

Node[identifier: value, cost, solution state].

K_Connector[identifier: marked state, cost].

KNode[node and k-connector identifiers: direction (Up or Down), cost].

Graph[(lists of nodes), (lists of kconnectors), (lists of knodes)].| **Null_Graph**

Figure 7.21 is a schematic of each constructor.

Construction Stage

The design process now changes in style and purpose from the analysis stage to the construction stage where the operations on the graph have to be defined. This follows the accepted idea that we create a special mathematics/calculus for our problem and this mathematics/calculus requires a set of complete operations (transformations and combinations) to work on the types of objects that the analysis of the task has proposed. Using the function notation for description, the general outline of the major operations can be listed in Table 7.4. These functions are the primitives from which all other operations may be constructed.

From these functions the final top-level view is given by the function **ao_solve**; it is the system level view of the And/Or graph search system (Fig. 7.22).

This function takes the parameters **list sym** and **?0** where **list sym** describes the environment in which the problem is specified, i.e. the rules, the goals and the cost function. **?0** is the starting value. The output is a **bool**, i.e. True or False, indicating if a solution is found or not. A side effect of the function is to draw the solution paths. For example, consider a toy world that represents the rules by which toys (letters in this case) can be swapped (Fig. 7.10). These rules would be as follows:

> x -> [c b a] thus x can be swapped for c b and a,
>
> c -> [d s] or [b m m] that is c can be swapped for d and s or b and 2 ms (different from the initial example in Fig. 7.10),
>
> b -> [m m] hence b is swapped for 2 ms,
>
> a -> [b b m] and a can be swapped for 2 bs and an m.

The purpose is to swap until all the toys are 'm's. The system will attempt to minimise the cost so 'm' is worth zero and all else is 10 units. This is the heuristic to aid finding the solution and is represented for our system as follows where QUERY shows what each function provides (Fig. 7.23):

Table 7.4 Major 'And/Or' operations

Function	Declaration	Description
expand	graph -> node -> list node	Expands a node by listing all the connecting nodes. Each sub-list groups the nodes together according to the intervening k-connectors
kexpand	graph -> node -> list kconnect	To enable expand to work a finer step of moving from a node to the list of k-connectors
nexpand	graph -> kconnect -> list node	Also required to enable expand is the next step from a k-connector to the list of nodes
rule_expand	rule -> node ->graph	A rule takes a node (a situation) and expands to a sub-graph
add_graphs	graph -> graph -> graph	This adds graphs together. It is a consequence of rule_expand
get_newnid	graph -> nid	Graphs need to be created from the elements of nodes and k-connectors
get_newkid	graph -> kid	as for get_newnid
term_test	value -> bool	This is a test that is applied to a node to determine if the goal has been reached
goal_test	(value -> bool) -> node -> bool	This applies term_test to a node
update_solved_state	(value -> bool) -> graph -> graph	This modifies the costings in the graph
test_solved	node -> bool	Determines if a particular node is solved (lead to a goal)
display_solved	graph -> node -> graph	Returns the sub-graph that is the solution path

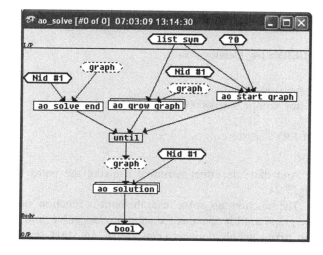

Fig. 7.22 Top-level function *ao_solve*

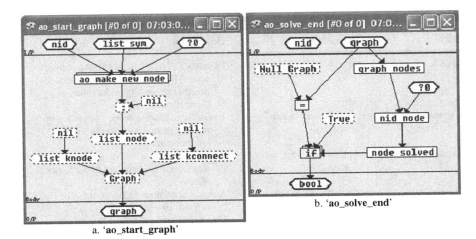

a. 'ao_start_graph'

b. 'ao_solve_end'

Fig. 7.23 Subsidiary functions to *ao_solve*

QUERY> toy_world
[toy_rule toy_term_test toy_cost]
QUERY> list_fdefs toy_rule

[
   [toy_rule ?0nil]
   [toy_rule 'x'[['c' 'b' 'a']]]
   [toy_rule 'c'[['d' 's']['b' 'm' 'm']]]
   [toy_rule 'b'[['m' 'm']]]
   [toy_rule 'a'[['b' 'b' 'm']]]
]
QUERY> list_fdefs toy_term_test

[
   [toy_term_test ?0 (= ?0 'm')]
]
QUERY> list_fdefs toy_cost

[
   [toy_cost ?0 #r10.000000]
   [toy_cost 'm' #r0.000000]
]
QUERY> ao_solve toy_world 'x'

True

And the side effect narrative showing the paths to the solution is given in Fig. 7.24.

The function '**ao_solve**' uses the built-in function '**until**' to loop around growing the graph until it contains the solution. '**ao_solve_end**' delivers '**True**' or '**False**', '**ao_grow_graph**' delivers a new graph, '**ao_start_graph**' delivers a starting graph,

Fig. 7.24 Output of *ao-solve*
for toy world

narrative

```
x -> [ c b a ]
  c -> [ b m m ]
    b -> [ m m ]
  b -> [ m m ]
  a -> [ b b m ]
    b -> [ m m ]
    b -> [ m m ]
```

and '**ao_solution**' shows the solution. The subsidiary functions are shown in Fig. 7.23.

There are two components to '**ao_grow_graph**'. The first is used in the general case, the second in the special case where the graph consists of one node only as can be seen in Fig. 7.25 and 7.26.

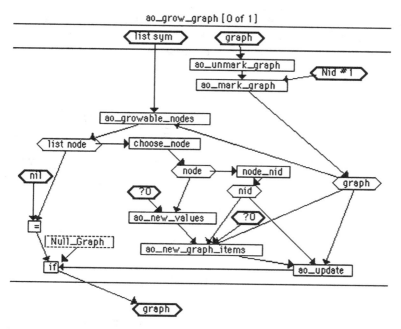

Fig. 7.25 The original growing a graph from rules: general case

Fig. 7.26 The original
growing a graph from rules:
special case of no
K-connectors

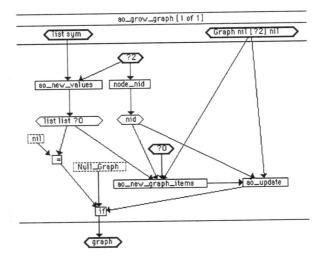

The difference can be seen in the pattern of the parameters. In general it is best
to try to avoid function graphs that are over-complicated. For instance, it is a good
idea to keep the computation involved in part of a function separate from its role in
the function. As an example of this change, look at '**ao_make_new_node**', used in
'**ao_start_graph**' in Fig. 7.27.

It would be cleaner to keep all components of Node at about the same level, i.e.
to rewrite as two functions. We can do this by using the schematic editing facilities. You can either cut and paste into a new window using the tool bar facilities
or highlight the subset of functions to be made into a function and then go to

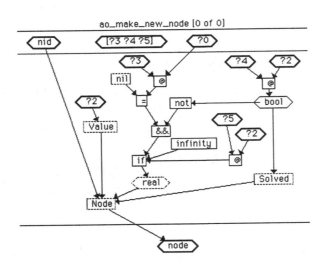

Fig. 7.27 Initial attempt at
making new nodes

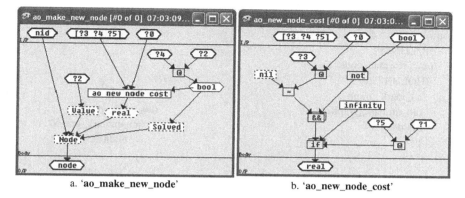

a. 'ao_make_new_node'   b. 'ao_new_node_cost'

Fig. 7.28 Second attempt at making a new node and keeping a conceptual level

edit menu and select 'copy selection to new window'. The new window can then be adapted to be a function and committed. The highlighted functions in the first window can be cut and replaced by the new function. When this is done we get Fig. 7.28.

The functional code generated in the general case is shown below. Note the wide use of HOLDN generated by the schematic as a means of retaining efficient operations.

Now the computation is separate, and '**ao_make_new_node**' is more general as the costing is now independent. Another example of simplification can be found in **ao_grow_graph.** It is a good candidate for simplification because there is just too much detail in the diagram. It can be replaced as shown in Fig. 7.29.

With a little redesign, '**ao_node_graph**' will simplify the other component of '**ao_grow_graph**' and we get Fig. 7.30.

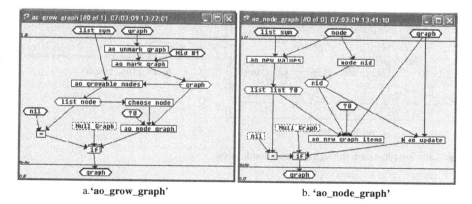

a.'ao_grow_graph'   b. 'ao_node_graph'

Fig. 7.29 Second attempt at growing a graph and simplification

```
ao_grow_graph?0?1::=                                                    )
   if(=nil                                                            )
    (HOLDN#5                                                        )
     (ao_growable_nodes?0                                         )
     (HOLDN#25                                                  )
      (ao_mark_graph                                  (HOLDN#25
       (ao_unmark_graph?1)                              (ao_mark_graph
        (Nid#1)                                           (ao_unmark_graph?1)
       )                                                   (Nid#1)
      )                                                   )
     )                                                  )
    )                                                );
   )
        Null_Graph                                 ao_grow_graph?0
    (ao_node_graph?0                                       (Graph nil
     (choose_node                                          (:?2nil)
      (HOLDN#5                                             nil)::=
       (ao_growable_nodes?0                               ao_node_graph?0?2
       (HOLDN#25                                          (Graph nil
        (ao_mark_graph                                    [?2]
         (ao_unmark_graph?1)                              Nil
          (Nid#1)                                  )
                                                   ;
```

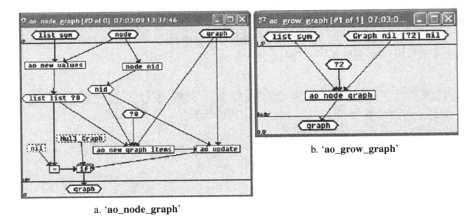

a. 'ao_node_graph'

Fig. 7.30 Simplification through concept modification

And the function, which grows a graph from a single node, has been quite clearly abstracted out.

In Summary

The environment of a Schema Interpreter such as Clarity fulfils the ideals of a specification language (in Chapter 1). The relational analysis is orientated to defining normalised objects that can also be interpreted as functions. Both relations and functions have a well-understood calculus and this suggests that some of this work could be incorporated into a design method. Errors in the schema are rare because the diagrams are kept simple and type checked. The diagrams also encourage the multi-layering of concept domains. The seemingly natural law that has emerged is that machine or library level functions will tend to devolve to the lower levels. At the same time there is always a simple description available at each stage. The approach is still evolving but even in its current form it provides a design method that is almost complete; you still need insight.

Exercises 7.1

1. Draw a Conceptual Model of the chest size problem in Chapter 6.
2. Generalise it to include alternative measurements such as collar size and arm length with price adjustment for non-normal combinations. Also include price.
3. Take the function '**chest_aux**' as described in Chapter 6 (Fig. 6.7) and turn it into a recursive function.
4. Make this function non-recursive by using a higher-order function (e.g. '**foldr**')
5. Adapted '**Chest2**' to include the generalisations and to print out an invoice.

Questions 7.1

1. Give one advantage and one disadvantage of a functional language compared with an imperative language.
2. Why don't you need any special de-bugging tools for Clarity?
3. Why should the model of a problem domain be represented by extensional functions?
4. What is the difference between a relational database and a functional database?
5. What is a 'malignant side effect'?
6. In what ways can evaluation be controlled and why should this control be needed?
7. What can insure a solution, if it exists, to the graph search method of problem solving and why?

Project: Learning from Defeat

Oxo2: The Game Player That Learns: A Continuation

Develop a Simple Learning Strategy

We will not use the GPS in this project but we will show how to add a little interest
to the OXO game. We will make some modifications to allow x to remember, for
a given state of the grid, one move that resulted in a win. For example, if the grid
looks like this:

```
x . x          1 2 3
. o o          4 5 6
x o .          7 8 9
```

and x happens to choose square 2 it wins. It will remember that for [#1 #3 #7] the
best play is #2.

If, in another game, the grid looks like this:

```
x o x          1 2 3
. o o          4 5 6
x . .          7 8 9
```

x will 'remember' that square 2 would be a winning move, but x cannot make that
move. If x happens to choose square 4 and wins, it will still remember that for [#1
#3 #7] the best play is #2. From a GPS point of view the OXO program can learn
'winning' transformations.

Looking for a Win

Look at '**best_play**' in Diagram 7.1. The general version will be used if there is no
match, and returns #0, which means there is no known best play here for a given
list. If the grid is empty, the input parameter to '**best_play**' is '**nil**' and the list is
empty then we allow x to occupy the centre of the grid. Here we cheat a little by
using some pre-knowledge. An alternative is to choose a square a random.

(1) *Define the function **best_play**.

Other components of '**best_play**' will be built up as more games are played. This
is OXO's memory.

Diagram 7.1 'best_play'
memory function

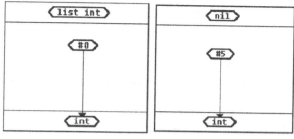

a. 'best_play' general.   b. 'best_play' specific.

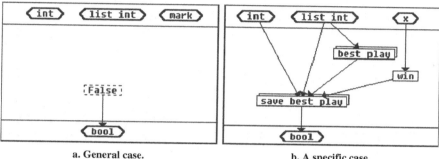

a. General case.   b. A specific case.

Diagram 7.2 'save_play'

Remembering the Winning Moves

Look at function '**save_play**' in Diagram 7.2.

The first parameter is the chosen square. The second parameter is the list of squares already taken by the player, and the third parameter is the mark, x or o. If '**best_play**' returns #0, then this play has not been saved so far. In addition, the play will only be worth saving if x has won. So the last two parameters to '**save_best_play**' must be #0 and '**True**' because '**win**' returns '**True**'.

Look at **save_best_play** in Diagram 7.3.

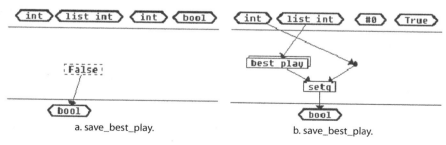

a. save_best_play.   b. save_best_play.

Diagram 7.3 'save_best_play'

The 'best play' is saved only when the last two parameters match #0 and 'True'. The saving is done by using 'setq', for example, if the first two parameters are #2 and [#1 #3 #7] then 'best_play [#1 #3 #7]' would return #2.

(2) *Define the function **save_best_play**.

(3) *Define the function **save_play**.

Choosing the Winning Move

The function '**choose_for** x' has changed in Diagram 7.4. There is more to do than choosing '**any_free_square**'. Working from the top, we find out '**where** x' is already, and a list of integers is returned, representing the squares. Then we look for a best play for that list by calling '**best_play**', which will match if that play has been remembered from a previous game. The function '**best_play**' will either return a number from #1 to #9 or #0. We can say '**x** will make a **choice**' (i.e. '**x_choice**') depending on that number.

The function '**x_choice**', in Diagram 7.5, is quite straightforward. If there is a best play, choose it, otherwise choose any free square as in Version 1.

This is a good opportunity to illustrate the difference between 'if' and 'pattern-match'. The function '**choose_for**' in Diagram 7.4 could have been constructed like that in Diagram 7.6 instead of using the function '**x_choice**'. '**best_play**' returns an integer, which is tested against #0, and 'if' used to determine which result to return.

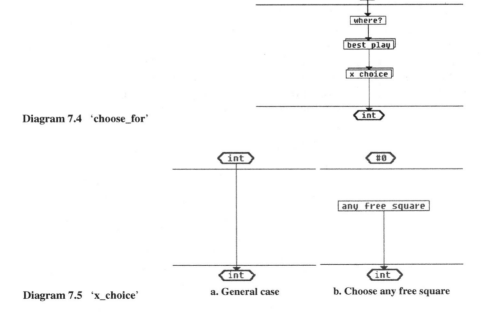

Diagram 7.4 'choose_for'

Diagram 7.5 'x_choice'   **a. General case**   **b. Choose any free square**

Diagram 7.6 'choose_for'
(an alternative using '**if**')

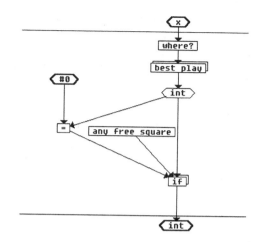

(4) *Define the function ' **x_choice**'.
(5) *Amend the function ' **choose_for** ' as in Diagram 7.6

Pulling It All Together

Lastly, we must add a new component to the function '**play**' for x. Look at Diagram 7.7.

The function '**progN**' has four tasks to do in order.

First, find out where x is BEFORE making a choice. It is important as it is this list that is saved in '**best_play**', not the new list with the latest choice added to it. If we did not do this first, then '**save_play**' would get the wrong parameter, as the saving is done after the choice is made, and then '**where?**' would return the new list.

This kind of situation can be complicated and cause errors that are sometimes difficult to find.

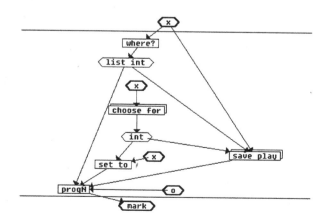

Diagram 7.7 'play' (extra
component)

The next task for '**progN**' is to choose a square for x and to set it to x.

Then call '**save_play**', which will save the choice if x has won, and the play is not already saved.

Lastly '**progN**' returns o for the next play in the game.

(6) *Add a new component to play as shown in Diagram 7.7

So if you play '**oxo**' now, it will learn from the games you play on how to find a winning move. If you wish to keep its learning for each session then you should save the database. That way, all the extra components of '**best_play**' will be retained until next time. If you want '**oxo**' to forget all it has learnt then type in the control window:

QUERY>forget best_play
True

Finally for Stage 2

Save your database and call it '**OXO2A**'.

Create a network view by opening a network window, go to the find 'menu' and click on 'Create/Update network from database'. This may require a little rearranging and the deletion of some functions to look neat. A proposed arrangement is shown Diagram 7.8. When you are satisfied with its appearance, commit it as before. Other views of the network, showing different functionality, can be created in separate network windows.

However, we can do better than this if we could remember all the winning combinations rather than just the first one. This is done in OXO version 3.

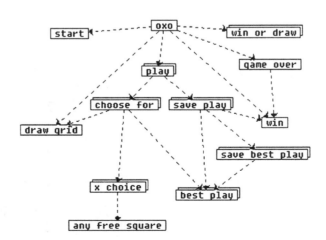

Diagram 7.8 Network of selected functions for '**OXO2A**'

Oxo3: The Game Player That Learns: Another Improvement

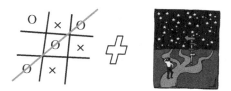

Improve the Simple Learning Strategy

In **Stage 2**, **version 2**, if x remembers that #2 is a winning play if you have squares [#1 #3 #7], then winning with #4 later in the game is not remembered.

Remembering All the Winning Moves

In this version of the game, we can remember both. We replace the function 'best_play' with 'best_plays'. For any of the squares already taken, we remember a list of winning plays rather than a single play.

(1) *Define the function 'best_plays' in Diagram 7.9.

Look at 'save_play' in Diagram 7.10, where 'best_play' is replaced by 'best_plays', and 'save_best_play' is replaced by 'save_best_plays'.

The function 'save_best_plays' in Diagram 7.11 needs some explanation.

The second component uses the built-in function 'filter', which filters out all the numbers in the third parameter that are not equal to the first parameter. For example, 'filter (!= #3) [#1 #3 #7]' will return [#1 #7]. Then the built-in Constructor ':' (where the colon here is pronounced 'cons'[6]) is used to attach this number to the head of the filtered list. For example ': #3 [#1 #7]' returns [#3 #1 #7]. This is to ensure that there are no repeated numbers in the list. If #3 had not already been in the list, this function would have the effect of adding it to the list.

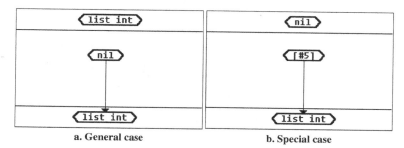

a. General case   b. Special case

Diagram 7.9 'best_plays'

---

[6] This comes from the list processing language 'LISP'.

Diagram 7.10 'save_play' (amended)

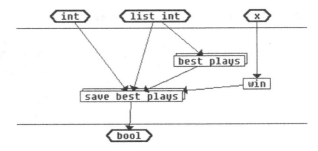

The third component is the case where there are no best plays yet for a given grid state for x. This component merely makes a list of one number by adding it to the empty list **nil**.

(2) *Define the function '**save_best_plays**' in Diagram 7.11.

(3) *Amend the function '**save_play**' in Diagram 7.10.

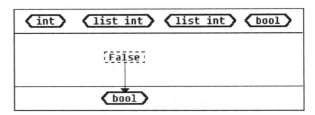

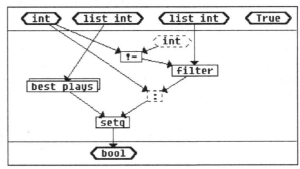

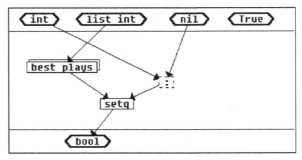

Diagram 7.11
'save_best_plays'

Selecting the Best

The function 'choose_for' x will be changed as in Diagram 7.12. The function 'best_plays' will return a list of remembered winning squares. These have to be 'filter'ed to find the **empty** squares (see Diagram 7.13). The function 'empty' returns **True** if a square is empty. Then x has to choose from a list of empty squares. This new function, 'x_choiceL' in Diagram 7.14 is similar to 'x_choice'. If the list is empty, choose the head, i.e. the first in the list. Otherwise, choose any free square.

(4) *Define the function 'empty' Diagram 7.13.

(5) *Define the function 'x_choiceL' Diagram 7.14.

(6) *Amend the function 'choose_for' Diagram 7.12.

You are now ready to play OXO. After a while **oxo** begins to find most of the winning moves. However, we can still do better than this. Try the stage 4.

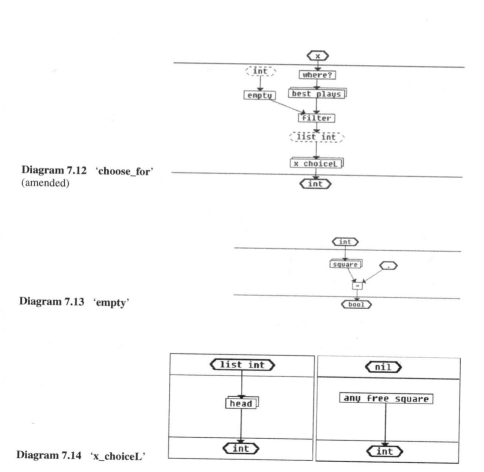

Diagram 7.12 'choose_for' (amended)

Diagram 7.13 'empty'

Diagram 7.14 'x_choiceL'

Diagram 7.15 Network of
selected functions for OXO3

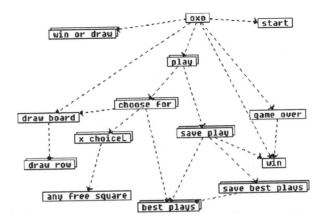

Finally for Stage 3

Save your database and call it 'OXO3A'. Create a network view by opening a network window, go to the find 'menu' and click on 'Create/Update network from
database'. This may require a little rearranging and the deletion of some functions
to look neat. A proposed arrangement is shown in Diagram 7.15. When you are
satisfied with its appearance, commit it just like a function window. Other views
of the network, showing different functionality, can be created in separate network
windows.

Oxo4: The Game Player That Does Even Better

Learning from Opponents and Using Tactics

In this version, x not only remembers its own winning choices, but those of o too.
This is achieved by simply amending the function '**play**' as in Diagram 7.16 to
proceed in the same way for both x and o.

Making Things Symmetrical

In Diagram 7.16 the symbol '**?0**' stands for '**mark**' since this is a way of referring
to the first parameter to the function '**play**'.

Diagram 7.16 'play'

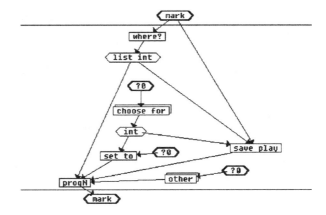

(1) *Amend the general function '**play**' as in Diagram 7.16

(2) *Remove the special case for **x** in '**play** '.

Now x will learn from o so all the user's winning moves will be remembered too. This will not be any advantage unless x has the same grid state as o had when o won. This will never happen if x always takes the centre first. For example, '**best_plays [#1 #2]**' will probably return **[#3]** after a few games, but x will never have **[#1 #2]**. The player x will always have #5 plus some other numbers. Player o will never have #5.

(3) *Remove the special case for '**nil**' in '**best_play**'.

Finally for Stage 4

Save your data base and call it 'OXO4A'. Create a network view by opening a network window, go to the find 'menu' and click on 'Create/Update network from

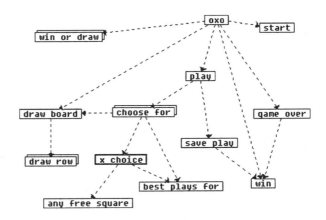

Diagram 7.17 Network of selected function for OXO4

database'. This may require a little rearranging and the deletion of some functions to look neat. A proposed arrangement is shown Diagram 7.17. When you are satisfied with its appearance, commit it just like a function window. Other views of the network, showing different functionality, can be created in separate network windows.

Oxo5: Hindering the Opponent

In this final version of the game, if x cannot win it tries to stop o from winning. It does this by looking for a winning move for o, i.e. choosing as if it were o and thus blocking the winning move for o.

Combining the Effort

As we need to look at the best plays for o as well as x, we introduce a new function, '**best_plays_for**' in Diagram 7.18. This will be familiar as part of '**choose_for**' in **Version 4**.

(4) *Define '**best_plays_for**' in Diagram 7.18.

The function '**choose_for x**' will be amended as in Diagram 7.19.
This function '**choose_fo r**' calls the function '**x_choice_fo r**' instead of '**x_choice L**' as in **Version 3** and **Version 4**. The function '**x_choice L**' had two components, essentially a winning move for x or any free square. The function '**x_choice_fo r**' has three components to correspond to three situations: a winning move for x, a winning move for o, or any free square.

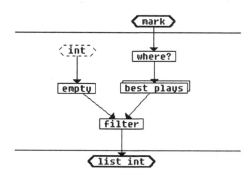

Diagram 7.18
'best_plays_for'

Diagram 7.19 'choose for'
(amended)

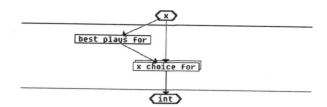

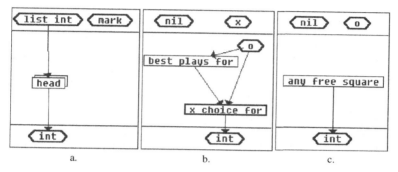

Diagram 7.20 'x_choice_for'

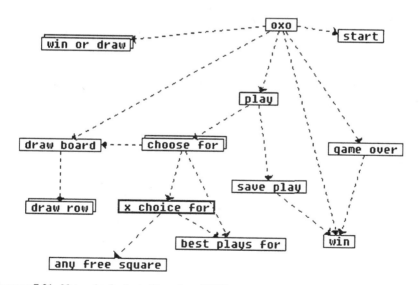

Diagram 7.21 Network of selected functions OXO5

Look at '**x_choice_for**' in Diagram 7.20. On the first call, the '**mark**' is '**x**'. If the list is not empty, there is a winning move for x, and the first in the list is taken. If the list is empty, '**x_choice_for**' will be called with the '**mark**' set to '**o**'. If the list is not empty, the first one will be chosen. If the list of winning moves for o is empty, any free square is chosen.

(5) *Define the function '**x_choice_for**' in Diagram 7.20.

(6) *Amend the function '**choice_for**' in Diagram 7.19.

You are all ready to play a smart oxo player that can only become smarter.

Finally for Stage 5

Save your database and call it 'OXO5A'. Create a network view as shown in Diagram 7.21.

References

Addis, T. R. (1985) '*Designing Knowledge-Based Systems*' Prentice-Hall, Upper Saddle River, NJ, ISBN 0-13-201823-3.

Date, C. J. (1995) '*An Introduction to Database Systems*' Sixth edition, Addis-Wesley Publishing Company, Boston, MA, ISBN 0-201-82458-2.

Newell, A. and Simon, H. A. (1963) *GPS, a Program that Simulates Human Thought. Computers and Thought* edited by Feigenbaum, E. A. and Fieldman, J., McGraw-Hill Book Company, New York, Library of Congress Catalog Card Number 63-17596.

Newell, A., Shaw, J. C. and Simon, H. A. (1963) '*Empirical Explorations with the logic theory machine: a case study in heuristics*', Computers and Thought, editied by Feigenbaum, E. A. and Fieldman, J., McGraw-Hill Book Company, Library of Congress Catalog Card Number 63-17596.

Nilson, N. J., (1998) '*Artificial Intelligence: A new Synthesis*', Morgan Kaufmann publishers Inc, San Mateo, California, ISBN 1-55860-535-5.

Chapter 8
Adult Things

> *When I was a child, I spake as a child, I understood as a child, I thought as a child; but when I became a man I put away childish things.*
>
> Corinthians 13, 11

Introduction

The essential purpose behind Clarity is to provide a design environment within which designs and ideas can be created, changed and explored with minimum effort. The price for this flexibility is an over simplified input/output and reduction in performance. However, once a suitable solution has been found then these limitations can be side stepped by using a visual development language, such as MSVC, that can be integrated with the Faith interpreter and the creation of one's own C++ code to replace some of the interpreted functions. This means that any Clarity developed program can always be extended to incorporate any functionality that a computer system can provide. There really are no limitations.

In addition to the possibility of creating your own functions, there is some useful functionality that extends the development environment. Some of these extra features are available via menu items and some are provided as built-in functions. Since our philosophy is that everything you can do with a computer should be possible in the language we have made, in some cases the features are available in both forms.

Graphics Operations

gr_operations

For the purposes of developing ideas quickly without the need to construct a full graphics interface a simple graphics window is provided. There is a set of functions that will allow simple shapes to be constructed and have some limited movement

T. Addis, J. Addis, *Drawing Programs: The Theory and Practice of Schematic Functional Programming*, DOI 10.1007/978-1-84882-618-2_8,
© Springer-Verlag London Limited 2010

provided by the rapid redrawing of sequences of diagrams. This set includes setting the colour for the graphics operations. It is possible to have a set of graphics windows in which a drawing can be created by using a set of primitives. The graphics window normally chosen by default is #1 otherwise the command

> QUERY> gr_setcurrwin #2
> True

will set the next gr_ function to the graphic 2 window. In this way you can draw different drawings in separate windows. Figure 8.1 shows a function '**drawGrid**' that produces a grid in graphics window 1 (the default).

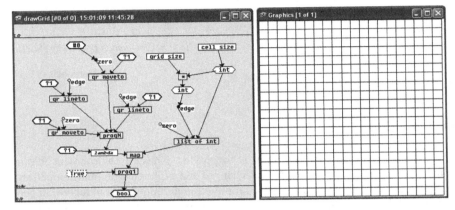

Fig. 8.1 '**drawGrid**' generates a grid in a graphics window

> QUERY> drawGrid
> True

Note that

> QUERY> list_of_int #0 (* grid_size cell_size) cell_size
> [#0 #20 #40 #60 #80 #100 #120 #140 #160 #180 #200 #220 #240
> #260 #280 #300 #320 #340 #360 #380 #400]

> QUERY> cell_size
> #20

> QUERY> grid_size
> #20

The graphics functions work as though you were guiding a mechanically operated pen over a sheet of paper. This means that the start position is always where the pen was left. This is so that only the destination is needed in order to draw a line with '**gr_lineto**' <x> <y>. The position (#0 #0), by computer standards, is the top left hand corner of the graphics window. Positive positions move to the right and down (Fig. 8.2).

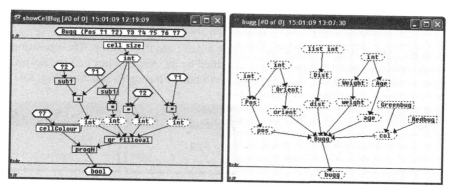

Fig. 8.2 'showCellBug' displays a *green* or *red circle* in the graphics window

Fig. 8.3 The result of
'showCellBug'

There are also a few primitive figures, such as ovals, rectangles and triangles both filled and unfilled, that can be displayed. These are designed to follow a simple scheme based on their position. The following query will show a green circle in the second cell on the first line. The circle will fill the 20×20 cell and will appear as shown in Fig. 8.3:

> QUERY> showCellBug (Bugg (Pos #1 #2) #1 #2 #3 #2 Greenbug)
> True

In this example '**Bugg**' is a constructor that packages the information about a bug, such as its position, size and colour. Text can also be written where the start position is specified by the parameters as follows:

> QUERY> gr_forecolor Black
> True
> QUERY> gr_text #85 #10 "A Green Bug"
> True

Figure 8.3 shows the result. Movement is achieved by redrawing. The original object image needs to be removed and this may be done by either clearing the graphics window each time using 'gr_clear' or by overwriting the original figure with (gr_forecolor White) before drawing it again in its new position.

btn_operations

There are a set of operations that put out tick boxes onto the desktop. Their position is specified by a parameter and each is identified by an integer. They can be 'ticked' or 'un-ticked' manually by clicking in the small box or through a function (Fig. 8.4).

Fig. 8. 4 Buttons on the desktop

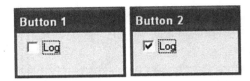

- '**btn_open**' opens a button with a given name and position.

  QUERY> btn_open #1 ["Log" #100 #100 #80 #80]
  True

- '**btn_test**' returns True if the button is checked, False otherwise.

  QUERY> btn_test #1
  False

- '**btn_set**' switches on the check in a button.

  QUERY> btn_set #2
  True

- '**btn_reset**' switches off the check in a button.

  QUERY> btn_reset #1
  True

- '**btn_attr**' returns button attributes, i.e. name and position.

  QUERY> btn_attr #1
  ["fred" #675 #95 #112 #64]

- '**btn_close**' deletes a button.

  QUERY> btn_close #1
  True

Dialog

Interaction with the terminal is clearly an important activity and as we have seen it is not too easy to create a comfortable interface with our current primitives. We have enhanced the primitive '**getchar**' to '**getline**' and also provided a special dialog box (see Fig. 8.5).

Fig. 8.5 Dialog window for
collecting information

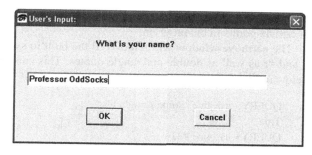

- ' **getline**' reads a string of characters from the keyboard.

  QUERY> getline
  "Hello"

- ' **gr_dialog**' pops up a modal dialog box and returns the user entered text as a
  string or the null string ("") if cancelled.

  QUERY> gr_dialog "What is your name?"
  "Professor OddSocks"

  To match '**getline**' we have instead of '**putchar**':

- ' **putline**' output a string of characters to the control window.

  QUERY> putline "Hello"
  HelloTrue

- ' **print**' prints a string, real, integer, list or symbol to the control window.

  QUERY> print [#24 'w' "jim"]
  [#24 'w' "jim"]True

  For programming we can also use for error messages (as well as the above):

- '**error**' prints an error message in the control window. The output is also the error
  message. Output is classed as generic.

  QUERY> error "Wrong type"
  User error: Wrong type
  (error "Wrong type")

Narrative Window (nar_)

Text has its own window, as we have seen. This is another facility for quick
development of ideas where the initial user interface can be simple. This window
provides a separate output for text to that of the control window. It can be used

effectively for debugging since it allows the programmer to insert print statements at critical points in the program.

The narrative window will remove all the built in syntactic constructors such as # and #r as well as double and single quotes. This can be seen from the examples below in Fig. 8.6.

QUERY> nar_line "Some straight text"
True
QUERY> nar_line #32
True
QUERY> nar_line ["Mixed type in a list" #54 #r3.72 'A' (add1 #45)]
True
QUERY> nar_line "all good men"
True
QUERY> nar_text "come to the aid of the party"
True

Fig. 8.6 The narrative window

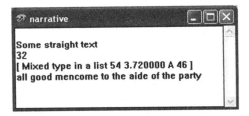

To help with the creation of messages there are string manipulation functions that treat every string as though it were a list of characters. So '**str_head**' will return the first character in the string and '**str_tail**' the string without the first character. Most of the list operations are represented in this group of functions. Another set of functions that are useful are the casting functions '**str_to_words**' and '**words_to_str**' which uses the space character to delineate words. '**str_concat**' is another useful function.

Automatic Junction Insertion for Dependency Networks

Junctions serve the purpose of reducing the complexity of a diagram. In the case of networks there is a facility that will automatically find all the places where a junction will simplify the diagram and insert it. The general rule is that where there are many to many links then these can be reduced by introducing a node. If there are 'n' sources and 'm' sinks then normally this will require n*m links. Using a node, this reduces to n+m links. The process may need to be repeated because the nodes

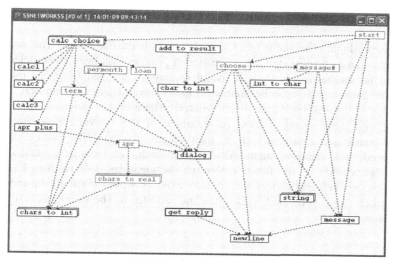

a. Hand-drawn before inserted junction

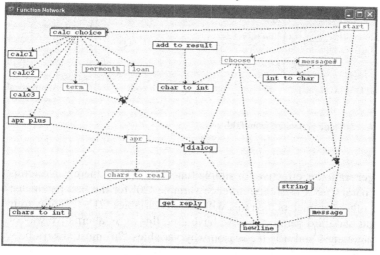

b. Redrawn with inserted junction.

Fig. 8.7 Changes made by automatic junction redrawing

will form new links which may need further reduction so the process can then be repeated on the resulting diagram until no further changes can be made. The menu item 'Redraw Window with Junctions' under 'Features' will perform the task. The original diagram is not replaced by the new one unless you overwrite it through 'commit'. The result can be seen in Fig. 8.7a and b after some rearrangement.

Converting Faith Code to Clarity Diagrams

Sometimes all that is available of a Clarity program is the Faith code. This is likely to occur when a stand-alone Clarity-developed program has been constructed and exported to another machine. It is useful to convert selected functions into the schematic form and this can be done with the 'Faith to Clarity' menu item under 'File' during the display of the Faith window. There is the option of converting all the Faith code to schematics. An example of this conversion is shown in Fig. 8.8 beside a comparison with the hand-created diagram. The Faith code in a highlighted Faith Window (menu Window/new/Faith code) can be generated in a component window of the function through the menu by 'File/Faith to Clarity'. If the function schematic does not already exist as would normally be the case then a schematic is generated. This schematic can then be shown by displaying the function as normal.

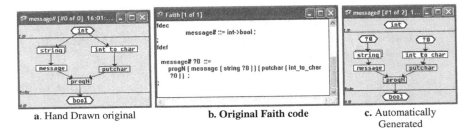

a. Hand Drawn original	b. Original Faith code	c. Automatically Generated

Fig. 8.8 A schematic generated from faith code

This generation is effective for simple functions. Where there is a reference to a function parameter it uses the reference variable '?0' for the first parameter and if there are other parameters then this will use the variables '?1', '?2', etc. to indicate the second and third parameters. We have used this as an alternative way of referencing parameters and it is *the* reason why variables '?n' must always be with an 'n' larger than the number of parameters to avoid confusion with this use of such a variable.

The other inconvenience of the generation is that the HoldN lozenge will be deconstructed by the analysis of the Faith code and then regenerated into its component parts in the new schematic. This deconstruction can be rectified by manually merging all HoldN lozenges that have their first input with the same integer and deleting the redundant input structures. In Fig. 8.9 the integer is #13 (green) and merging as described will remove the redundancy of the function 'choose'. Also for the other HoldN the integer is #15 (red) and here we can remove the repetition of all the functions stemming upwards from 'fix' by a further merge so that we end up with Fig. 8.9a.

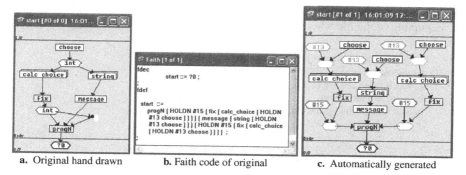

a. Original hand drawn   **b.** Faith code of original   **c.** Automatically generated

Fig. 8.9 The problem with '**HoldN**' in schematic generation

File Operations

Basics

Figure 8.10 shows sets of file communication functions. The initial operation is normally the need to open a file for reading or writing. So the function

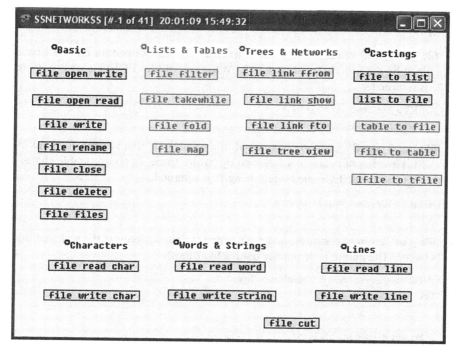

Fig. 8.10 File operations organised according to type

- **'file_open_read'** will open a file for reading only. This starts reading at the beginning of the file where the file named "rainbow" contains (say):

  My heart leaps up when I behold
  A rainbow in the sky:
  So was it when my life began,
  So is it now I am a man,
  So be it when I shall grow old,
  Or let me die!

  QUERY> file_open_read "rainbow"
  True

- **'file_open_write'** opens a new file for writing. If the file exists it returns False. Once written to, a file can only be removed via the operating system or using the function **'file_delete'**.

  QUERY> file_open_write "new1"
  True

- **'file_read_char'** reads the next character in a named file that is open for read. If the file is not opened the function is not evaluated. At end of file the EOF (decode #−1) character is returned.

  QUERY> file_read_char "rainbow"
  'M'

- **'file_read_line'** reads the next line in a named file that is open for read. A line is defined by the decoded character #13. At the end of file (EOF) the empty string "" is returned.

  QUERY> file_read_line "rainbow"
  "y heart leaps up when I behold"

- **'file_read_word'** reads the next word in a named file that is open for read. A word is a string of characters followed by 'white space' (a non-printable character). At end of file EOF the empty string "" is returned.

  QUERY> file_read_word "rainbow"
  "A"

- **'file_cut'** given two strings, and a file name (rainbow), returns the text that lies between. The output is in another named file (lines).

  QUERY> file_cut "So" "," "rainbow" "lines"
  "lines"

  So was it when my life began,
  So is it now I am a man,
  So be it when I shall grow old,

- **'file_close'** closes a given file if open for read or write. Returns False if no file open of given name.

  QUERY> file_close "rainbow"
  True

- **'file_write'** writes an expression to a named file that is open for write. All single and double quotes, '#' and '?' marks are retained. The files may have different extensions and as such will behave differently. We have

  .ddb are Faith files,
  .seg are picture segment files,
  .tmp are temporary and can always be written to but will overwrite the contents,
  .add can always be appended to.

    QUERY> file_write "Table1" (nar_line "Good man")
    True

- **'file_write_char'** writes the next character in a named file that is open for write.

  QUERY> file_write_char "new1" 'A'
  True

- **'file_write_line'** writes the next string followed by a new line in a named file that is open for write.

  QUERY> file_write_line "new1" "rainbow in the sky"
  True

- **'file_write_string'** writes the next string in a named file that is open for write.

  QUERY> file_write_string "new1" "So be it when I shall grow old"
  True

The file "new1" after the previous 3 function calls will be

    A rainbow in the sky
    So be it when I shall grow old

Lists and Tables

The file can be treated like a list of objects. An example of what this means is illustrated in the description of **'file_filter'**. The purpose of **'file_filter'** is to filter words, lines or characters through a specified function from one file to another. The first parameter is a string and is one of the three possible strings "*word*", "*line*" or "*char*". This specifies the atomic units (objects) to be considered (see **'file_read_line'**, etc.

for definitions of the atomic units). The second parameter is a filter function to be applied to these units. The last two parameters are the input file and the output file. The function returns the output file when finished. A null string ("") is returned if failure.

QUERY> file_filter "word" (!="So") "rainbow" "new2"
"new2"

The file "new2":

My heart leaps up when I behold
A rainbow in the sky:
was it when my life began,
is it now I am a man,
be it when I shall grow old,
Or let me die!

The list processing operations that are represented for files are those that can be done in sequence such as 'map', 'takewhile', 'fold' and 'filter'. Other operations such as 'zip' which involves the merging of two files were considered too expensive at the time to be useful. The reason was that these operations are to handle exceptionally long lists.

A table is different from a list in that it is a list of lists. Such a table is intended to be compatible with such things as spread sheets or SQL relations or statistics tables. The function 'table_to_file' converts a list of lists to a table, with items separated by a given separator, True/False to specify if strings are to be enclosed in double quotes, and lists separated by new lines. This gives sufficient flexibility to cover many table formats.

QUERY> table_to_file (decode #9) False [["Start" "Stop" "Hours"] [#1000
#1800 #r6.0] [#1130 #2200 #r10.5]] "Table1"
"Table1"

The file "Table1" contains

Start	Stop	Hours
1000	1800	6.000000
1130	2200	10.500000

And in reverse we have 'file_to_table' which reads a file in a table format (with a given separator) into a list of lists of strings.

QUERY> file_to_table (decode #9) "Table1"
[["Start" "Stop" "Hours"] ["1000" "1800" "6.000000"] ["1130" "2200" "10.500000"]]

Note that #9 decoded is a 'Tab'

QUERY> decode #9
' '

Trees and Networks

This set of file operations were derived from an earlier set which predated the use of the NETWORK window. The advantage of these functions over the more direct NETWORK window is that the results can be cascaded to produce results which are particularly useful for debugging. The original (non-file) set was

- **'link_build'** – builds a representation of the function and constructor linkages of the current database without showing them. Returns an identifier for further processing. The detail of what 'Linkage' looks like is hidden and for the purpose of these set of functions it was, at the time, not important to know.

  QUERY> link_build
  (Linkage #1)

- **'link_ffrom'** – filters out all links emanating from the given symbol where 'letter_ct' is a predefined function that counts the number of letters in a word.

  QUERY> link_ffrom (Linkage #1) letter_ct
  (Linkage #2)

- **'link_fto'** – filters out all links converging to the given symbol.

  QUERY> link_fto (Linkage #1)*
  (Linkage #3)

- **'link_show'** – displays the linkage. In this example it is all the connections from the function 'letter_ct' and to the function '*'

  QUERY> link_show (Linkage #3)
  True

In the case of the file operations a file takes the role of (Linkage n). The files are text files and contain lines of pairs of symbols. Suppose we had a file called 'linkfile1.txt' that contained the list of pairs (they could be words) shown in Fig. 8.11a, then the call

QUERY> **file_link_show** "linkfile1.txt"
True

will display the graph in a NETWORK window as shown in Fig. 8.11b. Since it is a NETWORK window the network can be redistributed and coloured. The file 'linkfile1.txt' can then be used by **'file_link_ffrom'** to generate a children's file which if we use 'a' as our starting symbol will be simply be a copy of the original file because it is the root of this network.

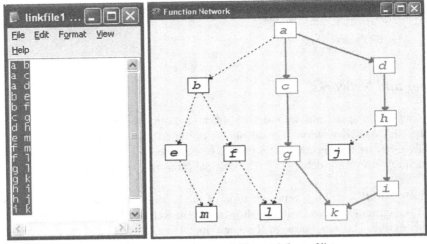

| a. List of symbols in text file | b. The graph form of list |

Fig. 8.11   Creating and displaying a network

QUERY> **file_link_ffrom** "linkfile1.txt" "a" "linkfile2.txt"
"linkfile2.txt"

QUERY> **file_link_fto** "linkfile2.txt" "k" "linkfile3.txt"
"linkfile3.txt"

The function '**file_link_show**' of 'linkfile3.txt' will display just the sub-graph shown in red in Fig. **8.11**b. The function '**File_tree_view**' will display a tree version of the graph in an expandable file style window. So that

QUERY> **file_tree_view** "linkfile3.txt"
True

will become as shown in Fig. 8.12 (Tree view of red sub-graph (a → (d → (h → (j (i → k))))((c → (g → k)))))

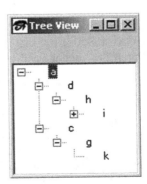

Fig. 8.12   Tree view of red
sub-graph

Casting and Code Generation

One of the most important operations is 'casting' where one type of object can be 'cast' into another. We have already come across castings such as 'fix' and 'float' but there are many more that allow some rather elegant ways to solve problems. Figure 8.13 gives a map of the castings between established types. This does not include the file castings that would naturally continue with the list to file and list to table transformations.

Many of the castings are designed to allow the generation of Faith code . The target type is an expression (expr). Faith can be generated initially as lists either by hand or by a function. In this form it can be manipulated using the list functions and then at the point when it has to be used it can be preceded by a list to expression transformation. This is sometimes referred to evaluation deferral. A simple example is

> QUERY> list_to_expr (:*[[add1 #34] [sub1 #23]])
> #770

Here the round brackets are evaluated first and then the square brackets are, in effect, changed to be round brackets and thus evaluated. Also note that variables (e.g. '?2') can be generated to be used so that functions may be created, defined and then used. This allows a different level of programming which can be very useful. It is also worth noting that the function 'quote' prevents the evaluation of an expression. (see eval and @)

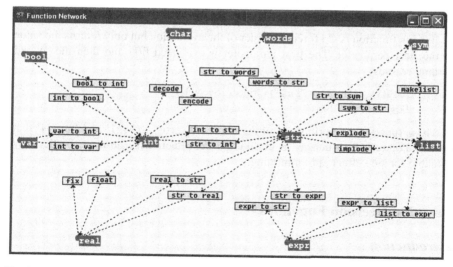

Fig. 8.13 A map of castings. Does not include file castings

QUERY> first (Pair (quote (+ #1 #2)) #5)
(+ #1 #2)

and 'eval' evaluates a quoted function.

QUERY> eval (quote (add1 #5))
#6

A primitive version of this evaluation is '@' which applies a function to a variable which at the query level seems pointless since

QUERY> @ + ?0
(+ ?0)

is the same as

QUERY> + ?0
(+ ?0)

Where it is important is when defining a higher-order function where the application of a function is embodied in a variable.

Loosely related to @ is !@ which forces an order of evaluation but only returns the value of the first parameter. The second parameter is evaluated first and then the first parameter. So if we define a function '**printstr**' in a Faith window, thus

fdec printstr ::= str -> str;;
fdef printstr ?0 ::= if (print ?0) ?0 (" ");;

then

QUERY> !@ (printstr "First") (printstr "Second")
"Second""First""First"

Its twin function is @! forces an order of the evaluation but only returns the value of the **first** parameter. The **first** parameter is evaluated first and then the second parameter, thus

QUERY> @! (printstr "First") (printstr "Second")
"First""Second""First"

These functions are primitives of the family of 'prog', 'prog1' and 'progN' that provide controlled sequences of evaluations for functions. These are particularly valuable for side effect   programming.

Bayesian Decision Functions

Introduction

One of the valuable tools that can be used in decision making is the use of Bayesian classification It uses countable or at least potentially countable features and objects in order to be able to make rational decisions based on experience.

The Reverend Thomas Bayes FRS (1701–1761) produced a theorem that involved determining a probability from the assumption that in ignorance all values are likely to occur. This assumption caused the acceptance of his theorem to be delayed until halfway through the twentieth century (Bellhouse 2004). In its modern form it is considered as simply conditional probability and has been primarily used in pattern recognition and decision theory.

The Bayesian Theory of Classification [→ Page 285]

The Bayesian Theory of Classification is devised from the elements of Decision theory. Central to the theoretical treatment of Decision theory is the loss function $\lambda(i/j)$, where i is any one of R hypotheses and j is any one of the same set of hypotheses. This function represents the loss (in terms of units) incurred when the decision is made that the state of the world is i when, in fact, it is j. In terms of pattern recognition, this represents the loss that occurs when the 'machine' places a pattern that actually belongs to category j into category i.

One of the simplest expressions of this function is

$$\lambda(i/j) = 1 - \delta_{ij} \tag{1}$$

where $\delta_{ij} = 1$ when $i = j$ (Kronecker delta function).

$$= 0 \text{ otherwise.}$$

This states that the loss when wrong will be 1 unit and that there will be no loss when correct. If a machine classifies patterns such that the average value of $\lambda(i/j)$ is minimized, the machine is said to be optimum.

A pattern of evidence can be represented as a vector X in the feature space, where the features are observations that represent the different items of evidence. The probability of a pattern of evidence X implies a hypothesis i, where i is one of R hypotheses, will be represented by the symbol $P(X/i)$, and the probability of the ith hypothesis will be given as $P(i)$.

Now, it is likely that the features chosen are not perfect for distinguishing a state of affairs given a pattern of evidence, and there will be an overlapping of the hypotheses' boundaries. The probability of a hypothesis j given a particular evidence pattern X will be represented by $P(j/X)$.

If the decision i is made (the basis for making this decision is immaterial at this point), then the conditional average loss $L(i/X)$ will be

$$L(i/X) = {}_{j=1}\Sigma^R \lambda(i/j)P(j/X) \tag{2}$$

This will be the average loss (in units) for making this decision given the particular pattern X. Combining Equations (1) and (2)

$$L(i/X) = {}_{j=1}\Sigma^R(1 - \delta_{ij})P(j/X)$$

and this becomes

$$L(i/X) = 1 - P(i/X) \tag{3}$$

Therefore, to minimize the expected loss for a particular decision i, *i should be chosen so as to maximize P(i/X)*.

Now P(i/X) can be estimated by using Bayes' rule , which is

$$P(i/X) = \frac{P(i/X).P(i)}{P(X)} \tag{4}$$

Now if X is described by the features $x_1, x_2, x_3, , \ldots x_d, \ldots x_D$, then

$$P(X/i) = P(x_1/i).P(x_2/x_1, i).P(x_3/x_1, x_2, i). \ldots etc$$

and

$$P(X) = P(x_1).P(x_2/x_1).P(x_3/x_1, x_2). \ldots etc$$

therefore

$$P(i/X) = \frac{P(i).P(x_1/i).P(x_2/x_1, i)}{P(x_1) P(x_2/x_1)} \ldots\ldots\ldots \tag{5}$$

This would take considerable computing power if X has many dimensions, and there would need to be a large number of examples of each i to ensure the correct determination of some of the more obscure probabilities.

If the transformations on the measurements (observations) are chosen so that the features are independent of each other, then Equation (5) can be greatly simplified

$$P'(i/X) = \frac{P(i).P(x_1/i).P(x_2/i) P(x_3/i)}{P(x_1)P(x_2)P(x_3)} \ldots\ldots\ldots etc$$

This means that dimension transformation that result in x_n must do the work of correlation.

If logs are taken and log (P'(i/X)) is considered as a discriminant function G(i/X), then

$$G(i/X) = {}_{k=1}\Sigma^D log(P(x_k/i)) - {}_{k=1}\Sigma^D log(P(x_k)) + log(P(i))$$

Since ${}_{k=1}\Sigma^D log(P(x_k))$ is a constant for each of the k hypotheses,

$$G'(i/X) = {}_{k=1}\Sigma^D log(P(x_k/i)) + log(P(i))$$

This is an extension of Bayes' rule in log form. It is a simple linear equation where the impact of all the evidence is the log sum of the impacts made by each observation separately. The only requirement is that the observations must behave as though they were independent. The individual elements ($\log P(x_k/i)$) can be cal-culated for any 'pattern of evidence', and if there are several hypotheses to choose from then maximum $G'(i/X)$ is selected.

*The Bayesian Functions in Operation

Since the conceptual interface to the world should be defined in terms of construc-tors so Fig. 8.14 shows an example of their use for classifying fruit in this way.

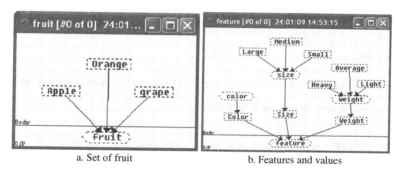

a. Set of fruit   b. Features and values

Fig. 8.14 Setting up for Bayesian classification

The function '**prob_learn**' modifies the internal probability tables through the presentation of an example of a class of object and its list of feature value pairs (not type pairs). The first parameter is an enumerated constructor that represents the class of objects taken from a set of classes. The second parameter is a list of constructor value pairs where the constructor is a feature and the value is one drawn from a set of values. Initially we might need to reset the internal tables. The function '**prob_reset**' clears the probability tables of all values.

QUERY> prob_reset
True

QUERY> prob_learn Apple [(Color Red)(Size Small)]
True

QUERY> prob_learn Orange [(Color Red)(Size Large)]
True

QUERY> prob_learn Apple [(Color Green)(Size Large)]
True

QUERY> prob_learn Orange [(Color Green)(Size Small)]
True
QUERY> prob_learn Orange [(Color Green)(Size Medium)]
True

The function 'prob_classify' will, given a list of feature value pairs (not type pairs), calculate the discrimination value G'(i/X) of this combination of feature values determined from the information given.

QUERY> prob_classify [(Color Green)(Size Small)]
[(Pair Apple #r0.416667) (Pair Orange #r0.555556)]

Other functions are

- 'prob_getclass' the probability of a class (first parameter) is returned (see prob_learn for further context).

  QUERY> prob_getclass Apple
  #r0.400000

- 'prob_getcond' the conditional probability (feature value given class is returned.

  QUERY> prob_getcond (Color Red) Apple
  #r0.500000

- 'prob_getfeat' the probability of a feature value pair (not type pair) for all classes is returned.

  QUERY> prob_getfeat (Size Small)
  #r0.400000

Sometimes it is useful to be able to start with a set of probabilities and to this end there are three useful functions:

- 'prob_setclass' the probability of a class (first parameter), given no further information, is pre-set to second parameter. The head of the list is the new sum of the individual probabilities of each class. The tail of the list is pairs (type pair) of the class constructor and their respective probabilities.

  QUERY> prob_setclass Apple #r0.7
  [#r1.300000 (Pair Apple #r0.700000) (Pair Orange #r0.600000)]

- 'prob_setcond' the conditional probability (feature value given a class) is pre-set. The first parameter is a constructor/value pair. The second is a class and the last the probability to be set.

  QUERY> prob_setcond (Color Red) Orange #r0.9
  [#r1.566667 (Pair (Color Red) #r0.900000) (Pair (Color Green) #r0.666667)]

- **'prob_setfeat'** the probability of a feature value pair (not type '**pair**') without any further information (i.e. across all classes) (first parameter) is pre-set (second parameter).

  QUERY> prob_setfeat (Size Small) #r0.3
  [#r0.900000 (Pair (Size Small) #r0.300000) (Pair (Size Large) #r0.400000) (Pair (Size Medium) #r0.200000)]

Matrix Operations and Linear Simultaneous Equations

Although list operations perform many of the operations required for Matrix manipulation, where a matrix is simply a list of lists (or a table), it seems neater to express these as special functions without eliminating the list operations. Of particular value is the function for solving simultaneous equations .

- 'mat_minus' subtracts second matrix from the first.

  QUERY> mat_minus [[#10 #5] [#20 #8]] [[#10 #4] [#19 #8]]
  [[#0 #1] [#1 #0]]

- 'mat_plus' adds two matrices together.

  QUERY> mat_plus [[#10 #5] [#20 #8]] [[#10 #4] [#19 #8]]
  [[#20 #9] [#39 #16]]

- 'mat_times' multiplies two matrices together.

  QUERY> mat_times [[#2] [#1]] [[#2 #1]]
  [[#r4.000000 #r2.000000] [#r2.000000 #r1.000000]]

- 'mat_trans' transposes a matrix.

  QUERY> mat_trans [[#3 #2] [#2 #1] [#1 #0]]
  [[#r3.000000 #r2.000000 #r1.000000] [#r2.000000 #r1.000000 #r0.000000]]

- 'mat_solve' solves a set of linear equations that are expressed in the form of a matrix. If the matrix has more equations than variables and the equations are consistent then a single result is given. If the equations are inconsistent the NIL is returned. If there are fewer equations than variables then a reduced matrix (indicating the constraints between the variables) is returned. To solve the pair of equations

  $2x + 5y = 16$ and $3x - y = 7$ for x and y:
  QUERY> mat_solve [[#2 #5 #16] [#3 #-1 #7]]
  [[#r3.000000 #r2.000000]]

When not enough information

$2x + y + z = 1.2$ and $x + 2y - z = 0.3$:
QUERY> mat_solve [[#2 #1 #1 #r1.2] [#1 #2 #-1 #r0.3]]
[[#r1.000000 #r0.500000 #r0.500000 #r0.600000]]

This function has been used extensively in the calculations of forces on bridges built of rods.

Set Operations

Sets are simply lists of objects, usually of the same kind or type. Lists are assumed to be non-redundant in the sense that no object appears more than once. The function '**mkset**' ensures that this is the case. Otherwise the functions for set operations are '**set_union**', '**set_subtract**' and '**set_intersect**'. They all follow the same pattern.

- '**set_intersect**' set operation, intersection of two sets.

    QUERY> set_intersect ['a' 'b' 'c'] ['b' 'c' 'd']
    ['b' 'c']

Switches

Each switch is literally a single computer bit. Currently 3 K words have been reserved giving 96,000 switches ranging from 0 to 95,999. A switch is used as a global flag and has been used to define different states of a complex simulation.

- '**sw_set**' uses #-1 to specify all of them. This sets the switch(es) to 'True'

    QUERY> sw_set #-1
    True

- '**sw_reset**' resets the switch(es) as for sw_set.

    QUERY> sw_reset #333
    True

- '**sw_test**' tests a switch.

    QUERY> sw_test #334
    False

Project: Using Faith with Clarity

Loans: A Loans Calculation Program

Introduction

This program will calculate different factors, depending on the user's choice, relating to a loan, over a period measured in months, at a given rate of interest (to 2 decimal places). If, for example, the user chooses the **monthly repayment,** the system will ask the amount to be borrowed, how long the loan has to run and the interest rate. It will return the monthly repayment. The main function is called **start** (see Diagram 8.1.).

The program will require a lot of interaction with the user and some calculations. The interactions will involve strings of characters, e.g. "Please choose one of the following calculations:" The calculations will use the internal representations of integers and decimal numbers, so conversion functions are used. [In the ClarityPro, these conversions and a function 'dialog' are available as built-in functions.]

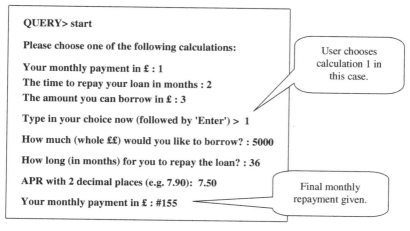

> **QUERY> start**
>
> **Please choose one of the following calculations:**
>
> **Your monthly payment in £ : 1**
> **The time to repay your loan in months : 2**
> **The amount you can borrow in £ : 3**
>
> **Type in your choice now (followed by 'Enter') > 1**
>
> **How much (whole ££) would you like to borrow? : 5000**
>
> **How long (in months) for you to repay the loan? : 36**
>
> **APR with 2 decimal places (e.g. 7.90): 7.50**
>
> **Your monthly payment in £ : #155**

User chooses calculation 1 in this case.

Final monthly repayment given.

Diagram 8.1 The user interface for function '**start**'

Conversions

One of the simplest of these conversions is function '**char_to_int**' in Diagram 8.2. (Also defined in OXO.)

    The function '**char_to_int**' converts the character representation of a number, e.g. '7' into the internal representation of an integer e.g. #7. The difference is the way it is stored by the computer.

    (1) *Define the function **char_to_int** in Diagram 8.2.

Building on this function, we can define a function to translate a list of characters into an integer. For example ['4' '5'] transforms into #45.

    Look at function '**chars_to_int**' in Diagram 8.3.

    This function uses a running-total returned by the function '**result**', which is initially set to zero. Then for each item in the list, the function '**add_to_result**' multiplies '**result**' by 10 and adds the new item. So for ['4' '5'] the steps are as follows:

        result = 0;
        result = 0 * 10 + 4 = 4;
        result = 4 * 10 + 5 = 45;

    (2) *Define the function '**result**' in Diagram 8.4.

    (3) *Define the function '**add_to_result**' in Diagram 8.5.

    (4) *Define the function '**chars_to_int**' in Diagram 8.3.

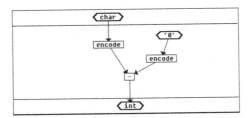

Diagram 8.2 Function '**char_to_int**'

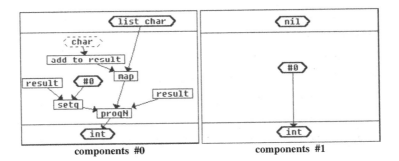

components #0   components #1

Diagram 8.3 Function '**chars_to_int**'

Diagram 8.4 'result'

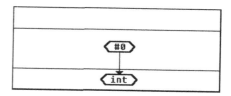

Diagram 8.5 'add_to_result'

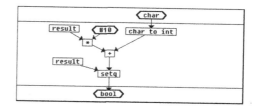

Putting out Messages

As there are various messages to print out, we will make use of a function called **'string'**, which will return different strings, given different integer input parameters. This will make a neater diagram for the functions that use these strings. The strings may also be edited easily.

Look at function **'string'** in Diagram 8.6. Two components are given, but we need to define a further **four** components, according to the list of additional values

'string #2' returns "The time to repay your loan in months:"
'string #3' returns "The amount you can borrow in £:"
'string #4' returns "Please choose one of the following calculations:"
'string #5' returns "Type in your choice now (followed by 'Enter')>"

(5) *Define all 6 components of the function **'string'** in Diagram 8.6 plus additions.

There are some more simple printing functions to define.

(6) *Define the function **'newline'** in Diagram 8.7.

(7) *Define the function **'message'** in Diagram 8.8.

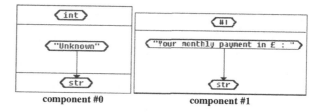

Diagram 8.6 The function 'string'

component #0   component #1

The function '**message#**' in Diagram 8.9 prints a message, followed by the character form of its integer identifier, to print out the choices described above.

This function makes use of function '**int_to_char**' in Diagram 8.10, which does the opposite of function '**char_to_int**'.

(8) *Define the function '**int_to_char**' in Diagram 8.10.

(9) *Define the function '**message#**' in Diagram 8.9.

Getting Input from the User

As was stated earlier, this program relies on a certain amount of interaction, and that brings us to the function '**dialog**' in Diagram 8.11. This function prints a message, e.g. "What is your name? and then keeps reading characters until the 'Enter' key is pressed. Characters can be deleted by using the 'Backspace' key, and the printed

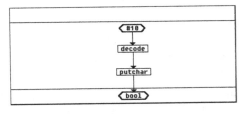

Diagram 8.7 The function '**newline**'

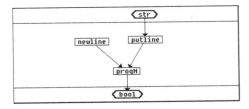

Diagram 8.8 The function '**message**'

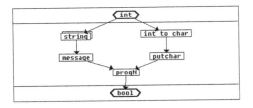

Diagram 8.9 '**message#**'

Diagram 8.10 The function
'int_to_char'

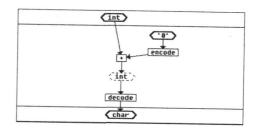

Diagram 8.11 The function
'dialog'

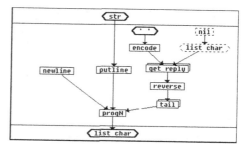

character '–' will indicate the deletion. The function returns the list of characters read. For example,

QUERY> dialog "What is your name?"
What is your name? Jannn–icc-e
['J' 'a' 'n' 'i' 'c' 'e']

The function that keeps reading characters and adding them to a list is '**get_reply**' in Diagram 8.12. This function takes an integer as input because it cannot match an 'Enter' key or 'Backspace' key as an input parameter, but its integer code can be matched. There are four components of '**get_reply**'.

Look carefully at '**get_reply**'. The input parameters are the integer code for the character and the list of characters already read. In component #0, we are dealing with an ordinary printable character. The built-in function '**decode**' turns it into a character and '**putchar**' prints it for the user. Then the constructor ':' (cons) adds it to the head of the list of characters, and '**get_reply**' is called again. The first parameter to '**get_reply**' will be the new character read from the user with '**getchar**', which is then '**encode**'d into its internal integer form. The second parameter is the new list of characters, with the latest one at the front.

We have to start with something, so in '**dialog**', we call '**get_reply**' with the 'space' character and an empty list (although it does not matter which character we use).

Therefore, if the user types the word 'fred', the list is built up like this:

[' '], ['f' ' '], ['r' 'f' ' '], ['e' 'r' 'f' ' '], ['d' 'e' 'r' 'f' ' ']

Which is why '**dialog**' then '**reverse**'s the list and takes the '**tail**', that is everything except the first item.

Getting back to '**get_reply**' we see that component #1 deals with 'Backspace',
which has an internal code of #8. We print ''−' to indicate a deleted character, and
carry on to the next read with only the tail of the list so far, i.e. we lose the last
character read. Component #2 deals with the case where someone types 'Backspace'
as the first character. Component #3 deals with the 'Enter' key, which has internal
code #13. A '**newline**' is printed and the list of characters returned.

 (10) *Define the function '**get_reply**' in Diagram 8.12.

 (11) *Define the function '**dialog**' in Diagram 8.11.

We can now consider the function that will print the choices for the user, and will
return the user's choice as an integer. This is the function '**choose**' in Diagram 8.13.

The function '**choose**' will print '**string #4**', followed by '**strings #1**', '**#2**' **and**
'**#3**' with their identifiers. Then the function **dialog** will be called to return a list
of characters, but we are only expecting one, so the **head** of the list is taken. This
character is converted to its integer equivalent and returned.

 (12) *Define the function '**choose**' in Diagram 8.13.

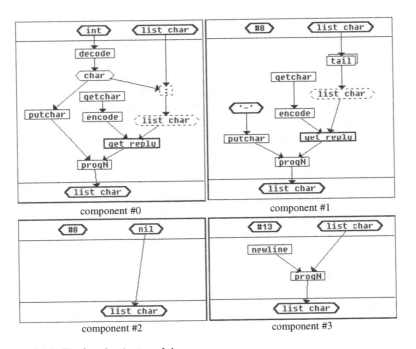

Diagram 8.12   The function '**get_reply**'

Diagram 8.13 The function
'**choose**'

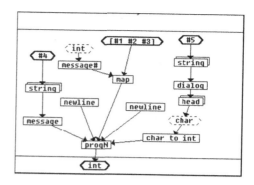

Diagram 8.14 The function
'**start**'

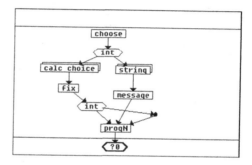

Doing the Calculations

It is time to look at the main function '**start**' in Diagram 8.14.

Evaluating the parameters of '**progN**' from left to right, the first function to be called is '**choose**', which, as we have seen, prints out choices for the user, and returns that choice as an integer. The function '**calc_choice**' will perform the appropriate calculation, then the string associated with the choice is printed followed by the result, which is an integer.

Look at the function **calc_choice** in Diagram 8.15.

The only choices are #1, #2 and #3. Component #0 is there for completeness. '**power**' is a built-in function, e.g. 'power #r2.3 #2' returns #r5.29. All three calculations '**calc1**', '**calc2**' and '**calc3**' depend on the functions '**loan**', '**apr_plus**', '**term**' and '**permonth**' (e.g. Diagram 8.16, 8.17, 8.18, and 8.19). They all involve a dialog with the user.

(13) *Define the function '**loan**' in Diagram 8.16.

(14) *Define the function '**term**' in Diagram 8.17.

(15) *Define the function '**permonth**' in Diagram 8.18.

The function '**apr**' in Diagram 8.19 uses the conversion function '**chars_to_real**' in Diagram 8.20.

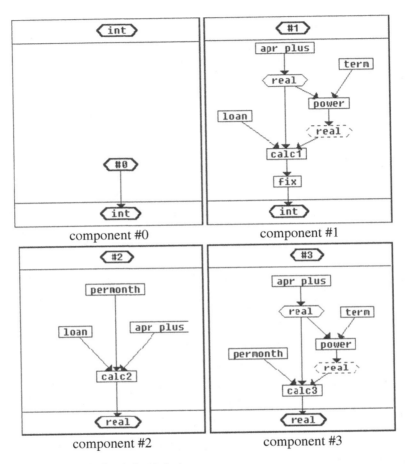

component #0   component #1

component #2   component #3

Diagram 8.15 The function '**calc_choice**'

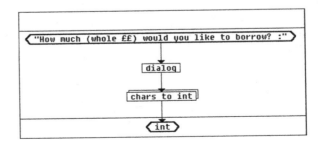

Diagram 8.16 The function
'**loan**'

Diagram 8.17 The function
'term'

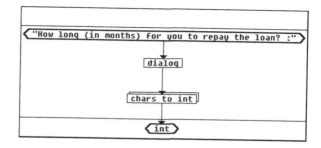

Diagram 8.18 The function
'permonth'

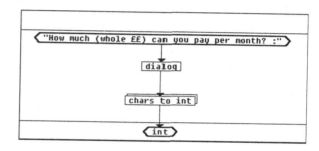

Diagram 8.19 The function
'apr'

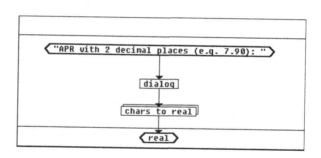

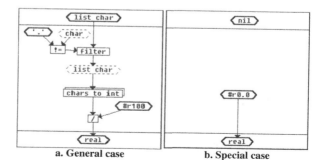

Diagram 8.20 The function
'chars_to_real'

a. General case   b. Special case

We are assuming that the user will type in the APR with exactly two decimal places, as requested. So we will have a list of characters, e.g. ['5' '.' '5' '0']. To convert this to a real number, we 'filter' out the '.', convert to an integer with 'chars_to_int', and then divide by the 'real' #r100, to return a real number #r5.50.

NB: If we divide by the integer #100 the answer would be an integer, in this example, #5, which is not what we want. If there is a real involved in the arithmetic, then a real is returned.

(16) *Define the function 'chars_to_real' in Diagram 8.20.

(17) *Define the function 'apr' in Diagram 8.19.

The function 'apr_plus' is defined because it is used in all three calculations.

(18) *Define the function apr_plus in Diagram 8.21.

The calculations themselves show how it is possible to put an expression into a parameter lozenge. Now look at 'calc1' in Diagram 8.22, which is called from 'calc_choice #1'.

The function 'calc1' is called with three parameters: an integer and two reals. These three parameters are represented inside the expression by the variables ?0, ?1 and ?2 respectively. These act in the same way as x, y and z in mathematics. The expression is in *pre-fix* form, i.e. instead of writing for example '?0 + ?1' we write '+ ?0 ?1'. '?0 + ?1' is *in-fix* form and is more familiar. It is fine for two parameters but for three or more pre-fix form is a consistent way of writing expressions. The expression in 'calc1' in Diagram 8.22 would be more familiar in *in-fix* form as

(?0 * (?2 * (#1 – ?1))) / (#1 – ?2)

(19) *Define 'calc1' in Diagram 8.22.

(20) *Define 'calc3' in Diagram 8.23.

However, 'calc2' in Diagram 8.24 needs a little more explaining. If you choose how much to *borrow* and how long to pay, your monthly payments can be calculated and have no limit. If you choose how much to *pay* per month, and how long for then the amount you can borrow on that basis can be calculated. But if you specify some very large amount to borrow and a small monthly repayment, it is possible that it will

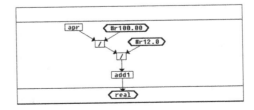

Diagram 8.21 The function 'apr_plus'

Diagram 8.22 The function 'calc1'

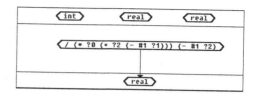

Diagram 8.23 The function 'calc3'

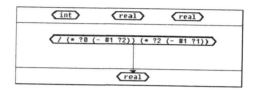

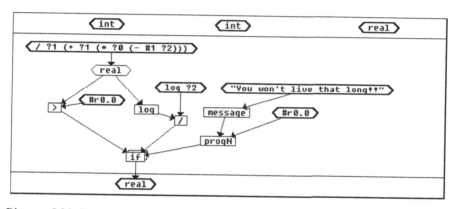

Diagram 8.24 The function 'calc2'

never be paid back, i.e. you will not even keep up with the interest. This amounts to a check which is made in **calc2** before calculating the result.

(21) *Define **'calc2'** in Diagram 8.24.

(22) *Define **calc_choice** in Diagram 8.15.

(23) *Define **start** in Diagram 8.14.

You can now test your program by typing 'start' in the control window after the prompt QUERY> (see Diagram 8.1).

Finally

Save your data base and call it 'Loans' then create a network view by opening a network window, go to the find 'menu' and click on 'Create/Update network from database'. This may require a little rearranging and the deletion of some functions to look neat. Two proposed arrangements are shown in Diagram 8.25 and in Diagram 8.26. These different networks describe the different functionality required by the program 'Loans'. When you are satisfied with the appearance of each network, commit them just like different components of a function window. Of course you might like to produce other views of the network, showing further distinctions of the functionality.

The popular functions '**chars_to_int**', '**dialog**', and '**string**' have been left out of **Network 1**, to make it clearer. They have been placed on **Network 2**, along with their parent functions and descendent functions. Colours can also be chosen (say red) to show those functions that appear in both networks. Just highlight the functions (and arrows) and go to the colour menu. Chose the colour you want.

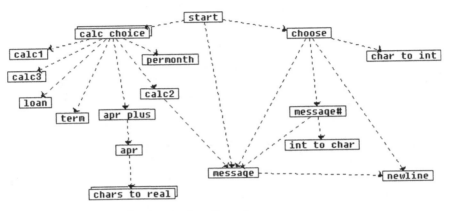

Diagram 8.25   **Network #1** of the database '**Loans**'

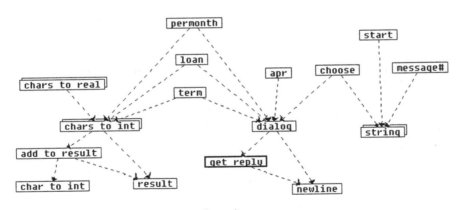

Diagram 8.26   **Network #2** of database '**Loans**'

References

Bellhouse D.R. (2004) '*The Reverend Thomas Bayes, FRS: A Biography to Celebrate the Tercentenary of His Birth*' Statistical Science Vol. 19, No. 1, pp. 3–43.

Chapter 9
Higher-Order Programming and Lower Level Activity

For now we see through a glass darkly;
but then face to face; now I know in part;
but then shall I know even as also I am known.
Corinthians 13, 12

Special Function Classes

Introduction

In the built-in window ('help') that shows all the library functions the 300+ functions have been grouped according to their speciality. Some we have already described in detail in Chapter 8 but there are many others worth at least mentioning. Some groups such as Boolean and Boolean Hybrids, which refer to functions that test, are not detailed in this book since many of them would be expected to be available for any programming language (e.g. arithmetic functions). Here we describe briefly some useful groups of functions that are not always found in other programming languages.

There is another area of programming that needs to be covered. Clarity has been built in the imperative language of C and C++. We have shown that although a functional language is formally complete it does not relate physically to the world except through side effects. Side effects are often the real reason for programming in that computers are needed to link with the external world so that information can be broadcast and mechanisms controlled. The way this is achieved with Clarity is by ready made built-in functions (e.g. 'print') but this immediately puts a barrier to further uses. We can overcome this barrier by creating new library functions in an imperative language, a language that links intimately with the physical structure of the computer.

We will first cover functions that emulate the imperative form of programming. Then we will go on to links with the operating system and how to extend the library. Finally we will summarise the source code and the underlying structure of Clarity. With this knowledge anything is possible.

T. Addis, J. Addis, *Drawing Programs: The Theory and Practice of Schematic Functional Programming*, DOI 10.1007/978-1-84882-618-2_9,
© Springer-Verlag London Limited 2010

Function and Constructor Handling

These functions provide a means of manipulating other functions before they are evaluated. Some have already been introduced such as '@', 'progN' and "quote". Some of the other important function handlers are described here but it is worth looking at the complete group under the function 'help'.

Information

- 'bagN' list of function values for the function specified as an argument (see 'range').

      fdec place ::= str ->str;;
      fdef
          place "Tom"::= "Aldbourne";
          place "Jan" ::= "Aldbourne";
          place "David" ::= "Bath";

      ;
  QUERY> bagN place
  ["Aldbourne" "Aldbourne" "Bath"]

- 'inventoryf' returns a set of unique values that are used by the function given as a parameter (sym). The integer (int) specifies the parameter number. #0 is the function name and #1 is the first parameter. The greatest integer that can give a response would be the 'body' of the function. Integers higher than that are undefined. This uses 'list_fdefs' and there is a danger of infinite recursion in some cases.
  See example, for bagN

      QUERY> inventoryf place #1
      ["Tom" "Jan" "David"]

- 'inverse' returns a list of the parameters of all the components of a function that returns the given value, inverse mapping. This is limited to extensional functions with a single parameter (see inverseN).

      QUERY> inverse place "Aldbourne"
      ["Tom" "Jan"]

- 'list_children' lists the functions that are called by the given function. NB: The information is taken from the database, not from memory. See also 'list_parents'.

      QUERY> list_children "factorial"
      ["sub1" "*"]

- 'list_fdefs' lists all the components of a function where each component is in list form (see 'assertl')

      QUERY> list_fdefs place
      [[place "Tom" "Aldbourne"] [place "Jan" "Aldbourne"] [place "David" "Bath"]]

- **'list_parents'** lists the functions that call the given function. NB: The information is taken from the database, not from memory. See also **'list_children'**.

  QUERY> list_parents "factorial"
  ["main"]

- **'show'** displays the Clarity function component window that represents the expression.

  QUERY> show (factorial #0)
  True

- **'tdefs'** returns a list of lists of str which expresses the definition of a type (sym) (see ftypes).

  QUERY> tdefs pair
  [["Pair" "?0" "?1"]]

Manipulators

- **'compose'** puts functions together. Each function must have a single argument only. Also see the casting function **'combine'**.

  QUERY> compose log10 sqrt add1 #99
  #1

- **'match'** finds the bindings of two expressions. This is Unification as required for logic programming and A* search for searching for logic proofs (also see **'matchq'**):

  QUERY> match (?0 ?1 ?2) (#1 ?1 #3)
  [[?0 #1] [?2 #3]]

- **'permute'** exchanges the argument positions of a two argument function.

  QUERY> permute power #5 #2
  #32

Creators

- **'assert'** asserts a function from parameters but evaluates these parameters before definition. There is a family of assert functions: **'assertl'**, **'assertlcdec'**, **'assertlfdec'**, **'assertq'** and **'assertql'**; also see **'set'** and **'setq'**.

  fdec GP_of ::= str ->str;;
  fdef
    GP_of ?0 ::= "Unknown";
    GP_of "Smith" ::= "Symon";
    GP_of "Booth" ::= "Wills";
  ;

QUERY> assert GP_of "Davies" "Wills"
True
QUERY> GP_of "Davies"
"Wills"

- 'set' similar to assert but function is given as a single parameter.

    QUERY> set constant "Time"
    True

- 'deny' removes a specified function component in FAITH but not CLARITY (use remove component for the Clarity function window).
  See example for 'assert'

    QUERY> deny [GP_of "Booth"]
    True
    QUERY> GP_of "Booth"
    "Unknown"

- 'denyall' removes all traces of a function in FAITH but not CLARITY and returns 'False' if not done. Note that 'known' is a built-in function which provides a test before a function is called. If the result is 'False' it means it is not known and should not be used.
  See examples, for 'assert'

    QUERY> denyall GP_of
    True
    QUERY> known "GP_of"
    False
    QUERY> denyall (quote coord)
    True
    QUERY> known "coord"
    False

- 'forget' removes all traces of special, i.e. extensional , cases of a function in FAITH but not in CLARITY and returns 'False' if not done.
  See example for assert:

    QUERY> forget GP_of
    True
    QUERY> GP_of "Smith"
    "Unknown"
    QUERY> GP_of "Booth"
    "Unknown"

- 'newtdec' declares a new data type and if successful will return 'True'.

    QUERY> newtdec "weekday" "enum"
    True

QUERY> newtdec "number" "nonlex"
True

- 'nlcreate' creates a new lexical type instance and populates a data type with enumerated instances.
  See examples, for 'newtdec'

    QUERY> nlcreate weekday "Sunday"
    Sunday
    QUERY> nlcreate number "one"
    one

- 'remember' makes an extensional component of a function (sym) such that it 'remembers' the result. The function can have any number of parameters. This means that the extensional component will be returned next time this function is called. The function MUST be a user defined function. Also 'keep' is similar but takes one parameter, which is an expression.

    fdec series : := real ->real; ;
    fdef series ?0 : := + (#1) (* ?0 (+ (#1) ?0)) ; ;
    QUERY> remember series #r0.5
    #r1.750000
    QUERY> list_fdefs series
    [[series ?0 (+ #1 (* ?0 (+ #1 ?0)))] [series #r0.500000 #r1.750000]]

Generators

These are functions that generate data.

- 'factors' generates a list of the factors of an integer

    QUERY> factors #345
    [#3 #5 #15 #23 #69 #115]

- 'index' generates a list of numbers 0 → list length

    QUERY> index ['a' 'b' 'c']
    [#0 #1 #2]

- 'list_of_int' returns a list of integers from the first to the second arguments in steps of the third argument

    QUERY> list_of_int #2 #13 #3
    [#2 #5 #8 #11]

- 'rand' returns a random number. Note that 'srand' (no parameters) seeds the random number generator with date and time.

    QUERY> rand
    #16838

- 'repeat' returns a list of size int of ?0. ?0 is evaluated each time. Note that 'replicate' is the same but evaluates only once and then the result is replicated.

  QUERY> repeat #3 rand
  [#10113 #17515 #31051]
  QUERY> replicate #3 rand
  [#5758 #5758 #5758]

Combinators

These are special functions used by the Faith interpreter for mapping a functional language on to an imperative machine. It provides an alternative form of the Faith code that is more efficient than using it directly. Details of this can be seen in Field and Harrison's book (Field and Harrison 1988, (also see Reade 1989)). They can be used directly for programming and on occasions they appear when some functions can only be partially interpreted. The problem is that it is a range of capital letters that are reserved and so cannot be used for other things. Each of the combinators has a name that describes its transformation.

- 'B' is the Compositor $(?1 \rightarrow ?2) \rightarrow (?0 \rightarrow ?1) \rightarrow ?0 \rightarrow ?2$

  QUERY> B add1 sqrt #400
  #21

- 'C' is the Permutator $(?0 \rightarrow ?1 \rightarrow ?2) \rightarrow ?0 \rightarrow ?1 \rightarrow ?2$

  QUERY> C / #4 #20
  #5

- 'I' is the Identity $?0 \rightarrow ?0$

  QUERY> I 'a'
  'a'

- 'K' is the Cancellator $?0 \rightarrow ?1 \rightarrow ?0$

  QUERY> K "yes" "no"
  "yes"

- 'S' is the Distributor $(?0 \rightarrow ?1 \rightarrow ?2) \rightarrow (?0 \rightarrow ?1) \rightarrow ?0 \rightarrow ?2$

  QUERY> S + add1 #5
  #11

System

Interacting directly with the system from within a program can be useful for such things as triggering other programs or making the computer system respond or collect information about the system. System functions themselves can be grouped.

Database

- 'create' creates a new database.
- 'close' clears the main memory of user's database

>   QUERY> close
>   True

- 'commit' saves the current database

>   QUERY> create "extra"
>   Created :extra.ddb
>   True
>   QUERY> open "extra"
>   Loading extra.ddb...Loaded
>   True
>   fdec triArea ::= real->real->real ;;
>   fdef triArea ?0 ?1 ::= * (/ ?0 #2) ?1 ;;
>   QUERY> commit
>   True

- 'load' reads into main memory a user's database. When load and open (see below) are used this way, the contents of the Faith window can be misleading. See example for commit

>   QUERY> close
>   True
>   QUERY> known "triArea"
>   False
>   QUERY> load "extra"
>   Loading: extra.ddb...Loaded.
>   True
>   QUERY> known "triArea"
>   True

- 'open' opens a user's database

>   QUERY> close
>   True
>   QUERY> open "extra"
>   Loading extra.ddb...Loaded
>   True

Function

- 'delay' introduces a delay in 1/60th of a second.

>   QUERY> delay #60
>   True

- 'dump' prints information on a symbol, information on all symbols if argument is "fdef" or all symbol names if argument is "fdec". Note the use of combinators.

```
QUERY> dump "triArea"
*** triArea :FUNCTION arity:2, max_var:1
TYPES real->real->real
:DEFS
 :(@#1 (@#1triArea#1?0#1) ?1#1)
 1:(@(@B*)(@(@C/)#2))   (@(@*(@(@/?0)#2))?1)
END-DEFS
True
```

- 'escape' allows the user to escape from the function evaluation loop when 'esc' key is pressed. Also see '**trace**'.

  ```
  QUERY> escape True
  True
  ```

- '**export**' exports a list of functions and their dependences as a standalone database (.ddb) with .seg file.

  ```
  QUERY> export ["expert"]
  ```

  It will then list all the dependencies and open up a file-saving window for you to name the database and say where you want it kept.

- '**gc**' performs garbage collect on the nodes of the evaluation tree. This activity is normally triggered automatically by the interpreter. The problem is that the triggering can cause unexpected delays as large amounts of memory are scanned and cleaned. Calling the function under the programmers control will reduce such surprises.

  ```
  QUERY> gc
  True
  ```

- '**import**' opens a file accessing window for you to choose the database to load.

- '**sysbeep**' sounds the warning noise.

  ```
  QUERY> sysbeep
  True
  ```

- '**trace**' traces the spine of the apply tree during evaluation.

  ```
  QUERY> trace True
  redex :True
  True
  ```

- '**user**' calls a function that has been coded by the user as part of an application extension, a DLL. The function is called by name from inside the DLL. Its parameters are always passed as a list of strings, for example

  ```
  QUERY> user "UsersDLL.dll" "average" ["1" "2" "3" "4"]
  "2.500000"
  ```

The answer is always returned as a single string.

For information on how to create and use a simple DLL interface to Clarity, see the section "Writing Application Extensions: (DLLs)" – Page 316.

External

- **'exec'** executes an expression at system level.

    QUERY> exec "C:\Clarity\clarity.exe"
    True

- **'exit'** will exit the Clarity program.

- **'remote'** This function executes an application, waits for the result, and then outputs this result as a list of string. This is explained on Page 315 – "Adding users' own code".

Time

- **'time_year'** gives the year as an integer, e.g. #9 (i.e. 2009).

    QUERY> time_year
    #9

- **'time_month'** gives the month as an integer, e.g. #1 (i.e. January)

    QUERY> time_month
    #1

Other time functions follow exactly the same pattern: **'time_dayofmonth'**, **'time_dayofweek'**, **'time_hour'**, **'time_minute'** and **'time_second'**.

Client/Server Facilities

Overview of Network and Machine Organisation

If there is another Clarity running on the same or a different computer capable of communicating across a network then two or more Claritys can be linked together. This provides the facility to send queries to Clarity on a different machine and receive a result back. A query can be any function where such a function may represent complex processes. It is possible to have real parallel processing by using a set of networked computers.

There are certain conditions that should be established before you start. The firewall must be set up to accept ClarityPro or at most be switched off entirely. The latter is fine provided you are isolated from the World Wide Web or other external potential dangers. With windows XP and later there is the requirement that all the computers on the network with which you wish to set up communication should be logged-on with all the same user name and password. It would also be advisable that each is logged on as a single user.

All the machines can be set up to have several Claritys running (see Fig. 9.1). Each of the Claritys (e.g. 1 and 2) can be both a client and a server. The client requests a job to be done and the server does the job. The path between a particular Clarity on a machine and another Clarity on (possibly) a different machine is defined by the IP address of the machine (e.g. 192.168.0.102) or alternatively the name of the machine (e.g. Sidney), a port number (e.g. 3001) and a socket number (e.g. 182). The port number is assigned by the user to identify each Clarity (in this case) in a machine. The same port number can be used in different machines. The socket number is generated locally by the machine's system to identify the separate requests made to that particular Clarity (e.g. Clarity 1). Each path is a named service (e.g. MathsCalcs) and will include the client's socket number. So the path MathsCalcs from a Client to a Server will be, for example, 136-224- (3001-192.168.0.102). Although a path can be used many times, once set up and named, the paths that share the same machine will queue jobs to be done in sequence. Paths for different machines will be done in parallel.

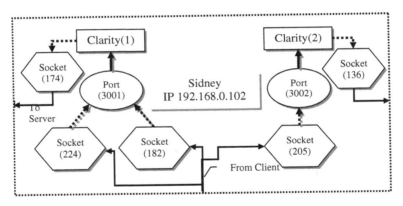

Fig. 9.1   An example of the internal networking organisation

Manual Networking

There are two ways of achieving communication. The first is manually via a pull-down menu with the following choices:

- Control/Client Connect
- Control/Client Disconnect
- Control/Server Listen
- Control/Server Stop

The first requirement is to create at least one server in order to provide a service to be requested. Go to the menu of the Clarity to be designated a Server. Note that a Server can also be a Client. Then click on the following:

Control/Server Listen

This will produce the request box as shown in Fig. 9.2 where a particular active Clarity (the server and Clarity 1 in the example) will perform whatever tasks required within its range of active functions. For functions above and beyond the library functions a database must be loaded. This loading of a database can be one of the first requested tasks.

Fig. 9.2 The request for port number

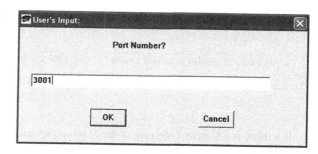

In ClarityPro the control window will display

QUERY> Server attempting to listen
      Server is listening at port 3001

If you then chose to be a client (say Clarity 2) and want to have a function performed on your behalf by another machine and the other machine is set up to listen then you go to menu

'Control/Client Connect'

This triggers off a sequence of requests for information as shown in Fig. 9.3. The first is the unique name you want to give to the communication link for a particular Clarity on a particular machine; this is the particular path name adopted for all future communication (e.g. MathsCalcs) with that Clarity. The second request is the IP address of the machine (or you can use the computer network name) on the network that identifies the machine you want. The third is the port number used by the server to link a particular Clarity. The last request is a time limit you will impose before you give up listening for an answer. This is because while you are listening you are not doing your own processing. The server will assign, privately, a socket number for this particular task. Other sockets are used for other tasks from (possibly) different machines that are using this particular Clarity on this particular service machine.

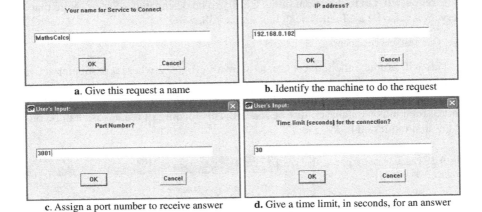

a. Give this request a name   b. Identify the machine to do the request

c. Assign a port number to receive answer   d. Give a time limit, in seconds, for an answer

Fig. 9.3 Sequence of information requests for client connect

If a there is a Clarity listening at the machine specified by the IP address on port number 3001 (Fig. 9.3c) then you will get in the Client's control window

> QUERY> Client initiating a connection ...
>   Client has made the connection

You are then ready to make a request for a service from this machine. This can be done manually in the control window using the function 'joblist', such as

> QUERY> joblist #30 [(Job (sqrt #r2345) "MathsCalcs") (Job (nar_line "Thanks for the use of your PC") "MathsCalcs")]

The first parameter of 'joblist' is a time-out limit in seconds for all the jobs to be completed in the list. Each element of the list is a type 'job' indicated by the constructor 'Job'. Job has two parameters. The first is the task to be done and the second by which server. The task name (e.g. 'sqrt') must be known by both the server and the client. These jobs must be specifiable without failing the local interpretation checks. However, the function name may be recognised by both but be defined differently and thus associated with different processes in the client than in the server. In our example this is not the case since we are using library functions and these tend to remain the same. The above joblist will find the square-root of #r2345 and will print out a message at the server end to say 'Thanks ...' with the result 'True' being returned in the answer list at the client end.

On the server the control window will report

> QUERY> Server attempting to listen
>   Server is listening at port 3001
>   Client has requested a connection
>   Server accepted connection, socket= 224

Data is available for reading, socket=224
Data is available for reading, socket=224

Note the two different acknowledgements for each task to be done. The results will be returned in a list in the same order as the original jobs.

[#r48.425201 True]

This networking operation makes very clear the distinction between side effects and function results. Only side effects can be requested to happen at the server. These will be the actual computation to perform the function and other machine actions such as printing out a message.

At the end of all the jobs to be done and when networking to this server is no longer required, then

Control/Client Disconnect

can be called. The result will be a request for which service you want to disconnect as shown in Fig. 9.4.

The control window will report the following:

QUERY> Client has closed connection, socket=136
You may reconnect when server is listening

Fig. 9.4 A request for service disconnection

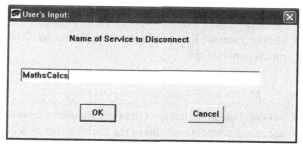

When stopping the server from listening and 'Control/Server Stop' is called from the menu then this produces the simple response in the server's control window

QUERY> Server is closing all sockets

Networking Through User Functions

There are a set of built-in library functions devoted to network communication. In summary these are:

- **client_connect** Local area network functions to share tasks. Tries to establish a connection to a service. Parameters are a name chosen by the client, the server IP address, the server port number and the timeout.

    QUERY> client_connect "maths" "166.266.26.86" #1027 #50
    True

- **client_disconnect**– Local area network functions to share tasks. Breaks the connection to a named service.

  QUERY> client_disconnect "maths"
  True

- **client_getfile**– For client/server applications. The client gets a file from the named service; the other parameters are the names of the local and remote files, and the timeout.

  QUERY> client_getfile "maths" "myfile" "yourfile" #20
  True

- **client_putfile**– For client/server applications. The client sends a file to the named service; the other parameters are the names of the local and remote files, and the timeout.

  QUERY> client_putfile "maths" "myfile" "yourfile" #20
  True

- **joblist**– For client/server applications. A client sends a list of jobs to various services. The parameters are timeout and the list of Jobs, each of which consists of an expression to evaluate and the name of the service.

  QUERY> joblist #30 [(Job (sqrt #r2345) "maths")]
  [#r48.425201]

- **server_conns**– For client/server applications. Returns the number of current client connections.

  QUERY> server_conns
  #1

- **server_listen**– Local area network functions to share tasks. Listens for requests for client connections. Takes the port number as a parameter.

  QUERY> server_listen #1027
  True

- **server_stop**– Local area network functions to share tasks. Breaks the client connections, and stops listening.

  QUERY> server_stop
  True

Figure 9.5a and b are two examples of client to server communication. In Fig. 9.5b a set of service names are used so that the same named database (ddb) is loaded on all of them. If the services are on separate machines then this will happen in parallel. The 'joblist' will be returned when all the services have responded or when time-out is exceeded. In this case the function 'load' responds 'True' when successful.

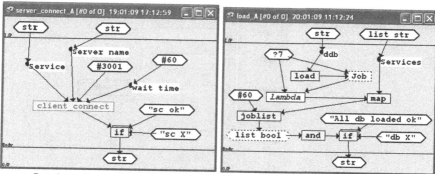

a. Opening a Connection with a server   **b. Loading a database on several servers**

Fig. 9.5 Two examples of client to server communication

Adding Users' Own Code: Extending the Library

A Simple Approach

A very simple approach to extending the functionality of Clarity is to use the function **'remote'**. The mode of communication between Clarity and another program can be through files. The function **'remote'** executes an application, waits for the result, and then outputs this result as a list of string. The application must be written to expect an input file of information and must write its results onto an output file, terminated by **'$$$$'** (indicating end of file). The function **'remote'** waits for this output file to be complete, in this example it prints the results as a list, and finally deletes the file.

The input and output file names are quite specific. For example, if the application is called **'fred'**, remote will generate an input file from the input parameters called *'fred1.txt'*. The application must expect to read a file of this name. The application should be written to generate an output file called *'fred2.txt'*. The last parameter is the timeout in seconds, in case of any problems.

An Example

```
QUERY> remote "ParaRect" ["2" "3" "4"] #20
["52" "24"]
QUERY> remote "ParaRect" [] #15
["1012" "2184"]
```

'remote' generates file ParaRect1.txt from its input parameter list

```
2
3
4
```

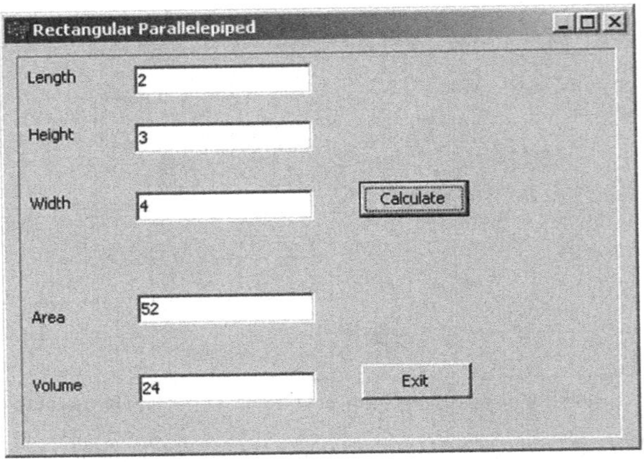

Fig. 9.6 A form generated by
application 'ParaRect.exe'

And then executes 'ParaRect.exe', which in this example produces the form in
Fig. 9.6. 'ParaRect' was built using Borland Developer Studio 2006. The form is
shown after the user has pressed the "Calculate" button. In this case, if '**remote**'
is called with no parameters then the user is expected to type them in. 'ParaRect'
generates this file ParaRect2.txt (the $$$$ is vital)

```
52
24
$$$$
```

The function '**remote**' uses this file to generate its output results list.

Writing Application Extensions: (DLLs)

It is possible to extend the functionality of Clarity by including C or C++ code
written by the user and included in the style of a DLL. The functions are accessed
from Clarity via the built-in function **user** which takes as parameters the library, the
function, and its parameters, for example

```
QUERY> user "UsersDLL.dll" "mnemonic"["Read" "Only" "Memory"]
"ROM"
```

Here the DLL is called 'UsersDLL.dll', the function is '**mnemonic**', and the
parameters to that function are in the list ["Read" "Only" "Memory"].
There is a standard interface to be adhered to, so that there is no confusion
about parameter types. The input is always a list of parameter strings, which may
be empty, and the output is always a single string. The input has to be correctly
interpreted by the DLL code, and the output has to be correctly interpreted by
Clarity. Below is an example of a C++ file 'userlib.cpp'. This is used as part
of a Borland project to build a DLL that contains some simple functions. The
procedure to be followed is also included as comments at the beginning of the file.

```
/*————————————————————————————

    userlib.cpp JJTA 27Apr07
    This file is used to create the dll "UsersDLL.dll", with a Borland Developer Studio
2006 project to create a dll. The dependencies are as follows:

    UsersDLL.dll

            UsersDLL.bpf
            userlib.cpp
            VCLINIT.cpp


The file contains functions written by the user. Although each function may require
different parameters (integers, floats, file names etc) they must always be given
(from Clarity) in STRING form. It is up to the user function to translate them into
the form required for processing. The examples below make this clearer.

Here are some examples of calling the functions in "userlib.cpp" from Clarity:

QUERY> user "UsersDLL.dll" "test" ["fred" "john"]
"fred"
QUERY> user "UsersDLL.dll" "average" ["1" "2" "3" "4"]
"2.500000"
QUERY> user "UsersDLL.dll" "mnemonic" ["Read" "Only" "Memory"]
"ROM"
QUERY> user "UsersDLL.dll" "rms_value" ["1.0" "2.0" "3.0"]
"2.160247"

This file can be used as a template for creating further funct ions. Always return the
reply as a string, and deal with the string in Clarity, e.g. with the built-in
functions str_to_int, str_to_real etc..
            ————————————————————————*/


#include <windows.h>
#include <string.h>
#include <stdio.h>
#include <stdlib.h>
#include <math.h>


#define EXPORT __declspec(dllexport)
        static char reply[256]; use this for the return parameter

/* —————————————— Function Descriptions —————————— */

extern "C" EXPORT char* far pascal test(char *values [ ], int count);
extern "C" EXPORT char* far pascal average(char *values [ ], int count);
extern "C" EXPORT char* far pascal mnemonic(char *values [ ], int count);
extern "C" EXPORT char* far pascal rms_value(char *values [ ], int count);
```

```
/*—————————Add further function descriptions here—————————*/

int WINAPI DllMain (HINSTANCE hInstance, DWORD fdwReason, PVOID pvReserved)
{
    return TRUE ;
}

/* ——————————— Function Definitions ——————————— */

char* far pascal test(char * values[], int count)
{
/* Simply returns the first parameter */
    strcpy(reply, values[0]);
    return(reply);

}

/* ——————————————————————————————————————— */

char * far pascal average(char * values[], int count)
{
/* Find the average of a list of numbers, assuming they are integers */
    float acc = 0.0;
    int i, num;
    if(count == 0) return NULL;
    for(i=0; i<count; i++) {
            sscanf(values[i], "%d", &num);
            acc += num;
    }
    acc = acc / count;
    sprintf(reply, "%f", acc);
    return(reply);

}
/* ——————————————————————————————————————— */
char * far pascal mnemonic(char * values[], int count)
{
/* make a mnemonic by taking the first letter of each of a list of strings */
    int i;
    if(count == 0) return NULL;
        for (i=0; i<count; i++)
        reply [i] = values[i][0];
    reply [count] = '\0';
    return (reply);

}
/* ——————————————————————————————————————— */
        double sqrt(double x);
```

```
char * far pascal rms_value(char * values[], int count)
{
/* Find the root mean square of a list of numbers, assuming they are floats * /
        float acc = 0.0;
        int i;
    float num;
    double root;

    if (count == 0) return NULL;
        for (i = 0; i < count; i ++) {
            sscanf (values [i], "% f", &num);
            acc += num * num;
        }
    acc = acc / count;
    root = std::sqrt ((double) acc);
    sprintf (reply, "%f", root);
    return (reply);
}
/* ————————Add further function definitions here ———————— */
```

Creating an Interface to Clarity

Sometimes we may want to design a special interface to a function that has already been created using Clarity, and which we have stored in a ddb. For example, a nice interface to the Sudoku problem would be a grid of squares to be filled in by the user, and where the solution appears. The interface in Fig. 9.7 was built using Borland Developer Studio 2006. It can be used for general queries to Clarity, and also specifically to solve a Sudoku problem.

There are three edit boxes, labelled **QUERY>**, **REPLY** and **MESSAGES**, and called edtQuery, edtReply, and edtMessages, and two buttons, labelled **Evaluate** and **Quit**, for the purposes of sending a general query to Clarity, receiving the reply, and specifying an area for any messages from Clarity that occur during the evaluation of the query. For example, if the user types the query **+ #4 #5** and presses the **Evaluate** button, the reply **#9** is received.

Type the query **help** for a list of all the available built-in functions. They can be ordered alphabetically. Double-click on their icons for information on how to use them.

The function that evaluates the queries in ClarityDLL is **ask_query**, which takes three parameters, all strings. The first is a null-terminated string for the query itself, the second is the area for the reply, and the third is the area for any messages from Clarity.

The event function for clicking the **Evaluate** button is **OnEvaluate()**. This means that the code in **OnEvaluate()** is executed when the user presses **Evaluate**.

Fig. 9.7 An user-designed
interface to Clarity

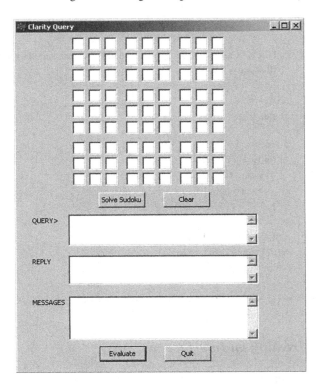

The code shown in Fig. 9.8 should be added to **OnEvaluate()**.

The ClarityDLL.**lib** file should be included as part of the project to create the executable and ClarityDLL.dll should be in the same directory as the interface code.

If the database 'sudoku81' is in the same directory as the interface it can then be loaded by pressing the **Solve Sudoku** button. This action will also read the values in the grid, call 'solve_sudoku' with a list of strings, and insert the solution back into the grid. The function '**solve_sudoku**' takes a list of 9 "row" strings as input and returns a list of 81 integers for the solution. For example, if we were to run ClarityPro, load sudoku81, we can call via the Control Window '**solve_sudoku**' like this:

QUERY> solve_sudoku ["009062050" "200001000" "005090603" "120000000" "803000204" "000000087" "708020900" "000800005" "090340800"]

[#3 #8 #9 #4 #6 #2 #7 #5 #1 #2 #7 #6 #5 #3 #1 #4 #9 #8 #4 #1 #5 #7 #9 #8 #6 #2 #3 #1 #2 #7 #6 #8 #4 #5 #3 #9 #8
#5 #3 #9 #1 #7 #2 #6 #4 #9 #6 #4 #2 #5 #3 #1 #8 #7 #7 #3 #8 #1 #2 #5 #9 #4 #6 #6 #4 #2 #8 #7 #9 #3 #1 #5 #5 #9
#1 #3 #4 #6 #8 #7 #2]

This function was added solely for the purpose of this interface instead of '**setup_squares**' and '**solve_it**'.

```
      static char query[1000];
      static char reply[5000];
      static char messages[5000];

      extern  "C" _declspec(dllexport)
              void far pascal ask_query(char *query, char *reply,
char *messages);

void __fastcall TForm1::OnEvaluate(TObject *Sender)
{
      int len;

      sprintf(query, "%s", edtQuery->Text);
      len = strlen(query);
      if(query[len-1] == '\n') {
              if(query[len-2] == '\r')
                      query[len-2] = '\0';
      }

      ask_query(query, reply, messages);
      edtReply->Text = reply;
      edtMessages->Text = messages;
}
```

Fig. 9.8 The C++ code

Adding Users' Own Code

Any Clarity query can be called from this interface, including user functions defined in a DLL, as described in the section above entitled "Writing Application Extensions". The DLL can be created using the same development environment as that used to create the simple interface. Make sure that the way the parameters are handled inside the function code matches the list of parameters. Always return the reply as a <u>string</u>, and deal with the string in Clarity, i.e. with the built-in casting functions such as '**str_to_int**', '**str_to_real**', etc.

Opening a Database

Suppose a database has been created using Clarity as for example **sudoku81.ddb**. To load it we type in the Control Window

    QUERY>   **load "sudoku81"**

And then we have access to all the functions in the ddb. (However, in the example interface, sudoku81 is loaded once, the first time **Solve Sudoku** is pressed.) In Figs. 9.9 and 9.10 the interface is shown before and after **Solve Sudoku** is pressed.

We will not go into the details of this implementation since it is all standard C++ development. We hope that we have provided sufficient information for the reader to complete an interface to 'sudoku'.

Fig. 9.9 Filling in the given numbers

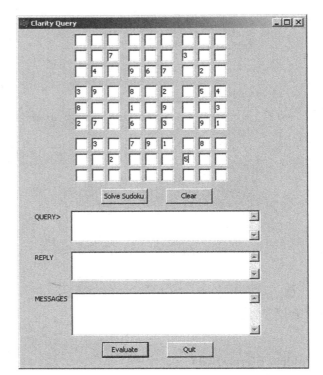

The advantage of this approach is that the same interface can be used for any further development of 'Sudoku81'. For an example of further development see Chapter 10.

Some Additional Features

Importing and Exporting Databases

In addition to opening, creating and saving databases it is possible to import and export parts or all of a program. 'Export to Database . . .' under menu 'Filters' will export any set of highlighted functions *and their dependencies* to a file. 'Import Database . . .' under menu 'File' will import a named database (program). Clashes of function names are detected and will trigger a pop-up menu of possible actions that might resolve the encountered clash.

This feature is valuable at the end of a development project when we require a clean database (program) devoid of all the redundant functions that have been used during its evolution to the final version.

Fig. 9.10 The solution

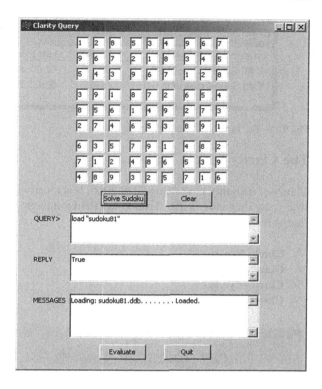

Stacking Windows

Function and network windows can be stacked automatically by menu item 'Stack' under 'Window'. This helps to tidy up the work space. However, all open windows are also listed under menu/window.

Re-numbering and Naming Function Components

Function components can be 'Renumbered' under 'Find'. Normally, the order of the components does not really matter but when there are several hundred components it is useful to use the numbering as a form of indexing for data management purposes. This also relates to component naming where the index will display this name. The naming is done by

Menu/Find/Name or Rename

The index is displayed by double clicking on the background of any one of the function's components. Each component can also be associated with an annotation window. This choice of junction labels provides a complete self-documentation service. This is ideal for also keeping validation tests and results of functions during the development phase. An example of an index for the function 'factorial' is shown in Fig. 9.11.

Component # (and Name)	Parame...	Last Modified	
#0 General Case N > 0	?0	02:03:09 12:10:18	
#1 Special case of N = 0	(#0)	02:03:09 12:11:30	

Fig. 9.11   The Index for 'factorial'

The Clarity Source Code

Clarity is currently built using BDS 2006. It is mostly written in C, using C++ only where the demands of the development environment must be satisfied. There are four versions of Clarity:

> **ClarityPro.exe**
> **ClarityLite.exe**
> **ClarityEye.exe**
> **ClarityDLL.dll**

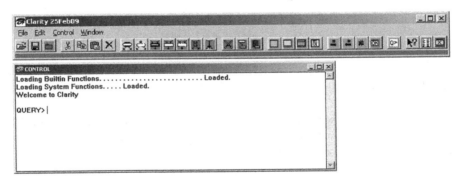

Fig. 9.12   ClarityPro with full functionality and libraries

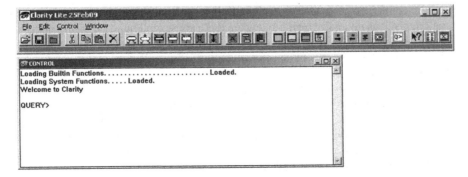

Fig. 9.13   Some functionality is disabled for ClarityLite

ClarityDLL is a dll, to be used with a user-defined interface, as described on page 25 – "Creating an Interface to Clarity".

ClarityPro will look like Fig. 9.12 on opening. All built-in functions are available.

ClarityLite will look like Fig. 9.13. A limited number of built-ins are available (see Fig. 9.14).

ClarityEye will look like Fig. 9.15. The functionality is restricted. It is intended to be used for queries only.

Function Name/Recency	Function Types	Group
!	int->list ?0 ->?0	List
!=	?0->?0->bool	Boolean
$	list ?0 ->int	List
%	int->int->int	Maths (.
&&	bool->bool->bool	Boolean
*	?0->?1->?2	Maths (.
+	?0->?1->?2	Maths (.
-	?0->?1->?2	Maths (.

Fig. 9.14 Reduced library for ClarityLite

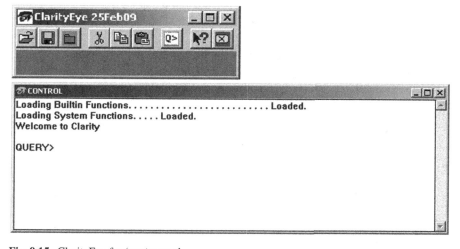

Fig. 9.15 ClarityEye for '**customers**'

The C Files and Header Files

The structure of the Faith and Clarity interpreters with their libraries is described under the following group of files. There are two header files of particular interest:

target.h and platform.h

target.h can be edited to produce the different target versions described above, and some others besides.

platform.h can be edited to produce versions of Clarity to run on different platforms, e.g. Windows applications and Apple Mac applications. The latter development ceased before the Apple Mac System X. Some transformations were completed but only for the early non-Intel chip versions.

The following files describe the C or C++ source code files grouped, in general and according to function.

> *ClaritySdiApp.cpp* Contains the main entry point for Clarity, WinMain(). It does the initialisation, and starts the message handling.
>
> *clr_*.c* For drawing functions in Clarity, creating and interpreting the Clarity forms – Function, Constructor and Network.
>
> *net_*.c* Generating and displaying the function network diagrams.
>
> *pdecs.c, pfdef.c, plhs.c.* Storing newly created functions in memory as part of a database.
>
> *symbols.c, f_free.c, f_remove.c* Dealing with the internal symbol table.

To query a function, the expression is parsed, and an apply tree built (Field and Harrison 1988). This is then evaluated in an expansion and reduction process

> *cint.c, parse.c, parser.c and putils.c.* The files involved in parsing.
>
> *evaluate.c, comb.c, enum.c, futils.c, matcher.c, mem.c* The files involved in the evaluation process of expanding and reducing the apply tree.
>
> *bi_*.c* For handling the built-in functions
>
> *print.c, printall.c* Printing out the results of the query evaluation.
>
> *f_dbops.c commit.c* To save newly created functions in memory to a database as a file.
>
> *X_*.c* These cross-platform files contain code for two versions of Clarity, Windows and Apple Mac. They mostly relate to interaction with the user in the form of menus, buttons, graphics, etc.
>
> *mainDLLc.c, callquery.c, globals.c* Extra files involved in making Clarity-DLL.dll, which replace ClaritySdiApp.cpp.

Project: Problem Solving

Sudoku: Searching for Answers

Introduction

The Sudoku square is represented by a 9 X 9 grid that has a few integers apparently randomly distributed. It will be noticed that the grid is subdivided into 3×3 smaller grids. The purpose of the game is to fill in the blank squares with the integers 1–9 so that each small sub-grid contains the entire number set and so do each row or column (see Fig. 9.16a and b).

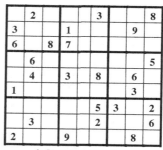

a. Easy Problem   b. Very Hard Problem

Fig. 9.16 Two examples of a Sudoku problem

Prototyping: A Controlled Approach to Design

In this project we wish to introduce the mechanism of prototyping. This allows a designer to design from the network diagram. It also provides a useful memory aid by keeping track of what has been done, type checking and what has still to be done. In this process the network and function windows will generate prototype schema for you to fill in. As a project we will simply provide the Clarity schema and an explanation of some of the important functions so that you can try out this technique. While using prototyping it is possible to create the functions in any order but it will not be possible to test them until all the supporting functions are present. A good approach is to create a network of the functions such as shown in Diagram 9.1a.

The names will remain in *italic* until they have been defined by you. The process of prototyping will start with the call

Menu/Find/Create Functions from Network

This action will generate a prototype schema for all the functions in the network. The record of this is shown in the Control Window (see Diagram 9.1b). The prototype schema for the function 'reduce' will appear after double clicking on the 'reduce' box in the network window (see Diagram 9.2a). From the schema shown in the project collection of schema the details can be filled in (see Diagram 9.2b). This will include extra functions not given in the original network and when committed a series of tests will be done by Clarity in order to collect information about the

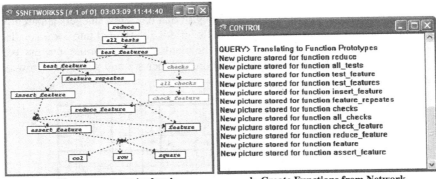

a. The core process 'reduce'   **b. Create Functions from Network**

Diagram 9.1   The first steps to prototyping from the network

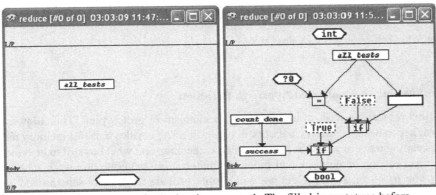

a. The initial prototype for 'reduce'   b. The filled-in prototype before
commitment

Diagram 9.2   A prototype

coherence of the definition. In this case the commitment is started for (say) function '**reduce**' by clicking

Menu/OK

This will respond with a set of choices, the top choice being 'Replace Component'. Click this and the set of tests for the prototype commences. Each stage will require further OKs and 'Replace Component' until all the tests are accepted (see Diagram 9.4a).

Diagram 9.3a shows the function '**reduce**' after all the type checking has been completed and the 'holdN' function inserted. This level of completion is marked by the function '**reduce**' not being in italic (see Diagram 9.3b). When the database is saved at this stage then the children of '**reduce**' can be found:

Menu/Filters/Children

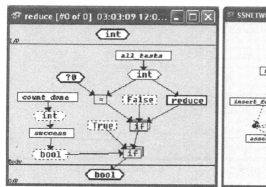
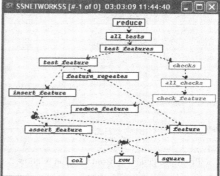

| a. The prototype after commitment | b. The resulting Network |

Diagram 9.3 Completed coherence check

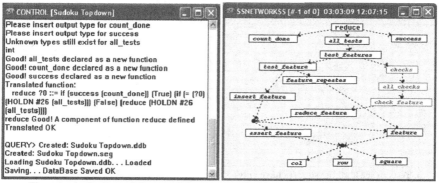

| a. The auto-checks done while committing | b. After save, the children can be found |

Diagram 9.4 Saving the database and new tasks found to be done

The record of what is done is given in the control window as shown in Diagram 9.4a. The resulting new functions are displayed in Diagram 9.4b. New prototypes are generated by this process from information drawn from the function window Diagram 9.3a. The junctions in the network will also carry the information to the prototype schema generation as shown in Diagram 9.5b.

The new functions can also set up a train of development. Once (say) '**count_ done**' is written and all the type demands are satisfied, the database saved, then a new addition to the evolving network can be found through Menu/Filter/Children. Note that if the children are already in the network then the link will be made and the new information added to the prototype 'square' (see Diagram 9.7a).

The function '**count_done**' (see Diagram 9.6) can now be completed with the functions '**done**' (see Diagram 9.8c) and '**square**' (see Diagram 9.7b). The function '**success**' simply determines if all the squares have been resolved by adding

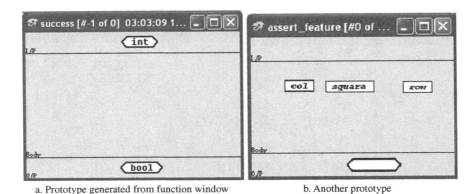

a. Prototype generated from function window   b. Another prototype

Diagram 9.5 Other prototypes generated

a. Tests to see if all the squares have only   b. Further children generated
one number,

Diagram 9.6 Expanding new elements of the problem

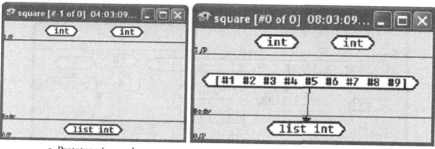

a. Prototype 'square'

b. Original version of 'square'

Diagram 9.7 The new information is added to the prototype square

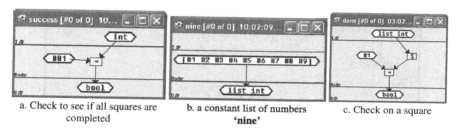

a. Check to see if all squares are
completed

b. a constant list of numbers
'nine'

c. Check on a square

Diagram 9.8 The other functions can now be completed

checking that the sum of all the associated numbers with each square adds to 81. So this branch will not lead to any further development but **'success'** will be used by other functions such as the top level function **'solve_it'**.

We will now describe the main functions used to solve a Sudoku puzzle. The interface problem can be resolved in many ways by using some of the techniques described in this chapter. We used this simple interface so we can just get the main problem solver working. The top function for this simple interface is shown in Diagram 9.9. The function **'set_row'** simply takes the string provided by the user via **'gr_dialog'** and creates a new set of squares for a line. Squares not fixed by the user remain as the general case and therefore have all nine numbers assigned as shown in Diagram 9.7b.

The Collection of Functions

Diagram 9.10 shows the top level functions that represent an overview of the whole problem solving process. The function **'setup_square'** resets the grid of squares to empty and allows the user to input a new problem to be solved. At this stage every small square in the grid will have associated with it all nine possible numbers except those that have been specified by the user in setting up a specific problem to be solved. The function **'solve_it'** finds a solution to the problem and prints it out using **'show_square'**.

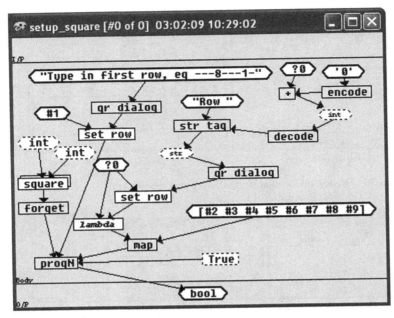

Diagram 9.9 A Function for setting up the initial problem state

The Diagram 9.10 was generated after the program was created and then it was processed by

Menu/Features/Redraw Window with Junctions

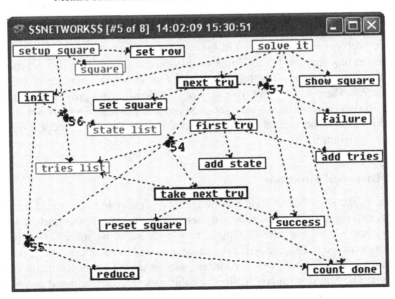

Diagram 9.10 Top level functions for Sudoku

This reduces the number of lines by detecting the many-to-many used-on relationships. The junctions may be useful concepts as can be found through the reduction of the many-to-many functional dependency relationships in the process of normalisation of a set of relations (Addis 1985). The junctions are numbered automatically and we have the following four new concepts discovered:

54: Stack, where potential solution paths are stored.
55: The Solution Path.
56: Potential Problem States.
57: Current problem state.

As we have proposed in Chapter 7 we usually make the problem state a set of extensional functions. In this case it is the single function '**square**' along with the '**state_list**' and '**tries_list**'as shown in Diagram 9.10. The theory for solving this problem is that every blank square is potentially capable of containing any one of the nine numbers (see Diagram 9.7b). The numbers are just labels, so there will be no arithmetic involved. The technique will be to identify the numbers in the list that can be eliminated because they already exist in the same square, row or column. So the general strategy is to '**reduce**' these lists of numbers by analysis, until each square is represented by a list of only one integer (see Diagram 9.3a). When that occurs the puzzle is solved (see Diagram 9.8a) and the goal state reached. Since there are likely to be many scans of square over the range 1–9 the constant '**nine**' is declared for that purpose (see Diagram 9.8b). The first thing the '**solve_it**' function does is to call the function '**init**'(see Diagram 9.11). The function '**init**' initiates two lists that help keep track of what states have been visited.

The function '**count_done**' adds up the number of labels (numbers) for the whole grid (see Diagram 9.12a). If this equals '81' (test done by function '**success**', Diagram 9.8a) then this returns '**True**' showing that the goal has been achieved. Otherwise the function '**reduce**' (see Diagram 9.3a) will reduce the list of possibilities for each square by using the rules of Sudoku via the function '**all_tests**' (see

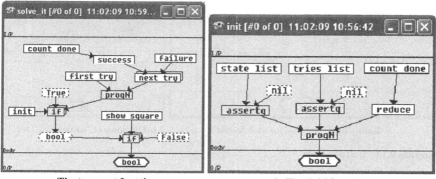

| a. The top most function | b. The 'init' function |

Diagram 9.11 The top function and first action

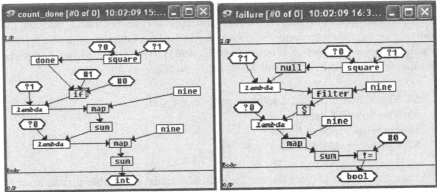

a. Checking each small square   b. Fail to find a solution

Diagram 9.12   Check and fail of problem

Diagram 9.13a). These rules, contained in function '**all_tests**', will test each row, column and 3∗3 box associated with every square in the grid. If a unique integer appears on only one list, then that square must have that value. This reduction is repeated until no more squares can be solved this way. If it cannot be solved by this straight forward elimination then a new path will be explored, derived from the stack, until there are no further possibilities. At this point '**failure**' to find a solution is reached. Otherwise '**next_try**' is tried (see Diagram 9.13b).

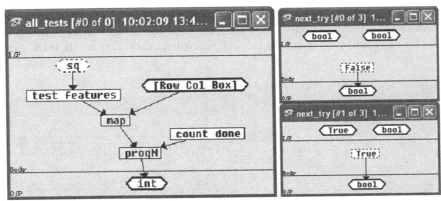

a. Testing for completion for each feature   b. Unknown or 'success' is 'True'

Diagram 9.13   Trail and error

The function '**next_try**' is pattern sensitive to '**success**' and '**failure**' outcomes (see Diagrams 9.13b and 9.14). If the result is '**success**' = '**True**' then whatever 'failure' might be the result will be '**True**' and the answer '**square**' will be printed. Otherwise, if the 'success' = 'False' and 'failure' = 'False' then '**first_try**' will be attempted followed by further tests (see Diagram 9.14a). The function '**first_try**' will attempt to go back to the '**tries_list**' to what numbers and squares can be attempted next (see Diagram 9.15a). The final condition considered is no success and also nothing to try next (see Diagram 9.15b). In this case all the attempts at this level are forgotten and the world state is reset to the last no-failure state from the '**state_list**' (see Diagrams 9.14b and 9.15b).

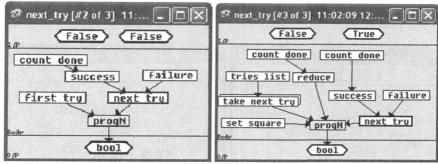

a. No 'success' but still numbers to try   b. No 'success' and no numbers left

Diagram 9.14   What to do when there is no '**success**'

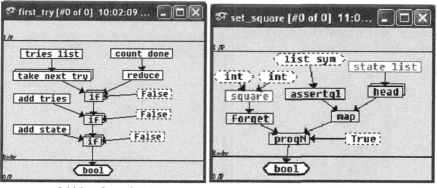

a. Initial try for each state   b. Reset to previous state

Diagram 9.15   What may be attempted next

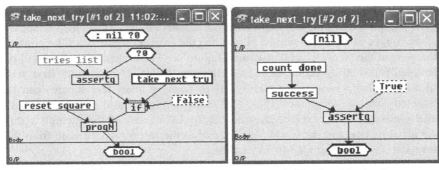

a. Nothing at this level   b. Nothing at top level

Diagram 9.16 Two possibilities on trying something else

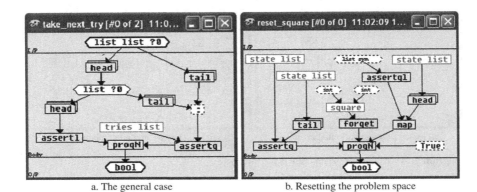

a. The general case   b. Resetting the problem space

Diagram 9.17 General case for trying and resetting of current state to null

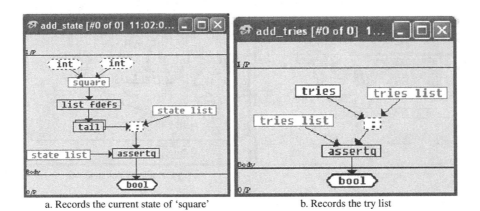

a. Records the current state of 'square'   b. Records the try list

Diagram 9.18 Recording states and tries

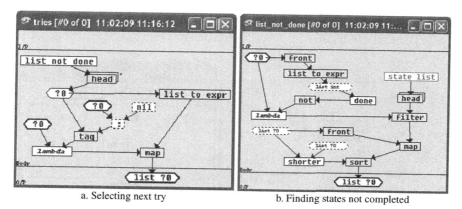

a. Selecting next try   b. Finding states not completed

Diagram 9.19 Selecting a list of things to try

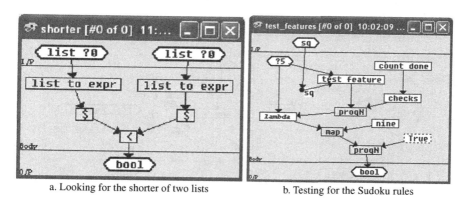

a. Looking for the shorter of two lists   b. Testing for the Sudoku rules

Diagram 9.20 Selecting shortest list and testing for Sudoku constraints

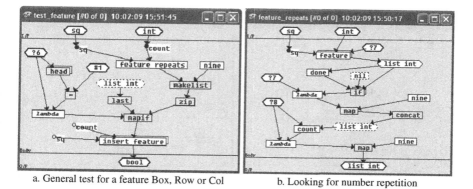

a. General test for a feature Box, Row or Col   b. Looking for number repetition

Diagram 9.21 Starting the chain of tests for all the features of Row, Box and Col

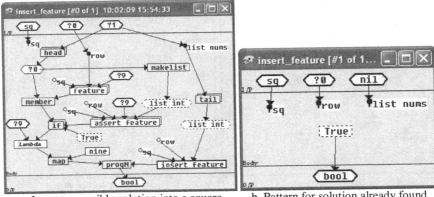

a. Inserts a possible solution into a square   b. Pattern for solution already found

Diagram 9.22   Inserting solutions into the matrix of squares

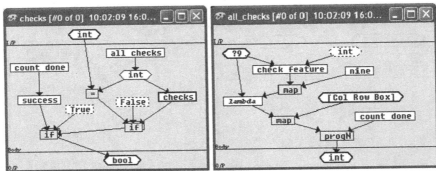

a. Starting all the required checks if not   b. Checking each feature in turn
   finished

Diagram 9.23   Starting the consistency checking

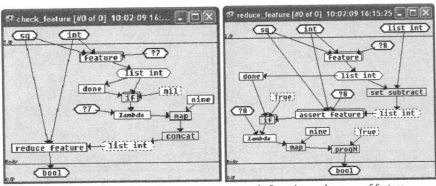

a. Attempt to reduce the number list   b. Scanning each square of feature

Diagram 9.24   Reduction testing

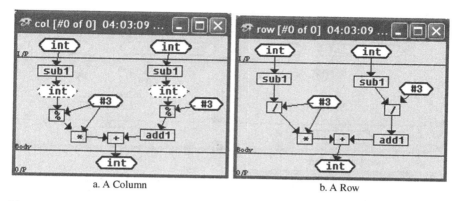

Diagram 9.25 Two feature definitions of a box in terms of a 'square' index

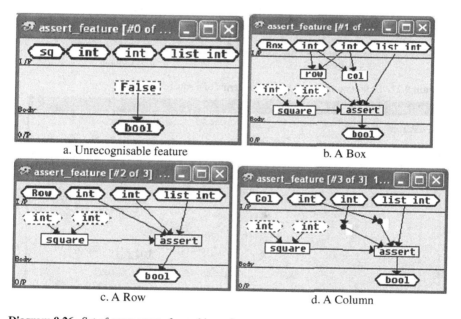

Diagram 9.26 Set of components for making a feature

The square index in Diagram 9.25 gives a row and col parameter in a 9×9 square of a box in position (int, int), e.g. box(3, 5) has row 2 and col 8 (Diagrams 9.27 and 9.28).

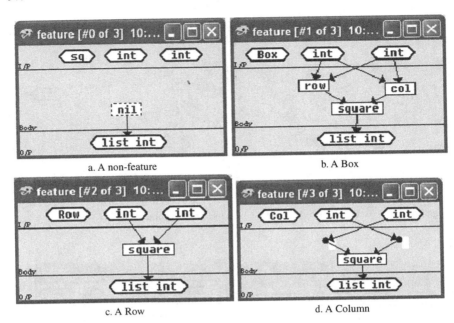

a. A non-feature   b. A Box

c. A Row   d. A Column

Diagram 9.27   Definition of all the features in terms of a square

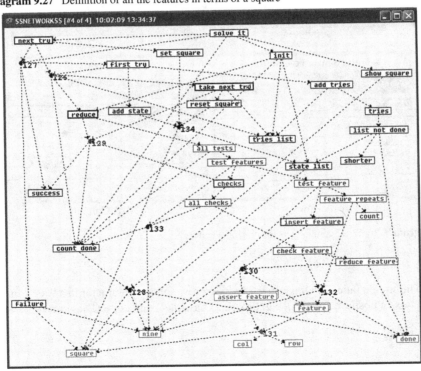

Diagram 9.28   Complete overview of Sudoku '**solve-it**'

References

1. Addis T. R. (1985) *'Designing Knowledge-Based Systems'*, Kogan Page, London, ISBN 0-85038-859-7, ISBN 1-85091-251-3 also Prentice-Hall, Englewood Cliffs, NJ (1986) ISBN 0-13-201823-3.
2. Field A. J. and Harrison P. G. (1988) *'Functional Programming'* Addison-Wesley Ltd, Boston, MA, ISBN 0-201-19249-7.
3. Reade C. (1989) *'Elements of Functional Programming'*, Addison-Wesley Ltd, Boston, MA, ISBN 0-201-12915-9.

Chapter 10
Programming with Uncertainty: Theories, Models and Programs

And now abideth faith, hope, charity, these three;
but the greatest of these is charity

Corinthians 13, 13

Models and Programs [→ Page 349]

We have seen in Chapter 7 how problem solving mechanisms can be constructed from a general problem solver (GPS). The key to this is that the problem solving activity is captured by functions that allow transformations to occur to a model of a problem domain. The problem domain therefore has to be modelled. However, this modelling is not an arbitrary activity since the kind of implementation depends very much on the problem to be solved and the representation used. There are many features of the problem domain that are not going to be valuable in the problem solving process. But to know this suggests that some notion of what is considered to be a solution is already known by the model designer. Further, to be able to do the abstraction of the right collection of features, no matter how simple, suggests that there is already some theory, regardless of how primitive, of the problem domain.

Once created the model also has to rely on a human agent (the user) who must also be able to understand how to interact with the model. Such interactions may, for example, require the user to perform actions in the problem domain. To have such ability the user must be able to share the same, or at least a similar, theory to that of the designer of the system. So the best one might expect from a computer model is it to be an aid or intellectual assistant to an already knowledgeable user. The position of model in the scheme of activities is shown in Fig. 10.1.

The process of deriving the model from the theory depends on abduction and abstraction (Peirce 1934, 1966, Addis 1987, 1989, 1990, Addis and Gooding 2008, Gooding 1990, 1996, Gooding and Addis 2008, Magnani 1998, 2001, Magnani et al. 1998). In summary, Charles S. Peirce proposed an alternative description of how we gain useful knowledge of the world. His proposal suggested that there were three different ways in which conclusions can be arrived at from observations of the world. The first is through abduction which is concerned with noticing puzzling

T. Addis, J. Addis, *Drawing Programs: The Theory and Practice of Schematic Functional Programming*, DOI 10.1007/978-1-84882-618-2_10,
© Springer-Verlag London Limited 2010

Fig. 10.1 The role of a
model with respect to a
problem domain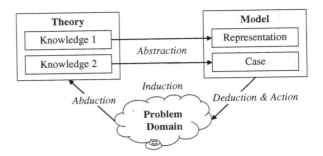

and unexplained phenomena and to create a plausible and useful explanation of
these observations. How this is done is (ironically) not explained although a sub-set
of this activity has been described by others as an inverse implication (Charniak
1975). So in this case you might have A → B, B therefore possibly A where A
is a known hypothesis. How the hypothesis gets known is not usually explained.
The next stage is to use the normal deductive process to make predictions. It is the
predictions that determine if the theory is useful. Finally there is a modified view of
the normal induction. This view takes induction simply as the comparison between
these predictions and of actual observations.

The normal view of induction is that it is an inference to a generalisation (or
theory) from examples (Langley et al 1987). Peirce has split this normal view into
Abduction which is the generalisation process via a theory and a new version of
induction which is the observation of examples to support the generalisation. His
pragmatic description of a theory or generalisation is that it should serve a purpose
and in particular it should make the world a less surprising place. This is an excellent definition because it immediately gives a mechanism that can assess a theory
without reference to the rather abstract notion of 'truth'. We will come back to this
later in this chapter when discussing 'belief' as a technical measure. The model in
our diagram Fig.10.1 is a particular 'case' (or example) of a theory (Knowledge 2)
given in terms of some 'representation' scheme (Knowledge 1). The model is used
deductively to infer the results with which we are interested. Induction is used with
the results of the model and further observations to either confirm (justify) the model
or to stimulate a modification to the model.

The account we described by Newell and Simon as the GPS was a derivative
of a human problem-solving model (Newell and Simon 1956, 1973). In essence,
the theory states that problem solving is a process of exploring a "problem space"
for a solution. A problem space can be visualised as a directed graph. The nodes
of the graph represent the different possible states of a problem. There is usually a
single start state that indicates the current situation and a set of termination states
that indicate the desired result. The arrows that go from node to node represent the
actions that are available to an agent (the problem solver) in that state and these
actions transform the problem from one state to the next. Problem solving is the
discovery of a path from the start state to a termination state. The solution is the
sequence of transformations (arcs) that make up the path.

The theory has its foundations in utility theory (Luce and Raiffa 1957). Utility theory is a means through which choices can be assessed (their utility) and decisions can be made. The utility of a state in Newell and Simon's version of decision theory is a measure of the proximity that a solution state has in terms of the estimated number of transformations needed to reach it from the start position. Each transformation has a cost, possibly in a measure of effort, so that the minimum cost path is always the ideal solution. It is this utility, a measure of summated and estimated cost, that guides the inference system to select a route to a solution.

We can say that the computer model of a problem solver is expected to consist of three elements that are related to different kinds of knowledge:

1. a 'representation' that describes a set of problem states and has the potential to describe all the problem states (the abstraction of the problem),
2. a 'set of transformations' that describes how any given state can be transformed to a new state (the deductive system),
3. a 'heuristic' that provides guidance to a search algorithm through the problem space (the heuristic knowledge).

These elements may be represented in a wide variety of forms depending on the knowledge representation scheme used (e.g. clauses, rules).

The appeal of Newell and Simon's theory, and as we illustrated in Chapter 7, is that the states of the problem can be represented as propositions. These propositions are formal representations of natural sentences that are written, thus

All(x) Elephant(x) -> Colour(Grey,x)
Exists(y) Name(Dumbo,y) and Elephant(y)

and the transformation from one state to the next is the application of deductive inference to selected propositions drawn from a database of propositions. The deductive inference step is an extension of Modus Ponens (all A are B, X is an A therefore X is a B) called Resolution. The only requirement is that the propositions must be normalised into clauses, a process that can also be done automatically.

The Role of a Model

As an illustration of a model and how it is normally used, consider the process of designing a simple slide as shown in Fig. 10.2. Such a slide may form part of the transportation system for a product in a factory. This product will have specific dimensions, weight and composition. After the drawing of a sketch that shows the spatial relationship of the product to the slide we now need to determine the acceleration of the product down the slide so that the velocity may be calculated at its point of reception.

Fig. 10.2 A spatial
representation of a slide

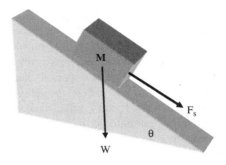

To do this we make reference to Newton's 'Theory' of Dynamics. Some aspects of this theory[1] may be presented as a series of statements; thus

T1. Every Body travels in a straight line unless a force acts upon it.
T2. Momentum is the product of mass and velocity.
T3. Force is the rate of change of momentum.
T4. For every action there is an equal and opposite reaction.
T5. Gravity is an acceleration caused by the mutual attraction of mass.
T6. Weight is a force due to gravity.
T7. Forces (and hence velocities) will add as vectors.

From this theory, a dynamic model may be constructed using the 'representation' of mathematics. In this case a first attempt will appear as

M1. A Body of mass M is on the slide.
M2. The slide is at angle θ with respect to the horizontal.
M3. The weight of the Body is $W = M*G$ where G is the acceleration due to gravity.
M4. The force down the slide $Fs = W*\mathrm{Sin}(\theta)$.

The slide is constructed as a particular 'case' where an angle and mass are chosen. It is found that the actual acceleration is much less than that predicted. After checking the calculations, reference is then made back to the 'Theory'. The 'Theory' restricts the set of possible explanations for this discrepancy to that of a 'force' and this guides the designer to create a better model. In this case, the 'Theory' limits the set of possible proposals to the existence of other 'forces' acting on the Body. Another single force can 'explain' the discrepancy between the model and the observations; this force is usually referred to as *friction*.

---

[1] A theory in this book does not necessarily mean a formal theory. Any set of statements that forms some coherent description of the world that can be used to "render facts likely" (Peirce, 1934) will be considered a theory. A theory is a set of propositions that reduces the uncertainty in the world for an agent.

The notion of friction does not come directly from the Theory but is an interpretation of both experience (i.e. there is a recognizable feeling of resistance when moving the Body on the slide which becomes greater with increased pressure between the surfaces) and the theory (i.e. only forces can influence the motion of a Body). The process that generates the insight (that these disparate experiences and concepts should be amalgamated into a simple causal element identified as friction) is "abductive" inference. An important component of abduction is that the agent interacts with the world. The Model is modified, thus

M4'. The force down the slide Fs' $= W^*[Sin(\theta - K^*Cos(\theta)]$

where K is the coefficient of friction for the materials in contact.

The coefficient of friction K is a concept that has evolved from the need to adjust the model to fit the observations; it is a form of tweaking so that the observations will fit the model. However, the notion of friction does not and cannot emerge from only the manipulation of the sentences that make up the theory; it is not discoverable by formal analytic means such as logic and deduction.

A precise relationship between a theory and a model cannot be easily defined as they both represent an infinite range of possible interpretations and share many of the same properties (c.f. Aris 1978). However, we may consider that there is a continuum of theories and models ranging from the non-specific (most general) to the identification of unique cases. The relationship between a theory and a model is that a model will be associated with a more specific set of situations (cases) than a theory. The slide example could represent an infinite number of cases that are constrained by the model. It could represent a child sliding on a sledge down a hill or the launching of a lifeboat. On the other hand, the theory of dynamics can be applied to pendulums, planets and billiards. In line with our use in functional programming, the complete range of cases derivable from a model or theory will be called the "extension" of the model or theory and the model or theory, from which a case is derived, is called its "intension". The problem is that both extensions, in principle, are infinite; their cardinality is infinite.

Figure 10.3 shows the model as the end product of two simultaneous processes; the empirical abstraction of significant features from the world and the description abducted from the formal world. In the formal case there are several stages of abduction so that the model emerges from a potentially infinite set of possibilities that may be presumed to exist within the abstract world of human imagination. In the empirical case the model is also the end product of several stages of abstraction of what is an infinite set of possible distinctions. The model can capture only a subset of the possible features of an artefact (i.e. it does not, in the above case, show the colour, texture, smell or structure of the materials); it is a subset that is coherent and must serve a particular purpose. A model and a theory both together encapsulate an understanding of the world that is the result of purpose and experience. A model and its associated theory is 'declarative knowledge' if the model relates to at least one feasible artefact (i.e. can be constructed). What is feasible and the method used to

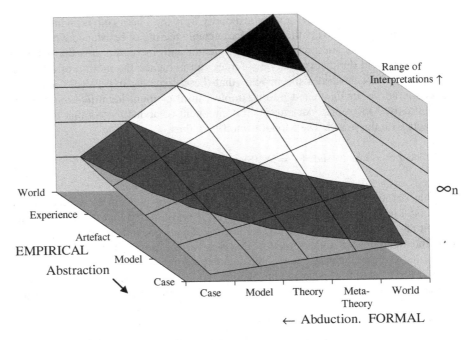

Fig. 10.3 The Model as a point of contact between Theory and Artefact

make such a judgement (such as the comparison of predictions with observations) is another form of inductive inference.

Since the number of cases for a model is much less than the number of cases for a theory because it is a subset and since both numbers are infinite then what we are dealing with here are transfinite numbers. The z-axis of Fig. 10.3 is an ordinal and increasing arrangement of these transfinite numbers (∞_n) What we are comparing is the relative volume of cases.

In the example of the slide the mathematical model will describe the active forces of interest provided the right combination of calculations is applied. The right combination of calculations is selected by the mathematician given the purpose of the model. This understanding of how to use the model to make appropriate predictions is 'heuristic knowledge'. The design of this slide (the artefact) has utilised two models: the model of forces represented in mathematical terms and the model of spatial relationships that uses a scaled projection of the slide onto two-dimensions. The two models are two different abstractions from experience and two different abductions from theory. The models are related in that there is a clear mapping between points of contact. In this case the points of contact are the angle of the slope and the direction of the forces acting on the Body.[2] Other design tasks, such

---

[2] However, the triangle of forces is not shown.

as the construction of VLSI chips, will use nine or ten different models to represent different abstractions of the same object. Each of the models is related to some theory that uses a generalisation of the characteristics to be controlled and formed in the design. A theory is only useful if it provides this control. The control is incorporated in the constraints (lawful behaviour) and in the procedures for deriving the consequences of any design decision within the domain of the theory. Hence the laws of electronics (e.g. Ohm's law) provide a means through which particular circuits may have predictable performance.

The theory for the slide example involves both the representation scheme (mathematics) and the generalisation of a particular aspect of the world (dynamics). The theory is made explicit by the model in the form of equations (case). The model is influenced by both the theory and the artefact. The model is interrogated through calculations by a mathematician (usually the same person as the designer) who may use a calculator or tables. The engineer must be able to interface with the artefact (construct) through measurements (e.g. the angle of slope and the acceleration) in order to provide observations that can be compared with the predictions of the designer; the artefact must engage the model. The mathematician, engineer and designer indicate the skills (tacit knowledge) required to progress a simple design.

Although the model is the main component to be altered in the design process, the effectiveness of both the theory and the artefact are continually under review. The theory will always be modified since models can rarely be made adequate to reflect the artefacts and an artefact will always be reconsidered in the light of predicted performance and the achievement of the purpose. This shows the value of a model. None of this can begin unless there are both the beginnings of a theory and the inklings of an artefact from which a case model can be created. However, modifing a theory would seem to require the existence of a meta-theory which has the same relationship to the theory as that the theory has to the model. Model, theory and meta-theory will be referred to as different 'levels' of knowledge. So we can conclude that a theory is abducted from a meta-theory and supported through induction by experience with its models. How this terminates is not clear but the ultimate limitation must be determined by the inbuilt flexibility of the human mind. However, see Addis (1990) for a wider discussion of this view of design.

∗ Solving Sudoku

As a means of illustrating some of our modelling techniques we have fully explained a Sudoku puzzle solver in Chapter 9 in the Project section. Sudoku has become a very popular passtime for those that want an alternative to crossword puzzles. The advantages of Sudoku for us is that it illustrates many of the issues we have covered concerning modelling. For those unfamiliar with the game, the Sudoku square is represented by a 9×9 grid that has a few integers apparently randomly distributed (see Fig. 10.4, see also Chapter 9). It will be noticed that the grid is subdivided into

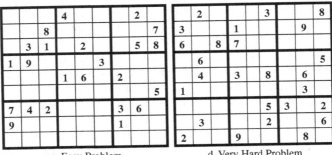

c. Easy Problem   d. Very Hard Problem

Fig. 10.4 Two examples of a Sudoku problem

3×3 smaller grids (boxes). The purpose of the game is to fill in the blank squares with the integers 1–9 so that each small sub-grid contains the entire number set and so do each row or column.

What makes the 'hard' Sudoku puzzles 'difficult' is that they require some trial and error process. This means that a path has to be chosen to see if it leads to a solution. For this to work a list of 'failed' attempts must be kept to prevent repeating a mistake and a list of states needs to be kept so that on a failed attempt it is possible to reset the grid to the point of trying another possible route to the solution. A transformation from one state to the next is the choice of number to place in an empty square. This choice has to obey the Sudoku constraints.

The selection of a number is primarily done by the function '**reduce**'. This will look for all those squares that have numbers that are so constrained by the rules that only one answer is possible. Most 'easy' problems will need no further processing except to continue cycling round as the new numbers lead to new squares with a unique number. The 'hard' problems will involve some uncertainty in this process as some situation will appear when simple elimination is not possible. In this case a choice has to be taken from a small list of possibilities and if this does not lead to a solution it requires resetting to when the choice was made and trying another route. For this purpose a '**state_list**' of the successive states of the grid is maintained. Each state also records the current list of integers associated with each square, and a trace of all the attempts at solving the puzzle. The trace of attempts is the list of numbers tried for each square and this information is held in the function '**tries_list**' (see Project Chapter 9).

The fixed heuristic for solving the hard problems is to choose a square with the shortest list, and then choose the first integer on that list so that the reduction process can be tried again. A failure, tested by function '**failure**', is indicated by one of the lists associated with a square being reduced to nil. In this case, the previous state of the squares must be retrieved (**head** of **state_list**), and the next item in this list is tried. If there is only one integer left, it must be that one and another reduction can take place. If there is a solution this process will find it. Figure 10.5b gives a solution to the starting condition of numbers 1–9 set in the diagonal as shown in

9	2	7	5	4	3	6	1	8
3	5	4	1	8	6	2	9	7
6	1	8	7	2	9	4	5	3
8	6	3	4	9	1	7	2	5
7	4	2	3	5	8	1	6	9
1	9	5	2	6	7	8	3	4
4	8	9	6	1	5	3	7	2
5	3	1	8	7	2	9	4	6
2	7	6	9	3	4	5	8	1

1	4	9	8	7	5	3	2	6
6	2	7	3	1	4	9	5	8
5	8	3	6	2	9	1	7	4
2	6	1	4	9	8	5	3	7
3	9	8	2	5	7	6	4	1
7	5	4	1	3	6	8	9	2
4	3	2	9	8	1	7	6	5
9	1	5	7	6	2	4	8	3
8	7	6	5	4	3	2	1	9

a. **The solution for Very Hard**   **A Solution with diagonal 1 to 9**
problem

Fig. 10.5 Two Sudoku solutions

red. On inspection, there can be more than one solution. For example if the yellow squares in Fig. 10.5b are exchanged with the orange squares along the same row then this would be an alternative solution or the transpose of the grid along the diagonal. There are several other sets of pairs where this can be done.

An Introduction to Game Theory [→ Page 364]

The Problem of the 'Best' Choice

The problem with the Sudoku program is that its method of making a decision is fixed. It will always cycle through the tests in exactly the same way and will always chose the shortest list to pursue an alternative set of possibilities. The list themselves will always be examined in numeric sequence. The solution shown in Fig. 10.5b is likely to be one of many possibilities but these will never be discovered no matter how often the program is run. In some puzzles there is also the possibility that a solution, even if it exists, will never be found since the same paths to a solution will always be made and this may lead to a dead end. It turns out, from game theory (Luce and Raiffa 1957), that always choosing the optimum path is not necessarily the best way of getting a solution. In some cases it is sub-optimum.

There is also another issue in that the occasional random change in strategy is a useful means of exploring your environment and that can be very useful for survival. There is also another age old trap of *local optima* that can also be resolved by random moves. You can get *local optima* where the problem solving path is always chosen so as to improve the current position and never choosing a route that seems to take the position further away from a solution. In the case of Sudoku, we have so far, always chosen the squares that have the fewest potential lists of numbers to be reduced. This is because the solution for a particular square is when the list consists of a single number; the shorter the list the nearer a solution. The problem with this approach is that it can reach *local optima* where no final solution can be found.

For Sudoku this situation is unlikely to occur but for the Tiles problem described in Chapter 7 it is possible.

If we are to make a random move then what is the best way to assess when to apply this jump? It must be done before the final solution is done simply because there is then no need for it; you have reached your goal. To do it at other times requires some theory. We start with examining some simple games.

The Old Shell Game

This is a well-known game where a 'pea' or small round token is placed under one of three identical shells A, B and C. The shells are moved around and the problem for the punter is to say where the pea is. He has to place a bet of, say, €25 with the possibility of winning €40 from the showman if he gets it right otherwise he loses his money. The rational approach is to draw up a table of gains and losses for each of the possibilities. This table is referred to as the Pay-off Matrix. Figure 10.6a shows this matrix. We would expect to have for each possibility two values: what the punter wins or loses and what the showman wins or loses. However, in this case the loss of one is exactly the gain of the other. This is known as a Zero Sum Game (Fig. 10.6b) so that the Punter wins what the Showman loses, etc. So the number in each position could be seen as negated for the showman. Figure 10.6b is another example shown all from A's view. What A wins, B loses. In the shell game we do not have any information so, if it is *fair*, then the chance of winning are one third. The expected or average winnings less the losses over a long period for any particular move can be estimated as

$$(€40 - €25 - €25)/3 = -€3.33$$

This does not look like a game to enter into but if you do win the first time the best bet is to never play the game ever again.

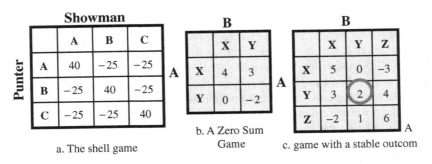

Fig. 10.6 Payoff matrices for different games

Principles of Maximising

We assume that a reasonable player will always choose a move that will maximise the pay-off so what a reasoning player does is "*do as well as possible*". In some games this is very clear because there is a *Dominant Strategy*. In Fig. 10.6c we have the situation that:

- A chooses **Y** because no matter what B does A will do well.
- B wants to *minimise* the pay-off to A so B also chooses **Y**.

So we have the 'Rationality Principle' such that players will always use the dominant strategy because we assume the other player is 'rational'. In this case the centre cell is the equilibrium cell because if either player changes row or column they will be worse off. There are other strategies. These are

- **MaxiMax:** Choose highest possible outcome
- **MaxiMin:** Avoid worst payoff
- **Maximum Average:** Go for highest average
- **MiniMax Regret:** Minimise the regret

They are all shown in Fig. 10.7a. However, all these strategies will pick the *Dominant Strategy* if one exists.

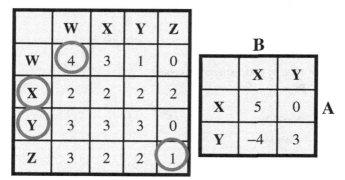

a. Different applied strategies   b. No stable outcome

Fig. 10.7 Pay-off matrices for different strategies

Probabilistic Strategies

Consider Fig. 10.7b. Here we have an unstable situation because there does not seem to be any rational grounds to choose one action over the other. A may choose X because there is no chance of losing only a possible chance of winning. However, B, being rational will consider this, so will choose Action Y because there will be no loss. A will realise that B is rational so with a 'double think' in progress A will choose Y with the hope of winning a positive return. B, in turn, will have already considered this possibility so will choose X instead with the hope of winning through A's double-think. A, on the other hand, being aware of his opponents potential will change his mind and go for X after all. This loop of analysis will go on forever. Since there is no telling where it might end the best strategy is to be random and, say, toss a coin. In this way your opponent will never know what you are doing and there is a chance you might win. If the game is repeated many times A's expected win can be calculated by the sum of the potential winnings multiplied by the probability of the winning happening.

$$5 \times 0.5 - 4 \times 0.5 = 0.5 \text{ for action X by B}$$
$$0 \times 0.5 + 3 \times 0.5 = 1.5 \text{ for action Y by B}$$

If B is applying the same strategy of coin tossing then the expected gain for A will be

$$0.5 \times 0.5 + 1.5 \times 0.5 = 1$$

However, is there a 'best' probability (biased coin) that could improve on this expectation for A? The answer is 'yes' and it will be maximum if the two expectations for B's X and Y moves are equal. This gives us a chance to calculate through a set of three simultaneous equations where x and y are the probabilities of winning; z is the expected win

$$5x - 4y = z, \ 3y = z, \ x + y = 1$$
$$5x - 4y = 3y \text{ both expectations equal}$$
$$5x = 3y + 4y$$
$$= 7y$$
$$x = 7/5y$$

Now $$y = (1-x)$$

$$x = 7/5 \ (1-x)$$
$$x = (7-7x)/5$$
$$5x = 7-7x$$
$$5x + 7x = 7$$
$$12x = 7$$

$$\underline{x = 7/12} \text{ and so } \underline{\mathbf{y = 5/12}}$$

So the expected pay-off will be 1.25 instead of 1 which is a definite improvement. This calculation is the 'Maximum Security Level' (MSL) and is the preferred probability (or relative frequency if repeated) of selecting the different actions.

Choosing Actions (or Calculating a Heuristic)

This is fine if you have a set of utilities (e.g. money) that clearly states what you can gain or lose upon states of the game. In the case of Sudoku the choices do not have a utility as such but they might have a probability of finding a direct route to a solution and not a blind choice that requires backtracking. So is it possible to make a calculation from such a set of probabilities?

Essentially we are in the same position of a mixed strategy situation since we are dealing with what we could consider as the probabilistic choice of a mythical opponent. If we are faced with two possible actions both of which could lead to a WIN or a LOSE than how do we chose which one to take? In the case of two choices and given no information we might as well toss a coin. If we are given some information we can use this to our advantage. For example, the most likely information we will have is some estimate of the probability of success for each of the actions. Here we can use the same trick as was used in Bayes rule by making an imaginary pay-off (of -1) if we select wrongly (LOSE) and (0) if we get it right (WIN). Consider a simple two choice problem where we have to choose between two actions X or Y as shown in Fig. 10.8 where f_x and f_y are the frequency of doing action X and Y respectively.

Action (Maximum Security Level)	WIN	LOSE
X (f_x)	$P_x \times (0)$	$(1 - P_x) \times (-1)$
Y (f_y)	$P_y \times (0)$	$(1 - P_y) \times (-1)$

Fig. 10.8 Pay-off matrix for an unstable game

Then the expected loss for action X where P_x is the probability of a WIN assuming a zero sum game.

$$= P_x \times (0) + (1-P_x) \times (-1)$$
$$= -(1-P_x)$$

Maximum Security Level (MSL)

Let f_y be the frequency of choosing action Y and f_x be the frequency of choosing action X. Then,

$(1-P_x) \times f_x = (1-P_y) \times f_y$ because **both** expected payoffs must be equal for 'best' f_y and f_x.

But $f_y = 1-f_x$ because you have to do something so

$(1-P_x) \times f_x = (1-P_y) \times (1-f_x)$

So (after manipulation) $f_x = (1-P_y) / \{(1-P_x) + (1-P_y)\}$

It follows that $\quad\quad f_y = (1-P_x) / \{(1-P_x) + (1-P_y)\}$

Generalised MSL for Actions

Most problems will have more than two choices and where there is no opponent the appropriate action can only be determined on probability grounds or on the basis of some information such as a heuristic or model or theory. First we need to know how to determine the MSL for several actions. Some games may have more than one outcome such as win, lose and draw. Further, some puzzles can have more than one solution. In the Sudoku case we will usually have only one solution but there may be good or bad routes to this solution.

Multiple Simultaneous Equations Matrix

Because we are dealing with the case that an outcome is either a win or lose we can take **pairs** of expected losses (say actions for X_n, X_{n+1}) that are **equal** where the probability of a win for X_n is P_n and for X_{n+1} is P_{n+1}. The probability that should be invoked for action X_n is f_n such that the sum f_n will add to 1. It adds up to 1 because we can only take one action for the choice. We then have an expected pay-off for each pair and each pair will be equal for the MSL. For example X_1 and X_2 will be

$$(1 - P1) \times f1 = (1 - P2) \times f2$$
$$(1 - P1) \times f1 - (1 - P2) \times f2 = 0$$

This equation will be labelled $X_{1\text{-}2}$. We also have the equation for all pairings

$$\Sigma f_n = 1 \rightarrow \Sigma f_n - 1 = 0$$

We need to solve for each f_n and we have 'n' equations which is just enough. In matrix form for solving equations using the function '**mat_solve**', we require a table of coefficients for all the equations as shown in Fig. 10.9.

We therefore have four equations with four unknowns so the probabilities to apply to actions can be calculated.

	f1	f2	f3	f4	=
	1	1	1	1	1
$X_{1\text{-}2}$	(1–P1)	–(1–P2)	0	0	0
$X_{2\text{-}3}$	0	(1–P2)	–(1–P3)	0	0
$X_{3\text{-}4}$	0	0	(1–P3)	–(1–P4)	0

Fig. 10.9 Coefficient matrix for 'mat_solve'

Implementing MSL

The main problem in implementing the calculation for MSL is to translate a set of probabilities into a form that can be solved by '**mat_solve**'. These probabilities do not necessarily add up to 1 because the results are independent but the answer to MSL does have to add up to 1 because only a single action can be chosen at a time. Figure 10.10a shows the overview network for the calculation. The process is simple (see Fig. 10.10b) in that the list of probabilities of winning outcomes are listed for all possible choices, these are organized into a matrix framework initiated by the function '**matrix_frame**'. This function creates a matrix that has the right dimensions to layout all the coefficients for '**mat_solve**' with the first line all of '1's.

Once the frame has been created then it is filled in by repeated use of the function 'pairwise _place' (see Figs. 10.11 and 10.12). This takes the first two probabilities and the first line as shown in Fig. 10.9. It then generates the equation as shown

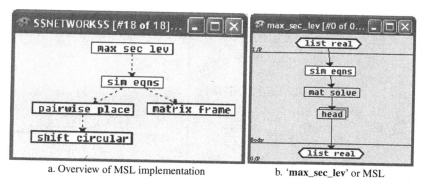

a. Overview of MSL implementation   b. '**max_sec_lev**' or MSL

Fig. 10.10 Network and main function 'max_sec_lev'

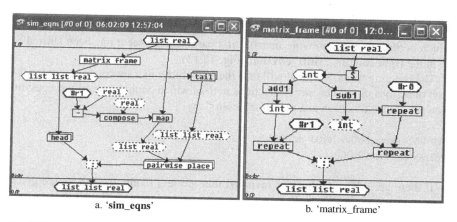

a. '**sim_eqns**'   b. 'matrix_frame'

Fig. 10.11 Top level of MSL

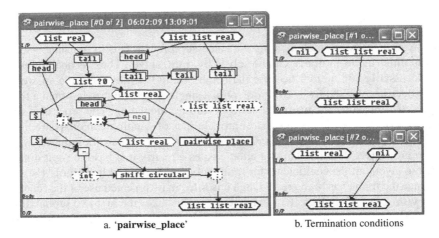

a. 'pairwise_place'   b. Termination conditions

Fig. 10.12   The placing of equations in the matrix

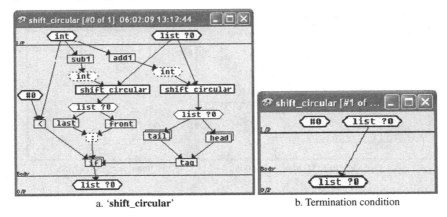

a. 'shift_circular'   b. Termination condition

Fig. 10.13   Moving through the sub-equations

which is placed in the growing matrix (first parameter) after it has been shifted to be in the right column ('**shift_circula**r' Fig. 10.13).

The function '**max_sec_lev**' will take the probability of a successful outcome for a set of actions. So if there are two actions both of which could be equally successful then the choice of action is a toss of the coin.

QUERY> max_sec_lev [#r0.9 #r0.9]
[#r0.500000 #r0.500000]

If there are other possibilities involved that are less likely, then these are given their chance even if it is small.

QUERY> max_sec_lev [#r0.9 #r0.9 #r0.5 #r0.1]
[#r0.432692 #r0.432692 #r0.086538 #r0.048077]

To see how this function behaves in general then you can take a pair of probabilities and change one of them over a wide range and leave the other constant. This is only indicative of the trends since the behaviour of the equation with multiple choices is not simple. The following query will generate a list of 100 points between 0 and 1 to test '**max_sec_lev**' for action probability of success pairs [0.01 0.5] to [1.0 0.5].

QUERY> map nar_line (zip [(map(*#r0.01)(list_of_int #1 #100 #1))
(map(lambda ?7(head(**max_sec_lev** [?7 #r0.5])))(map(*#r0.01)
(list_of_int #1 #100 #1)))])

The results Fig. 10.14 show three distributions where the alternative success probabilities are from 0.1, 0.5 and 0.9. As expected the 0.5 action probability is achieved when the two success probabilities are equal (see red circles on graph).

The results shown in Fig. 10.14 also seem to fit Empirical studies, as referenced by Gonzalez R. and Wu G. (1999), where people tend to overweight small probabilities and underweight large probabilities during the process of decision making. This has often been taken as a distortion of human perception but in fact it would seem that this 'distortion' has positive survival value. This is because it not only optimises the achieving of success in the long run but also the opportunity to learn about the world as well. This is particularly important since the non-formal world changes and so do the probabilities of success.

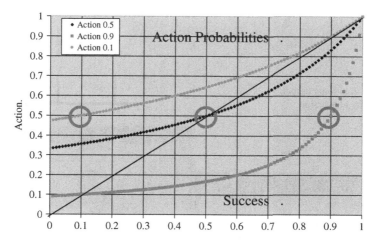

Fig. 10.14 Three series of results for 0.1, 0.5 and 0.9 probabilities success

The Act of Choosing

We now need a function that will take the result of MSL and return a choice in accordance to the probability distribution. The function '**happen**' chooses as specified by

the 'probability' distribution represented by the list of probabilities. These probabilities are expected to sum to 1. However, if the distribution list sums to zero it is
considered that no result is possible given the event. In this case the null result is
returned. The null result is defined as #0. The choice is indicated by giving the list
position, thus

QUERY> happen [#r0.2 #r0.3 #r0.5]

#1

QUERY> happen [#r0.2 #r0.3 #r0.5]

#3

QUERY> happen [#r0.2 #r0.3 #r0.5]

#2

Implementing this process involves a random number to probability conversion
based on the physical mechanism shown in Fig. 10.15. Here the position of the
ball with respect to the upper six slots is determined by the throw of a dice. In this
example the dice has come up with '3'. The probabilities are selected by relative
width of the three lower slots. If the total width of the mechanism is taken as 1
then the three slot positions in the figure would represent 0.167, 0.333 and 0.5. The
program network shown in Fig. 10.16a is a generalisation of this and will work for
any random number up to 512 instead of just 6 (Fig. 10.17).

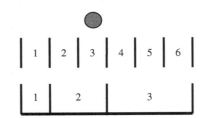

Fig. 10.15 Random number
to probability conversion

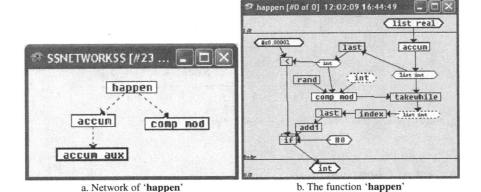

a. Network of 'happen'   b. The function 'happen'

Fig. 10.16 A function for choosing from a list of mutually exclusive possibilities

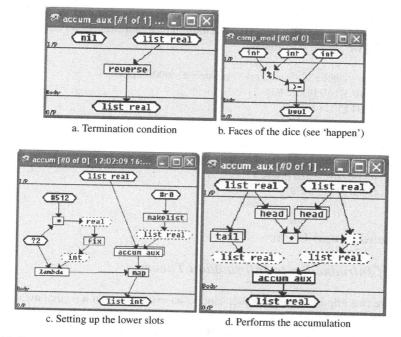

a. Termination condition　　　　　b. Faces of the dice (see 'happen')

c. Setting up the lower slots　　　　d. Performs the accumulation

Fig. 10.17 Accumulating the probabilities and selecting a random cut of the range

So for 10,000 examples of 'happen', for the same distribution, the tendency is for the count of choices to reflect the distribution probabilities. So for happen [#r0.2 #r0.3 #r0.5] we have the following:

QUERY> map (lambda ?7 ($(filter (= ?7) (repeat #10000(**happen**
[#r0.2 #r0.3 #r0.5]))))))[#1 #2 #3]
　　[#1994 #3074 #5056]

And for Fig. 10.15 we have

QUERY> map (lambda ?8 ($(filter (= ?8) (repeat #10000(**happen**
[#r0.167 #r0.333 #r0.5]))))))[#1 #2 #3]
　　[#1650 #3315 #4997]

The process is that the probabilities are accumulated from the first to the last. The results are multiplied by 512 and changed to integers. The final result will be an increasing list of integers thus [0, 102, 256, 512]. A random number is generated between 0 and 512 (in this case) and then the list is scanned from lowest to highest until the random integer is greater or equal to the list integer. Where it stops is the choice. The number 512 can be increased to give a larger number of potential choices.

So for 10,000 examples of 'happen', for the same distribution, the tendency is for the count of choices to reflect the distribution probabilities. So for happen [#r0.2 #r0.3 #r0.5] we have the following:

QUERY> map (lambda ?7 ($(filter (= ?7) (repeat #10000(**happen** [#r0.2 #r0.3 #r0.5])))))) [#1 #2 #3]
       [#1994 #3074 #5056]

And from Fig. 10.15

QUERY> map (lambda ?8 ($(filter (= ?8) (repeat #10000(**happen** [#r0.167 #r0.333 #r0.5])))))) [#1 #2 #3]
       [#1650 #3315 #4997]

Information and Choice

A Brief Introduction to Information Theory

There are two important insights that support an explanation of a formal measure of information. The first is the pragmatic definition of a hypothesis or theory given by Charles S Peirce (1934, 1966). The second is the mathematical theory of communication by Claude E. Shannon and Warren Weaver (1964; first published circa 1948). Peirce founded the American philosophy of Pragmatics. Central to this philosophy was that an argument to support a Hypothesis or Theory should not necessarily involve the notion of Truth, as such, but it should always be concerned with Usefulness. Within this framework, a theory or hypothesis is only useful if it serves a purpose. Within science this purpose is primarily to *make the world a less surprising place*; it reduces uncertainty. A nice example of this was given by Peirce's friend William James (1842–1910). He had gone on a picnic with a group of friends in a wood. He decided to go for a walk and when he came back he found his friends in a heated argument. He describes the problem as follows:

> The *corpus* of the dispute was a squirrel – a live squirrel supposed to be clinging to one side of a tree-trunk; while over against the trees opposite side a human being was imagined to stand. This human witness tries to get sight of the squirrel by moving rapidly round the tree, but no matter how fast he goes, the squirrel moves as fast in the opposite direction and always keeps the tree between himself and the man, so that never a glimpse of him is caught. The resultant metaphysical problem is this: *Does the man go round the squirrel or not?*

From this he describes the pragmatic method as

- "... to try to interpret each notion by tracing its respective practical consequences."
- ".... Whenever a dispute is serious, we ought to be able to show some practical difference that must follow from one side or the other's being right."

In the case of the squirrel it depends what you want 'to go round' to mean. If you mean that the man is first to the North, then West and then South, East and back to North then the answer is 'yes'. If you want it to mean that the man first is in front, then to the side followed by back, side and front of the squirrel then the answer is 'no'.

We have taken the pragmatic view in this book so that the term 'belief' has a practical meaning. It is associated with a model of the world that can be used to predict a person's actions in response to circumstance reflected in the model. The Belief a person has in a model is measured by the probability of the person's observed actions as interpreted by that model being acted upon.

Shannon and Weaver, on the other hand, were primarily interested in developing a useful theory of communication. In particular they had the model of a telegraph system which transmitted a series of characters down a cable where each represents a message. In this case the measure of information is taken to be *one's freedom of choice when one selects a message*. If there is no freedom of choice, then the ability for the receiver of the message to predict what the message will be is certain. The wider the message transmitter has for choice from the selection of messages the greater the uncertainty. We can thus say that

- *Uncertainty* is a measure of information and will be inversely proportional to the probability.

That is *uncertainty* will increase when the probability (p) of predicting an event decreases. So we can say that a certain event provides no surprises and thus no information

- We also require that information should be additive.

However, we have the problem that probabilities multiply. A solution to this is to take the logarithm of the probability so that multiplication becomes addition. This has the satisfactory consequence that it fits other psychometric related measures such as for sound (the decibel).

So we have the following:

Uncertainty as a measure of information is $= \log(1/p)$

This equation only tells us of the uncertainty of a single event for a particular message with probability (p):

- What we want is some kind of measure for a whole set of messages

This is because it is only in the context of a set that such a probability has an uncertainty; it is a set from which a choice can be made. The minimum set of choices can only be two items and the maximum uncertainty with two items will be when they are equally probable:

- We require a unit of information to be the simplest choice with maximum uncertainty.

To make the measure to be equal to 1 for the minimum choice condition it requires that the log has to be to the base of '2'. In information terms this is called a 'bit' and as shown in Fig. 10.18 the log of 1 will be 0 with the log of 0.5 being -1 for such a base. Also note that for any base log(1/p) is equal to −log(p). So

$$\text{Uncertainty}(p) = - \log_2(p)$$

To make a measure of the set we can take the expected (or average) uncertainty. This means adding up the uncertainty for each message where each has been multiplied by the probability of occurrence for that message. This results in

$$\text{Expected uncertainty} = - \Sigma_n p_n \log_2(p_n)$$

Expected uncertainty is referred to as *Entropy* and is measured in bits. The antilog$_2$ of this result will return an equivalent probability that will be the expected uncertainty in terms of probability of guessing the message correctly before it arrives.

Fig. 10.18 The change in uncertainty of a single event wrt to event probability

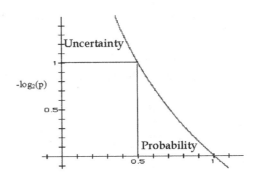

* Using Information to Choose

There are several places where choices are made in the Sudoku problem (see Fig. 10.19a). A choice of square to be resolved if it has more than one number associated with it and a number from that list 'to try' for a solution if there is no immediate resolution found by the function '**reduce**'. In this function '**reduce**' there is the order in which the checks are carried out and if there is a failure then there is a range of states to go back to and try again. We will just look at the choice of a square (see Figs. 10.20 and 10.21)

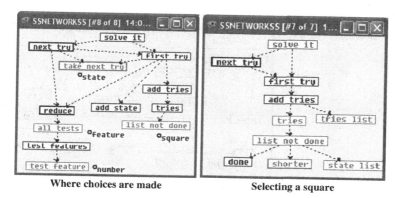

Fig. 10.19 The places to consider improving search

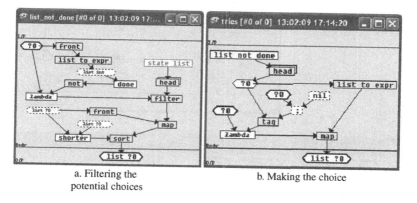

a. Filtering the potential choices

b. Making the choice

Fig. 10.20 The fixed mechanism for choosing a square to resolve

To calculate the entropy for each square the function takes each integer on the squares list and determines where else it is being used in the box, column or row. The maximum possible will be 3×9 less the 2 extra on the square itself; a total of 25. The number of repetitions of a number divided by 25 gives the probability of it occurring. It is this set of probabilities that define the entropy of the square. This is then used to calculate the maximum security level over all the potential squares. The function 'happen' then chooses one of them as described. The function 'tries' no longer needs to make the choice so 'head' can be deleted. The only other addition is the function 'srand' in the function 'init' so that the random number generator 'rand' will not simply repeat its initial sequence each time the Sudoku program is called. In practice it becomes effectively random. Figure 10.22 shows the new functions required for this improved choice.

On implementation the new Sudoku program is slower for normal Sudoku problems that are designed for people to solve and have only a single solution. However for problems that may have several solutions, such as shown in Fig. 10.5, it is on average faster and will tend to find different solutions each time it is run.

Fig. 10.21 Opening the choice to select using entropy

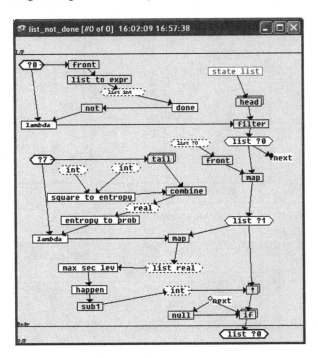

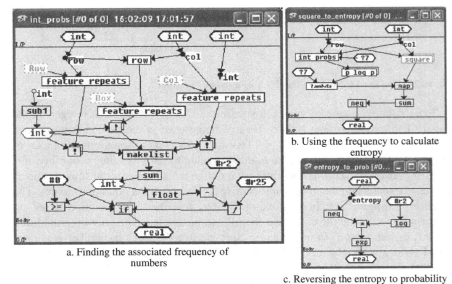

a. Finding the associated frequency of numbers

b. Using the frequency to calculate entropy

c. Reversing the entropy to probability

Fig. 10.22 New procedures for choice

Belief Adjustment [→ Page 372]

We introduced Bayes' Rule in Chapter 8 as a built-in library function. It was originally concerned with arriving at a support for a theory through accumulating evidence. Normally, Bayes' Rule assumes a constant and unchanging world. In practice the world in which we live changes and even what counts as evidence can also change (see irrational sets (Addis et al. 2008)). So whatever features we have chosen, a program needs to be designed to accept change. We can make the assumption that, relative to the number of events that can occur during a process, all changes in the world will be gradual. What exactly we mean by 'gradual' will become clear.

In practice a scientist (say) is always reluctant to give up a useful theory despite a run of apparently falsifying observations (for examples see Gooding and Addis 1999, 2008). This observation is normal in scientific practice (see, e.g., Kuhn 1962, 1974, 1977a, and Lakatos 1970). There is another Bayesian assumption that may be questioned in that it requires that the order in which events occur should be irrelevant. This is very unlikely to be the case in an ever changing world except for short periods of time.

People will tend to have a set of beliefs about the world they live in. These beliefs are hypotheses, theories or models about the world. They also govern how people will act to world events or even determine what events are perceived. The consequences of people's actions may not be the outcome expected and as such these unexpected results will throw some doubt on their beliefs about the world. As we have shown a good survival strategy is to have a random component in behaviour. So if we are trying to assess the range of belief in associated models then a different sequence of actions will produce different patterns of belief-revision (Gooding and Addis 2008).

Figure 10.23 shows two possibilities (A and B) of keeping track of an event that will happen (1) or not happen (0) with a changing probability. Since the event is random you need a big enough sample that will ensure that a significant change in

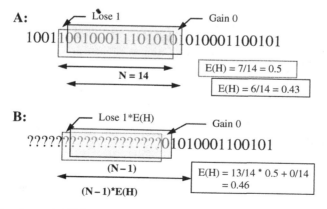

Fig. 10.23 Running probabilities with and without memory of recent events

probability is detected but not too big that it will mask the change or too small that the randomness itself is detected. Small sample theory can be used to consider what that might be and M. J. Moroney (1963 (1951)) is a very good source on all matters statistical and S. Ashcroft and C. Pereira (2002) has associated software. In practice, it depends on what turns out to be useful and in human belief models a sample of seven has worked well.

In the example A (Fig. 10.23) we keep a moving window of 14 samples. When a new sample appears, we move the window forward in time. We do this by dropping the oldest sample and add the most recent to the list. In this example the average number of (1)s change from 0.5 to 0.43. In example B we do not have any memory except for the current probability. If we imagined we had a sample N (such as 14) then when we drop the oldest sample we do not know if that is going to be a (1) or (0). We do know that if the average is probability is p (say 0.5) then the expected sum of N will be N.p (say 14 × 0.5) so since we dropped one our expected current sum will be (N−1).p (say 13 × 0.5). We know what our new event (e), which is (0) in this case. So our new sum is the expected sum for one less plus the current situation {(N−1).p + 0} and to get the new average (expected p) we need to divide this by N (the sample size). This becomes

$$p_n = \{(N-1).p_{(n-1)} + e\}/N$$

Where (n) is the new time and (n−1) is the previous time. The value of (e) will be either (1) or (0) depending on what happens. Since the amount of change to (p) is governed by the value of N we can call 1/N flexibility. The larger N is the smaller the change per time sample and the so the smaller the flexibility.

Figure 10.24 shows that the different flexibilities (Flex) govern the amount of influence a past event has on the present. Since the scale is logarithmic this influence of a past event never (in theory) disappears altogether but this influence does drop off quite rapidly as event time moves forward. We now consider how this might be used in practice.

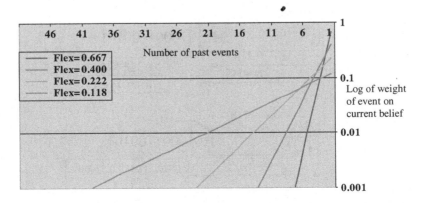

Fig. 10.24 The relative influence of past events on the present

The Impact of Evidence: Hypotheses and Theories

It is the fate of all scientists to eventually be proved wrong or at best shown to be misguided. It is a wise scientist to assume that hypotheses should not, in practice, achieve absolute certainty and should remain hypothetical: scientists will classify these hypotheses as a necessary postulate. So a hypothesis cannot be wholly, irretrievably disbelieved if there is counter evidence but it can simply be re-labelled as an artefact, a fiction or non-fact, as a non-existent entity (phlogiston, the ether), or as a false (though once-believed) principle (e.g. the immutability of chemical elements and of biological species).

To call something a *hypothesis*, H is to say that there is some *empirical* support for it (H) given the evidence (R_e.). See Fig. 10.25 which shows where the evidence from experiments enter into the cycle of events. This support is a 'probability' in the sense that it is an expected chance that the hypothesis is correct and thus can be acted upon with the confidence suggested by this expectation; it is a 'belief'. We will label this $E_{n-1}(H/R_e)$ where n is the current numbered event and n–1 the previous event so E_{n-1} is the situation just before further evidence is available. As you might expect, it has a value that lies somewhere between 0 and 1 for each hypothesis H. It is also assumed that these hypotheses are mutually exclusive in that only one of them can be chosen when considering an action and only one of them will eventually be selected as representing the world and so the sum of these values will add up to 1. Given a new result (R_e) from carrying out an experiment (or action) e then the expected probability concerning a particular hypothesis can be modified to $E_n(H)$ by following equation (see Addis 1985, p. 260):

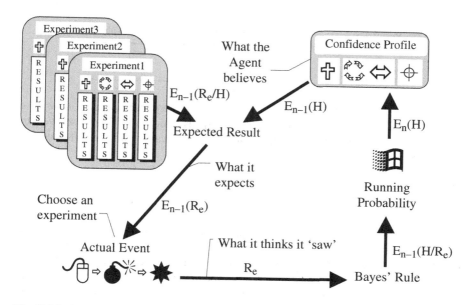

Fig. 10.25 Belief adjustment derived from experimental results

$$E_n(H) = \frac{(N-1).E_{n-1}(H) + E_{n-1}(H/R_e)}{N}$$

This is using the equation we derived earlier but substituting $E_{n-1}(H/R_e)$ for (e). $E_{n-1}(H/R_e)$ is derived from using Bayes rule, where

$$E_{n-1}(H/R_e) = \{E_{n-1}(R_e/H)\}/\{E_{n-1}(R_e)\}$$

and

$$E_{n-1}(R_e/H) = p(H).p(R_e/H)$$

This gets round the problems of Bayes rule by simply using it as a conversion process to get our updating expectations in the right form for the running probability. We now consider a simple example.

A Simple Example of Confidence Adjustment

Given a coin that is to be thrown we might consider two possible hypotheses:

- H_1. The coin is good
- H_2. The coin is double headed

Result	P(Result/H1)	P(Result/H2)
Heads	0.5	1.0
Tails	0.5	0.0

According to Peirce, knowing that one of these hypotheses is true "*makes the world a less surprising place*". Treating Entropy as a measure of surprise, we can calculate the difference made by 'knowing' H_2 is the case from the difference in entropy of the two situations:

Entropy of $H_1 = -(0.5 \, Log_2 \, (0.5) + 0.5 \, Log_2 \, (0.5)) = -((-0.5) + (-0.5)) = 1 \, bit$
Entropy of $H_2 = -(1.0 \, Log_2 \, (1.0) + 0.0 \, Log_2 \, (0.0)) = -((-0.0) + (-0.0)) = 0 \, bit$

So the difference made by 'knowing H_2 rather than H_1 is the case' is $(1 - 0) = 1$ bit.

Since someone or something needs to have the beliefs about the world we will use the generic term 'agent'. So the effect of the new information is mediated by an agent's current beliefs about the world. Suppose that the initial confidences that an agent has in each of these hypotheses are

	Agent
$E_{n-1}(H_1)$	**0.8**
$E_{n-1}(H_2)$	**0.2**
Total	**1.0**

Then we can calculate the effect of an experiment (tossing the coin) as follows. Using

$$E_{n-1}(H) = \frac{(N-1).E_{n-1}(H) + E_{n-1}(H/R_e)}{N}$$

Agent			
$E_{n-1}(R_e/H) = E_{n-1}(H) * P(R_e/H)$	E(Head/H)	E(Tail/H)	Total
$E_{n-1}(H1) * P(Result/H1)$	$0.8 * 0.5 = 0.4$	$0.8 * 0.5 = 0.4$	**0.8**
$E_{n-1}(H2) * P(Result/H2)$	$0.2 * 1.0 = 0.2$	$0.2 * 0.0 = 0.0$	**0.2**
E(R)	**0.6**	**0.4**	**1.0**

We can then calculate

Agent		
E(H/R)	Head Occurs	Tail Occurs
$E_n(H1/R)$	$0.4/0.6 = 0.67$	$0.4/0.4 = 1.0$
$E_n(H2/R)$	$0.2/0.6 = 0.33$	$0.0/0.4 = 0.0$
Total	**1.0**	**1.0**

So from the update equation, we have

$$E_n(H) = \frac{(N-1).E_{n-1}(H) + E_{n-1}(H/R_e)}{N}$$

If we let $N = 4$ so $(N-1)/N = 3/4 = 0.75$ and $1/N = 0.25$ for an agent's flexibility, then

Agent		
	Head Occurs	Tail Occurs
$E_n(H1)$	$0.75 * 0.8 + 0.25*0.67 = \mathbf{0.77}$	$0.75 * 0.8 + 0.25*1.0 = \mathbf{0.85}$
$E_n(H2)$	$0.75 * 0.2 + 0.25*0.33 = \mathbf{0.23}$	$0.75 * 0.2 + 0.25*0.0 = \mathbf{0.15}$
Total	**1.0**	**1.0**

It is important to note that whereas on a purely Bayesian model the appearance of a tail could eliminate the belief that the coin is double headed (H_2), this model does not produce such a conclusion. This response is not as irrational as it might appear since it keeps open the possibility of alternative explanations, e.g. that there has been a switch of the coin (say, for a double-tailed coin) or an observational error. This is more like what is required for scientific investigation as suggested by David Gooding and others (1990, Tweney 1985, Matthews 2004).

* Belief Adjustment and Learning

For the moment imagine scientists who have a set of theories about a particular aspect of the world. They have available a set of experiments that they can choose to perform which will help test which of the theories is the most useful in terms of its ability to make predictions about the world. The notion of a theory here can be extended to other things besides scientific theories held by scientists. It could be our internal model of someone we are speaking to. In this case, the experiments are sentences we construct and the results are the responses we get from the other person (Addis and Billinge 2004, Billinge and Addis 2008). However, for this particular explanation it is clearer to use the science model of discovery.

Figure 10.25 shows where the different parts of the equation for adjustment come from. The confidence profile is the set of probabilities that represent the range of beliefs in different hypotheses. For convenience we will call these probabilities 'beliefs'. The symbols used in the diagram relate to the historical set of hypotheses (circa 1843) during Faradays investigation of electromagnetism (see for more detail Gooding 1990, Gooding and Addis 2008, Addis and Gooding 2008). Every experiment will have a range of results associated with it that are specific to each hypothesis. A good experiment should be expected to consistently produce quite distinct results for each hypothesis. A bad experiment will be unpredictable for all hypotheses. An experiment is chosen and the results (R_e) of the experiment are observed. Using the known probability of that result given a hypothesis $E(R_e/H)$ and Bayes Rule then for each hypothesis a probability of it being that hypothesis that 'caused' the result $E(H/R_e)$ can be calculated; Bayes' rule is equivalent to a casting function since it converts $E_{n-1}(R_e/H)$ to $E_{n-1}(H/R_e)$. This probability is used in the running probability equation to adjust the belief. This calculation was played out with the coin toss experiment above.

A Belief Keyword Retrieval System

The problem with keyword systems is that to be used effectively you need to know what keywords to use. The difficulty arises from not knowing how people describe a particular item, what words they use or even how they might have organised their information. The retrieval systems used for the World Wide Web are fast and effective. With a bit of experience it is possible to home in on items that match your requirement. What you do not know is what you may have missed due to the item not using the keywords you have chosen and that might be a better fit for your requirements. One of the solutions that might deal with this problem is a 'semantic' system that extends each keyword to include similar keywords and integrates the combination of keywords used to home in on some kind of common subset. This can fail because not only do different people see a word to mean many different things but time and culture will change the meaning of words. The word 'cool', for example, has had many different meanings in our lifetime. Other approaches have taken this into account by employing a dynamic list of 'uses' of words. Also they record the way keywords have been used successfully together. This gives a form of practical 'meaning' to a word.

In all these cases the user has to know at least some of the keywords within the retrieval system that are appropriate for the item required. For areas of specialisation, as might be found in a University, someone external to the area will have some difficulty in even guessing one appropriate keyword. One answer to this is a menu system where general areas of specialisation are presented which lead onto more detailed areas until after several moves you are guided to the required information. The problem with this is that any mistake at any level will lead to the wrong item. Further, not all levels will be interpreted correctly or even understood.

One possible solution is for the system to engage in some kind of 'conversation' with the user with the purpose of trying to elicit what is wanted. This cannot be done by a natural language since the problem of natural language understanding by a machine has not been generally resolved. The tree/menu approach is a kind of simple 'conversation' but is too rigid in the way it works.

Implementing a Belief Retrieval System

It is possible to treat the situation as a discovery process where the items or at least the item class could be discovered as though it is a scientific theory. Here we can create a simple analogy where the item class is a theory, the keywords are different experiments and the 'result' of a keyword is either 'present' or 'absent'. This works well with the belief system since the entire item classes can be pre-designated in the same way that theories are pre-specified for the system. All the bits of the equations can be found out from the database so that the probability of a keyword being present or absent for any class can be derived from all the items recorded that belong to that class. From this and the relative number of items in a class an initial estimate of the probability (belief) of a class can be assumed. This might be later modified from monitoring user requests. This latter process reflects something of the mechanism of semantic retrieval mentioned above.

Such a system (called PRIZE) was tested in 2002 to see if this approach was in principle workable for the University of Portsmouth. It used a database of the Universities expertise and skills. This database was intended to be an online tool for people outside the university to find an expert. The work was never published or used. However, a commercial version of it has been adapted and is being used to help expert systems' knowledge base to be developed by the experts without the use of a knowledge engineer.

The PRIZE system was a database of people whose skills were defined as a list of keywords. The keywords are chosen by each individual and where a keyword is a phrase, such as "Artificial Intelligence". For this exercise no attempt was made to detect spelling mistakes, variants of the same word and similes. Each person is a researcher and was thus considered to belong to a research group (Group) even if it was only a group of one. Of all the staff this was a subset of 350 people belonging to 102 groups in 21 departments of five faculties. The group belongs to department and each department belongs to a faculty. Normally research groups can belong to more than one department but this was testing the principle so that complication was ignored.

The SFD graph Fig. 10.26 shows the dependences between objects. This means that there three choices for what may replace a 'theory'. We can shift our definition of what is meant by 'theory' from Group to Dept to Faculty. The first stage would be to take the broader category of Faculty and when that has been reached to explore Dept and then the Group and finally the Person. A Person's desirable properties are characterised by a set of Results for every Keyword. However, only the keywords that are 'present' are stored. All the people are examples of the Group to which they belong. It is the accumulation of these people and their Keywords that makes each group an example of a Dept and so on. The people and their Keywords also provide the probabilities of a result given a theory for each Keyword and the probability of a Result. These three bits of information are sufficient to provide the raw material for a Belief System. A small range of keywords, derived from the level of confidence for each class (Group, Dept or Faculty) can be assessed as to their importance to distinguish between the classes and then offered to the user. The user can then say which of these should be present and which should be absent in the person they are interested in finding. All the others offered that have not been chosen are considered experiments not performed. The results given by the user are then used to modify the initial set of 'beliefs' as for the running probability (Fig. 10.25). This will then reflect back on the next set of experiments to be offered.

In practice, the stepping down to a different class such as Dept was found not to be necessary. There is an alternative way of assessing the keywords and that is for their ability to divide a database into components that will home in on a specific item. Unlike the keywords as experiments that go for minimum entropy, keywords to

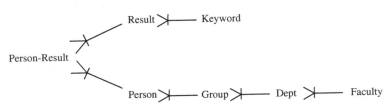

Fig. 10.26 An SFD graph of the 'objects' for PRIZE

identify should have maximum entropy. These will have maximum spread over class and will also occur frequently. Such a list is offered under a separate heading for the user to choose to use with the standard approach to retrieve data. The technique uses best hits and is conditional on a chosen Faculty (or Dept, etc.) derived from the first few belief revision cycles. In practice we found that one or two cycles of belief revision was sufficient to home in on a short list of about 5–15 people.

The advantage of belief revision is that if the system seems to be moving away from the desired results then the user can continue with other keywords and the system will shift as the effect of any wrong decisions fade. In the final implementation the sorting was done by a user built_in (prefixed 'ubi_') 'ubi_order_setups'. This takes a single integer parameter #1 that represents the 'faculty' level. The function accesses the current 'confidence' and 'occurrence_prob' and calculates from these the new 'perceived entropy' or result expectation ($E_{n-1}(R_e)$) as shown in Fig. 10.25 and then sorts them. We found the library Bayesian functions were awkward to use and so we constructed our own versions. This is an extensive calculation since every keyword is an experiment. From this sorted list the set of *search keywords* (green window in Fig. 10.27) and the best 15 are displayed for using to adjust belief. The *best keywords* for normal retrieval are calculated by the function 'order_keys' in the pink window Fig. 10.27. Finally, the *possible faculties* are calculated by 'best_model', ordered and displayed in the mauve window.

In the control window 'init_query' resets PRIZE to the start condition. Each of the three levels of theories of Faculty, Dept, and Group is set to the initial expectations based on relative numbers of people in them. The total number of theories at each level is listed. The function 'get_best' with the level number #1 (Faculty) is then called and calculates and displays in the three-coloured windows information for the user about keywords and possible faculties. The number given is some test information and not relevant to the user. There are then two optional queries that can be repeated with an optional 'get_best' in between

```
QUERY> ans_best #1 #1 [#512 #9 #296 #160]
    [["Faculty of Technology" #r0.918627]
    ["University of Portsmouth Business School" #r0.027610]
    ["Faculty of Science" #r0.026305]
    ["Faculty of Humanities and Social Sciences" #r0.015111]
    ["Faculty of the Environment" #r0.013992]]

QUERY> ans_best #0 #1 [#723 #2 #48 #223 #45]
    [["Faculty of Technology" #r0.919914]
    ["University of Portsmouth Business School" #r0.026360]
    ["Faculty of Science" #r0.026024]
    ["Faculty of Humanities and Social Sciences" #r0.014524]
    ["Faculty of the Environment" #r0.013742]]
```

The first query 'ans_best' with the first parameter #1 chooses a list of keywords by using their internal code given in the windows that help identify positively the person, the user is after. The second option is with the first parameter #0 to indicate

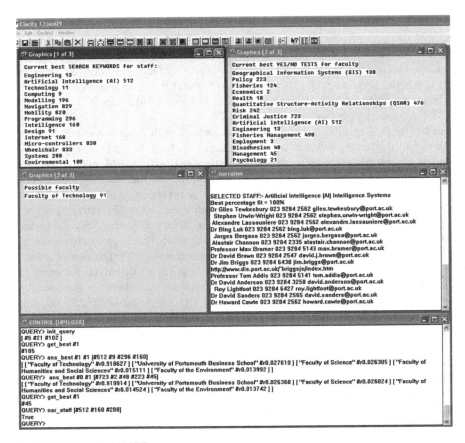

Fig. 10.27 Output of PRIZE

the keywords that definitely do not identify the person. These keywords are automatically remembered and removed from any further Search Keywords offered. The number gives after the faculty name is the confidence (belief) in this being the correct choice for the user and gives a guide as to when to stop refining the search. In this case we would have stopped after the first request.

The last stage is to use a selection of the offered keywords to identify an individual and these are displayed in the white window. There are 14 possible hits and they are all relevant for expertise in Intelligent Systems. The response times for this trial system are: '**init_query**'=15 secs, '**get_best**'=5 secs, '**ans_best**'=1 sec and '**nar_staff**' ≪ 1 sec using a 1.8 GHz Mac-mini under boot-camp.

There is certainly a different 'feel' with such a retrieval system. There is a feeling that it is positively on your side and really trying to help. The interface is a bit crude since it uses only what is easily available with the Clarity library. However, it was sufficient to demonstrate that the principle worked and was effective. In 2008 the commercial version was built for a very specific purpose and has proved to be useful. The interface was created through a C++ compiler and called as a DLL from Clarity (see chapter 9). Alongside the belief system is a tree accessing retrieval system that reflects the structure of the organisation. This is actually preferred because it is quicker to respond and the people using it are familiar with the structure. Occasionally, they cannot find what they want and the belief system has usually succeeded where the tree approach has failed. Most naive users prefer the belief system until they get used to the organisation they are dealing with. It provides a smooth transition from one retrieval mechanism to another. Once the speed of response of the belief system has been improved the reason for using the alternative approach may disappear.

Final Word

Although this is the last chapter of the book it is not the end of development for Clarity or schematic languages derived from it. In Chapter 9 we have shown how the existing system can be extended and how visual languages that are used to design interfaces can be integrated. This is a clumsy process and it would be so much neater to have a more direct access to these design languages so that it flowed naturally with Clarity. There are many links of this kind such as integrating spreadsheets and relational databases both of which are functional languages that have been well established. There are also small things such as bringing the Faith to Clarity translator up to date so that it can handle the '**HOLDN**' function in a more natural way. There are a large number of special functions that could be made built-ins, such as all the statistical functions.

One of the characteristics we have found with using Clarity over the last 20 years is that there is a style of programming that is distinct from text based languages. The solutions are subtly different and the structures of the programs are influenced by diagram appearance. We also find that we do not write a program as such but what we do is simply develop an environment that suits our interests and create solutions that build upon our previous work. The effect is that Clarity behaves like an emulation of a unique operating system for a functional machine. This would suggest an interesting development.

As for any system that is alive and well there will be change and adaption. Much more change than we can handle and it is for this reason that we are giving away Clarity in all its forms, example databases and source code. At the time of publishing this will be found at the publisher's web site www.springer.com/978-1-84882-617 or www.clarity-support.com.

References

Addis T. R. (1985) '*Designing Knowledge-Based Systems*' Kogan Page, London, ISBN 0-85038-859-7, ISBN 1-85091-251-3 also Prentice-Hall, Englewood Cliffs, NJ(1986) ISBN 0-13-201823-3.

Addis T. R. (1987) '*A Framework for Knowledge Elicitation*', The First European Workshop on Knowledge Acquisition for Knowledge-Based Systems, September, Reading University.

Addis T. R. (1989) '*The Science of Knowledge: A Research Programme for Knowledge Engineering*', The Third European Workshop on Knowledge Acquisition for Knowledge-Based Systems, July, Paris.

Addis T. R. (1990) '*Knowledge for Design*', Knowledge Acquisition, Vol. 2, pp. 95–105, Academic Press.

Addis T. R., Addis J. T, Billinge D., Gooding D. and Visscher B-F. (2008) '*The Abductive Loop: Tracking Irrational Sets*', Special issue of Foundations of Science, Vol. 13, No. 1, pp. 5–16, March, ISSN 1233-1821.

Addis, T. and Billinge, D. (2005), '*Music to Our Ears: A Required Paradigm Shift in Computer Science* presented at *ECAP04*', University of Pavia, Italy, in Computing, Philosophy and Cognition, ed Manani L. and Dossena R. Vol. 4 ISBN 1-904987-24-9, pp 147–162, pub College Publications.

Addis, T. R. and Gooding, D. C. (1999) '*Learning as Collective Belief-Revision: Simulating Reasoning About Disparate Phenomena*', in: Proceedings: AISB'99 Symposium on Scientific Creativity, pp. 19–28.

Addis, T. R. and Gooding, D. C. (2008) '*Simulation Methods for an Abductive System in Science.*' Special issue: Tracking Irrational Sets, Science, Technology, Ethics in Foundations of Science. ISSN 1233-182, Springer, Netherlands.

Aris R. (1978) *Mathematical Modelling Techniques*. Research Notes in Mathematics 24, Pitman, London.

Ashcroft S. and Pereira C. (2002) '*Practical Statistics for the Biological Sciences: Simple Pathways to Statistical Analysis*' Palgrave Macmillan, Basingstoke, ISBN-10: 0333960440.

Billinge D. and Addis T. R. (2008) *Seeking Allies: Modelling How Listeners Choose Their Musical Friends*, Special issue of Foundations of Science, Vol. 13, No. 1, pp. 53–66, March, ISSN 1233-1821.

Charniak E. (1988) '*Motivation Analysis, Abductive Unification and Non-Monotonic Equality*', Artificial Intelligence, 34, pp 275–296.

Gonzalez R. and Wu G. (1999) *On the Shape of the Probability Weighting Function*, Cognitive Psychology, Vol. 38, No. 1, pp. 129–166, February.

Gooding D. C. and Addis T. R. (2008) *Modelling Experiments as Mediating Models*, Special issue of Foundations of Science, Vol. 13, No. 1, pp. 17–36, ISSN 1233-1821.

Gooding, D. and Addis, T. R. (1999) '*A Simulation of Model-Based Reasoning About Disparate Phenomena*', in: Magnani et al., eds., pp. 103–124 in Model-Based Reasoning, Scientific Discovery, Kluwer Academic, NY.

Gooding, D. C. (1990) '*Experiment and the Making of Meaning*', Kluwer Academic, Dordrecht and Boston.

Gooding, D. C. (1996) *Creative Rationality: Towards an Abductive Model of Scientific Change*, in: Philosophica: Creativity, Rationality and Scientific Change, J. Meheus, ed., Vol. 58: 73–101 ISSN 0379-8402, pub Ghent University.

Kuhn, T. S. (1962) *The Structure of Scientific Revolutions*, Chicago University Press, Chicago, IL, 2nd edition (1970).

Kuhn, T. S. (1974) '*Second Thoughts on Paradigms*', in Kuhn, ed. (1977), pp. 293–319. The Essential Tension. ed Kuhn T.S, ISBN 0-226-45806-7, The University of Chicago Press, 1977.

Kuhn, T. S. (1977a) '*Objectivity, Value Judgement and Theory Choice*', in Kuhn, ed. (1977), pp. 320–339.

Kuhn, T. S. ed. (1977b) '*The Essential Tension*', Chicago University Press, Chicago, IL.

Lakatos, I. (1970) '*Falsification and the Methodology of Scientific Research Programmes*, in I. Lakatos and A. Musgrave, eds., Criticism and the Growth of Knowledge, Cambridge University Press, Cambridge, pp. 91–196.

Langley P., Simon H. A., Bradshaw G. L. and Zytkow J. M. (1987) '*Scientific Discovery: Computational Exploration of the Creative Process*', MIT Press, Cambridge, MA.

Luce R. D. and Raiffa H. (1957) *'Games and Decisions: Introduction and Critical Survey'*. John Wiley & Sons Ltd, New York.

Magnani, L. (2001) *Abduction, Reason and Science,* Kluwer Academic, Dordrecht.

Magnani, L., Nersessian, N. and Thagard, P., eds. (1998) *'Model-Based Reasoning in Scientific Discovery'*, Kluwer, Dordrecht / Plenum, New York.

Magnani, L. (1998) *'Model-Based Creative Abduction'*, in Magnani et al., eds., pp. 219–237.

Matthews, R. (2004) *'Opposites Detract'*, New Scientist, Vol. 181, No. 2438, pp. 39–43.

Moroney M. J. (1963) *'Facts from Figures'*, 3rd edition, Penguin Books, Baltimore, MD.

Newell A. and Simon H. A. (1956). *'The Logic Theory Machine'*. IRE Transactions on Information Theory, Sept IT-2(3), pp 61–79.

Newell A. and Simon H. A. (1973) *'Human Problem Solving'*. Prentice-Hall, Englewood Cliffs, NJ.

Peirce C. S. (1934) *'Scientific Method'*, in Collected papers of C. S. Peirce, Vol. VII, ed A. W. Burks, Cambridge: Harvard University Press.

Peirce, C. (1966) *'The fixation of belief'*, in Weiner, P. P., ed. Charles S. Peirce: Selected Writings. Dover, New York, pp. 92–260.

Shannon, C. E. and Weaver W. (1964) *'The Mathematical Theory of Communication'*, University of Illinois Press, Urbana, IL (first published 1949).

Tweney, R. D. (1985) *'Faraday's Discovery Of Induction: A Cognitive Approach*, in D. Gooding and F. James, eds., Faraday Rediscovered, Macmillan, London: / APA Press, New York, pp. 189–209.

DOI 10.1007/978-1-84882-618-2_11

ERRATUM

Erratum to: Drawing Programs: The Theory and Practice of Schematic Functional Programming

Tom Addis and Jan Addis

ISBN: 978-1-84882-617-5

© Springer-Verlag London Limited

In the "Preface" section, the web site path of University of Portsmouth has been printed incorrectly as "http://userweb.port.ac.uk/_addist/978-1-84882-617-5.zip". Hence please read the web site path as "http://userweb.port.ac.uk/~addist/978-1-84882-617-5.zip".

Appendix A: A BNF Description of the Functional Data Language Faith: The *Faith Code* Window

Fdb Section

<fdb section>	*::= <fdb commands> <terminator>*
<fdb commands>	*::= <fdb command> <fdb commands>	<empty>*
<fdb command>	*::= <declaration section> |*
	<definition section> |
	<query> |
	<dbport> |
	<memory events>
<terminator>	*::= ;*
<empty>	*::=*

Function and Constructor Declarations

<declaration section>	::= fdec <declarations> <terminator>	
	cdec <declarations> <terminator>	
	tdec <tdeclarations> <terminator>
<declarations>	::= <declaration> <declarations>	<empty>
<tdeclarations>	::= <tdeclaration> <tdeclarations>	<empty>
<declaration>	::= <function name> <is> <types> <terminator>
<tdeclaration>	::= <function name> <is> <typeop> <terminator>
<function name>	::= <symbol>
<is>	::= ::=
<types>	::= <type> <to> <types>	<type>
<typeop>	::= typeop <int val>	nonlex	enum
<to>	::= ->
<type> <variable>	::= <function type>	<list type>	<pair type>	<basic type>	
<function type>	::= (<types>)
<list type>	::= (list <type>)

T. Addis, J. Addis, *Drawing Programs: The Theory and Practice of Schematic Functional Programming*, DOI 10.1007/978-1-84882-618-2,
© Springer-Verlag London Limited 2010

`<pair type>`	`::= (pair <type> <type>)`
`<basic type>`	`::= int	real	char	str	bool`
`<variable>`	`::= ?<natural number>`

Function Expressions

`<expression>`	`::= <fexpression>	<lambda expression>	<holdn expression>	` `<constant>`
`<fexpression>`	`::= <function name> <arguments>	<combinator>` `<arguments>`
`<lambda expression>`	`::= lambda <variable> <expression>`
`<holdn expression>`	`::= HOLDN <int val> <expression>`
`<arguments>`	`::= <argument> <arguments>	<empty>`
`<argument>`	`::= <constant>	<list arg>	(<expression>)	<function name> |` `<variable>`
`<constant>`	`::= <int val>	<real val>	<char val>	<str val>	<bool val>`
`<list arg>`	`::= [<arguments>]	(makelist <arguments>)	` `(: <argument> <list arg>)	nil`
`<int val>`	`::= #<integer>`
`<real val>`	`::= #r<real>`
`<char val>`	`::= '<char>'`
`<str val>`	`::= "<chars>"`
`<bool val>`	`::= True	False`
`<chars>`	`::= <char> <chars>	`
`<chars>`	`::= <char> <chars>	<empty>`

Function Definitions

`<definition section>`	`::= fdef <definitions> <terminator>`
`<definitions>`	`::= <definition><definitions>	<empty>`
`<definition>`	`::= <fexpression> <is> <expression> <terminator>`

The *Control Window*

| `<query>` | `::= <expression> <cterminator> | <constant> <cterminator>` |
| `<dbport>` | `::= load <file name> <cterminator> |`
`open <file name> <cterminator> |`
`create <file name> <cterminator> |`
`exec <file name> <cterminator> |`
`close <cterminator> |`
`commit <cterminator>` |

\<cterminator\>	::= \<terminator\> | \<newline\>
\<file name\>	::= \<str val\>
\<memory events\>	::= trace \<bool val\> \<terminator\> |
	dump \<str val\> \<terminator\> | dump \<terminator\> |
	gc \<terminator\>

Basics

\<integer\> and \<real\> are read by C's scanf, they are terminated by any of the characters:

: ; newline space ( ) [ ]

They are not terminated by '–'. The following are valid:

\<integer\>	0 –1 –100001 100021
\<real\>	3.14 2.0 –24.5 36.7e-15
\<character\>	any printable character
\<symbol\>	any sequence of printable characters except combinators and the following

reserved symbols:

::= ; -> ( ) [ ] cdec, tdec, fdec, fdef, load trace open, creat, exec, close, commit,

lambda int real char str bool list pair and any other built in library functions

\<combinator\>	::= B | C | I | K | S

Appendix B: An Extension of Faith to the Schematic Language Clarity

A Schematic Extension of BNF

The underlying structure of the Clarity schematic language is an acyclic bipartite directed graph. The graph relates to the Faith code and this will be given in terms of the BNF structure descriptors (Appendix A). The two types of node are a collection of functions (F) and a collection of types (T). The nodes are connected via an input mapping I and an output mapping O. The input mapping I maps a type node t_j **to** a collection of function nodes $I(t_j)$. The output mapping O maps a type node t_j **to** a collection of function nodes $O(t_j)$. A schema consists of a four-tuple, thus

$$\text{<Schema>} = (F, T, I, O)$$

The degrees of freedom of these mappings are governed by a syntax that will be expressed in terms of a graphical extension of BNF. This extension introduces a second dimension into the normal BNF meta-language that shows the context-dependent cardinality constraints of the mappings. A graph that represents a Clarity schema will be described such that the input mapping for a node is always placed above the description of that node and the output mapping will always be placed below. The resultant triple will be treated as single BNF symbol:

<input mapping cardinality to node>
<node>

We will illustrate a mapping <mapping> by a collection of arrows. The input mapping will converge onto a node and the output mapping will diverge away from the node. A single arrow represents a 2-tuple either input { f_i,t_j } or output { t_j,f_k } which maps a single node i or j onto another j or k.

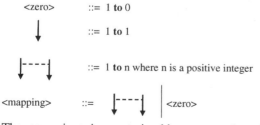

<pre>
<zero>   ::= 1 to 0

              ::= 1 to 1

              ::= 1 to n where n is a positive integer

<mapping>   ::= | <zero>
</pre>

The <mapping> is constrained by <types> (see Appendix A)

The Constructor Window

The window consists of two domains. A bottom strip is the output domain and the remaining top part is the declaration domain.

<declaration schema> ::= (F ∋ <constructor node>, T ∋ <c_type node>, I, O)

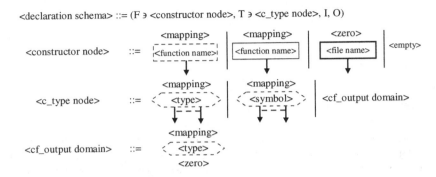

The Function Window

The function window consists of three domains. The top strip is the input domain and the bottom strip is the output domain. The middle domain is the body of the function.

<function schema> ::= (F ∋ <f_function node>, T ∋ <f_type node>, I, O)

<f_type node> ::= <input node> | <output domain> | <ftype> | <htype> | <ptype> | <junction>

<f_function node> ::= <function node> | <junction> | <empty>

<input domain>   ::=   <input node><input domain> | <empty>

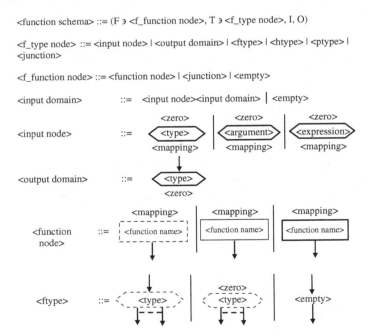

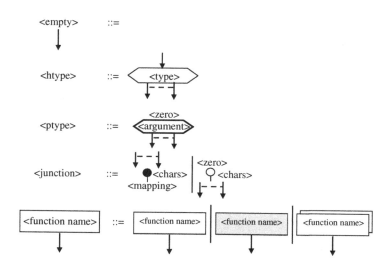

The Network Window

The network window has only one domain . A Clarity program can be designed as a collection of functions without regard to the individual functional schemas. The schema is simply a directed graph that may contain cycles. The mappings J and K are now from function to function (no type nodes involved). The input function J maps a function node f_l to a collection of function nodes $J(f_l)$. The output mapping maps a function node f_l to a collection of function nodes $K(f_l)$.

<network schema> ::= (F <net_function node>, J, K)

<net_function> ::= <n_function> | <n_junction> | <empty>

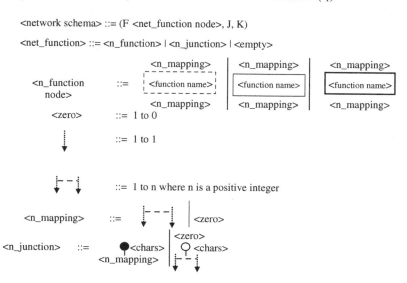

Appendix C: The .seg File Structure

An Example .seg File

The following file represents one picture.
$$$$ marks the end of file.

LINE 1 gives a general description:-
name = display_type,
Component Number = 0,
number of picture segments = 17,
picture type = 1 (Function),
Text size = 12,
Top left corner = (10,40),
width = 400,
Height = 320,
Time of last update = 964077692 (seconds since some date),
No of lines of annotation = 2.
Optional field: Title = <string> Note words are sepertated by '~'
e.g."This~is~the~first~component"

LINES 2 and 3 are the annotation lines.
Then the lines come in groups of 3 (unless there is annotation), representing each picture segment.

LINE 4
segment name (also label) = bool,
segment number = 1,
segment type = 1 (lozenge),
style = 2 (BOLD),
top left, bottom right = (197,298) (241, 313)
(If there is annotation, there would be another integer,
and that number of lines of annotation following.)

LINE 5

"Backward" connections, i.e. connection from B13 = connection from segment 13

LINE 6

"Forward" connections, i.e. connection to. There are none here.

Note that segment 13 is:

> I/O 13 3 0 207 247 217 298
>
> B11
> F1
> I/O means it is an arrow.
> 13 = segment number
> type 3 = arrow,
> style = 0 = SOLID.
> top left, bottom right = (207, 247), (217, 298)
> 1 connection from segment 11
> 1 connection to segment 1 (see LINE 4)

Segment file example:

display_type 0 17 1 12 10 40 400 320 964077692 2
Display all vehicles of a particular type, e.g.
QUERY> display_type Car
bool 1 1 2 197 298 241 313
B13

sym 2 1 2 78 7 114 22

F6
filter 3 2 0 160 158 220 173

B10B17
F15
veh_match 4 2 0 34 74 118 89
B6B7
F9
veh 5 1 1 152 48 188 63

F7
I/O 6 3 0 93 22 78 74
B2
F4

I/O 7 3 0 152 60 103 74
B5
F4
bool 8 1 1 107 119 151 134
B9
F10
I/O 9 3 0 84 89 120 119
B4
F8
I/O 10 3 0 140 134 178 158
B8
F3
display 11 2 0 172 232 240 247
B12
F13
I/O 12 3 0 202 211 205 232
B14
F11
I/O 13 3 0 207 247 217 298
B11
F1
list~veh 14 1 1 164 196 240 211
B15
F12
I/O 15 3 0 192 173 199 196
B3
F14
vehicles 16 2 0 216 78 292 93

F17
I/O 17 3 0 248 93 196 158
B16
F3
$$$$

End of Segement File Example

Note: the built-in function 'display' will display ALL the pictures in a .seg file, e.g. QUERY> display "abc.seg" or QUERY> display "abc". If the database with the networks in is already open, you just need to select a network window (the green one) and type '<CTRL>n'. You have to save the database to keep the network up-to-date.

Index